F.-X. Godts C.SS.R.

ON THE FEWNESS OF THE SAVED

THE TEACHING OF THE SAINTS

VERY USEFUL AS SPIRITUAL READING FOR THE CLERGY

THIRD EDITION

EXPANDED AND REVISED

Translated by John S. Daly, France, from Latin to English in the year 2017

"There are fewer who are saved."

(Saint Thomas)

"The more common opinion holds that the majority even of the faithful are damned."

(Saint Alphonsus)

"Plazza, or to be more accurate Gravina, asserts in Chapter V of his *De Paradiso*: 'It is probable that the elect among mankind are far more numerous than the reprobate.' — But it must be admitted that it was precisely this Chapter V that was condemned by decree of the Congregation of the Index, 22nd May 1772."

(Hugo von Hürter, S.J.)
1899

Translated by John S. Daly, France,
from Latin to English in the year 2017.

Text translation from Latin to English, and typesetting,
Copyright © 2017 by MOS, Inc., Pekin, Indiana.

Printed and bound in the United States of America.

Published by

Refuge of Sinners Publishing, Inc.
5271 E Mann Rd - Pekin, IN. 47165
www.TraditionalCatholicPublishing.com
812-967-2531

APPROBATIONS

The book entitled *On the Fewness of the Saved — The Teaching of the Saints by F. X. Godts C.SS.R., third edition, expanded and revised,* has been examined and approved by two theologians of our Congregation appointed for this purpose and by the authority received from the most Reverend Father General M. Raus we authorize its publication.

Brussels, 5th May 1899
J. R. Van Aertselaer C.SS.R.
Superior of the Belgian Province

IMPRIMATUR

Mechlin, 29th July 1899

H. J. DE CLERCK,

VIC. GEN.

Prayer Request

Would the reader kindly remember in their prayers the person who generously donated the cost of the translation of this work from Latin to English and wishes to remain anonymous, but is certainly known to God.

DEDICATION

To Blessed
Clement-Mary Hofbauer

distinguished propagator of
the Congregation of the Most Holy Redeemer
who
by his tireless efforts succeeded in strengthening the enfeebled faith
and sadly diminished Catholic spirit of the people of his day and was
for this reason hailed by Pius VII as an *apostolic man* and a *pillar of the
Church*[1]
this *vindication* of the doctrine of the Saints *is humbly dedicated* by

THE AUTHOR

[1] Office, Matins, Lesson VI.

CONTENTS

SUMMARY OF THE STATE OF THE QUESTION

1

ARE THE MAJORITY of the ENTIRE HUMAN RACE, taken as a whole, damned, as a result of their mortal sins?

YES, answers the whole of Tradition, attested by 73 Fathers, Doctors and Saints of the Church and 28 Scriptural exegetes. This doctrine is stated by some theologians to be de fide, while others call it more than merely true, universal, certain; "and not a single Father can be found," notes Estius, "to have written otherwise."

PROBABLY NOT, answers GRAVINA, although he grants that the common view is the more probable, but his work was, notwithstanding this, "condemned outright" by order of the Sacred Congregation of the Index.

CERTAINLY NOT, reply Bougaud, Mauran and Fr. Castelein, who, to defend their opinion, are obliged so far to expand the soul of the Church as to contend that a very great number of pagans, Mahometans, heretics, schismatics etc., are saved.

2

Are the majority of ADULT CATHOLICS damned as a result of their evil life?[1]

YES, reply, once again, all the Fathers, Doctors and Saints who have considered the specific question of Catholics, as do all the Theologians and Exegetes of the times previous to Protestantism — an opinion Saint Alphonsus calls the more common.

PROBABLY NOT, reply a few theologians later than the XVIth century, in company with Suárez. Their main argument is that, "although Catholics for the most part are sinners who repeatedly fall back into their sins, nevertheless they receive the last sacraments fruitfully and die a holy death."

CERTAINLY NOT, reply Bougaud, Mauran and Fr. Castelein.

PREFACE TO THE THIRD EDITION

GENTLE READER,

I

You will readily understand that this book is not an attack but a defence. Against the attacks of a handful of Progressives I am defending the heritage of our Fathers: their time-honoured interpretation of certain scriptural texts, their time-honoured doctrine of the fewness of the saved, their time-honoured method of preaching on hell and on the fear of God and their time-honoured moral principles. Specifically I am safeguarding the doctrine of Saint Ignatius and of 35 *beati* and other theologians of the Society of Jesus.

This study is entitled "On the Fewness of the Saved" because Saint Thomas attests and the teaching of all the centuries attests that "those who are saved are fewer", and Our Lord Himself attests that "few there are who find … the narrow way that leadeth to life."

The second half of its title is: "The Teaching of the Saints". By *the Saints* I understand the missioners and successors of the Apostles whose preaching has been examined and approved by the Church; the Holy Doctors and the other holy Fathers of the Church whose authority in the science of salvation, which is the *science of the Saints*, is of the greatest weight.

I have deliberately refrained from citing those Saints who are not so remarkable for learning, such as Saint Benedict Joseph Labre,

Blessed Gerard Majella and others to whom, as his beloved little ones, the Heavenly Father revealed the great wisdom which He has hidden from the wise and prudent of this world; I mention only those whom the Holy Ghost has established as prophets, Evangelists, pastors and doctors until the consummation of the world to build up the body of Christ.

I have also refrained from citing female saints although of some of them I am happy to say with the Church herself "Grant that we may be nourished by her heavenly doctrine and instructed by the sentiment of her pious devotion."[2] I shall be quoting on page 82 the words of the Vicar of Christ teaching that God has vouchsafed to his saints the benefit of greater divine light.

Finally the subtitle of this little book is "Very useful as spiritual reading for the clergy" — both for their own sanctification and that of the souls entrusted to them. This is because it is very well adapted to inculcating that fear of the Lord which is for all men the beginning of wisdom and of eternal life and of which the clergy, more than the other faithful, stand in such great need. For "the reading of the Holy Gospel warns us to take great care lest we who are known to have received more than others in this world be for that reason more gravely judged by the world's Creator. For where gifts are greater, fuller account must be rendered of them."[3]

Indeed, as the pious Cardinal Bona remarks, "There is no keener stimulus to correct sinful behaviour and bring our life into conformity with the norm of the Gospel than that terrible and awe-inspiring statement: *many are called but few are chosen...* So since the elect are few, and perhaps far fewer than we think, we ought to withdraw from the multitude and live with the small number of the Saints, elect and innocent."[4] And this is especially applicable to priests

---

[2] *Roman Breviary*, Collect for the Feast of Saint Teresa [of Avila].

[3] Saint Gregory the Great, Homily 9 *On the Gospel*; *Roman Breviary*, Office of a Bishop and Confessor, Lesson VII.

[4] See below, p. 151 et seq.

as their vocation requires them to be the salt of the earth and the light of the world.

Reading this book will also prove of the highest value in procuring the salvation of souls. For after the example of the saints, and especially of Saint Ignatius, the fear of God should be greatly impressed upon the faithful, even what is called *servile fear*, for as Fr. von Hummelauer notes, "Meditation on Hell, in the mind of the Holy Father, flows in its entirety from the affection of perfect love."[5]

II

For seventeen centuries the doctrine of the fewness of the saved was in tranquil possession without even a single discordant voice ever being raised on the subject. As Estius remarks, "Even among the faithful the authority of both Scripture and the Fathers teaches that the bad are more numerous than the good and hence the reprobate more numerous than the elect, and not a single one of the Fathers can be found to have written otherwise." (See below, page 130) This opinion is so certain, says this excellent theologian, that "I do not think that any Christian could be found to oppose it." (See p. 130)

Towards the end of the XVIth century some writers disturbed this admirable and unanimous consensus as is shown by the words of Vasquez (p. 129).

It was about that time that Suárez wrote, "In absolute terms, speaking of all men who have existed or shall exist from the beginning of the word to its end, the common and true opinion is that number of the reprobate is greater," and of Christians, "the commoner opinion is that more Christians are reprobate than predestined," but when he comes to speak of Catholics, he says "it seems to me more likely that the greater number are saved under the law of grace" He includes baptized infants among those so saved. "This is because, in the first place, of those who die before reaching adult-

---

[5] Hummelauer, Franz von (1842-1914), *Meditationum et Contemplationum S. Ignatii Puncta*, p. 104.

hood, the great majority die with Baptism." (See below p. 134) But the reasons he gives to justify his opinion as at least likely were very soon contradicted and refuted by outstanding writers, notable among them being Cornelius a Lapidè, Recupito and other writers even of the Society of Jesus, as well as the celebrated Cardinal Bona (p. 148).

From that period the opinion that the greater number of Catholics are saved began to enjoy some measure of extrinsic probability on account of the authority of Suárez, while the opinion that the greater part of mankind is damned continued to enjoy the same absolute authority as before.

While the opinion of Suárez found some followers, it also aroused energetic opposition. For instance on 16th July 1695, the Louvain Doctor Steyaert championed the following thesis: "the *narrow gate* referred to in Matthew VII, 13 denotes the gate of the Christian Religion as it is practised by the bulk of the faithful (without requiring any further rigours)". But this was contradicted by another Louvain Doctor, Verschuren, who published a small work entitled "Defence of the Strait Way, demonstrating, against Doctor Steyaert, that a greater number of adult faithful are damned than are saved." (See below, p. 163).

In the middle of the eighteenth century, Alessandro Borgia, bishop of Fermo, preached a sermon, to the scandal of his listeners, on the great number of Christians who are saved, in the course of which he said: "This number is small in comparison with the number of the whole of mankind but not from the standpoint of Christians alone." The learned Foggini was swift to publish against this claim a book entitled "Assertion and Demonstration of the Striking Agreement of the Fathers of the Church concerning the fewness of adult believers who are saved in comparison with the number of believers who are reprobate."

III

Hitherto the debate had related exclusively to the greater or lesser number of *Catholics* who are saved.

The first writer who dared to brave the unanimous consensus of the Fathers and Doctors by asserting — albeit only as *probable* — the opinion that the greater part *of the entire human race* is saved, was Fr. Gravina, S.J., of Palermo. (See below, p. 41) The professors of the Palermo Seminary raised their voices and published articles against this unheard of novelty, but Gravina stood his ground until his opinion was finally condemned outright by the Sacred Congregation of the Index in 1772.

In 1767 the same Congregation had already condemned, pending correction, a work by Marmontel entitled *Bélisaire*, in which it was also alleged that the majority of men are saved.

While this debate was raging at Palermo, in the year 1767 — so five years before the condemnation of Gravina — the Spanish Jesuit Genér wrote in his *Theologia dogmatico-scholastica*: "Among *the whole of mankind*, the number of the predestined is much greater, and hence the number of the reprobate is much less, *than the common opinion holds.*"

How great is this number in the opinion of Genér? He himself states: "*Perhaps*, at least, the non-reprobate in comparison with the reprobate are at the lowest count equal in number."[6]

But, as I have said, at this time Gravina was not yet on the Index.

IV

In our own days, however, three authors have gone beyond the opinion of Gravina, claiming not merely as a probable opinion but as absolutely *certain*, that the majority of the human race is saved.

The first of these was Bougaud, Vicar-General of Orléans, in his work *Le Christianisme et le Temps Présent*, published without ecclesiastical approval.

The second was the Rev. Victor Mauran, parish priest of Marseilles, in another work which appeared without approval.[7] It is

---

[6] Vol. II, p. 342 *et seq*.

probable that both of these writers were unaware of the condemnation of Gravina.

The third was the Rev. Fr. Auguste Castelein S.J., who in the year 1898 published in the secular review *La Revue Générale* five articles — needless to say without the approval of his order or of the ordinary of the publisher — entitled : *Le rigorisme et le nombre des élus*. The doctrine of these articles was very ably refuted by the Rev. Fr. Coppin C.SS.R. in his book *La question de l'Évangile : Seigneur, y en aura-t-il peu de sauvés, ou considérations sur l'écrit du R. P. Castelein, etc.* Other refutations of this Progressive were written by the Rev. F. Chatel in the periodical *Revue des Âmes Pieuses* and by the Olivetan Fathers of France in the *Bulletin de Notre-Dame de la Sainte Espérance.*

Fr. Castelein assembled his articles into a book which he published in November of the same year under the title *Le Rigorisme et la Doctrine du Salut.* The Catholic daily *Le Bien Public* recommended it in the following terms : "To Fr. Castelein's considerable theological authority is added that of the Rev. Fr. Petit, Provincial of the Order and that of the Cardinal-Archbishop who gave their *Imprimatur* to the book. Fr. Castelein's doctrine is not a novelty. It is *in conformity with the constant tradition of the Church.*" (23rd November 1898)

Whoever wrote this was clearly unacquainted with Foggini's work "Assertion and Demonstration of the Striking Agreement of the Fathers of the Church concerning the fewness of adult believers who are saved in comparison with the number of believers who are reprobate", just as Fr. Castelein was unaware of the condemnation of Gravina until after the appearance of his book.

But it had certainly come to his attention a few months later when, with no new approval of his Order or the Ordinary, he published a second edition entitled *Le Rigorisme, le Nombre des Élus et la Doctrine du Salut, second edition, revised and expanded.* For therein, on

---

[7] *L'humanité dans la vie future — élus et sauvés,* by the Rev. Victor Mauran parish priest of les Accates (Marseille), Librairie Verdot and from the author. No date of publication stated.

note 2 to page 285, he writes: "Let no one appeal, as an argument against my thesis, to the inclusion on the *Index* of the work,…" And he goes on to dismiss that condemnation in the following terms: "Many other motives may explain why this work was placed on the Index."

It was against this edition, which is worse than the first, that I wrote a small study *On the Fewness of the Saved…*, from which I suppressed, out of charity, the name of the author and the title of the work I was opposing. One thousand copies of the first edition of this work were published, but already 1300 subscribers were calling for it before it had left the presses so a second edition, slightly expanded, was immediately printed.

In addition to congratulations, further information and precious additional material poured in from the clergy, both secular and religious, so I set my hand to producing a third edition of my study which is now before you. It is indeed both "expanded and revised", for in addition to the parallel between the teaching of Fr. Castelein and that of Gravina (Chapter II), it adduces a list of the Saints, Doctors and Fathers of the Church expanded from 25 to 73; a list of Theologians up from 35 to 74 and a list of Exegetes to the number of 28 instead of 12. It further demonstrates how falsely certain theologians and exegetes have been cited in favour of the Progressives' cause. It vindicates the traditional text concerning the *strait way* and the *few that are saved*, etc. It sets out the symbolic meaning of the eight who were saved from the Flood and the four who were saved from Sodom, as well as of the two who alone entered the Promised Land. I have treated more fully of the Soul of the Church and the state of the Church during the early centuries of Christianity, the current extension of redeeming grace, etc. Hence this third edition is much fuller than the two former editions.

V

My reason for writing was not only to defend a speculative truth but also to defend *practical conduct*. The mathematical number of the saved, which is known to God alone, is relatively unimportant; what matters much more for the missioner,[8] as a learned professor of Dogmatic Theology writes to me, is "the moral and practical truth which must preside, in accordance with the laws of divine providence, over the direction and guidance of individuals to reach their last end."

What most roused my zeal against Fr. Castelein's pernicious book is my experience acquired in the pulpit and the confessional. How many of his book's readers have I not already seen smiling when mention was made of how widespread and perverse is the vice of impurity or of the eternal horrors of Hell! How often have I now had to face scepticism after preaching on the eternal truths! Now when I preach sacred Missions prominent figures who are in other respects pious and who ought to be setting an example to ordinary folk refuse to come to the sermons or to approach the confessional, saying that Missioners are Rigorists, Terrorists, and Pessimists.

And what awaits us later on when the sophistries by which Fr. Castelein endeavours to justify his errors have, with the passage of time, distilled their poison into so many souls? When many have been persuaded that the affair of salvation is a very easy business, even after a bad life, that Communion once a year is enough to keep us united with Christ, that the malice of sins of the flesh is not so great if they do not violate nature, that there are no strong grounds for fleeing *ordinary* mortal sins, for only the foulest forms of evil need be taken account of, that the dangers of the world and of evil exampled are to be disregarded, etc.

And such claims are set before the laity, in their vernacular tongue, in secular periodicals and newspapers as being the findings of the study of genuine theology, the doctrine of the Fathers and of the Church, the authentic meaning of Sacred Scripture! Those who

---

[8] Fr. Godts writes as a Redemptorist who has devoted his life to the apostolate of preaching parish missions. — Translator.

preach the contrary, i.e. sound doctrine, are to be spurned and fled from as Jansenists!

Yet the writer of these claims, though doubtless unwittingly, is precisely imitating the behaviour of the Jansenists, for as the pious, and hence despised, Massillon so rightly said, "One of the gravest wounds Jansenism inflicted on the Church has been, in my opinion, to encourage women and simple layfolk to discuss the loftiest and most incomprehensible mysteries, making them a topic of conversation and argument. This has led to irreligion. For the laity there is but a step from argument to doubt and from doubt to unbelief."[9]

No doubt this was not the intention of Fr. Castelein, but it is what he has contributed to bringing about. His book will convert no one and is certainly not what our generation had need of, for it takes no interest in the *strait way* that leads to salvation.

VI

There are those who accuse me of holding an extreme view too and who think that the truth lies midway between the two, namely that, "Nothing is known of the number of the elect; it is known only to God."

In absolute terms, i.e. if a specific number is meant, I admit this, but *relative* to the number of the damned, I deny it. Moreover, the Church, Saint Thomas and the others who state that we do not know the number of the elect are speaking exclusively in absolute terms. Otherwise how would it be possible for Saint Thomas to say in the same place "The number is known to God alone" and "those who are saved are fewer". Quite simply in the latter text he is speaking of the *relative* number.

As Recupito accurately writes in treating directly of the number of the predestined and of the reprobate:

[9] Cf. Rohrbacher, René François (1789-1856), *Histoire universelle de l'Église catholique*, bk. 89.

There are two subjects of debate: (a) certainty of the number and (b) whether the number of the predestinate is greater or lesser than the number of the reprobate. As to the first point, there are two kinds of number: the *counting* number and the *counted* number. The former is termed the *material* number since the fact that this or that thing is numbered bears a material relation to the number itself. The latter is termed the *formal* number and it is constituted by there being so many, but not more, of any particular thing. Hence one may be certain of the formal number but uncertain of the material number, or vice versa.

"In the divine intellect the material number of the predestinate and of the reprobate, as well as the formal number, is certain.[10]

As to the latter, the truer opinion seems to be that the number of the reprobate among the adult faithful is greater than the number of the predestinate.

When it is stated that knowledge of the number is reserved to God alone, this must be understood of such and such a determinate number, for instance that there are such and such a specific number of millions, but not of the magnitude of the number considered in general terms and in comparison with the number of the reprobate.[11]

This is how Hürter should be understood when he writes: "Nothing can be established with certainty of the number of the predestinate or of the reprobate."[12]

And the same applies to Perrone's footnote to the effect that "the Church has never defined anything on this subject; indeed she professes that she does not know the number of the elect."[13]

But this learned theologian goes astray when he audaciously asserts that "hence those who defend either opinion are guided only by conjectures."

---

[10] Recupito, Giulio Cesare, S.J. (1581-1647), *De numero prædestinatorum*, cap. I, pp. 1-2.

[11] *Ibid.*, cap. III, pp.8-9.

[12] Hürter, Hugo S.J. (1832-1914), *Theologiæ Dogmaticæ Compendium*, 1880, vol. II, p. 97, note 2.

[13] Perrone, Giovanni S.J. (1794-1876), *Tractatus de Deo Creatore*, n. 748, note; *Prælectiones Theologicæ*, Louvain, vol. III, p. 339.

This is true of Gravina, who himself admits that he is guided by *conjectures* and it also applies to some others of the Progressives, such as Faber, Bougaud and Mauran, for they explicitly say of their arguments: "These are not doctrines... These are bad arguments... The reader is requested to be indulgent towards this whimsy... Even if we are in error...." Etc. (See below, p. 317)

But it is quite false of the Saints, Doctors, Fathers, Theologians and Exegetes of whom I shall be citing a long list, all of whom base their teaching not on conjectures but on the Word of God, written and passed down, as well as on experience and sound reasoning.

VII

It may be objected, however, that no revelation has been made as to the fewness of the saved, so how can a tradition exist?

To this I reply:

1. The written revelation concerning the fewness of those who find the strait way and the fewness of the elect is certain, as will be abundantly demonstrated in what follows.

2. Many things are known by revelation passed down (tradition) which are not found in Scripture.

3. To show the divine origin of a doctrine it is not necessary to prove by the records of tradition that consensus has prevailed on the subject throughout *all* of the previous periods of history; it is sufficient for this consensus to have prevailed at *any* time. This is because, on account of the constant assistance of the Holy Ghost and the Church's immovable constancy in the same faith which this assistance necessarily produces, it is impossible for there ever to be a consensus in the Church in affirming a truth concerning which a negative consensus has previously existed. Hence for a theological demonstration of the apostolic origin of any doctrine it is enough to show that the Fathers of, e.g., the fourth or fifth century unanimously taught it, as applies in the present case, with no further need to

adduce explicit testimony of the same consensus in the apostolic or sub-apostolic times from the handful of surviving documents of this period.[14]

4. There is however, as to the issue we are examining, a tradition which is quite certain and which is derived from the early Christian centuries as will be shown at once. Let me first bring forth, as an argument from tradition alone, the IVth Book of Esdras, cited by Estius, John of Saint Thomas, Gonet, Suárez and others.

Throughout Chapter III of this work it is copiously shown that malice abounds in all the descendants of Adam and especially in the infidel nations. Then come the following explicit statements:

> And he (the Angel) answered me saying: The Most High has made this world for many but the world to come for few.
>
> But I will tell a parable before thee Esdras. As you will enquire of the earth and it will tell you that it will give much more earth for earthenware to be made but little dust of which gold is made, so is the action of the present world.
>
> Many indeed have been created but few shall be saved...
>
> For as the husbandman soweth upon the ground many seeds, and planteth many plants, but not all which were sown in time, are preserved, nor yet all that were planted, shall take root: so they also that are sown in the world, shall not all be saved. (Chapter VIII; 1-3, 41)
>
> I have spoken heretofore, and now I say, and hereafter will say: that they are more which perish then that shall be saved.
>
> As a flood is multiplied above, more then a drop. (Chapter IX; 15-16)

But the most important record which shows the early Christian tradition of the fewness of the saved is the ancient and constant doctrine of the two ways.

Our Lord Jesus Christ Himself, as is well known, used the figure of the two ways both in Matthew (who wrote his Gospel in the year 42 and in Luke who wrote in about the year 63. The figure was so

---

[14] Cf. *Theologia Mechlinensis, Demonstratio Catholica*, tract. *de Regula Fidei*, 1891, p. 358, q. 3.

familiar to the primitive Christians that they embodied it, so to speak, in a symbolic sign, viz. the letter Y.

1. A Christian record drafted towards the end of the first century is the book entitled the *Didache* or *Teaching of the Twelve Apostles* the authenticity, weight and widespread use of which among the primitive faithful are beyond question and recognized even by the more exacting critics.[15] Among the Greeks, Eusebius, Athanasius, and Nicephoras count this work among the apostolic writings, while among the Latins it is cited by Ruffinus among the inspired books; several Apostolic Fathers borrowed from it. Now this book opens with an exposition of the two ways, the one of life and the other of death, but which are widely different: "There are two ways in the world: the way of life and the way of death; the way of light and the way of darkness."

2. This *Teaching of the Twelve Apostles* is complemented and illustrated in the Homilies attributed to Saint Clement, which are mentioned by ancient writers of the Church and which, though not canonical scripture, are a genuine record of apostolic tradition. In the seventh homily we may read: "Knowing therefore these good and evil actions, I foretell to you, showing forth the two ways, of which those who travel along one perish while those who journey by the other, led on by God, are saved. So the way of those that perish is broad and very smooth and calls for no effort but leads to perdition whereas the way of the saved is narrow and rough and at length, after much labour, leads those who take it to salvation."[16]

3. Another record of the apostolic doctrine of the two ways is the Epistle commonly attributed to Saint Barnabas the Apostle. Already in Part I, Chapter 4, we read: "Consider the works of the evil way... Let us therefore take care not to be found, as it is written, *many called*

---

[15] Cf. Fessler, Bishop Josef (1813-72), *Institutiones Patrologiæ*, 1890, vol. I, p. 121.

[16] Homily VII, cap. VII; Migne, *Pat. Græc.*, vol. II, col. 222.

but few chosen."[17] And Part Two of this Epistle treats exclusively of *the two ways*:

> There are two ways of doctrine and of power, the one of light and the other of darkness. But there is a great difference between these two ways, for the angels of God are in charge of one of them, bearing light, while the angels of Satan are in charge of the other. (Chap. XVIII)
>
> So the way of light is this: if anyone wants to reach the assigned destination, let him strive to obtain it by his works. And so the knowledge we are given in this way of walking is: Thou shalt love thy Creator; thou shalt give glory to Him that has redeemed thee from death. Thou shalt be simple of heart and rich in spirit. Thou shalt not cleave to those who walk in the way of death. Thou shalt hate to do what does not please God. *Etc.* (Chap. XIX, *The way of light.*)

But the way of darkness is tortuous and accursed. For it is the way of eternal death with torture, in which are found those things which bring ruin upon the soul: idolatry, rashness, exaltation on account of power, hypocrisy, fickleness, adultery, homicide, robbery, pride. *Etc.*[18] (Chap. XX, *The way of darkness.*)

4. The *Ecclesiastical Canons of the Holy Apostles* belongs to much the same period. In their pages Saint John is cited as saying, "There are two ways, the one of life and the other of death… For the way of life is this: first, thou shalt love God who made thee with thy whole heart." Etc.

5. Close to them are the *Constitutions of the Holy Apostles*, where, in the prologue to Book VII, we read: "The Lord Jesus also deservedly said: No man can serve two masters." And of the two ways: "There is no resemblance between them, but a vast difference; indeed they are entirely distinct; and one is the way of natural life, while the other is devoted to death."

6. A famous record is the book of Saint Hermas entitled *The Shepherd*, written at the latest, says Fessler, around the year 150. "Truly a

---

[17] *Ibid.*, col. 734.

[18] *Ibid.*, coll. 775-779.

useful book," comments Saint Jerome, "and many of the ancient writers have made use of its testimonies."[19]

In Book 1, Vision 3, the building of the Church triumphant is described: six angels join together splendid stones, squared and polished, so as to construct a tower the joints of which should not be perceptible; but other stones to a great number, brought by many thousands of men, they cast forth and did not use them for the building.[20]

In Book III of the same work, Parables 3 and 4, men in the wayfaring state are compared to trees; in the wintertime living trees cannot be distinguished from dead ones, but in the summer those that are green stand out sharply from those that are dried up. So shall it be in the consummation of the world.[21]

7. Clement of Alexandria, (fl. 217), with his eclectic school, began to use the human wisdom of the philosophers to support Revelation, making especial use of Pythagoras whose character is particularly practical. Hence he writes in his *Stromata*, bk. 5, chap. 5, with regard to Pythagoras' symbols: "Moreover, as the Gospel, the Apostles and all the Prophets speak of the *two ways*, one of which they call *narrow* and *strait*, being hemmed in by precepts and prohibitions, whereas the other is called *broad* and *spacious*, in which free rain is given to pleasures and to anger ... Pythagoras too, when he admonishes his readers to take the royal road, does not hesitate to *forbid them to follow the judgement of the crowd* as being for the most part rash and incongruous."

8. Origen (fl. 254), the colleague of Clement of Alexandria and, like him, a disciple of Pythagoras, also interprets the figure of the two ways and the narrow gate which few find (see below, p. 116).

9. The Christian poet Ausonius composed verses upon the letter **Y** as being a figure invented by Pythagoras and bearing his name:

---

[19] *De viris illustribus*, cap. X ; Migne, *Pat. Græc.*, vol. II, col. 850.

[20] *Ibid.*, col. 902.

[21] *Ibid.*, col. 655.

> The Letter of Pythagoras, divided as it is into two prongs,
> Is seen to offer a symbol of human life.
> For the arduous path of virtue chooses the right hand fork
> And offers a difficult first approach to onlookers,
> But it affords rest to the fatigued upon the lofty summit.
> Gentle is the route displayed by the broad way,
> But when its bourne is reached
> It casts down headlong those it has ensnared
> And rolls them over the rough rocks.[22]

And when the same poet is speaking of the Greek and Latin monosyllabic letters, he introduces the letter Y personified and saying "I spread my arms apart for I am Pythagoras' two-pronged road-fork."[23]

10. In instructing the emperor Constantine about the two ways, Lactantius uses the same figure: "There are two ways, O Emperor Constantine, by which human life must advance. The one leads up to heaven and the other down to hell. The poet has evoked them in his songs and the philosophers in their disputations.... For they say that the course of man's life is like the letter Y and that every man, when he has reached the threshold of adolescence and come to the point at which 'the road divides into two paths,' hesitates for a moment, wondering which fork to choose...

For what need is there of the letter Y in matters contrary and diverse? But the better of the two (prongs) is turned to the rising of the sun and the worse to its setting, for he that follows truth and justice, when he

---

[22] Migne, *Pat. Græc.*, vol. IX, col. 54.
Littera Pythagoræ discrimine secta bicorni
Humanæ vitæ speciem præferre videtur.
Nam via virtutis dextrum petit ardua callem,
Difficilemque aditum primum spectantibus offert:
Sed requiem præbet fessis in vertice summo.
Molle ostentat iter via lata: sed ultima meta
Præcipitat captos, volvitque per ardua saxa.
[23] *Ibid.*, vol. XIX, col. 901. "Pythagoræ bivium ramis pateo ambiguis."

shall have received the reward of immortality, will enjoy everlasting light. *Etc.*[24]

I have deemed it superfluous to follow Lactantius through his long dissertation on the properties of each way; my point has been sufficiently made by citing this text against those who have the impudence to deny that there is any tradition as to the matter before us.

11. The great Saint Jerome several times approves the interpretation of Lactantius concerning the letter Y. For instance in his *Commentary on Ecclesiastes*, Chap. X, he writes: "Our Firmianus [Lactantius] also mentions the letter Y in his celebrated work entitled *The Institutions*, where he treats very fully of things of the right and of the left, i.e. of virtues and vices."[25]

And in writing to the Christian mother Laeta he supposes that the doctrine of the symbol Y is known to her: "But he that is a child and understands as a child, until he reaches the age of understanding and *the Pythagorean letter* confronts him with its road-fork, both his good acts and his bad are attributed to his parents."[26]

And again in the Epistle to Pamachius he says: "Lot, which means *declining*, chooses the level ground and, in terms of the Pythagorean letter, pursues rather such things as are easy and *leftward*."[27]

These texts may suffice to show the ancient tradition of the two ways and I am astonished at the effrontery of the Progressives in daring to deny it.

> O Timothy, keep that which is committed to thy trust, avoiding the profane novelties of words, and oppositions of knowledge falsely so called."[28]
> For there shall be a time, when they will not endure sound doctrine; but, according to their own desires, they will heap to themselves teach-

---

[24] Lactantius, *Divin. Instit.*, lib. VI., cap. III; Migne, *Pat. Lat.*, vol. VI, coll. 641, 642 and 644.

[25] Migne, *Pat. Lat.*, vol. XXIII, col. 1146.

[26] Epist. CVII; Migne, *Pat. Lat.*, vol. XXII, col. 873.

[27] Epist. LXVI; Migne, *Pat. Lat.*, col. 645.

[28] I Timothy, VI, 20.

ers, having itching ears: And will indeed turn away their hearing from the truth, but will be turned unto fables.[29]

Despise not the discourse of them that are ancient and wise, but acquaint thyself with their proverbs. For of them thou shalt learn wisdom, and instruction of understanding, and to serve great men without blame.[30]

...

After writing the foregoing I chanced upon a little work, recently republished, expressly to support and spread the doctrine of the greater number of the saved: *La Confiance en la miséricorde de Dieu* by Languet.

Concerning this excellent author, its editor writes: "A contemporary of Massillon, Languet seems to have shared this author's severe opinion, for he tells us that: 'One last motive for fear remains for just souls: it is what *faith* teaches us as to the fewness of the elect.'" This is clear, certain and salutary.

Now admire the dexterity with which the editor, a confrère of Fr. Castelein, manages in a few words first to entangle this salutary doctrine and then to change its meaning to the very opposite: "However it is certain that this doctrine does not belong to Catholic *dogma* and that it is a mere error caused by an exaggerated interpretation of *certain* texts of Holy Scripture." (p. 6)

Thus in a single stroke what the learned Archbishop Languet declares to be of faith is presented as an error due to his ignorance.

Yet,

1. When Languet, with many other theologians affirms that the fewness of the elect is of faith, as having been clearly enough revealed by God, he by no means says that it has been *defined de fide* or that it is a dogma imposed by the Church for the obligatory belief of all.

2. How does the Editor dare write: "this is an error"?

---

[29] II Timothy, IV, 3-4.

[30] Ecclesiasticus, VIII, 9-10.

3. How dare he add, and so vaguely, "caused by an exaggerated interpretation of *certain* texts of Holy Scripture" and accuse of ignorance the author of whom he has himself written, "He was admitted to the *Académie Française*. His polemical writings earned him a laudatory brief from the Sovereign Pontiff. Ever at war with the Jansenists he combated their discouraging doctrines with vigour and success." (p. 5)

Languet was influenced to embrace the common opinion not only by the genuine interpretation of Scripture but also by the authority of Tradition and by his daily experience of the life of the multitude, just as the Doctors and Theologians of all the centuries were before him.

But towards the end of this re-edition of his work, the title suddenly changes and in place of the authentic work of Archbishop Languet the unsuspecting reader is confronted with three chapters extracted from a work by a certain Loggero entitled *On the Number of the Elect*. And in their pages are found not the traditional doctrine taught by Languet on this topic but sophistries of the same kidney as those I am about to refute and no more convincing in their probative value.

Moreover, weighty theologians are quoted in such a way as to make unfair use of the various meanings of the word "elect" as used in some of their writings and thereby to encourage the unsuspecting reader to think that they teach that the number of the elect is great whereas in reality they teach the very opposite expressly and at length.

Finally, I note that this work, like those of Bougaud, Mauran and Fr. Castelein's second edition, appears without special approval. Granted it bears the inscription "under the auspices of the Belgian Episcopate", followed by the names of six members of our hierarchy, but there is no sign of the *Imprimatur* of the Superior of the Order or of the Ordinary of the place. Oh how many errors the propagators of the doctrine of the greater number of the elect would have avoided if they had observed to the letter the following golden rules of the Sacred Congregation of the Index:

XXXVI. Let religious remember that in addition to the Bishop's permission they are bound by the decree of the Sacred Council of Trent to obtain authorization to publish their work from the Prelate to whom they are subject.

XLI. All the faithful are bound to submit to ecclesiastical censorship at least those books which concern the Divine Scriptures, sacred Theology … or other religious or moral disciplines of the same kind as well as all writings in general which have special relevance to religion and moral uprightness.

XLIIII. Printers and Publishers are informed that new editions of a work that has already been approved require new approval.

CHAPTER ONE

THE SALUTARY DOCTRINE OF THE FEWNESS OF THE SAVED IS NOT MERELY SPECULATIVE, BUT LADEN WITH PRACTICAL CONSEQUENCES.

THE DOCTRINE of eternal salvation is like a good seed which the Redeemer of souls sowed in the field of His Church from the start both directly and through His Apostles, then, as time passed, through his servants and especially through His Holy Doctors. But Christ Himself foretold what would happen to this seed: "But while men were asleep, his enemy came and oversowed cockle among the wheat and went his way."[31] This cockle takes different forms in different periods.

1. In our own age, however, notwithstanding the claims of the Progressives, the cockle is no longer *Rigorism* as it was in the days of the Jansenists. As Pope Pius IX has said: "It was not without a most providential disposition of almighty God that, at the precise time when the doctrine of the Jansenists was dazzling novelty-mongers and the error was attracting many adherents by feigned beauty and leading them astray, Alphonsus-Maria arose and succeeded, but his

---

[31] Matthew, XIII, 25.

learned and painstaking writings, in *utterly* uprooting this Hell-sent pest and *banishing* it from the field of the Lord."[32]

The cockle of our own age is *Laxism*, due to ignorance of the faith especially in the popular schools, and to false principles concerning piety and the truly Christian life, etc., etc. This is attested by the Church's current watchman-in-chief, Pope Leo XIII: "It is all too obvious how many and how various are the means of corruption by which the malice of the world deceitfully strives to debilitate and indeed utterly uproot from souls the Christian faith and all that fosters observance of the divine law and encourages its fruitfulness; already the field of the Lord, as though struck with some foul pestilence, is all but become a wilderness by ignorance of the faith, errors and vices.... Hence there are grave grounds to lament the public schools deliberately organized to ignore, or revile, the name of God. Nor is the resulting laxness and apathy of the Catholic profession in many quarters less lamentable: if it is not yet open defection from the faith, it is certainly well on the way to reaching that stage when faith no longer accords in any respect with life."[33]

And with justice does Dom Guéranger deplore it that, "enfeebled by the continual search for ease and by outrageous demands on what we call our sentiment, we lack the courage to fulfil our duties! Is it not true to say that holiness is no longer understood? It astonishes and even gives scandal."[34]

Among the doctrines of the Saints which scandalize our lax age must be numbered their persuasion of *the fewness of the saved*, which is utterly true, scriptural and universal.

---

[32] Pope Pius IX, Apostolic Letter *Qui ecclesiæ suæ*, 7th July 1871, declaring Saint Alphonsus Liguori a Doctor of the Church.

[33] Encyclical *Magna Dei Matris*, 7th Sept., 1892.

[34] Guéranger, Dom Prosper (1805-1875), *The Liturgical Year*, 21st January, Feast of Saint Agnes.

Yet it is attacked by Bougaud in his *Le christianisme et les temps présents* (Vol. V, chap. 16), and by Fr. Castelein S.J. in his *Le rigorisme, le nombre des élus et la science du salut.*

I have no hesitation in joining my confrère Fr. Coppin in calling this book "a work of no value in terms of doctrine,"[35] — "with little excuse if any for its publication"[36] — and "highly pernicious to souls".[37]

Indeed with regard to this latter point:

1. It diminishes the reverence and submission owed to preachers and pious writers;

2. It weakens horror of sin;

3. It depreciates the genuine notion of the Christian life;

4. It contradicts the common doctrine of the Church concerning the world and its dangers relative to the salvation of souls;

5. It reduces readers' esteem for the Church and how necessary she is;

6. It deceives the faithful;

7. And it inspires them with the spirit of presumption.[38]

---

[35] "This book, in terms of the thesis it purports to establish, is *of no value.*" (*La question de l'Évangile*, etc., — *Considérations sur l'écrit du R. P. Castelein*, etc., pp. 292 and 309.)

[36] "Fr. Castelein has written his book *without the slightest reason*, for its stated goal of combating rigorism, a remnant of Jansenism and a terrorism redolent of Mohammed … is naught but a gigantic spectre created by his own imagination." (*Ibid.* p. 311)

[37] "*In its various tendencies* it is liable to *be harmful* to souls…. This book is *pernicious* to souls." (pp. 292, 308)

[38] *Ibid.*, pp. 308-330. Nonetheless the praises of this perverse book are sung. "This book is a capital work. — It corrects a great many errors. — It clears the ground. — Its clarity as to life and death are dazzling and comforting. It is eminently salutary that men as competent and authoritative as Fr. Castelein should raise their voices! How many prejudices will fall away before Fr. Castelein's readers!" And Fr. Castelein himself humbly observes of his won work that "One of America's main Catholic journals has reproduced it for its one hundred thousand readers. *My ideas are true and just. They are the fruit of deep study of Holy Scripture and of the teaching of our greatest theologians.* — I should not be embarrassed to reply to my

2. In their vain attempts to refute the universal doctrine of the Saints concerning the fewness of the saved, its adversaries tilt gleefully at the windmill of Massillon's celebrated sermon *On the fewness of the elect*, as if the collapse of a *false demonstration* of a doctrine sufficed for the doctrine itself to fall to the ground. But as Fr. Coppin has well remarked, "the illustrious Massillon is, if I may be allowed the expression, but the man of straw used by Father Castelein to attack those whom he calls *the Rigorists*."[39] Bougaud uses the same technique.

But Massillon's sermon has long since been refuted, among others by the celebrated Rohrbacher,[40] who shows that it is full of exaggerations and based on a false dilemma.

Here for example is a false reasoning it uses: to save one's soul a man must either preserve his baptismal innocence or else do penance after the fashion of the Saints, whose penance was heroic. But few are those who conserve their baptismal innocence and few indeed are those who do heroic penance. Therefore there are very few who are saved.

But I deny the *major* dilemma: for there is a third position which is not only possible but real, namely ordinary penance which, as all admit, is truly sufficient.

But the rejection of Massillon's defective logic leaves the universal doctrine of the Saints as to the fewness of the saved unshaken and in possession by virtue of its own weight.

3. Moreover the refutation of Massillon alone entails no refutation whatever of the countless other preachers who, unrebuked, indeed approved, by the Church, have taught the selfsame truth as Massillon though with more solid arguments. Among them, to name only

contradictors. I ask only that the attack should be learned and precise." (Forward to the second edition)

[39] *Op. cit.*, p. 8.

[40] *Histoire universelle de l'Église catholique*, livre 89; Paris, 1852, vol. 27, p. 361.

those of the French nationality, are: Lejeune, Loriot, Houdry, Bour-rée, Bretonneau, Dufay, Ballet, Surian, Jard, Collet, Griftet S.J., Girardot S.J., De la Tour, De Géry, Richard, Billot, de Bulonde, Doucet, Roy, Gamberd, de Rancé, Chenart, Chevassu, Brydaine, Card. Giraud, etc.[41] The same topic has been treated by the mass of Italian preachers in their Lenten sermons. Indeed it may be stated, in the words of Fr. Schrader, that, "the common and universal preaching exercised in any age belongs to the Church's ordinary magisterium."[42]

Neither does the refutation of Massillon entail the refutation of Saint Leonard of Port Maurice's famous sermon on the same topic. This Saint, as the Church herself attests, was a man whom God in His mercy "rendered powerful by *word* and deed to turn the obstinate hearts of sinners to repentance."[43] Moreover his sermon *On the Fewness of the Saved* was delivered at Rome, with immense fruit, during the pontificate of Benedict XIV who had a high opinion of the holy missioner; this very sermon was in fact at least implicitly approved by the Church in the examination of the works of the Servant of God preparatory to his beatification.

There can therefore be no question of saying of this sermon what Bougaud says about that of Massillon: "It was debated whether this sermon should be put on the Index and it is regrettable that it was not so condemned."[44] On the contrary it is noteworthy that a certain chapter (and study) arguing that the elect are more numerous was put on the Index and condemned outright, as we shall be seeing: "it shall be deleted" says the judgement.

4. And the pious reader should not deceive himself on the grounds that some writings of the Progressives concerning *the great number of*

---

[41] Migne, *Collection Intégrale et Universelle des Orateurs Sacrés*, and X; Villaume C.SS.R., *Tables générales.*

[42] Schrader, Clement, S.J., *De Theologia Generatim Commentarius*, p. 102.

[43] Collect for his feast, 28th November.

[44] *Le christianisme et les temps présents*, 4th ed., vol. V, p. 378.

the elect bear the approbation of their Superiors; the teaching expounded therein cannot be judged definitely sound merely because it is approved. For, as His Holiness Pope Leo XIII writes: "No one should imagine that it is lawful for one to adopt indiscriminately any opinions which he may by chance have found in books written by members of the Society of Jesus *and published with the permission of the superiors*.... The superiors-general have constantly opposed any such freedom and have not hesitated to declare often and clearly, *even in our own times*, that *greater diligence and severity would be desirable on the part of some of the appointed censors.*"[45]

But to return to Saint Leonard, whose sermon the Progressives neither refute nor denounce to the Index, but enshroud in discreet and total silence, this sterling Minister of the Word of God, had no wish, like a certain modern author, to "accomplish a salutary apostolate by striving to enlighten the faith of my readers in order to bring it into harmony with the demands of their reason and the needs of their heart."[46] Indeed his understanding of the apostolate of Jesus Christ was quite the opposite, and "the hearts of his listeners, however hardened and stony, were broken to repentance by the wondrous efficacy of his words and the most ardent zeal with which he pronounced them,"[47] especially by the sermon on the fewness of the elect. Neither did Saint Leonard discuss this topic in the pages of the worldly press or secular newspapers, but, as is fitting, in the chair of truth.

---

[45] The candid reader will also note that this edition of Fr. Castelein's book, which is entitled "second edition, revised and expanded" bears no specific approval. It left the presses in March 1899 yet the Ordinary's approval is dated ... 18th September 1898 and the diocesan approval 25th September, i.e. it is the same as served for the first edition. But the 1896 decree of the Congregation of the Index commands: "Printers and publishers should note that new editions of the same work that has once been approved require a new approval. (Rule 44)

[46] The quotation is from Fr. Castelein. — Translator.

[47] *Roman Breviary*, 28th November, Lesson 6.

The zealous missioner did not consider this sermon to be merely speculative, but highly practical, as the following excerpts will clearly show.

Here is one part of this very famous sermon :[48]

> The subject I will be treating today is a very grave one ; it has caused even the pillars of the Church to tremble, filled the greatest Saints with terror and populated the deserts with anchorites. The point of this instruction is to decide whether the number of Christians who are saved is greater or less than the number of Christians who are damned ; it will, I hope, produce in you a salutary fear of the judgments of God.
>
> Brothers, because of the love I have for you, I wish I were able to reassure you with the prospect of eternal happiness by saying to each of you : You are certain to go to paradise ; the greater number of Christians is saved, so you also will be saved. But how can I give you this sweet assurance …?
>
> … I will let the theologians and Fathers of the Church decide on the matter and declare that the greater number of Christian adults are damned… .
>
> It is not vain curiosity but salutary precaution to proclaim from the height of the pulpit certain truths which serve wonderfully to contain the insolence of libertines, who are always talking about the mercy of God and about how easy it is to convert, yet who live all the while plunged in all sorts of sins and are soundly sleeping on the road to hell. To disillusion them and waken them from their torpor, today let us examine this great question : Is the number of Christians who are saved greater than the number of Christians who are damned?

5. The practical utility of the subject is also recognized by the celebrated Dominican theologian Fr. Jean-Baptiste Gonet :

> Since we are debtors to the wise and to the unwise and in any event the solution to this question can be useful for arousing within us the fear of God which is the beginning of wisdom and the foundation of salvation, and is, as Saint Ambrose states, 'the rudder of the wave-tossed soul', I wish to show that the opinion which maintains that, of Christians and of the faithful, many more are reprobate than are chosen, agrees better with Holy Scripture, the Fathers and Ecclesiastical History than the

---

[48] Saint Leonard of Port-Maurice, Sermon XXIV, *On the Fewness of the Elect*.

other opinion according to which the number of the elect is greater than the number of the reprobate.[49]

This is confirmed by Estius, who writes:

> This doctrine is useful, so that amid so few elect, each person may realise what great care should be taken to work out his salvation by a good life in order to be found among those few.[50]

And among those whom I am attacking, Bougaud himself remarks: "Will the majority or only a minority be saved? The question is obscure and appears idle! Yet, it is not so, for it is the questions of the practical utility of Christianity."[51]

And in the same way Fr. Faber says: "Nevertheless, if I could persuade myself that the discussion had but little practical bearing on a holy life, I should eagerly avoid entering upon it."[52]

The utility of this examination is evident from daily experience. For we missioners and confessors, especially in great cities and in places where little piety is found, observe how prompt and eager souls are to seize on any notion which diminishes the terror of hell and how readily they "say to those who see: See not: and to them that behold: Behold not for us those things that are right: speak unto us pleasant things, see errors for us."[53]

6. Among these weak and delusive seers we may certainly not number Fr. Bourdaloue S.J., easily the prince of France's Christian orators. Here is what he wrote:

> *It is well-established that the number of the elect will be smaller and that there will be incomparably more reprobate.*

---

[49] *Clypeus Theologiæ Thomisticæ*, Tract. V, *De Præd.*, disp. IV, digr. ii; ed. Vivès, vol. II, p. 363.

[50] *In lib. sent.*, dist. 40, §23; 1662, p. 148.

[51] *Op. cit.*, 4th ed., vol. V, p. 362.

[52] *The Creator and the Creature*, 4th ed., p. 353.

[53] Isaias, XXX, 10.

Yet preachers still wonder whether it is appropriate to explain this truth to the people and to speak of it in the pulpit, because, forsooth, it is liable to trouble souls and cast them into discouragement.

But it would be just as well-founded to ask whether it is desirable to explain the Gospel to the people and to preach it from the pulpit. For, after all, what truth is more strongly emphasized in the Gospel than the fewness of the elect? What is there that the Saviour of the world in His divine instructions has declared more authentically, repeated oftener, given us more formally and more clearly to understand? *Many are called but few are chosen.* Thus does He end several of His parables. *The way that leads to perdition is broad and spacious*, He says elsewhere; *the majority choose it. But the way that leads to life is narrow; few there are who walk in it. Strive to enter by it.* Could anything be clearer than these words?

This is what the Son of God publicly taught. This is what He inculcated to His disciples. Are we better advised than He as to what is or is not fitting to be announced to the faithful?

Let us preach the Gospel and preach it without omission or edulcoration; let us preach it in all its entirety, in all its purity, in all its severity, in all its force. Woe to whoever shall be scandalized by it; he alone will bear the punishment for his scandal.

The illustrious preacher then goes on to reply in the following words to a few hackneyed objections:

We are told that the fewness of the elect is a truth that *makes men tremble!* Yet the Apostle explicitly calls on us to work out our salvation with fear and trembling.

We are told that this subject is one that troubles consciences! But consciences sometimes stand in great need of being troubled and it is better to wake them from their torpor by troubling them than to let them sleep on in idle and deceptive repose.

Or again we are told that the thought of so few elect is discouraging and leads to despair! True enough, this truth can indeed discourage and even lead to despair if it is badly understood, badly presented or exaggerated, and especially if it is advanced on the basis of false principles and erroneous opinions.

But let it only be accurately understood and presented in accordance with reality, contained within just limits and founded on sound principles, and far from leading to discouragement, nothing is more capable of moving us to make the final efforts needed to ensure our salvation and to take our place among the predestinate.

I acknowledge that there are certain versions of this doctrine of the fewness of the elect that cannot be preached without injury to Christian hope. For example, the claim that there will be few elect because God does not will the salvation of all men; or because Jesus Christ did not offer His death on the Cross for all, or does not give His grace to all. … This is why the Church has denounced such pernicious errors.

If I were to embark on a discourse concerning the fewness of the saved, this is what I think it ought essentially to contain. Before all else I would lay down the following principles:

1. We must all hope to be of the number of the elect…

2. We are all not only entitled but strictly bound to hope that we shall be among the elect…

3. There is no sinner who ought not to conserve this hope…

Having laid down these principles, I would go on to examine not *whether* there will be few elect, since Jesus-Christ has Himself expressly told us so in His Gospel; but *why* there will be few, namely because there are few — very few indeed — who walk in the way of salvation or who want to walk therein.

Next, taking the Gospel, and coming down to details, I would explain to whom salvation is promised.

Treated in this way, this important subject can produce no harmful effect but many very good ones.

To go further, even if there were some whom this subject led to despair, who would they be?

Those who do not *want* their salvation.

Those who are not determine to do all for the sake of their salvation.

Those who undertake to reconcile a life of softness, sensuality and convenience with salvation — a life without penance with salvation — those who seek to broaden as far as they can the path of salvation and who cannot bear to be told that this path is as narrow as it is in reality, because they cannot make up their minds to hold fast along so stony a track.

In any event, every wise and Christian listener will draw advantage from this thought of the fewness of the saved, and the consequent fear will teach him:

1. to redouble his vigilance and to fortify himself against dangers;

2. never to pass a single day in the state of mortal sin, but rather to hasten at once to use the remedy;

3. to separate himself from the multitude and hence from the world; to cut himself off from them, if not in fact – which is not possible for all – at least in spirit, in heart, in maxims, in sentiments and in behaviour;

4. to follow the minority of Christians truly worthy of the name, whose conduct is irreproachable and who are faithful to all their duties;

5. resolutely to choose the narrow way, for it is the one way that Jesus Christ Himself came to teach us; to make serious efforts, to persevere in the face of obstacles;

6. and finally, to solicit God's grace and commend his soul to God by constant and earnest prayer.

Happy the preacher who leaves his congregation in such holy dispositions! His labour has been to good purpose, and any subject capable of arousing such sentiments cannot but be most solid and most salutary.[54]

Such then was the how the holy preachers acted and spoke in the pulpit, convinced as they were that this doctrine is highly salutary.[55]

---

[54] *Pensées sur le salut, Petit nombre des élus*; Migne, *Collection Intégrale et Universelle des Orateurs Sacrés*, vol. XVI, col. 617.

[55] N.B. In addition to Bougaud and Fr. Castelein there is a third defender of the opinion that the greater number are to be saved: the Rev. Victor Mauran, parish priest of Marseilles, who published, without episcopal approval, a book entitled, *Élus et sauvés* which will be discussed later in more detail. But let the reader judge the worth of this contender from a single quotation (pp. 239-40): "The logic of Saint Thomas seems to me to be *clearly defective* here. It amounts to *begging the question*... The entire reasoning of the Saint comes down to saying that *what is not common is not common*. Such an argument is certainly of no great value."

CHAPTER TWO

ALTHOUGH THE NUMBER OF THE ELECT IS KNOWN TO
GOD ALONE, THE MIND OF THE CHURCH SEEMS TO BE
IN FAVOUR OF FEWNESS.

PREDESTINATION is so deep a mystery as to be impenetrable to the human intelligence.

"O God to whom alone is known the number of the elect to be placed in eternal happiness...", says the Church in the Secret *for the living and the dead*, and the words of this prayer of course constitute a norm of belief for us.

1. Yet the Spouse of Eternal truth seems to incline in favour of the fewness of the elect.

For on the one hand she has condemned a text which asserted, and purported to demonstrate, that : "it is probable that the elect among mankind are far more numerous than the reprobate."

And on the other she has approved the writings and sermons of many Saints who explicitly taught the fewness of the saved, even in respect of adult Catholics.

Whereas we seek in vain a single Saint who has taught that the majority of men are saved.

2. The condemned work just mentioned appears as Chapter Five in a posthumously published work by Fr. Benedict Plazza S.J., enti-

tled *Dissertatio anagogica, theologica, parænetica de Paradiso*,[56] published in Palermo in 1762. The chapter in question, however, was not written by Fr. Palazza but by his confrère Fr. Joseph Maria Gravina S.J. and is entitled *Concerning the Number of the Elect Among Mankind in Comparison with the Number of the Reprobate*. By its decree of 22nd May 1772 the Sacred Congregation of the Index declared this chapter to be **condemned outright** and the entire work forbidden until this chapter should be deleted.

"In this chapter," says the famous theologian Hürter, "it is unhesitatingly alleged that: *it is probable that the elect among mankind are far more numerous that the reprobate*. Indeed it is purportedly demonstrated by the clearest proofs derived from every source as well as by arguments from Holy Writ, the Fathers, the theologians both scholastic and ascetic, and from heavenly revelations in addition to *select* theological conjectures almost countless in number. – Yet there can be no denying that it was precisely this fifth chapter that was condemned."[57] Thus writes Hürter, and in another work referring to the same subject he says: "The final chapter of this book, concerning the number of the elect, which the author *strives to exaggerate*, was prohibited."[58]

So notwithstanding its vaunted collection of proofs, this chapter was condemned outright, precisely on account of its teaching.

3. But this condemnation, issued in the year 1772, was not the first to strike the laxist Gravina, leader of the sentimentalist school which he christened *Benignism*.

For in the great work of Saint Alphonsus[59] may be read the theses of lax probabilism condemned by Pope Clement XIII in 1761 as containing propositions "of which some are false, some temerarious

---

[56] I.e. *A Mystical, Theological and Advisory Dissertation on Paradise*. — Translator.

[57] Hürter, Hugo S.J., *op. cit.*, vol. II, n. 145, note 2 ; 3rd ed., p. 97.

[58] Hürter, Hugo S.J., *Nomenclator Literarius Theologiæ Catholicæ*, vol. II, n. 521 ; 1879 edition, p. 1254.

[59] Liguori, Saint Alphonsus, *Theologia Moralis*, lib. 1, tr. 1, n. 85.

and some offensive to pious ears." And, although these theses were published in the year 1760 by the parish priest of Avio in the diocese of Trent, they had been extracted in their entirety, almost word-for-word, from a work by Gravina published at Palermo in the year 1752 under the title *Conclusions concerning the Use and Abuse of the Probable Opinion*, and which can be found in Volume IV of the *Thesaurus Theologicus* of Zaccaria, pp. 335-350.

The reader is requested kindly to pay special attention in reading what now follows. The aforementioned decree condemning the eleven theses of lax probabilism says: "But [His Holiness] has judged that the one extracted from number X, namely *Probabilism which was highly familiar to Our Lord Jesus Christ...* should be proscribed as erroneous and proximate to heresy." And this very error, proximate to heresy, is taken from Gravina himself, who writes in the aforesaid study, "Without any trace of laxism I do indeed profess *Benignism*, but of a legitimate kind, i.e. that which is abundantly encouraged by both civil and pontifical law... and finally which is Christian, as it was *so dear and familiar to Our Lord Jesus Christ that nothing was more so!*"[60]

4. The same year in which Rome condemned this doctrine of the Sentimentalist Gravina, albeit without mentioning his name, saw the death, in the Jesuit college of Palermo, of Fr. Benedict Plazza. Over 80 at his death, he had begun a dissertation on Paradise which he left unfinished at his death, to be completed and published by his confrère Fr. Gravina. The latter explains that:

> For my part, being busy with other cares, chiefly literary, I would certainly have declined this task but for the fact that ... I had not only encouraged this elderly and infirm man to write this very book but also often incited and pressed him to complete it. The study is divided into three parts... Many were lacking in Part III for only its first chapter had all its numbered paragraphs complete. The author's intention had been

---

[60] Quoted by Zaccaria, Franceso Antonio (1714-95), *Thesaurus Theologicus*, vol. IV. p. 349, n. LIII.

for four further chapters to be added, the last of them on the number of the elect [i.e. the famous Chapter V destined to be condemned]... I had decided to delete it altogether...[61]

But Gravina did *not* delete it. After adding the other three missing chapters (pp. 404-518) to the last one (viz. Part III, Chapter I) completed by Fr. Plazza himself he begins, on p. 519, to set out the state, difficulty and usefulness of the question.

Then he sets about rendering his opinion *probable* by *conjectures* (for so he terms his own arguments) drawn from the Scriptures, the Fathers, the Exegetes, the Scholastics, the Ascetic theologians, the revelations of Saints Bridget, Catharine of Siena, Mechtilde, Gertrude, Mary-Magdalene de Pazzi and Margaret of Cortona, as well as Venerable Mary of Escobar.

After which he proceeds to confirm his view by the arguments or errors of the heterodox.

And next, on p. 677, he offers an appendix called *The theological problem*:

> Which of the two opinions is more glorious to Christ and more useful to us, the mild or the rigid?" And he concludes in favour of the mild opinion, especially "because man is more prone to despair than to presumption. (p. 682)

Finally, to maximize the credibility of his opinion, he adds three corollaries intended to add yet further weight to it.

> 1. As the opinion I am defending displeases heretics, it ought to be very pleasing to Catholics;
> 2. As this opinion displeases a handful of unlearned persons, it ought to be very pleasing to theologians;
> 3. As this opinion displeases those who are envious of our salvation, it ought to be very pleasing to those who are zealous for our salvation.

5. However the first of these corollaries is in disagreement with Gravina's own teaching. For in §X he corroborates his opinion by appealing to the "reasonings of the heterodox". He cites the *Book of*

---

[61] *Dissertatio anagogica*, etc., *Introd.* pp. III-VIII.

Dialogues published at Basel in 1554[62] and the apostate Vergerius.[63] The former work "was admittedly condemned by the Church both owing to hostility to the author who was a Calvinist miscreant and an apostate from the Catholic religion and because it is full of errors and heresies," is entitled *Concerning the extent of the blessed kingdom of God.*

6. It makes use of three arguments in particular:

1. otherwise the Devil would boast that he has shown himself more powerful in damning men than God in saving them;
2. otherwise the Scriptures would not have commended the riches and wealth of the divine Mercy in such exquisite words;
3. by the common consensus of the Fathers and the Theologians, in addition to the manifest faithful, there are also *occult* believers. (p. 637)

As we shall be seeing later, these same three arguments, or rather sophisms of heterodox writers, are also exploited by Bougaud, Mauran and Fr. Castelein as decisive proofs.

7. With regard to the second corollary, Gravina, leader of the Sentimentalists, admits that his opinion at first sight gives grave scandal to the unlearned as it teaches that crowds of pagans, Mahometans, heretics, schismatics and Jews obtain salvation. But he thinks that this is a scandal to the unlearned, not to theologians, who, as though by some conspiracy, are teaching (especially the younger ones against the Jansenists) that in addition to explicit faith there is an implicit faith which is sufficient for salvation. And he thinks that the agreement of theologians in this opinion or dogma is derived from a consensus of the Holy Fathers who he fondly imagines all agreed in

---

[62] Probably the work of that title by early French Protestant Reformer Sebastian Castellio (1515–1563). — Translator.
[63] Pietro Paolo Vergerio (1498-1565) was a Catholic bishop who apostatized to Protestantism. — Translator.

subscribing to this opinion. Hence he considers this scandal to be *pharisaical* or *scandal of the weak*.[64]

8. Gravina also published his study "On the number of the elect among mankind in comparison with the number of the reprobate" separately, i.e. not as a part of Plazza's *Dissertation*.[65] This is why Gravina's name is found twice in the Catalogue of the *Index of Forbidden Books*: first under the word *Dissertation* and secondly in its alphabetical place.[66]

9. Gravina and his disciples, under the name of *Benignists* which they had adopted, were attacked by Concina, by Camaldolese theologian Fr. Anton-Maria Gardini who published his work under the title *Theological dissertation against the novelties of Fr. Gravina S.J., who opens the doors of heaven not only to heretics and schismatics but also to Jews, Mahometans, etc.,*[67] etc., as well as by Fr. Cari and other writers.

It was inevitable that Gravina's work would be swiftly denounced to Rome and this indeed occurred while Pope Clement XIII was still reigning, but only in 1772 did the Index prohibit both the separately published work and Plazza's work, "until such time as Chapter V, composed by the editor Fr. J. M. Gravina, which is condemned outright, shall be deleted...."[68]

---

[64] The moral theologians define *pharisaical scandal* as that which is taken by mere hypocrisy and *scandal of the weak* (or "of the little ones") as scandal due only to ignorance or poor judgement on the part of the person scandalized. — Translator.

[65] "Die Abhandlung erschien auch separat: J. M. Gravina, *De electorum*, etc., Palermo, 1764." (Reusch, Franz Heinrich (1825-1900), *Der Index der verboten Bücher*, vol. II, p. 976)

[66] 1899 edition, pp. 116 and 169.

[67] *Dissertatio Theologica adversus novitates Patris J. M. Gravinæ S.J., cælum januas reserentis non solum hæreticis et schismaticis verum etiam Hebræis, mahomedanis, etc.* (Venice, 1767).

[68] Another book was also condemned and placed on the Index "until corrected"; Marmontel's *Bélisaire*, by decree of 25th May 1767. This work also argued in favour of the opinion that the damned will be in the minority. "Is it necessary for there to be so many reprobate?" — (Cf. *Bulletin de Notre-Dame de la S. Espérance* — April 1899, p. 258).

10. The naive reader may be moved to conclude that by virtue of this condemnation the mind of the Church appears to be in favour of the fewness of the elect.

"Not in the least!" reply the Progressives. "Let no one invoke as an argument against our thesis the fact that Fr. Plazza's [i.e. Gravina's] work *de Paradiso* was put on the Index because of its Chapter V in which the same thesis is defended. Many different motives *may* explain this condemnation, *for instance* the credence extended to visions that are unreliable and have scant probative value."[69] It is not the doctrine taught in the condemned chapter which is condemned, forsooth, but perhaps just the author's acceptance of private revelations which prove too little! But this is mere guesswork – entirely gratuitous and devoid of the least likelihood.

In fact, Pope Benedict XIV stipulates in his Constitution *Sollicita ac provida* the method to be observed in prohibiting books. Rule N° 19 says:

> But if a few ambiguous words have escaped an author who is in other respects Catholic and who is reputed to be of sound religious belief and practice, justice seems to require that his remarks be mildly interpreted insofar as is possible and understood in a favourable sense.

So if Gravina had really placed excessive reliance on an argument derived from revelations or any other source, it is scarcely credible that for this reason alone the Sacred Congregation would so severely strike a Catholic author if it had not deemed his *doctrine* in other respects worthy of censure. Surely it would simply have required that the chapter be *corrected* rather than *expunged*. How could the chapter's *deletion* have been exacted if its fundamental doctrine had been capable of any sound interpretation? Would the *work* have been condemned *outright*, i.e. utterly and entirely, if it were defending a Catholic position, albeit perhaps with quite inadequate arguments?

11. Moreover Fr. Castelein is entirely mistaken in his supposition. Gravina himself states quite clearly in §9 of the Prologue to his work

---

[69] Castelein, *op. cit.*, 2nd edition, p. 285, note.

what measure of credence he extends to the private revelations he cites. It is precisely that which may be given them according to the doctrine of Ven. Fr. Louis Blosius, a most learned man and outstanding for his knowledge particularly in the domain of ascetical theology, set out in his *Monile spirituale* in which he discusses the authority of private revelations.

And as a matter of fact this work of Blosius was never placed on the Index nor were its doctrines ever censured, so how can we believe that Gravina's work was condemned for following the same doctrine? Especially given that it places its chief reliance on the revelations of those very Saints whom Blosius especially recommends, viz. Saints Bridget, Catharine of Siena, Mechtilde and Gertrude.

Fr. Castelein is therefore quite mistaken and there can be no doubt that this chapter, written by the religious Fr. Gravina, was condemned on account of the teaching therein defended.

12. A Jesuit writer using the initials E.T. and writing in the newspaper *Le Patriote*, 19th March 1899, expressed himself in similar terms:

> I draw attention to the note concerning the fact that during the last century of a lengthy chapter added to Fr. Plazza's work and treating of a similar but much more emphatic thesis was placed on the *Index of Forbidden Books.*
>
> It is true that this chapter was condemned, but this is all too sufficiently explained, for anyone who consults the un-theological and even, to be frank, puerile arguments which it invoked and the account of more or less debatable visions which the author puts to ill use, as well as the exaggerated conclusions he purports to draw from such evidence. None of this restrained Fr. Monsabré and neither was there any reason for it to hold back our present author [viz. Fr. Castelein].

This is merely playing with words!

"A … chapter … treating of a similar … thesis…" Gravina's thesis is not 'similar' to Fr. Castelein's but identical. Gravina's aim is to prove that it is probable that the number of the elect among mankind is far greater than the number of the reprobate, in terms of the entire human race. This is quite clear from the propositions which distinguish the individual paragraphs, compared with N[os] 282-5. "And since the opinion to which I adhere," he says in N° 284, "is the first of these...." This first opinion is stated in N° 283: "the elect are greater in number than the reprobate, out of the whole of mankind." Fr. Castelein advances not a similar position but the very same one: "The conquest of Jesus-Christ among the whole of mankind will be far greater than the conquest of Satan... Christ will succeed in winning, out of all the people and every human environment, more elect than He will leave being among the reprobate". (2nd ed., pp. 267, 301).

"*But much more emphatic...*" Not only does Gravina not go further than Castelein, but in fact, when it comes to the claims he makes for the certainty of his thesis, it is Castelein who goes further than Gravina. Gravina calls his claims *likely*; he wants his own view to be considered probable while he admits that the opposing view is probable and indeed *more probable* (N° 453). Castelein, by contrast, disregarding the venerable authority of the Fathers and the theologians, writes: "The arguments adduced from Holy Scripture and from Catholic theology are incomparably weightier in favour of the elect being in the majority. The numerous, varied and clear texts assembled in these pages *ought to dissipate all doubt on the point.... I am convinced* that Christ will win ... incomparably more souls than He will allow to be snatched from Him." (2nd ed., p. 266) Let the reader judge for himself which of these claims is the more audacious.

"*This is all too sufficiently explained, for anyone who consults the un-theological and even puerile arguments ... which it invoked...*" Gravina made use of Holy Scripture, the Fathers, the Exegetes, the scholastic and ascetical theologians and private: all of which are sources whence a writer is much more entitled to adduce theological arguments than the writings of the pagan philosophers and poets. If, as applies in the case we are considering, the arguments found in their pages are in fact vain and worthless; if as a matter of fact, despite the author's best efforts, they contribute nothing to proving a thesis which is sound in itself, ought not this author rather to be pitied than to be ignominiously condemned and placed on the Index? Where should we be if every writer who defended a thesis with irrelevant arguments, even if the thesis itself was not only probable but true, was to be placed on the Index? After all, the Sacred Congregation of the Index exists to vindicate Catholic doctrine, not the rules of logic.

"*…the account of more or less debatable visions…*" Gravina cites the revelations of Saint Bridget which are approved by the Church, as well as the revelations of other Saints which are universally held to be authentic and are made available to all with the full knowledge and approval of the Church.

"*…which the author puts to ill use…*" He simply cites them, so wherein lies the abuse, unless perhaps it be in what follows, namely:

"*…as well as the exaggerated conclusions he purports to draw from such evidence.*" The *only* conclusion he claims to deduce from them is the very same thesis defended by Castelein, albeit in despite of the laws of reason, for in reality the passages he quotes prove nothing except that God is merciful. Once again allow me to enquire: is the Sacred Congregation of the Index there to safeguard logic?

13. "*… None of this restrained Fr. Monsabré.*" I should very much like to be told precisely where that eloquent apologist defends Fr. Castelein's position. The most likely place to look would seem to be his Conference N° 102: *The other world — the number of the elect,* which certainly treats of the *subject.* In its pages Fr. Monsabré addresses the following difficulty:

> We constantly hear references to the fewness of those who are saved… Does not this amount to an avowal that this great abundance of merciful initiatives is all but useless … and that a hostile empire is triumphing over God's sovereign power and frustrating the aims of His government?

But the orator replies that this claim is inadmissible because its premises, concerning the fewness of the elect, *are not sufficiently certain.* For (he says, in Part I) the opinion is that few are saved *out of the human race,* but another opinion, also probable,[70] is that *in absolute terms,* many are saved. For it is probable that the greater part of Catholics are saved if we count children who die before the age of reason, to whom we may add the children of heretics etc. and such adult heretics as are in good faith, the children of infidels who are baptized before death, infidel adults who have observed in good faith the law of nature insofar as God has enlightened them, and finally such of the impious as grace wins over at the instant of death. "I think that with all these elements of salvation we can reach *a considerable number,* able to do honour to the divine mercy." So, in absolute terms, many men are saved, at least probably, which is all that Monsabré intended to show, namely that *it is not certain that few are saved.*

But now the orator moves on to discuss Fr. Castelein's *comparative* thesis. "Would you claim, gentlemen, *that the number of the elect, no matter how great it may be, is less than the number of the reprobate?* — **What does it matter?** You can no longer accuse God's government of failure. God willed the salvation of all... Not having obtained the triumph of His mercy over these rebels, He is sure of the triumph of His justice. No matter how many of these proud souls there may be, they cannot outweigh the immense army of the elect. A single saved soul is a masterpiece in which all the divine perfections act together, in concert with human freedom; a single creature glorified and admitted to the beatific vision is a marvel of beauty more astonishing and more ravishing than all the wonders of heaven and earth together. Yet there are those who would dishonour the author of this marvel by reproaching Him with the numerical quantity of the wretches who have deformed themselves by

---

[70] The word *probable* here and throughout this book is used in its technical theological meaning. In theology an opinion is called *probable* if "it is based on grave foundation of reason or authority which is sufficient to win the assent of a prudent man but does not exclude some fear that the contrary may prove correct". Thus two conflicting opinions may *both* be "probable". (Saint Alphonsus Liguori, *Theologia Moralis,* lib. I, cap. III, n. 40 et seq.) — Translator.

abusing the divine gifts and their own freedom? As well might one claim that mankind has no genius to boast of in our days because the number of genuine masterpieces does not match the number of the miserable specimens with which the world is flooded by those whose puny talent and poor taste are spurred by ambition. It is not a matter of counting, gentlemen, but a matter of weighing. A single saved soul weighs more in the balance of divine glory than the whole of Hell. '**Multo** sunt **plures** *gehennam ingredientes, sed* **majus** *est regnum cœlorum.*' [Many *more* are those who enter hell, but *greater* is the kingdom of heaven.] (Saint John Chrysostom)"

Thus the learned apologist not only does not hold Fr. Castelein's thesis, but he openly admits, to the contrary, that the *greater part of mankind* is damned, a fact which he mentions as an incidental difficulty, true in itself, but which he shows to have no weight against the case he is making. And indeed he shows this by an argument which also exposes beyond cavil the utter worthlessness of one of the main planks of Fr. Castelein's own case.

Then in Part II, venturing beyond the confines of the human race, he adds weight to his claim that absolutely speaking it is not certain that the number of the saved is few, given that (i) it is probable or at least possible that that the end of the world is not yet at all close and that all the nations of the globe may yet enter into humble submission to Christ and long remain so; (ii) it is certain that there are countless holy angels and it is at least possible that there are many elect among rational inhabitants of the stars or planets, and (iii) the present creation may not be the only one. These of course are no more than opinions and hypotheses, which serve to prove that no certain objection can be made against divine providence, for "in a matter which involves the very honour of God, I think that every consideration should be taken into account, be it certain, probable or merely possible."

Where then, I ask, does Fr. Monsabré adopt the position of Fr. Castelein? What is the meaning of E. T.'s words: "*None of this restrained Fr. Monsabré?*"

14. The Church, which in the *Roman Breviary* refers to the elect as: "a little flock, either in comparison with the greater number of the reprobate or rather out of devotion to humility…"[71] has never condemned, but rather approved, at least indirectly, the doctrine of Saint Alphonsus, Saint Leonard of Port-Maurice and of other holy Doctors and Fathers as well as Theologians, who have taught the fewness of the saved explicitly both in their writings and in their popular preaching. And this doctrine is held by all the Holy Fathers, so that it is rightly termed *the common opinion* by the best theologians and, as Estius has rightly written, "None of the Fathers can be found to have written otherwise."[72]

15. Here and now, relying on such authorities, I summon all the defenders together of the lax opinion, i.e. of the greater number of the elect, and I challenge them to show me a single canonized Saint who holds their opinion! I am aware that Sylvester, Suárez, Steyaert, etc. taught the salvation, not of the majority of mankind — for on that point they shared the common teaching that the majority of men are damned — but the salvation of the majority of Catholics alone; and I am aware that Bougaud, Mauran, Castelein and some recent authors hope for the salvation of *almost all* Catholics, as well as of the majority of the human race. But what is the authority of these theologians in comparison with that of the Saints? Let them adduce, I repeat, a single authentic text taken from the genuine writings of a single canonized Saint.

16. The gainsayers, it is true, invoke the names of two Saints, with certain vague statements attributed to them.

Bougaud writes, with regard to the salvation of the majority of *Catholics*:

> This was the opinion of Saint Francis de Sales. His companions, says Mgr. Camus, were once discussing the terrible Gospel text that 'Many

---

[71] Common of confessors who are not bishops, Lesson VII of the alternative lessons, taken from a sermon of Saint Bede the Venerable.

[72] See Chapter IV below for the full text.

are called but few are chosen.' He replied that in his view there would be few Catholics who would be damned ... that very few were lost.

This was the opinion of Saint Alphonsus de Liguori, whose great maxim was that it was very difficult for a Catholic to be lost.

So says Bougaud,[73] and the better to convince his readers he adds, in a note, the very words of our holy Father, in the original language: "*difficilmente si danna*", with the vague reference, "Letter 2".[74] What could be easier to verify! And Fr. Castelein, speaking in general of the opinion that the majority will be damned, asserts that "Many of the Fathers, *perhaps* [?] motivated by their *conjectures* [?] as to the history of the world as they then knew it after forty centuries of paganism, believed that the number of the reprobate would be greater than the number of the elect, but there is nothing obligatory about this opinion. Two celebrated doctors of *modern times*, Saint Francis de Sales and Saint Alphonsus de Liguori *appear* to incline in favour of the opposite view. And Saint Thomas Aquinas, although he follows the *old* opinion, etc." (p. 283)

Now let the reader see and judge for himself what the doctrine of the more recent Doctors of the Church was and whether Bougaud and Castelein are justified in citing them as opposed to the unanimous doctrine of the Saints of every century.

17. (a) With regard to our Father and Doctor Saint Alphonsus, *eight* authentic passages will be cited in the beginning of the following chapter in which our Patriarch expressly asserts the contrary:

1. *two* in which he says that "the more common opinion holds that the majority even of those who have faith are damned;"
2. and *six* other texts in which he asserts in general terms that the elect are a minority.

---

[73] *Op. cit.*, p. 373. — Also "E. T.", *Le Patriote*, 19th March, 1899.

[74] Bougaud appears to have transcribed this without acknowledgement from Faber's *The Creator and the Creature*, edition of 1881, p. 315, but the learned and trustworthy English author correctly states the opinion of Saint Alphonsus whereas Bougaud truncates it and falsifies it.

Yet notwithstanding such clarity, Bougaud declares: "Saint Alphonsus Liguori, whose great maxim was that it was very difficult for a Catholic to be lost: *difficilmente si danna*!"

How could so great a Doctor be guilty of such self-contradiction? To answer this question, we need only turn to the source cited: "Letter 2". The reference intended is to the second letter written by Saint Alphonsus to a recently consecrated bishop and it concerns the usefulness of sacred Missions. In this letter the most zealous Doctor asserts that it is difficult for *a Catholic who has properly listened to the Mission sermons* to be damned *if he dies within a year after the Mission*: "*Io tengo per certo, che di tutti coloro, che sono venuti alle prediche, se alcuno di loro muore fra l'anno, da ch'è stata la missione, difficilmente si danna.*"[75]

From this Bougaud concludes that the opinion of Saint Alphonsus, forever on his lips, was that it is difficult for *any Catholic at all* to be damned and consequently that the number of the elect among the faithful is greater than the number of the reprobate.

18. With regard to Saint Francis de Sales, two remarks should first be made:

(i) No authentic text has been adduced, taken from the *writings* of the Saint himself, but rather a *conversation* related by Camus. But this author Camus is of doubtful reputation.

(ii) The words adduced prove *too much* and therefore prove *nothing at all*.[76] For they imply that no Catholic, or practically no Catholic, could ever be damned: "He said that very few were lost, according to the remarkable statement that 'there is no condemnation to them that are in Christ Jesus.'[77] It is credible that the vocation to Christian-

---

[75] *Istruzione pratica degli Esercizi di missione, Opere ascetiche*, Turin, 1831, vol. X, parte II, p. 86.

[76] The author alludes to the axiom *Qui nimis probat nihi probat* — *he who proves too much proves nothing*. The meaning is that an argument which leads to aberrant conclusions is clearly unacceptable. It is not reasonable to accept some of its conclusions while rejecting others. — Translator.

[77] The author alludes to Rom. I, 8. "There is now therefore no condemnation to them that are in Christ Jesus, who walk not according to the flesh." — Translator.

ity, which is a work of God, is a perfect work, which leads to the end of all consummation, which is glory."

The Reader may therefore see how much trust should be accorded to Bougaud and Fr. Castelein when they impudently and uncritically oppose Saints Francis and Alphonsus, "two illustrious doctors of modern times", to the Fathers and Doctors of centuries past, for it is far from evident that they ever departed from the doctrine of Saint Thomas which Fr. Castelein calls "the *old* opinion".

Nor is it logical for Fr. Castelein to invoke Saint Francis, who is said to have been speaking *of Christians alone*, in favour of the opinion that the majority of the human race is saved. By what right does he dare to add: "Such was the sentiment of Saint Francis de Sales, and he even forbad unfavourable views concerning the salvation of those who, after a bad life, die with no outward sign of repentance…. And to confirm this *truth* [*sic*] he told how he had heard a preacher say, in speaking of the death of Luther, 'Who knows whether at the moment of his death God may not have touched him with His efficacious grace?' … From which the charitable prelate concluded that we ought never to despair of anyone's salvation." (2nd ed., p. 264)

Let me say it once again: "If these words are found in the authentic writings of Saint Francis de Sales, I will believe that such was really his opinion, but if our only source for them is Camus, I will not believe it. For Saint Francis, as a Doctor of the Church, was a "lover of the divine law" and a hater of its transgressors. We know what he wrote about the eternal salvation of men in general: "Men have become so perverse that from their very adolescence they have left the way of salvation and taken the road of perdition. Arriving at the age of reason, they choose the left-hand fork in the road."[78]

And with regard to the conclusion which Fr. Castelein draws from the opinion attributed to Saint Francis — "The Catholic Church shares this sentiment" (*ibid.* p. 265) — I find it very hard to admit it when I observe that so good a Mother as Holy Church re-

---

[78] *Sermon pour la Présentation de Notre-Dame*, 1839 edition, vol. II, p. 381, col. 2.

fuses ecclesiastical burial not only to deceased pagans, Jews, all infidels, apostates from the Christian faith, schismatics and public excommunicates, but also to Catholics who die by their own hand as a result of despair or anger *unless before death they give outward signs of repentance*, to manifest and public sinners who die without repentance and to those of whom it is publicly certain that they have not received the Sacraments of Confession and Communion and *have died with no sign of contrition*, etc.

19. I appeal to the Saints, not to theologians. I ask for the testimony of the Saints, not of Progressives. To the Saints I give the readiest credence and I confidently submit to their authority. There are five reasons for this:

(i) They were sent by God to teach us the way of salvation. Indeed, as Pope Pius IX says, "Jesus Christ Our Lord, having pledged never to be wanting to His Church, observing that it would be of the greatest utility to His immaculate Spouse, raises up men who are outstanding for *piety* and for *learning*, who, being filled with the Spirit of Understanding, pour forth like refreshing showers the eloquence of their wisdom."[79]

(ii) The Saints are the best Teachers on the subject of eternal salvation, having followed their Divine Master by *beginning to say and to do*.[80] Indeed they are eminent "among those who have both *done and taught* and whom Our Lord Jesus Christ has said shall be great in the kingdom of heaven. Offering an example of every virtue, they have enlightened, like a lantern placed upon the candlestick, all Christ's faithful who are in the house of God. What they have accomplished by holy works, the same have they taught by word of mouth and in writing."[81]

---

[79] Pope Pius IX, Apostolic Letter *Qui ecclesiæ suæ* of 7th July 1871, declaring Saint Alphonsus Liguori a Doctor of the Church.

[80] The allusion is to Acts I, 1: "The former treatise I made, O Theophilus, of all things which Jesus began *to do and to teach*...." — Translator.

[81] Cf. Decree of 23rd March 1871 on the same subject.

(iii) The Saints, better than many modern critics who have acquired their scriptural knowledge from German and Dutch rationalists, "have unlocked the mysteries of the Scriptures,"[82] by the help of the Holy Ghost who is the primary author of the Scriptures, who dwelt within them, whose living temples they were and by whom they were moved as true and genuine sons of God.

(iv) Because the Saints "attending exclusively to the glory of God and the spiritual well-being of men",[83] were immune from the disputes and prejudices of the schools. For they were Saints, elevated above vain and proud quibbling, drawing close, like the eagle, to eternal Light and considering all things in the brightness of this Light and judging all matters with upright and wise judgement in accordance with the spirit of God.

(v) Finally, the Saints appear to me to be heroes, perfect men, the heads of the human race in terms of talent and knowledge.

So let us with great reverence heed the words of the Saints, who are God's intimate friends.

20. And in this way we shall obey the warnings given by our Holy Father Pope Leo XIII on 30th December 1892 to the Society of Jesus concerning *the profession of the teaching of Saint Thomas*:

Having gravely considered, since the beginning of Our pontificate, in the accomplishment of Our apostolic duty, the prevailing hostility to the Church and the practical shipwreck of human society in matters of the greatest importance, We have located the main cause of this disaster in the fact that the certain *principles* and established rules by which the path to the Christian faith is fortified have been everywhere disregarded and almost despised, while *a lust for novelty has set in* which, *under the pretence of doctrinal progress*, resists and obstructs the wisdom passed down by God. It has not been difficult to identify the appropriate remedies, namely the

---

[82] *Ibid.*

[83] Pope Pius IX, Apostolic Letter *Qui ecclesiæ suæ* of 7th July 1871, declaring Saint Alphonsus Liguori a Doctor of the Church.

necessity of returning to the sources of sound doctrine which ought never to have been abandoned.[84]

21. Now the sources of sound doctrine are the writings of the Saints and in using them we shall also be following the advice of Saint Ignatius, who "in many places in the Constitutions [of the Society of Jesus] stipulated that solid and sound doctrine was to be followed, indeed the sounder and more approved doctrine." [85] Moreover in the *Spiritual Exercises* he indicates this rule to be observed *"in order that we may truly share the sentiments of the orthodox Church"* :

> "Eleventh Rule. To praise both positive and *scholastic* learning. Because, as it is more proper to the ancient *Holy* Doctors, such as Saint Jerome, Saint Augustine and Saint Gregory, *and the like*, to move hearts to love and worship God; so it is more proper to Saint Thomas, Saint Bonaventure, to the Master of the Sentences, and to other more recent theologians, to transmit the dogmas necessary for salvation with greater exactitude and to define them more suitably for our times and those to come in order to refute errors and heresies. For these Doctors, as they are more recent, are not only endowed with understanding of the Sacred Scripture and guided by the writings of the ancient authors, but also, illuminated by divine light, make happy use of the canons and decrees of Councils, and of the Constitutions of holy Church to promote our salvation."[86]

---

[84] Pope Leo XIII, *Gravissime nos*, 30th Dec. 1892; *Acta*, Vatican edition, vol. XII, p. 366.

[85] *Ibid.*, p. 368.

[86] Meursius, J., *Exercitia spiritualia S. P. Ignatii Loyolæ*, Antwerp, 1635, p. 140.

CHAPTER THREE

<hr>

The Authentic Opinions of Many Saints and Fathers of the Church

<hr>

I. Post-Patristic Saints

I WILL BEGIN this catalogue with some more recent Saints, and in first place a Doctor of the Church:

1. SAINT ALPHONSUS LIGUORI (1696-1787)

This mild and learned Saint was far from being a "Rigorist" or a "terrorist"; on the contrary, as Popes Pius VII, Pius IX and Leo XIII bear witness, he followed the path of moderation:

"He shed light on what was obscure and clarified what was doubtful, paving a safe path amid the complexity of theological opinions whether too lax or too rigid. Looking only to the glory of God and the salvation of men's souls, he wrote a great many books, filled with sacred learning and piety,"[87] so that it may "be most truly declared that there is no single one of the errors of our days which has not been at least to a great extent refuted by Saint Alphonsus."[88]

Here then is an assortment of well-known statements extracted from the works of this celebrated Doctor of modern times.

---

[87] Pius IX, Decree of 23rd March 1871.

[88] Pius IX, Apostolic Letter *Qui ecclesiæ suæ*, 7th July 1871.

(i) The more common opinion holds that the majority, even of the faithful, are damned.[89]

(ii) The more common opinion affirms that the greater part, even of the faithful, are damned.[90]

(iii) Let us recall what the Gospel states: "Narrow is the way, etc." The path to heaven is narrow and, to use a familiar expression, carriages cannot get through, so wanting to go to heaven in a carriage is tantamount to abandoning hope of arriving at all. "Few there are who find it," for very few are willing to do violence to themselves in order to resist temptations.[91]

(iv) The number of the reprobate is much greater than that of the elect.[92]

(v) We read in the Gospel that the elect are a very small number by comparison with the reprobate.[93]

(vi) The number of the reprobate exceeds the number of the elect.[94]

(vii) We know that the elect are few in number.[95]

(viii) I read in the Scriptures that the elect are few in number and that they are called the little flock.[96]

Indeed the general sentiment of all the works of the most zealous Doctor is not, as Bougaud absurdly claimed, that it is hard for a Catholic to be damned, but that, on the contrary, the path to heaven is narrow and found by few, that a large majority of adult Catholics live all but continuously in the state of mortal sin and that a man ordinarily dies in the state in which he habitually lives, etc.

---

[89] *Theologia Moralis*, lib. IV, tr. 2, cap. 2, n. 130.

[90] *Preparation for Death*, consideration 17, point 2.

[91] Sermon for the 3rd Sunday of Advent. See French translation by Fr. Eugène Pladys, p. 38.

[92] *The History of Heresies and their Refutation*, Chap. XIII, art. 2. See French translation of the Saint's *Œuvres Dogmatiques* by Fr. Jacques, vol. V, p. 505.

[93] *Ibid.*, p. 507.

[94] *De l'espérance chrétienne, ibid.*, vol. VIII, p. 501.

[95] *Ibid.*, p. 502.

[96] *Ibid.*, p. 503.

2. SAINT LEONARD OF PORT MAURICE (1676-1751)

After the most zealous Doctor Saint Alphonsus, it will be well worth our while to listen to his contemporary, Saint Leonard of Port Maurice, preaching in the following terms the fewness of the saved:

To resolve the doubt before us, let us place side-by-side all the Holy Fathers, both Greek and Latin and all the most learned theologians.... Then, attend not to what *I* am going to say but to what is going to be said by these great minds who serve as lighthouses in the Church of God to enlighten others and ensure that they do not go astray on the road that leads to heaven.

Note that our subject here is not the whole of the human race, nor even all Catholics, but only all *Catholic adults*.

Two eminent cardinals, Cajetan and Bellarmine, following the learned John of Avila,[97] agree in expressing their dissent from the opinion of the libertines and openly declare their conviction that the majority of adult Christians are damned.

Suárez, after consulting all the authorities, after weighing up the whole matter, writes these words: "The more common opinion holds that, among Christians, there are more reprobate than elect — *Communior sententia tenet ex Christianis plures esse reprobos quam prædestinatos.*"[98]

And if you add to the authority of the theologians that of the Greek and Latin Fathers you will find them, so to speak, all unanimous. This is the opinion of Saint Theodore, Saint Basil, Saint Ephrem and of Saint John Chrysostom.

Indeed, according to Baronius, it was the common opinion of the Greek Fathers that this truth had been expressly revealed to Saint Simon Stylites and that it was to place the capital affair of his salvation in greater security that he decided to spend forty uninterrupted years living atop a pillar, exposed to all the inclemency of the weather, a dazzling prodigy of holiness and of penance.

Turn now to the Latin Fathers and you will find a Saint Gregory, informing you unambiguously that "many come to faith but few reach the kingdom of heaven — *ad fidem plures perveniunt, ad regnum cæleste pauci*

---

[97] Beatified 1893. — Translator.

[98] Cf. the complete text of Suárez in Chapter IV below. Suárez makes this statement with regard to Christians in general, but not with regard to Catholics.

perducuntur," and Saint Anselm echoes him, saying that "there are few who are saved — *ut videtur, pauci sunt qui salvantur.*"

Saint Augustine is even more explicit. He concludes: "There are therefore few who are saved in comparison with those who perish — *pauci ergo sunt qui salvantur in comparatione multorum periturorum.*"

But nothing is more terrible than Saint Jerome's remark, uttered at the close of his life in the presence of his disciples: "Of one hundred thousand Christians of consistently bad life there is barely one who obtains pardon — *vix de centum millibus quorum mala semper fuit vita meretur habere indulgentiam unus.*"[99]

Saint Leonard confirms the sayings of these Saints with a terrifying argument which ought to inspire us priests with a salutary fear of sins and its occasions and the greatest zeal for acquiring holiness:

Let us examine the various states in particular and you will understand that one must either renounce reason, experience and the instinct of the faithful or else recognize that most Catholics are damned. I ask you: is there any state in the world more favourable to salvation than that of priests? Yet we find the great Chrysostom concluding, with tears, that, in the light of the far from exemplary life of so many priests, there are few priests who are saved and many who are damned — *Non arbitror inter sacerdotes multos esse qui salvi fiant, sed multo plures qui pereant.*"[100]

3. VEN. JANUARIUS SARNELLI C.SS.R. (1702-44)

The credit and esteem due to this outstanding servant of God are sufficiently attested by the fact that his merits and virtues were praised and made known by Saint Alphonsus, Doctor of the Church and his spiritual father.

His zeal for the conversion of sinners was ardent and he showed it by seeking after the most lost sheep of all, viz. prostitutes, who not only lose their own souls but attract a great many others to sin — he also showed it by his writings, which enabled him to do good even to those far distant from him in space or time, according to his own

---

[99] Saint Leonard, *op. cit.*, pp. 177-179.
[100] *Ibid.*, p. 182.

statement: "I want to preach until the day of the last judgement". Apostolic men instructed by reading them at once win countless souls to God.[101]

This most zealous and learned Apostle includes in his work *The World Sanctified* a special meditation on the greater number of the faithful who are damned. It is entitled *The majority of the faithful are damned*,[102] and begins:

Consider how countless Christians hurl themselves into the abyss of eternal torments. The more common opinion of the Greek and Latin Doctors, who are the oracles of the Church and the interpreters of the sacred mysteries — an opinion founded on the divine Scriptures and on reason — is that *the majority of the faithful who die after attaining the use of reason are damned.* For someone to be saved he must abstain from sin. But, alas! how many evils are committed! For someone to be saved he must do good. But how little good is in fact done and how badly it is done!

Then, speaking of the self-deceit of so many Catholics in making bad confessions, he quotes Saint Chrysostom to the effect that such a confession is but "*stage penance*".[103]

Finally he concludes by exhorting his readers:

Meditate on the fact that while we are alive we are called *wayfarers*, because we are journeying towards the Fatherland; we are travelling towards either an eternity of blessedness or an eternity of damnation. Contemplate in imagination all the men of the whole world who are marching along with you between the two eternities. Countless are those who advance with swift foot towards the eternity of hell, while *very few are the Christians who advance towards the eternity of paradise.* And at such a terrible spectacle, weep over the damnation of so many unhappy souls. Then examine carefully the eternity you have been journeying towards for the greater part of your life and are now approaching. If you are running along with the crowd, you will be damned with the crowd. Take courage, therefore, and change course; enter on a new way of life.

---

[101] Cf. Sacred Congregation of Rites, *Process of Beatification, Positio super dubium*, nn. 34 and 35.

[102] *Opera omnia*, Naples, 1888, vol. II, p. 216. "La maggior parte dei fideli si danna."

[103] *Ibid.*, point 2, p. 217.

Perchance if you wait until you one day wish to, you will no longer be able to. *Strive to enter by the narrow gate; for many, I say to you, shall seek to enter, and shall not be able.* Take the greatest pains to make a good confession; many are damned because many confess ill. Bad confessions, alas! how many souls do you cast down into hell! Christians beware; confess your sins rightly and work out your salvation.[104]

4. VEN. CLAUDE DE LA COLOMBIÈRE S.J.[105] (1641–82)

To the canonized Saints I add this Servant of God whose cause has been introduced and whose writings, it is hoped, will soon be approved by Holy Church. Among other things, he teaches:

The fewness of the elect should not be grounds of fear for us; sins are all that prevent us from being of their number.

There are few predestined among Christians because predestination is necessarily followed by salvation. But it is no less necessarily followed by the works that make salvation sure.

Are you frightened to be told that of a hundred thousand barely one will be saved? What does it matter provided that you are the one? And if, on the other hand, of the same number *all* were saved *but one*, how wretched would you be if you were the unhappy exception!

"But if there are *many* elect, I have a *better chance* of being of their number," I hear you say. But you are mistaken. You would be right if, after admitting the good to salvation, one or two bad people were added to increase the number, or if some of the good were then eliminated to keep the number down. But this is not so: however few the predestined may be, the good are never excluded, and however many they may be, the evil will never be among them.

If you are good when only one man out of a hundred thousand is saved, you will be the one; if you are bad, even if only one out of a hundred thousand were reprobate, it would be you...

Ask yourself whether the path to heaven is well-trodden. All the elect must go by the narrow way, for it is the only path that leads to salvation...

---

[104] *Ibid.*, p. 219.
[105] Beatified 1929. — Translator.

In our days even those who embrace piety want to have all their comforts...

In order to ensure his salvation a man must live in that state in which he must die if he is to be saved. But how many will you find who are habitually in the state of grace or even who conserve their friendship with God for a few days in the year? It is not certain; indeed it is quite uncertain, whether they receive that friendship in their confessions: the frequency with which they fall back into their sins convinces me that they have little resolution and have left the sacred tribunal and the sacred banquet quite destitute of grace. What assurance can be had that one who lives in this way will reach heaven?

Much reliance is placed on what one intends to do at the hour of death. Confessions made at that time are better made, it is said, and I do not deny it. But there are many who do not confess at that moment at all. And as a matter of act the imminence of death tends to add nothing to a man's ordinary dispositions save trouble, horror and fear that is entirely natural in character, as is proved by the fact that when the danger is past and the fear dissipated, he goes back to his former way of life.

Does it astonish you to hear that of a hundred thousand Christians there are not ten who are saved? For my part, to the contrary, the more I consider the matter, the more I am astonished that of a hundred thousand there are as many as *three* who *are* saved.

And the reason for my surprise lies in the strong inclinations we have towards evil, the dreadful tendency that leads us towards the precipice, this tendency promoted by so many enemies, inviting us, pressing us; a world so corrupt, such deadly, frequent and terrible occasions; so constant a negligence in matters of salvation: at the sight of so many obstacles to which we fail to oppose strong-willed opposition, is it possible, I wonder, that there should be ten Christians out of a hundred thousand who are saved?[106]

And these terrible words were not uttered impromptu or in the excitement of an unprepared discourse, but calmly committed to writing by a learned and exceedingly pious man who was the director of conscience of Blessed Margaret-Mary Alacoque[107] and a friend of the most gentle Heart of Jesus. Fr. de la Colombière was certainly

---

[106] Migne, *Orateurs sacrés*, vol. VII, coll. 1589-91.
[107] Canonized 1920. — Translator.

not a Sentimentalist, but who would dare call him a Rigorist, a Terrorist or a Jansenist?

5. SAINT VINCENT DE PAUL (1581-1660)

Beloved of God and men, whose memory is in benediction, this lovable Saint openly declares:

> What is rare, and rarer than can be said, is to persevere. And this is why there are so few predestinate, so few who are saved; it is because, as the Son of God assures us, only he who perseveres will be saved.[108]

6. VEN. LOUIS DE PONTE[109] S.J. (1554-1624)

Fr. de Ponte passed his novitiate under Balthasar Alvarez who had been Saint Teresa of Avila's confessor; he went on to teach philosophy and theology, at times exercised the office of Novice-Master and Rector and was deemed worthy by that light of theology Fr. Suárez to be chosen as his director in the spiritual life.

> The other part of the statement is to be weighed: *Many are called, but few are chosen.* — Just as among the men of this world who are called by God to receive His faith and grace, *very many are the sinners*, who resist this vocation, *but few are the just*, who consent to it and are *chosen to reach heaven*, so too among the just themselves, who are called to a perfect life, many resist this vocation, living in a certain lukewarmness, content with a certain mediocrity, whereas few are elect and perfect; because what is precious is always rare. O infinite God, who callest all and invitest them to follow perfection, I beseech Thy Majesty to increase the number of the elect, so that many may be perfect as Thou art perfect. Grant also, O Lord, that I may be of their number by corresponding to my vocation, so that Thou mayest be glorified in me and through me, world without end. Amen.[110]

---

[108] *Sermon on Perseverance.*

[109] Also known as *Luis de la Puente.* — Translator.

[110] *Meditationes*, pars III, med. 54; ed. Lehmkuhl, S.J., vol. III, p. 495.

7. VEN. CARD. BELLARMINE S.J. (1542-1621)

This Venerable Cardinal and Servant of God, one day no doubt to be beatified,[111] glory of the Society of Jesus, explicitly states the exact position defended in these pages:

No one should be led by the statement that the elect from among the nations cannot be counted to think that the number of the elect will be greater than the number of the reprobate. For although the number of the elect among the nations will indeed be far greater than from among the Jews, it will certainly be less than the number of the elect, even adding Jews and Gentiles together.[112]

And a little later the learned and devout writer adds:

This can be confirmed from Isaias, who describes the fewness of those who shall be found among the saved at the end of the world using two similes — that of the vineyard after the grape harvest and that of the shaken olive-tree — which must both inspire the greatest horror.

Here are the words of Isaias concerning the consummation of the world: *Behold the Lord shall lay waste the earth, and shall strip it.* (XXIV,1) And a little later: *For it shall be thus in the midst of the earth, in the midst of the people, as if a few olives, that remain, should be shaken out of the olive tree: or grapes, when the vintage is ended.*

Thus the number of the reprobate will be like the multitude of olives which fall on the earth when the olive-tree is first shaken, whereas the fewness of the elect will be like the fewness of those olives which have escaped the hands of the harvesters and remained among the topmost branches, to be shaken down later, one by one.

Or again the multitude of the reprobate will be like the grape harvest in which many vats are filled with the bunches that are collected by many harvesters while the fewness of the elect will resemble the fewness of the bunches which, by oversight, are left behind on the vines after the end of the harvest.[113]

---

[111] Beatified 1923, Canonized 1930, Doctor of the Church 1931. — Translator.

[112] *De Gemitu Columbæ*, cap. VI; ed. Vivès, vol. VIII, p. 404, col. 3.

[113] *Op. cit.*, p. 405.

And in another work he writes, no less explicitly: "As the number of men who are damned is greater than the number of those who are to be saved..."[114]

8. BLESSED PETER CANISIUS S.J.[115] (1521-97)

This holy and very learned man writes, in his notes on the Gospel for Septuagesima Sunday:

> I confess and proclaim the just judgement of God, who avenges the contempt displayed by ungrateful mortals for His supreme goodness and grace by electing and taking up to glory only *few* of those called to His Church and who profess the faith.

And a little later he writes:

> But as Christ often declares in the Gospel that many are called but few are chosen, again and again I will take heed to myself by the example of those who, though they are called and thus remain within the vineyard and believe as the Church does, yet correspond badly to their calling and hence, like fruitless vine-branches, are cut off and cast forth to burn in the fires of hell.
>
> As though bewailing the fewness of the elect, Christ says: *How narrow is the gate, and strait is the way that leadeth to life: and few there are that find it!*[116] How much less will I allow myself to be influenced by the multitudinous crowd of sinners who think they are entitled to behave in accordance with their whims. For *the number of fools in infinite.*[117]

Such are the words of Blessed Canisius whose holiness together with his solid doctrine places him among the greatest theologians of the Society of Jesus.

9. SAINT THOMAS OF VILLANOVA (1488–1555)

This is how this eloquent and merciful preacher of the Gospel addresses the faithful:

[114] *De Arte moriendi*, lib. II, cap. III; *ibid.* vol. VIII, p. 496, col. 2.
[115] Canonized and declared Doctor of the Church 1925. — Translator.
[116] Matthew VII, 14.
[117] Ecclesiastes I, 15.

How greatly we all wish to know whether many are saved of those who live this common life of Christians. They go to Church; they hear Mass; they receive the Sacraments; they keep the faith undefiled. Does this ordinary life suffice for salvation? Oh how terrible are Our Lord's words: *Strive to enter by the narrow gate! for ... strait is the way that leadeth to life: and few there are that find it!* Here is the answer: Few are saved. But someone might yet think that these few who are saved are the faithful, as they were then and still are a minority, in comparison with the infidels. But pay attention to what He now goes on to say of the called and of the faithful: Many are called but few are chosen. Even of those who are called not only to the faith but by any kind of vocation. Alas! Alack! Of many who are called, few are chosen! What then? Should we despair? No: we are not told this to make us despair but to make us more diligently watchful. For even if we knew that only one was to be saved of all the vast crowd of us gathered here today, I ought to strive to be that one. Yet the question may be asked, why, when we are told that God is supremely merciful, does He allow so many to perish? I answer: "This is the perversity of the wicked, endeavouring to blame God for their own fault." What blasphemy! If many are damned, God is not the cause of damnation, but of salvation. As he said by the Prophet, "Thy destruction is thy own, O Israel: thy help only is in me."

We must note and be afraid when we hear that "many are called but few are chosen" and that few obtain the reward. How we ought to fear and be terrified at this warning! For who is it that gives it, if not the very steward who is charged to pay the labourers? Believe me, brethren; believe me, as I have often admonished you, often cried out to you: unless you strive manfully and go beyond the commonplace and ordinary way of living, you will not receive the reward. Woe to the wretched who have laboured and have lost the fruit of their labour, finding fire in return. Remember, brethren, that you are labourers and that you are sent to the vineyard. If a labourer spends the day in gaming and dancing, in eating and drinking, instead of working, what reward will he receive from his Lord at nightfall, save blows and beatings! For every one of us is a labourer, be he a mighty king, a bishop, a religious, a woman or anyone at all.[118]

---

[118] Point 3 of Sermon I for the XIXth Sunday after Pentecost and Point 2 of Sermon II for Septuagesima Sunday.

Thus spoke this eloquent and merciful Archbishop.

10. VEN. DENYS THE CARTHUSIAN (1402-71)

Commenting on Job XXI, 33, "he shall draw every man after him," he writes:

> This means that infernal punishment gathers into its clutches a great number of every class, rank and kind of men; indeed so many that the others seem few in comparison and the number is so great as to be called "all", as when the Apostle says "for *all* seek the things that are their own. [Philippians II, 21]"[119]

And in his work On the narrow way of salvation and on contempt of the world, commenting on the text Few there are that find it (Matthew VII), he says:

> Christ spoke these words, and what indeed could be said to us that would be more disagreeable or would sound more terrible? Undoubtedly it would have been quite enough to terrify our hearts if Christ had said no more than that the way of salvation is narrow, and the way of damnation broad, for this would imply that it is easy to be damned and hard to be saved. But by explicitly adding that there are few who find this narrow way of salvation and many who walk in the broad way of damnation, He *clearly indicates that few are saved and many are damned.*
>
> And He makes the same declaration more clearly in other passage, when He says, "Many are called but few are chosen." Who could fail to shudder and be filled with dread upon hearing these words, if he is truly a believer and possesses the enlightenment of faith? For the Christian faith is such and so great, so elevated and so arduous, that even if we knew that all men who ever had been, shall be or are at present upon earth were to be saved barring only one, every man living would rightly be filled with the greatest fear of being himself that one person to be damned and ought therefore to serve God with fear and reverence....
>
> From which you may note, beloved, how narrow and strait is the way of salvation... For the Apostle says: *And they that are Christ's have crucified*

---

[119] *Opera omnia, Enarrationes in Job*, cap. XXI, art. 47; Montreuil, 1897, vol. IV, p. 580.

their flesh with its vices and concupiscences.[120] — Those, therefore, who have *not* extinguished their vices and concupiscences or *chastised their body,*[121] do not belong to Christ."

And again, he says that *a widow…that liveth in pleasures, is dead while she is living.*[122] That is to say that she is alive, in terms of natural life, but dead by the death of guilt. But if it is a mortal sin for widows to live in pleasures, how much the more so is it *for clerics, monks and canons!* … I have recalled these texts…to prevent you from pinning foolish self-deception on the divine mercy or from becoming like to those who walk in the broad way.[123]

11. SAINT ANTONINUS (1389-1459)

Blessed is he whom thou hast chosen and taken to thee: he shall dwell in thy courts.[124] There is significance in the use of the singular: *blessed is he…,* for, as Our Saviour says in Matthew Chapter XX and again in Chapter XXII, *Many are called, but few chosen.*

And Saint Antoninus refutes by anticipation the argument of Fr. Castelein that "it is stated in Chapter VII of the Apocalypse of Saint John that the elect form an immense crowd which no man can number, whereas nothing of the kind is said of the damned."[125] Saint Antoninus says:

Nor is this statement contradicted by the words of John in Apocalypse VII *I saw a great crowd*, etc. For the elect, although their number is so great in itself as for it to be practically impossible for us to count them, yet by comparison with the reprobate they are few, just as the grains of sand in a sack are practically countless, yet very little compared with all the sand of the sea. In the same way the elect are few when measured against the perverse, and hence they are blessed indeed, in accordance with the

---

[120] Galatians V, 24.

[121] I Corinthians IX, 27.

[122] I Timothy V, 5-6.

[123] *Dionysii Carthusiensis Opera Selecta*, Liège, 1854, vol. I, pp. 21 and 36.

[124] Psalm LXIV, 5.

[125] *Op. cit.*, 2nd ed., p. 267.

words of Psalm LXIV : *Blessed is he whom thou hast chosen and taken to thee : he shall dwell in thy courts.*[126]

So speaks the holy Archbishop of Florence.

12. SAINT LAWRENCE JUSTINIAN (1381-1456)

This holy Patriarch writes, in his book On the Compunction and Lamentation of Christian Perfection :

They are few in number who devote themselves to inward meditation, for it is opposed to the works of the flesh and to the rebellion of the senses. Narrow indeed is the way of the spirit, which leads to perfection and to the possession of Christ, but broad is the way that indulges the pleasures of the flesh and *countless are they who travel by it.*[127]

13. SAINT BERNARDINO OF SIENA (1380-1444)

This zealous Apostle of the Name and the love of Jesus Christ explicitly addresses our subject in the following words of his 23rd sermon :

It is therefore clear why *many are called*, i.e. to the faith, or to glory or to grace, while only *few are chosen*, i.e. by contrast with the great number of the called.

For although the threshed grains are many, yet they are little in comparison with the mass of straw and chaff, which represent the wicked, whom the Lord will *bring to an evil end.*[128]

And in his treatise entitled *De speculo peccatorum* he writes :

The reason why many enter into eternal damnation by the wide gate and the broad way is the one given in Ecclesiastes I : *the perverse are hard to be corrected, and the number of fools is infinite.* — Alas, they think more of the present life than of the end that is to follow it... From which a simple

---

[126] *Summa Theologiæ*, I, t. IV, cap. VII ; Verona, 1740, vol. I, col. 26.

[127] *Opera*, Cologne, 1675, p. 395.

[128] *Opera*, Lyon, 1650, vol. II, p. 138.

conclusion may be deduced : there are many in the wayfaring state in this world, but few of them will be of the number of the saved.[129]

14. SAINT VINCENT FERRER (1350-1419)

This very great preacher posed the question "How is it that Christ says *few are called* when John (Apocalypse VII) says that they are countless?"

And the answer he gives his hearers is as follows :

The two statements agree by virtue of the distinction according to which we may speak of the elect either absolutely or comparatively.

Thus, in absolute terms, there are many elect, as John says.

But if we adopt the relative standpoint, comparing the elect with the number of the damned, then *they are few.* — In the same way as in a handful of sand there are many grains in absolute terms but few in comparison with those on the seashore, so the human race, on account of its great number, is compared with sand as may be seen in the promise made to Abraham when the Lord said to him : *I will multiply thy seed as the stars of heaven, and as the sand that is by the sea shore.* [Genesis XXII] Here God speaks of the handful, for *the souls of the just are in the hand of God* and in absolute terms are countless, as Saint John says, but *in comparison with the damned they are as nothing at all.*[130]

Christ says [Matthew VII] : *Enter ye in at the narrow gate : for wide is the gate, and broad is the way that leadeth to destruction, and many there are who go in thereat. How narrow is the gate, and strait is the way that leadeth to life : and few there are that find it !* Still fewer are they that having found it, follow it — and very few indeed are they who follow it to the end. The narrow gate of paradise is the will of God. He that would enter paradise must hold all else in check. The wide gate is self-will. The strait way that leads to life is penitential affliction while the broad way of hell is worldly living, eating well, drinking well, excess, pleasure-seeking, avenging injuries, etc.[131]

---

129 *Ibid.*, vol. III, p. 464.
130 Sermon I for Septuagesima Sunday ; Antwerp, 1570, p. 295.
131 *Ibid.*, Sermon VI, p. 318.

Then the same most eloquent Saint addresses and resolves the usual objection made on the grounds of the infinite mercy of God.

As everything naturally acts in accordance with its proper virtue ... and God is infinite in mercy, surely He ought to save infinite souls. How is it, then, that there are many called but few chosen, instead of infinite elect? To answer objections of this kind, note that God is indeed infinite in mercy, kindness and goodness and that He has done, even infinitely, all that He ought and could have done in order that all might be saved. So the reason why all are *not* saved is that all do not *want* to be saved, indeed few are they who accept to receive their salvation. Pay heed to this comparison: a King paid a most abundant ransom for the freedom of captives in Barbary, and prepared ships and galleys to bring them back to their homeland, but they did not want to leave. In the same way, Our Lord Jesus Christ has paid a most abundant ransom for men, even for infinite men if there were so many, and has prepared ships for them such as baptismal innocence, sacramental penance and universal obedience. But the nations refuse to abandon their captivity just as the Jews do not want to leave the captivity of the law of Moses, the descendants of Agar do want to leave the captivity of Mahomet, the proud do not want to leave the captivity of their pride, and the same applies to the others.[132]

15. BL. ALBERT THE GREAT[133] (C. 1200-1280)

Blessed Albert's commentaries on the Gospels take the form of succinct notes, which do not, however, obscure his teaching:

In Matthew xx, 16: *Many are called but few chosen...* — I Corinthians IX, 24: *Know you not that they that run in the race, all run indeed, but one receiveth the prize?* — Matthew XX, 14, yet more clearly: In this parable the Disciples are told that the king had cast only one guest out of the wedding feast; for this reason Christ indicates not the person excluded but the motive for his exclusion. For whoever are called but do not live agreeably to their election are cast off in the same way as that one. Hence He immediately adds: *For many are called, but few are chosen.* — Ecclesiastes I, 15: *The number of fools is infinite.*

---

[132] *Ibid.*, p. 319.
[133] Canonized 1931, Doctor of the Church 1931. — Translator.

In Luke XIII, 23: *And a certain man said to him: Lord, are they few that are saved? And He said to them* [for one had enquired on behalf of them all]: *Strive to enter by the narrow gate; for many, I say to you, shall seek to enter, and shall not be able.* And in verse 25 Christ gives the first reason [why few are saved]. *Many are called but few are chosen* — i.e. many profess the faith in words but deny it by their deeds. — Ecclesiastes I, 15: *The number of fools is infinite.*

16. SAINT THOMAS AQUINAS (1225-1274)

Let us now reverently attend, as is fitting, to the teaching of the Angelic Doctor, who is, as Holy Church says, "The prince of theologians and the norm of philosophers, the outstanding ornament of the Christian world and the light of the Church."[134]

The Sovereign Pontiff Pope Leo XIII commands:

The imprudent and rash departure from the wisdom of the Angelic Doctor is a thing foreign to Our wishes and full of danger. Events already bear all too clear witness to the tendency, when Thomas is disregarded, for the resulting intellectual chaos to give rise to monstrous opinions. The name of Thomas should therefore be sacred to all, and men should be ashamed not to follow the leadership of him to whom Jesus Christ declared, 'Thou hast written well of me.'[135]

This great Doctor it is who teaches most explicitly, notwithstanding the growls of the Progressives, that "there are fewer who are saved."

For in discussing "whether the number of the predestined is certain", he first states, in the traditional scholastic method, the arguments against his own position:

It seems that the number of the predestined is not certain, for...

Objection 3. The operation of God is more perfect than that of nature. But in the works of nature, good is found in the majority of things; defect and evil in the minority. If, then, the number of the saved were

---

[134] In the *Prayer to Saint Thomas Patron of Catholic Students*, enriched with an indulgence of 200 days by Pope Leo XIII, 13th July 1895.

[135] Letter to the Minister-General of the Order of Friars Minor, 25th Nov. 1898.

fixed by God at a certain figure, there would be more saved than lost Yet the contrary follows from Matthew VII, 13-14: "For wide is the gate, and broad the way that leadeth to destruction, and many there are who go in thereat. How narrow is the gate, and strait is the way that leadeth to life; and few there are who find it!" Therefore the number of those pre-ordained by God to be saved is not certain.

He then proceeds to refute this argument in the following terms:

> **On the contrary,** Augustine says (*De Corr. et Grat.*, Cap. 13): "The number of the predestined is certain, and can neither be increased nor diminished." [...]
>
> **Reply to Objection 3.** The good that is proportionate to the common state of nature is to be found in the majority; and is wanting in the minority. The good that exceeds the common state of nature is to be found in the minority, and is wanting in the majority. Thus it is clear that the majority of men have a sufficient knowledge for the guidance of life; and those who have not this knowledge are said to be half-witted or foolish; but they who attain to a profound knowledge of intelligible things are a very small minority in respect to the rest Since their eternal happiness, consisting in the vision of God, exceeds the common state of nature, and especially in so far as this is deprived of grace through the corruption of original sin, those who are saved are in the minority. In this especially, however, appears the mercy of God, that He has chosen some for salvation, from which *very many* in accordance with the common course and tendency of nature fall short.[136]

Moreover in his Exposition of Matthew XXII, the Angelic Doctor writes:

> He then concludes: *Many are called but few are chosen,* for some do not want to come, and others have no wedding garment. Hence it was said earlier (VII, 14): *Narrow is the way that leadeth to life and very few there are who find it.*[137]

And commenting on Chapter XII of the Epistle to the Romans, Lect. 2, he says:

---

[136] *Summa Theologiæ*, I, q. 23, a. 7, reply to objection 3.
[137] Parma, 1861, vol. X, p. 200, col. 2.

Although they are called *few* by comparison with the barren multitude of the damned, in accordance with the words of Matthew VII, *few there are that find it*, yet in absolute terms they are many.[138]

In the same way, when commenting on I Corinthians IX, 24: *Know you not that they that run in the race, all run indeed, but one receiveth the prize?* He says, "The first clause refers to the condition of men in the wayfaring state, the second to the multitude of those who are called, and the third to *the fewness of the elect.*"

The authority of Saint Thomas, the prince of theologians, considerably inconveniences the Progressives, so they do their best to weaken it. Fr. Castelein writes:

> Saint Thomas Aquinas, *although he follows the old opinion*, did not deem it well enough established and certain to devote to it an article of his *Summa Theologiæ* in which he addresses *almost all* the problems of theology.[139]

Thus in the first place he admits that Saint Thomas teaches the ancient and traditional opinion concerning the smaller number of the elect.

Secondly, it seems to the present writer that Saint Thomas did not devote an entire article to this question, not because he considered it less well established and certain, but because it would not have been

---

[138] *Ibid.*, vol. XIII, p. 123.

[139] Second edition, p. 283. — The Rev. Victor Mauran belittles the authority of Saint Thomas in a different way:

> "It is distressing to see such an opinion taught by Saint Thomas Aquinas." (Introduction, p. IX)

> "Saint Thomas should not be held entirely responsible for this harsh and severe doctrine. The Holy Doctor is simply conforming himself to the teaching of his day."

> "It must be admitted that the Middle Ages, with their great and terrible combats, could not be very favourable to *liberal* ideas."

> "The logic of the illustrious Saint seems to me to be *clearly defective* here. It amounts to *begging the question*... We have the right to deny it."

> "Such an argument is certainly of no great value." (p. 239.)

I do not think that such plainly ill-considered remarks call for refutation.

appropriate in an abridged summary — which is what the word *Summa* means — of theology. For the Divine Doctor wrote his *Summa* for theological novices, as he avows in his Prologue to the work: "My intention in this work is to set out what relates to the Christian religion in a way suited to the learning of *beginners*."

Finally there are countless truths, even of the greatest importance in theology, which Thomas teaches not in the body of his articles but only in the replies to objections. Who could ever imagine that Saint Thomas holds only those doctrines for certain and established which he expounds in the body of the articles of the *Summa* and that he considers those stated in the replies to be doubtful and unsure?

It is therefore quite astonishing to read of Saint Thomas that:

> In replying to a third objection made by the supporters of *the old opinion* on the greater number as to the reprobate, he therefore contents himself with proving that this opinion can be reconciled with his thesis concerning predestination. Thus Saint Thomas does not treat the question *ex professo*; he gives his readers to understand that this opinion may be held *as true, nothing more.*[140]

If the Angelic Doctor allows our opinion to be held as true, he therefore himself considers to opinion of the Progressives to be false, for he would certainly not have allowed an opinion to be held *as true* which he did not himself consider to be such. It must therefore be said outright that the Holy Doctor admits the fact on which the objection is based, namely that the number of the damned among mankind is greater, which he demonstrates with great lucidity not to be incompatible with the divine mercy; otherwise he would simply have denied the claim on which the objection is based.

Moreover we have already seen Fr. Castelein admit that Saint Thomas did in fact hold this "old opinion".

And in any event the three other passages quoted show that the *Summa* is not the only place in which the Angelic Doctor manifests his opinion as to the fewness of the elect.

---

[140] *Ibid.*, p. 284, note 1.

17. PSEUDO-AQUINAS
PERHAPS **THOMAS ANGLUS**[141]

The fewness of the elect finds a remarkable champion in the unknown author of the ancient Commentary entitled *Expositio in Septem Epistolas Canonicas*, sometimes attributed to Saint Thomas Aquinas, the Angelic Doctor, and sometimes to his fellow-Dominican Thomas the Englishman. The following passage is extracted from its remarks on the text of I Peter III, 20,"wherein a few, that is, eight souls, were saved" :

> Note that the ark represents the Church..., *in which few, in comparison with the damned, are saved,* for it is stated in Matthew VII : *narrow is the way that leadeth to life and few there are that find it* ; and yet fewer are those who *walk* along that way and very few indeed those who *persevere* in it.... Few are saved in the ark, to wit, just eight souls, by which the fewness of the elect is signified — Matthew XXII : *Many are called but few are chosen.*

> Note from this that the fewness of the saved was prefigured in the days of the *law of nature,* i.e. when all perished but eight who were saved in the Ark during the flood as is recounted in this passage.

> And it was prefigured again in the days of the *law of Moses,* when we read in Numbers XIV that of all those — some six hundred thousand — whom the Lord brought out of Egypt through the desert (which signifies penance), only two, Josue and Caleb, were to enter the promised land.

> The same thing again was prefigured *in the days of the Prophets,* when the children of Israel were led into captivity and few were left in the promised land.

> And *in the days of grace* it was expressly announced, in the words of Matthew XXII : *Many are called but few are chosen.*[142]

---

[141] The thirteenth century *Expositio in Septem Epistolas Canonicas* is today commonly attributed to Nicholas of Gorran (1232-c.1295). Whoever its author was this scriptural commentary has always been held in high esteem. — Translator.

[142] Parma, 1869, vol. XXIII, p. 268, col. 2.

18. SAINT BONAVENTURE
DOCTOR OF THE CHURCH
(1221-1274)

The Seraphic Doctor speaks in the following terms of God's role in the predestination of souls:

> When God damns and reproves, He acts according to justice; but when He predestines, He acts according to grace and mercy, which do not exclude justice. — Since, then, *all men*, in so far as they were but a mass of perdition, ought to be damned, it follows that *more are reproved than are chosen*, in order to show that salvation is due to a *special* grace, whereas damnation is due to *common* justice. No man may therefore complain of the Divine Will, for It accomplishes all most rightly; rather ought we in all things to give thanks and honour the government of Divine Providence.[143]

And in commenting on the Four Books of the Sentences, with regard to the text: "For many, both evil and good, hold high office in the Church; and would that there may not be more of them who are evil than are good." He writes:

> Conclusion 1. And this [election] is different from vocation, because grace is given to many who do not persevere; that is why they are said to be *called* but not *chosen*. This is what is referred to in the text of Matthew XXII: *Many are called, but few are chosen.*[144]

And in his second sermon on the conversion of Saint Paul he writes to the same effect:

> We read in Holy Scripture of a twofold election, the one eternal and the other temporal.
> By the first we are always prepared for grace and for glory.
> By the second we are called to grace but not always to glory.
> The first election is the same thing as predestination, by which we are written in the book of life.
> The second election is the same thing as temporal vocation, which although, in time, it is invariably to grace, is not always to glory, for not

---

[143] *Breviloquium*, I, cap. IX; Quaracchi, 1891, p. 218.
[144] *Lib. Sent.*, dist., 40, a. 3, q. 2, Lyon, 1668, vol. IV, p. 328.

all who are called in time are elect in eternity. *For many, says Our Lord, are called, but few are chosen.*[145]

19. SAINT ANTHONY OF PADUA[146] (1195-1231)

In his sermon on *The Lord's Supper*, Saint Anthony compares the divine vocation to a breakfast, to which many are called, while salvation he compares to a dinner-banquet for which only a few are chosen. He writes:

> Finally the dinner-banquet is represented, which is held for the blessed whom the Lord admits, after a good death, to the refreshment of eternal life, which is referred to in the words of Luke XIV: *A certain man made a great supper, and invited many,* etc.
>
> This supper is held in private, for only the small number of his intimate friends are admitted, while those who had been present at the breakfast are excluded.
>
> The breakfast is faith, where the dishes are the articles and the sacraments, to which many are admitted who do not remain for the dinner-banquet.
>
> Hence *many are called,* i.e. to the breakfast [of faith], *but few are chosen* for the banquet [of eternal life]. (Matthew XX and XXII)[147]

20. POPE INNOCENT III (c. 1160-1216)

Commenting on the parable of the labourers in the vineyard he says of the elect: "They are said to be few in comparison with the wicked, for *the perverse are hard to be corrected, and the number of fools is infinite.*" Then he adds, concerning others:

> Not all believe in the Gospel of Christ He that believeth not is already judged; hence as there are more unbelievers than faithful, undoubtedly *many are called but few are chosen,* since even of the faithful many are damned, to wit those who deny their faith by their works, *for it had been better for them not to have known the way of justice, than after they have known*

---

[145] *Ibid.*, vol. III, p. 240.

[146] Declared a Doctor of the Church in 1946. — Translator.

[147] *Opera completa*, p. 418.

it, to turn back …. (II Peter II, 21). So may the Steward of the vineyard, Jesus Christ, grant us not to be of their number![148]

Thus twenty Saints, Beati or Venerable Servants of God, later in date than the Fathers of the Church properly so called, explicitly hold our opinion. Let the Progressives, Bougaud, Mauran or Fr. Castelein, now name a single one who taught their view. But let us now move on to hear the Fathers of the Church.

II. FATHERS OF THE CHURCH

We now pass on to the list of the testimonies of the holy Fathers of the Church, but before beginning it will be useful to remind ourselves of what was recently said of the authority of the Fathers by Our most Holy Lord Pope Leo XIII:

> The authority of the Holy Fathers "who, after the Apostles, planted, irrigated, built, shepherded and nourished Holy Church"[149] is supreme whenever all explain *in one and the same way* some biblical testimony as pertaining to the doctrine of faith or morals; for from their very consensus it is clearly apparent that it was transmitted in the same way by the Apostles according to the Catholic Faith.
>
> The judgement of the Fathers is also to be highly esteemed when they exercise as it were *privately* the role of Doctors on the same subjects since not only does their knowledge of revealed doctrine and information on many other subjects useful for knowledge of the Apostolic books recommend them, but God Himself has afforded fuller assistance of divine light to these men outstanding for their holiness of life and zeal for truth. For which reason the exegete should be aware that his duty is reverently to follow in their footsteps and to show wise discernment in making use of their labours.[150]

Moreover, as will become superabundantly clear to the Reader, there exists as it were a consensus of the ancient Fathers of the Church in which it is unanimously agreed that a greater number of

---

[148] Sermon X for Septuagesima, *Pat. Lat.*, vol. CCXVII, col. 357.

[149] Saint Augustine, *Contra Julianum*, II, 10, 37.

[150] Encyclical *Providentissimus Deus* on the study of Holy Scripture, 18th Nov. 1893.

mankind are condemned to eternal torment than are admitted to eternal salvation. It is a terrible thing to have to say, but useful to know, so that no one may err, and it may be of the greatest comfort to those who endeavour to live with the few, for it is a distinct mark of predestination to conform one's life to the life of the few who are good.

I trust I may be allowed meanwhile to cite, as a warning to priests and seminarians, the words of a certain Synodal Letter of the bishops of France and of Germany to the bishops of Spain and thus to conclude:

> Abide within the limits of the Holy Fathers and beware of stirring up new cavils which have no use save to subvert listeners. For it is enough for you to follow in the footsteps of the Fathers and to adhere with firm faith to their sayings. For in Our Lord they were Teachers in the faith and Guides towards life.[151]

21. SAINT BERNARD OF CLAIRVAUX
DOCTOR OF THE CHURCH
(1090–1153)

This Father supposes in his third sermon for the Vigil of Christmas that the common verdict is very well known:

> For which of those who are even nominally believers is unaware that the Lord shall come, that He is to come to judge the living and the dead and to render unto each according to his works? This knowledge, my brethren, does not belong to all nor even to many, but to few — *for indeed there are few who are saved.*[152]

---

[151] Harduin, vol. IV, col. 895, Paris.

[152] *Pat. Lat.*, vol. CLXXXIII, col. 96.

22. HONORIUS OF AUTUN (1080-1154)
OR
GERHOH OF REICHERSBERG

All bowed down in the desert and only two entered with the multitude of the children of Israel… Thos who bowed down in the desert represent the *many called, who did not want to come*; the two who entered represent the actives and the contemplatives who are animated with twofold love and will enter into the rest of the Lord.[153]

23. RUPERT OF DEUTZ (C. 1075-C. 1129)

For many are called but few are chosen. In other words there are *many* in the present Church, who have become members and whose names are written in the book of confession, but *few* — which should fill us with dread — who are destined to escape the judgement represented by the Flood.[154]

24. CARDINAL GEOFFREY OF VENDÔME
(C. 1065-1132)

After His Resurrection He was seen only by the good, only by a small number and only for a short time. For only the good shall have the glory of the future resurrection … and they will be few in comparison with the wicked. For as He says in the Gospel: *Many are called, but few are chosen.*[155]

25. VEN. HILDEBERT OF LAVARDIN
ARCHBISHOP OF TOURS
(C. 1056-1134)

This devout Archbishop of Tours in his Sermon for Septuagesima expounds as follows the celebrated words of Saint Paul:

[153] Commentary on Psalm XCIV, verse XI; *Pat. Lat.*, vol. CXCIV, col. 580.

[154] *On Exodus*, lib. IV, cap. 29; *Pat. Lat.*, vol. CLXVII, col. 730.

[155] Sermon 5; *Pat. Lat.*, vol. CLVII, col. 357.

Know you not that they that run in the race, all run indeed, but one receiveth the prize?[156] The finishing-line of the track in the stadium measured out for the race represents the end of the present life which is given to us in which to run the race of our salvation, while the Lord warns us, saying: "Run, unhappy man, run, hasten while you have time lest you fall into death."

The fact that out of the great crowd of competitors only one won the prize while the others ran the race in vain signifies for us, my dearly beloved brethren, that *it is greatly to be feared* that all we who have entered the race for the crown *may yet be beaten by one.* Hence the Apostle goes on to warn: *So run that you may obtain.*[157]

26. ABBOT WERNER OF SAINT BLAISE
(†1126)

Abbot Werner was renowned for learning as well as for his great integrity of life in the XIIth century. Commenting on the text *For many are called but few are chosen*, he says: "This pertains not to the earlier saints but to the Gentiles, for many come to faith, many are within the Church, but *few reach the kingdom...* That many are condemned, both of the first and of the last, is added in the terrible verdict: *for many are called* to faith, *but few are chosen* for the kingdom.[158]

27. SAINT BRUNO OF SEGNI
(C.1048-1123)

The Abbot of Monte Cassino and Bishop of Segni writes as follows in his *Commentary on the Gospel of Matthew*, Part II, cap. VII:

As if answering someone who remarked "this way is narrow and these commandments are very hard to observe," He adds, *Enter ye in therefore at the narrow gate*: and he explains that, *the way is strait and the gate is narrow*, so that *few there are that find it.* Yet this is the way and the gate by which eternal life is reached. *For they are few who are saved, in comparison with those who are damned.* Hence the Lord says elsewhere: *For many are called but few*

---

[156] I Corinthians IX, 24.

[157] *Pat. Lat.*, vol. CLXXI, col. 420.

[158] *Pat. Lat.*, vol. CLVII, col. 846.

are chosen. Whereas the way and the gate that lead to perdition are very broad and spacious and there are therefore many that go in thereby.

Fasting, watching, abstaining from carnal desires and all pleasures, not doing one's own will – to whom would this not appear narrow and strait?

Whereas eating and drinking abundantly, yielding to the desires of the flesh and to every inclination to pleasure, restraining one's own will in nothing at all — to whom would this not appear broad and spacious?

This is why many walk along this way and many enter by this gate. But whither do they enter? They enter into the city of damnation, the college of death, the prison of suffering and the lake of every misery.[159]

And commenting on Matthew Chapter XX he says:

But the following words — *For many are called but few are chosen* — show us that *there are very few who are saved in comparison with those who, hour after hour, are called.*[160]

In addition, on Matthew XXII, *For many are called but few are chosen,* he says:

For many are called to the wedding feast, but few are ushered into the bridal chamber and glory of the King.[161]

And in his commentary on the first Book of the Sentences, cap. 2, concerning Noah's Ark, he writes:

This ark represents Holy Church, outside of which no one is saved and those who are found within which in the day of vengeance shall not perish. For many now seem to be within her, who will then be found outside her... The wicked are much more numerous than the good; those who seek earthly things more numerous than those who seek heavenly things. The way that leads to life is narrow, but the way that leads to damnation is broad.[162]

---

[159] *Pat. Lat.*, vol. CLXV, col. 129.
[160] *Ibid.*, col. 239.
[161] *Ibid.*, col. 253.
[162] *Ibid.*, col. 879.

28. EUTHYMIUS ZIGABENUS († C. 1122)

In his Chapter XLII *Concerning the reward of the hired labourers*, he expounds this parable in en entirely general way, not of the Jews and the Gentile Christians. And at the end he says: "Many indeed are called to faith, *but few accept.*"

The reference is to living faith, which is accompanied by observance of the commandments until the end and the keeping of the nuptial (baptismal) garment until the day of judgement.

> Let us hear and be horrified, all those of us who after being washed by the divine baptism have soiled our souls and lost our life, condemning ourselves not only to be expelled from the wedding feast but also to be cast down into most wretched torment. We must therefore take care of the inward dress, not the outward. For many are called, but few are chosen. He also says the same thing at the end of the parable concerning the wages of the hired labourers.[163]

29. SAINT ANSELM OF CANTERBURY
DOCTOR OF THE CHURCH
(C. 1033–1109)

In his letter to Odo and Lanzo, he writes:

> For *we are all certain*, as Truth Himself has said it, that of the many who are called, *few are chosen*, but how few they are, none of us knows, for the Truth has remained silent. For this reason, let anyone who does not yet live as the few live either join the few by correcting how he lives or else fear certain reprobation. And let whoever deems himself already to be of the few not confide too soon in the security of his election. For as none of us knows quite how few the elect will be, neither does anyone know if he is already among the few elect albeit he already resembles the few among the many who are called.[164]

This idea was so familiar to the Holy Doctor that he repeats it again and again and in almost the same words. Thus writing to some

---

[163] *Pat. Græc.*, vol. LXVI, coll. 253-255.
[164] Lib. I, Epist. II; *Pat. Lat.*, vol. CLVIII, col. 1065.

monks of the Abbey of Bec, he says: "For since among the many who are called there are few who are chosen, *we are all certain*, as the Truth Himself has said it, *etc.*[165]

And to the Countess Ida he writes:

Very dear friend in God! The Lord says, *Many are called, but few are chosen*. So never be sure that you must be numbered among the elect until you so love that there a few whose life bears comparison with yours; and even when you know that your are one of the few, continue to fear, for it still remains doubtful whether you will be of the few elect, until you see that you are of those few of whose election no doubt remains. For He who said: *Few are chosen*, precisely did not tell us *how few*; in order that no matter how great progress we may seem to have made, we may always deem that we have not yet reached beyond the very first stage of progress.[166]

30. PSEUDO-ANSELM
(PERHAPS HONORIUS OF AUTUN)

Next is an extract from the *Elucidarium*, Lib. II, capp. 18-19, *On the different states of the laity*, formerly attributed to Saint Anselm and included among his works:

Disciple: What do you think of soldiers?
Master: There are few who are good.
Disciple: What hope may merchants have?
Master: Little; for they acquire almost all that they have by fraud, perjury and excessive profit.
Disciple: What then of artisans?
Master: Almost all are lost, for whatever they make they use the utmost deceit.
Disciple: What do you say of public penitents?
Master: Call them not "penitents" but "mockers of God"; for they mock God and deceive themselves, rejoicing when they have done evil and exulting over the worst things.
Disciple: And of farmers what say you?

---

[165] *Ibid.*, col. 1114.
[166] Lib. III, Epist. XVIII; *Pat. Lat.*, vol. CLIX, col. 43.

Master : *In a great measure* they are saved, because they live simply and nourish God's people by the sweat of their brow.

Disciple : And what of children?

Master : Those that cannot yet speak, such as three-year-olds, so long as they have been baptized, are saved. But of those that are five years old or more, some are lost and some are saved.

Disciple : It seems that there are few who are saved.

Master : *Strait is the way that leadeth to life: and few there are that find it!* Yet as the dove chooses pure grains, so does Christ gather His elect from among all these kinds of person.[167]

31. OTHLO OF RATISBON (C. 1010-C.1072)

In his *De cursu spirituali* the Benedictine monk Othlo, of the abbey of Saint Emmeran's comments as follows on the words of the Apostle in I Corinthians IX, 24: *Know you not that they that run in the race, all run indeed, but one receiveth the prize?*

Special attention should be paid to the sharp contrast between "all" and "one". What should we take this "one" to signify except, of course, any *one* of the elect, persevering in the unity of faith and in the other virtues (the agreement of which makes them too a unity) and striving to be one and the same? — And what is represented by all those who run in the race but do not win the prize unless it be those who, although they reach the holy faith and get off to a good start in the accomplishment of good works, believe but for a time, but fall away in the hour of temptation by failing to persist in their good works?[168]

And later he writes :

Our Lord and Saviour ... wishing to save at least some of those who are on the road to damnation, dissuasively declares: *Many are called but few are chosen*, as much as to say : many indeed know how to do good, but few there are who in fact do it.[169]

---

[167] *Pat. Lat.*, vol. CLXXII, col. 1148.

[168] *De cursu spirituali*, cap. I; *Pat. Lat.*, vol. CXLVI, col. 141.

[169] *Ibid.*, cap. XIX, col. 211.

32. RALPH OF FLAIX
(XIITH CENTURY)

As we find ourselves in such a cloud of ignorance that scarcely anyone is able to find the way to the heavenly city, the Lord says: *Few there are that find it.* Hence none of the more simple, and still less the educated, ought to set up his own form of belief or rule of life; on the contrary the authority of the ancients and what they taught was to be believed or done must always be held to.[170]

33. SAINT PETER DAMIAN
DOCTOR OF THE CHURCH
(1007–1072)

Was Our Lord's celebrated warning to follow the narrow way addressed only to the Jews as some Progressives claim? Or does it concern all Christians of every age? This Doctor thinks the latter:

Although those who travel along it are diverse, there is but one road to be followed, namely that which Truth Itself paved for us, saying: *Strait is the way that leadeth to life and few there are that enter by it.* This way Our Lord Himself followed and He orders anyone who would follow Him to enter by the same way.[171]

34. THEOPHYLACT OF ACHRIDA
(† C.1070 OR C. 1108)

Commenting on Matthew XXII, 11: And the king went in to see the guests: and he saw there a man who had not on a wedding garment, etc., he writes:

Entry to the wedding feast is gained without judgement, for by grace alone we are all called, both good and bad; but the way of living of those who have entered will not thereafter escape scrutiny; rather will the King conduct a detailed examination of all those who after their entry into the faith shall be found to wear a soiled garment.

---

[170] *On Leviticus*, book V, chap. 4; cf. D. Ceillier: *Auteurs Sacrés*, vol. XIV p. 739.

[171] Sermon 32, *On Saint Apollinaris*; *Pat. Lat.*, vol. CXLIV, col. 677.

Let us therefore be filled with dread at this thought, for unless one's life is pure, faith alone will profit him nothing; not only will he be expelled from the wedding, but he will be cast into fire....

Many there are who deceive themselves with vain hope, thinking that they will reach the Kingdom of Heaven; already they are mingling in spirit with the choir of those who recline at the feast, filled with great self-esteem....

Many, however, *are called* — for God calls many, indeed all — *but few are chosen*; for *there are few who are saved* and who are worthy to be chosen by God.[172]

35. RATHERIUS
BISHOP OF VERONA
(C. 887-974)

In his first Sermon on the Ascension the Bishop preaches as follows:

There are those who build up the faith by their words but destroy it by how they behave. It is greatly to be feared that to these too apply the words spoken by Our Lord: *When the unclean spirit is gone out of a man, he walketh through places without water, seeking rest; and not finding, he saith: I will return into my house whence I came out. And when he is come, he findeth it swept and garnished. Then he goeth and taketh with him seven other spirits more wicked than himself, and entering in they dwell there. And the last state of that man becomes worse than the first.*[173] This is so true that if it applied to none of those who profess to believe and have been baptized, what would become of Our Lord's declaration: *Many are called but few are chosen?* For who are here referred to as *called* unless it be those who have entered the Church by Baptism? And who are referred to as the *few* that are *chosen* unless it be those who hold fast by their conduct to the sacrament they have received by faith? — And who are *not* among these *chosen* save they who have not been faithful to what they promised? And what was it that they promised? Let each one call back to mind what he either promised himself or what was promised on his behalf before his baptism.[174]

---

[172] *Pat. Græc.,* vol. CXXIII, col. 387.

[173] Luke XI, 24-26.

[174] *Pat. Lat.,* vol. CXXXVI, col. 737.

36. REMIGIUS OF AUXERRE (C. 841–908)

Commenting on the text of Psalm XXXIX, 6: *I have declared and I have spoken: they are multiplied above number*:

I, Christ, have declared, i.e. by work and by word: do penance, for the Kingdom of Heaven is at hand. — *They are multiplied above number* who come to the faith; they have come to exceed the number of the elect, for *many are called but few are chosen*. Many are found within the structure of the Church who easily fall back into the vanities of this world.[175]

37. SAINT PASCHASIUS RADBERTUS (785–865)

In Book IV of his Commentaries on Matthew: *Enter by the narrow gate*, he writes:

Although charity is called *broad*, yet it is narrow and *few* there are that find it, and, of those that find it, *fewer yet* who strive to enter by it....

For wide is the gate and broad the way that leadeth to destruction. This gate and way is sought by none but found by all, for we are born therein and even to those who turn their backs on it, it offers itself ever anew. Hence *rare* is he that sets his hand to the virtues, whereas sensual gratification, like an importunate harlot, is forever beckoning each of us to its delights. Hence *many there are who go in thereat*.

But *how narrow is the gate and strait the way that leadeth to life!* Hence it is that the bridegroom and the bride of the Canticles exclaim:

Who is she that goeth up by the desert, as a pillar of smoke of aromatical spices, of myrrh, and frankincense?[176] As though they were saying: *Who is this that goeth up* by the way that *few find?* And even if they find it, how narrow it is and shaped so as to resemble a pillar of smoke — one composed of aromatic spices and frankincense? By these aromatic spices Christ taught earlier that, bearing His mortification with us in our bodies, we should be a sacrifice of incense, so narrow as to resemble indeed a pillar of perfumes. This way of the desert, then, is found by *few*, but the way in which the people are massed is trodden by many. The way of the desert, in which Christ combated, is walked by *few*. They are called *few* in com-

---

[175] *Pat. Lat.*, vol. CXXXI, col. 354.

[176] Canticles III, 6.

parison with those who walk by the broad way. And thus the gate and way of life is narrow enough, and admits but *few*.[177]

And in Book X of the same work, he says:

Many are called but few are chosen. Those who are invited, therefore, are not said to be few, but those who are *chosen*; for the greatness of immense goodness is such as to extend the invitation to all without exception, but among those invited the discernment of judgement is exercised and the election of integrity of life is made.

And this declaration includes and concludes all those parables concerning the labour of the vineyard and the building of the house etc., in all of which what is sought is not the beginnings of works but the end.[178]

38. BISHOP HAYMO OF HALBERSTADT
(† 853)

In his Homily XXI for Septuagesima Sunday, he preaches as follows on the Gospel of the day (*At that time, Jesus said to his disciples this parable: The kingdom of heaven is like to a householder, who went out early in the morning to hire labourers into his vineyard. ... So shall the last be first, and the first last For many are called, but few chosen.*[179]

[177] *Pat. Lat.*, vol. CXX, p. 322.
[178] *Ibid.*, col. 749.
[179] The full text of the Gospel is as follows:
At that time, Jesus said to his disciples this parable: The kingdom of heaven is like to a householder, who went out early in the morning to hire labourers into his vineyard. And having agreed with the labourers for a penny a day, he sent them into his vineyard. And going out about the third hour, he saw others standing in the market-place idle. And he said to them: Go you also into my vineyard, and I will give you what shall be just. And they went their way. And again he went out about the sixth and the ninth hour, and did in like manner. But about the eleventh hour he went out and found others standing, and he saith to them: Why stand you there all the day idle? They said to him: Because no man has hired us. He saith to them: Go you also into my vineyard. And when evening was come, the Lord of the vineyard saith to the steward: Call the labourers and pay them their hire, beginning from the last even to the first. When therefore they were come, that came about the eleventh hour, they received every man a penny. But when the first also came, they thought that they should receive more: and they also received every man a penny.

So the kingdom of heaven in this passage represents the Church, which is said to be like a householder, in order to teach us to believe the unknown by means of a thing known.... So the vineyard of this householder is holy Church, which from the beginning of the world to its end brings forth as many saints as the vines bring forth fruit-bearing shoots. This vineyard was first planted among the people of the Jews, but after the Incarnation of the Lord, it expanded to the ends of the earth....

So shall the last be first, and the first last.... Here the rarity of the faith of the Jews is rebuked, as it is added: *For many are called, but few chosen.* This applies especially to the Gentiles, of whom many are called, but few are found to believe in the Lord....

But for us who follow a twofold understanding of this parable, morally each of us shall, when evening is come, reach the end of his life, and although some are called from this life before reaching manhood yet, even if their age does not correspond to evening, their death will have the same effect. In the evening, then, the labourers are summoned to receive their reward, for the elect receive the reward for their good works at the time when they are called forth from this life...

Thus the last shall be first and the first shall be last as we daily see happen in the Church, for some who are converted later to the Lord, by their inward fervour and pious devotion outstrip many of those who live in lukewarmness and negligence. *But the statement added at the close of the parable calls rather for fear than for explanation.* For we all know that we have been called, but we are still unaware whether we are of the elect. For God calls us in many ways, by faith.... But there are some who are strong in faith and bright in words of doctrine, but who are reproved from God's election because they are torpid in good works and, as the Apostle James says, *Faith without works is dead.*[180] Of these Paul writes to Titus and the Lord says in the Gospel: *Not every one that saith to me, Lord, Lord, shall enter into the kingdom of heaven: but he that doth the will of my Fa-*

And receiving it, they murmured against the master of the house, saying: These last have worked but one hour, and thou hast made them equal to us that have borne the burden of the day and the heats. But he answering one of them, said: Friend, I have done thee no wrong: didst thou not agree with me for a penny? Take what is thine, and go thy way: I will also give to this last as to thee. Or, is it not lawful for me to do what I will? Is thy eye evil, because I am good? So shall the last be first, and the first last. For many are called, but few chosen. — Translator.

[180] James II, 14-17.

ther who is in heaven, he shall enter into the kingdom of heaven. These are they who shall say on the Day of Judgement: *Lord, have not we prophesied in thy name, and cast out devils in thy name, and done many miracles in thy name?* And to whom it will be answered: *I never knew you: depart from me, you that work iniquity*.[181, 182]

39. CHRISTIAN OF STAVELOT (FL. 864)

The following passage is taken from his Exposition of the Gospel of Saint Matthew (Chapter VII, 13-14):

Enter ye in at the narrow gate. There is a metaphor here, for the gate represents the way of the commandments of Christ

Wide is the gate, and broad is the way that leadeth to destruction. This means the pleasures of this world, which are met with spontaneously as the body delights therein; they need be neither sought nor learnt, which is why *there are many who go in thereat.*

How narrow is the gate, and strait is the way that leadeth to life! That is to say that it is very demanding, by fasting, by patience, by love for one's enemies, to traverse this world and reach eternal life. *Narrow is the way*: for which reason the Psalmist says: *I have kept hard ways.*[183]

And few there are that find it. He says that there are few who find it, and not all of those who find it travel by it...

Similarly, in another passage, Our Lord says: *Many are called, but few are chosen.* They are *called*, because they have become Christians, but they deny God by their way of living — there are *few chosen*.[184]

The same writer comments as follows on Matthew, XXII, 14:

For many are called: i.e. from among both the Jews and the Gentiles. *But few are chosen.* A fearful declaration, for there are few who serve God without stain and we offend God in many ways without noticing.

It is also possible to understand the words *Many are called* of Christians alone, for they are called by preaching, but do not follow by works. The greater part of them walk in the broad way.[185]

---

[181] Matthew VII, 21-3.

[182] *Pat. Lat.*, vol. CXVIII, coll. 154-163.

[183] Psalm XVI, 4.

[184] *Pat. Lat.*, vol. CVI, col. 1320.

40. JONAS OF ORLÉANS (760-843)

In his work *On Instruction of the Laity*, Book I, Chapter 20 is entitled "How many respect the Christian profession in words, but neglect it in their actions". Therein Bishop Jonas writes:

> For the lovers of the world, the way is broad and spacious — and leads
> to death; but for the lovers of Christ the way is strait and narrow, and
> leads to life. For, very sad to say, those in the Church in our times who
> are advancing by the broad and spacious way towards death are greater
> in number than those who strive to enter by the strait and narrow way
> that leads to life. And the reason for this is that the words written by the
> Apostle to Timothy appear to be fulfilled: *Know also this, that, in the last
> days, shall come dangerous times. Men shall be lovers of themselves*, etc.[186] And
> as he writes in another passage: *For all seek the things that are their own; not
> the things that are Jesus Christ's.*[187] For I have clearly observed that the
> Christian profession in modern times is not so devoutly and religiously
> observed by the majority as it was by the primitive Christians.[188]

This is the opposite of what Fr. Castelein thinks, for, as we shall
be seeing later, he prefers the fervour of the Christians of our own
day to the state of the primitive Church.

41. AMBROSE AUTPERT (†C. 778)

In Book IV, 15 of his Exposition of the Apocalypse, commenting
on Chapter VII, verse 14: *These are they who are come out of great tribula-
tion*, he writes:

> Hence absolutely, hence certainly, all who are of the elect will be tried
> by great tribulation, as they *know not whether they be worthy of love or ha-
> tred*;[189] and hence they mourn and lament and injure themselves with
> their continual weeping. — Rare are such men! — To which not I but
> the Lord replies: *Many are called but few are chosen.*

---

[185] *Ibid.*, col. 1423,
[186] II Timothy III, 1-2.
[187] Philippians II, 21.
[188] *Pat. Lat.*, vol. CVI, col. 166.
[189] Ecclesiastes IX, 1.

And in Book VII, 25 :

> Because in his mercy the Lord *calls many*, but, in deference to justice,
> *chooses few*, as He Himself says : *Many are called but few are chosen*, who
> would not fear whether he may not fail to be of the number of the elect?
> And although we know that we are called and live among the saints, we
> are quite ignorant of whether we are elect and belong to the number of
> the chosen, as Solomon bears witness, saying : *Man knoweth not whether he*
> *be worthy of love or hatred.*

And in his book *On Avarice*, N° 14, he replies by anticipation in
the following words to the objections of today's Progressives :

> Perchance those for whom we adduce such passages from the divine
> Scriptures may say : *Behold, thou hast terrified us and now we have all but suc-*
> *cumbed to despair. If these things be so, which of us shall be saved? What ought we*
> *to do?*
>
> I reply not in my words but in those of Our Lord : *Enter by the narrow*
> *way*, etc. Our Lord proposed but two gates and two ways. He said that
> by the broad and spacious way many travel to perdition ; while by the
> narrow gate and strait way, *few* enter into life. He did not mention any
> *other* gate or way.
>
> You may seek a third way wherever you wish, to walk and go in by,
> but be not deceived : you will not find one, for no other way to life ex-
> ists. There is only one ; go in by it.[190]

42. THEOPHYLACIAS
ARCHDEACON OF THE HOLY SEE (†752)

In his letter catalogued as N° 83 in the collection of the Letters of
Saint Boniface Archbishop of Mainz, Theophylacias writes :

> Hitherto, not without grave Davidic sadness, have I been compelled
> by inner sorrow of heart to sing those canticles : *Annuntiavi et locutus sum :*
> *multiplicati sunt super numerum* — *I have declared and I have spoken : they are*
> *multiplied above number* ;[191] for *many* come to faith, but *few* are led on to

---

[190] *Pat. Lat.*, vol. LXXXIX, col. 1289.
[191] Psalm XXXIX, 6.

the number of the elect, as the Lord Himself publicly declares, saying: *Many are called but few are chosen.*[192]

43. SAINT BEDE THE VENERABLE[193]
(C. 672-745)

Commenting on Matthew XX, 16: *For many are called but few are chosen*, he glosses: "Since many are called to faith, but few are led on to the heavenly kingdom."[194]

And commenting on Matthew VII, 13: *Enter ye in at the narrow gate: for wide is the gate, and broad is the way that leadeth to destruction, and many there are who go in thereat*, he writes:

> Broad is the way that tends towards the pleasures of the world; there is no need to seek it or to find it, for these things are spontaneously met with; but not all find the narrow path, nor do those who find it at once enter on it; indeed many turn back in the middle of the journey of truth, being ensnared by the gratifications of the world.[195]

And on Luke:

> On the Day of Judgement, ever to be remembered with fear, when the same Creator shall appear in the form of the Son of man, *so great will be the rarity of the elect* that the ruin of the world is spurred on apace, not by the clamour of believers unjustly by condemned but by the torpor of believers who are justly condemned.[196]

44. SAINT ISIDORE OF SEVILLE
DOCTOR OF THE CHURCH
(C. 560-636)

In his *Book of Questions on Numbers*, Question 42, he writes;

---

[192] *Pat. Lat.*, vol. LXXXIX, col. 782.

[193] Pope Leo XIII declared Saint Bede a Doctor of the Church in November 1899, shortly after the publication of Fr. Godts's work. — Translator.

[194] *Pat. Lat.*, vol. XCII, col. 88.

[195] *Ibid.*, col. 37.

[196] *Ibid.*, col. 551.

Now the fact that six hundred thousand men able to bear arms are numbered as having gone out of Egypt, while no more than two of them entered the Land of Promise, is a figure showing that many attain Faith by Baptism, but *very few reach the heavenly fatherland* according to the Gospel image that *many are called but few are chosen.*[197]

45.— ANTIOCHUS OF PALESTINE
(†VIITH CENTURY)

In his Homily 94 he writes :

It is far preferable to dwell with few who are good rather than with the numerous multitude of the useless, as indeed the divine Scriptures inform us...

At the end of the world, the angels shall go out, and shall separate the wicked from among the just, and shall cast them into the furnace of fire : there shall be weeping and gnashing of teeth;[198] *for many are called but few are chosen;*[199] *for wide is the gate, and broad is the way that leadeth to destruction, and many there are who go in thereat.*[200]

Hence of the *few* who are pious and good He says : *For narrow is the gate,* and the way hedged in with bramble-thorns, that leadeth to life, and *few* there are that enter by it. And again : *Fear not, little flock, for it hath pleased your Father to give you a kingdom.*[201, 202]

46. SAINT GREGORY THE GREAT
DOCTOR OF THE CHURCH
(540-604)

Here is how this celebrated Doctor of the Church spoke in his Homily 38 *on the Gospel,* N[os] 8 and 14 :

It ought not to frighten you that in the Church there are many bad and few good. The ark amid the waters of the flood was broad in the

---

[197] *Pat. Lat.,* vol. LXXXIII, col. 358.
[198] Matthew XIII, 49-50.
[199] Matthew XXII, 14.
[200] Matthew VII, 13.
[201] Luke XII, 32.
[202] *Pat. Græc.,* vol. LXXXIX, col. 1719.

parts which contained the beasts and narrow in the quarters reserved for men, for Holy Church contains many who are carnal and few who are spiritual… *What ought often to be repeated and always remembered without ever being forgotten* is that: *Many are called but few are chosen.*[203]

It is clear how much importance the Holy Doctor attaches to this truth, for he inculcates it in various other places also.[204] I shall include here one further example taken from his Homily XIX, N° 5 *on the Gospel* containing the words: *Many are called but few are chosen.*

> For many come to faith, yet few are brought to the heavenly kingdom. For behold how many of us there are assembled for today's feast: we fill the structure of the Church, but who knows how few of us there may be who are numbered among the flock of God's elect?[205]

Thus Saint Gregory did not fear to preach openly to the people the fewness of the saved; he was at quite the opposite pole to the carnal prudence of the Progressives.

47. SAINT CÆSARIUS OF ARLES (C. 470-543)

This holy Bishop wrote two sermons *On the two ways: the broad and the narrow.* In the one numbered 68, after exhorting his listeners to choose the narrow way, whereby to mount towards paradise, he so depicts those who travel along each way as to make it clear, upon examination of what men aspire to, that *there are more in the broad way than in the narrow and hence that more are damned.*

And since he is preaching to Christians and applies this parable to them, he is very far indeed from sharing Fr. Castelein's false and lax interpretation: "The terrible passage about the *narrow way* and the *few who find it* concerns a specific and exceptional situation — the state of decadence and corruption which characterized the Jewish people at the Coming of the Messiah.[206] Does it follow that after the

---

[203] *Pat. Lat.*, vol. LXXVI, coll. 1280 and 1090.

[204] Verschuren, *Arcta via*, p. 79 (see below).

[205] *Pat. Lat.*, vol. LXXVI, col. 1157.

[206] *Op. cit.*, p. 35.

preaching of the Gospel and in the visible kingdom of the Messiah this narrow way will bear but a small number of the faithful while the great mass marches on to death by the broad path of its vices obstinately held onto?[207]

Cæsarius therefore says:

But perhaps some may be wondering who are those who, with perilous joy, go down by the broad way, and who are those who laboriously go up by the strait and narrow way.

All lovers of the world, the proud, the avaricious, robbers, the envious, the drunken, adulterers, those who use double weights and measures, those who harbour hatred in their hearts, those who render evil for evil, those who love spectacles of bloodshed, passion and shamefulness, *are all proved to be going down by the broad way.* Whereas those who are chaste and sober, merciful, faithful to justice, cheerfully and promptly giving alms according to their means and harbouring no hatred of any man in their hearts are going upwards towards the things above, by the strait and narrow way. And although they seem yet to dwell in body upon earth, the Apostle declares that their conversation is in heaven, so that when the priest calls out *Sursum corda!* they may confidently reply *Habemus ad Dominum!*[208]

And in Sermon 67 he says:

Over the strait and narrow way Christ presides; but in charge of the broad and spacious way is the devil. Christ invites men to His kingdom; the devil summons them to hell. Those who open only their bodily eyes are deceived by the broad and spacious way, but if we pay attention with the eyes of the heart we find our safety in the hard and harsh way.[209]

48.— POPE SAINT HORMISDAS (c. 450-523)

In his epistle 23, addressed to all the Catholics of the East, and which may be found in the Acts of the second session of the Fifth Council, as reported by Baronius under year 518, N° 2, he says:

[207] *Ibid.,* p. 36.
[208] *Pat. Lat.,* among the works of Saint Augustine, vol. XXXIX, col. 1876, n. 3.
[209] *Ibid.,* col. 1874, n. 2.

What scope is there for reward where there is no merit of virtue? The gate is narrow but the kingdoms within are extensive; *by few is access gained*, but they are the approved. Are not these words beacons for those whom they instruct that: *they will persecute you and scourge you in their synagogues*.[210]

49. RURICIUS OF LIMOGES (C. 440–510)

In his Epistle XVI to Turencius:

Just as what is good is rare, so what is eternal is arduous. For we have Our Lord's assurance that the way that leads to hell is a smooth and downward one, whereas that which raises men to glory is narrow and harder to travel. Wherefore, if not that *many* travel by the former and *few* by the latter?[211]

50. SALVIAN (FL. 464)

I cheerfully grant my opponents that this devout priest was, as it were, the Jeremias of his day. Let them by all means take some of his gloominess with a pinch of salt; the fact remains and cannot be denied that he clearly entertained no hope of the salvation of the majority of men or even of adult Catholics, at least in his own day, and that is enough for what I am setting out to prove. In Book III of his work *On Divine Government*, he writes:

What I have to say is heavy and woeful. The very Church of God, which ought in all things to be pleasing to God, what is it if not exasperating to God? For apart from a very small number who flee evils, what do we find among the whole body of Christians if not a cesspit of vices? (…)

I will go further. It is easier to find men guilty of all evils than only some; easier to find men guilty of graver crimes than lesser ones — I mean it is easier to find men who have committed both great *and* small sins, rather than only smaller ones without the greater. For such disgraceful behaviour has infected almost the whole Christian people, so

---

[210] *Pat. Lat.*, vol. LXIII, col. 416 (cf. Matthew X, 17).
[211] Vol. LVIII, col. 98.

that in the whole body of the Church it is considered to be a species of sanctity to be merely *less* vicious than the rest.[212]

51. SAINT LEO THE GREAT
DOCTOR OF THE CHURCH
(C. 400–461)

Here is what he says in Sermon XLIX, cap. II :

In all respects therefore the pronouncement of Truth Himself is fulfilled, informing us that the way that leads to life is narrow and arduous, so that while the broad road that leads men on to hell *is constantly trodden by dense crowds, rare are the footfalls of the few* who enter by the paths of salvation.

And the reason why the left-hand path is more frequented than the right-hand one is simply that the multitude of men are inclined to worldly joys and bodily goods.... Hence, while those who aspire after visible thing are *countless, scarcely anyone* is found to prefer what is eternal to what is temporal.[213]

52. SAINT ISIDORE OF PELUSIUM
(† Vᵀᴴ CENTURY)

Writing to the priest Eusebius, he says :

If, as you write, the devotion of kings towards God is a rebuke to the irreverence of certain bishops, and the excessive honour shown them enfeebles them, while their yearning for honour and for pleasure has supplied the matter for a banquet, you should take care that the matter be not a scandal to you. For not all suffer from these diseases as there are some who desire to live an apostolic life. If on the other hand you were to say that these latter are all too rare, I would not contradict you. Let us rather admire the foreknowledge of Our Saviour who said : *Many are called but few are chosen.*[214]

---

[212] *Pat. Lat.,* vol. LIII. col. 66.

[213] *Pat. Lat.,* vol. LIV, col. 302.

[214] *Sancti Isidori Pelusiani Epistolarum Liber Quintus,* Epist. 89 ; *Pat. Græc.,* vol. LXXVIII, col. 1378

What is here said of bishops is applicable *a fortiori* to the faithful in general.

53. SAINT PETER CHRYSOLOGUS
DOCTOR OF THE CHURCH
(C. 380-C.450)

The great number of the blossoms gives hope of a great harvest of fruit, but so many are cut off by the blasts of the wind that *very few persevere* to yield their fruit. In the same way the believers in Christ seem to be many when the Church is at peace, but when the storm of persecution blows, few are found in the fruit of martyrdom.[215]

54. SAINT CYRIL OF ALEXANDRIA
DOCTOR OF THE CHURCH
(C. 375-444)

In Book II of his commentary on Isaias, he comments on chapter XXIV, 6: Therefore the dwellers in the earth shall be poor and few men shall be left:[216]

As the earth has become accursed on account of the great iniquity found in it, hence unexpectedly made destitute, they will scarcely escape in safety, for those that are left will be *few* and easily counted. This concerns the literal meaning and the outward aspect of what is recounted. But for the inward meaning I say once again that ... *few* shall be left, i.e. few who have pleased God in justice and have acquired riches by their noble and valiant conduct. They are few, in accordance with the statement of Our Saviour, that *many are called but few are chosen*.[217]

---

[215] Serm. 97; *Pat. Lat.*, vol. LII, col. 472.

[216] Saint Cyril follows the Greek Septuagint version, which differs somewhat in this passage from the Vulgate and consequently from our English Catholic Bibles. — Translator.

[217] *Pat. Græc., vol.* LXX, col. 539.

55. JOHN CASSIAN (C.360-435)

This celebrated Abbot of Marseille, whom his contemporary, Saint Castor the Bishop, describes in Book IV, chap. 38 of his *De Cænobiorum Institutis* as "adorned with a special glory of holiness", writes as follows concerning *the few who are to be imitated*:

> By many tribulations we must enter the Kingdom of God. For *narrow is the gate and strait is the way that leadeth to life, and few there are that find it.* Consider yourself therefore to have been made one of the few that are chosen and do not allow your fervour to be cooled by the example of the lukewarmness of the masses, but rather *live as the few in order that you may be found worthy to enter with the few into the Kingdom of God. For many are called, but few are chosen,* and *little is the flock* to which *it hath pleased the Father to give his inheritance.*[218]

56. SAINT NILUS THE ABBOT[219] († C.450)

> Narrow is the gate and strait is the way that leadeth to life and few there are that locate it. If then they that find it are *few, fewer still* will they be who are able to go in by it, for some do not go in on account of their own negligence.[220]

57. SAINT AUGUSTINE OF HIPPO
DOCTOR OF THE CHURCH
(354-430)

In several of his writings Saint Augustine, the greatest of the Church's Doctors, very explicitly states the position I am defending. For instance, in his *Contra Manichæum*, cap. 16, where he treats of how to catechize a pagan so that the behaviour of the Church's bad members may not deter him from embracing the Catholic faith, he says:

---

[218] *Pat. Lat.*, vol. XLIX, col. 196.

[219] Also known as Saint Nilus of Sinai or Saint Nilus the Elder. — Translator.

[220] *Epistolarum Liber Primus*, Epist. 159; *Pat. Græc.*, vol. LXXIX, col. 147.

Would he know that the inheritance of God is *with the few* while the signs of its participation are *with many*; that holiness of life is communicated *with few* but the holiness of the sacrament *with many*? (...)

And these few He calls few by comparison with the great number of the wicked, although they are very many considered in themselves, spread throughout the world and growing up amid the cockle and with the chaff until harvest-time and the day of winnowing.[221]

And in his *Contra Cresconium Donatistam*, lib. III, cap. 66, he says:

The sea is full of bitter waves and full of sweet fish.... You have adduced from the Gospel the passage *For there are few who are saved* (Luke XIII, 23). Now explain how it is that the Lord Himself says *how narrow is the gate and strait is the way that leadeth to life and few there are that find it* (Matthew VII, 14), when elsewhere he says *Many shall come from the east and the west, and shall sit down with Abraham, and Isaac, and Jacob in the kingdom of heaven* (*ibid.*, VII, 11). And how it is that in the Apocalypse it is stated that their number is so great that no man may count it. ... How can the same people be both few and many? There is no escape to be found by saying that one is true and the other false, for both are utterances of divine Truth; but rather the self-same good and true Christians, who are many in themselves, *are also likewise few in comparison with those who are wicked and false.* In the same way the abundant grain with which a great barn is filled is yet said to be little in comparison with the chaff.[222]

And in book IV, chapter 53 of the same work he writes:

Indeed they are many in themselves, but the same are few when compared with the far greater number to be punished with the devil.[223]

And in his Sermon CXI, also sometimes called *de Verbis Domini* XXXII, he says:

Indeed there are few who are saved. Remember the question asked in the Gospel: *Lord, are they few that are saved?*[224] How does Our Lord answer this? He does not say: "There are not few but many who are

---

[221] *Pat. Lat.*, vol. XLII, col. 291.

[222] *Pat. Lat.*, vol. XLIII, col. 537.

[223] *Ibid.*, col. 582.

[224] Luke XIII, 23.

saved." No, indeed. But what *does* He say? *Strive to enter by the narrow gate!* So when you hear: *There are few who are saved*, the Lord has confirmed it. There are few who enter by the narrow gate. And elsewhere He says: *Narrow and strait is the way that leads to life and few there are that go in by it, but broad and spacious is the way that leadeth to destruction, and many there are who go in thereat.*[225] What comfort then can be found in belonging to an immense multitude? Hear me, ye few. I know that you are many who hear and few that heed. I see the threshing-floor and I look for the grain, but scarcely is any grain to be seen when the floor is being trodden by the ox, but afterwards it will be winnowed out. *There are few who are saved, in comparison with the many who perish.*[226]

Are not all these passages as clear as day?

58. SAINT JEROME
DOCTOR OF THE CHURCH
(C.340-420)

Saint Jerome comments as follows on Isaias XXIV, 13-15:

So few will be the saints, of whom our Lord says in the Gospel *Many are called but few are chosen* that their fewness is compared with those very rare olives of which the merest handful lingers in the topmost branches after the olive-trees have been shaken and harvested. And with how, after the grape-harvest, the poor, pressed by need, go round the empty vines to collect a handful of single grapes here and there.[227]

And in Book II of his work against the Pelagians he comments on the Gospel text *Few there are that find it* by enquiring:

Do you wish to known how easy are the commandments of God? Heed what is said: *How narrow is the gate and how strait is the way that leadeth to life and few there are that find it.* He does not say: *who go in thereat,* for this is exceedingly difficult; He says: *who find it.* Few find it and *many fewer go in by it.*[228]

---

[225] Matthew VII, 13.
[226] *Pat. Lat.,* vol. XXXVIII, col. 641-2.
[227] *Pat. Lat.,* vol. XXIV, col. 294.
[228] *Pat. Lat.,* vol. XXIII, col. 573.

59. PSEUDO-JEROME
PROBABLY SAINT PAULINUS

An ancient author[229] not certainly identified, instructing the noble matron Celantia, writes:

> And those who confess themselves disciples of the Truth do not follow *the crowd* in its errors. Our Saviour certainly shows forth in the Gospel two ways of behaving and two distinct paths of life leading to different destinations....

> See how great is the separation and difference between these two ways, the one leading to death and the other to life. The former is trodden and followed by many, the latter is scarcely found by a few.... If we prefer present comforts to those of the future, we are travelling by the broad way. We are accompanied by the many and tightly crowded together with cohorts of similar men.... But if we trample all cupidity underfoot and strive to be rich in virtues alone, we are climbing the narrow way; such conduct is adopted by few and it is very rare and difficult to find suitable companions on this path.[230]

60. SAINT JOHN CHRYSOSTOM
DOCTOR OF THE CHURCH
(C. 347-407)

The holy and golden-tongued Orator sets out his convictions in his celebrated Homily XXIV on the Acts of the Apostles, pronounced before the Christian people of Antioch.

> I say this not because I despise you for being so numerous but because I would have all to be approved, placing no trust in numbers: *Many more are they who go down into hell....*

> How many do you think there are in our city who will obtain salvation? What I have to say is disagreeable, but must be said. Among so many thousands [There were easily a hundred thousand and more at An-

---

[229] This letter is found among those attributed to Saint Jerome. See Migne: *Pat. Lat.*, vol. XXII, col, 1204. Erasmus and others think that it can be attributed to Saint Paulinus while others think it is the work of Sulpicius Severus. In any event it is an ancient document of respectable authority.

[230] *Ibid.*, col. 1209.

tioch, notes Cornelius à Lapide][231] *there are not a hundred who will reach sal-vation, and even of that number I am not sure.* How great is the wickedness of our youth and how great the idleness of their elders![232]

Concerning this famous passage of the Holy Doctor some say, with the author of the *Theologia Mechliniensis*,[233] "This is said by way of exaggeration, and not absolutely — if they frequent vain specta-cles, follow lusts, vices, etc., as is clear from the words used."[234] Oth-ers question the authenticity of all Saint Chrysostom's homilies on the Acts of the Apostles, on account of their stylistic poverty and a certain appearance of contradiction. But the Benedictine editors con-sider them to be genuine.[235] Moreover we have already seen the Venerable Fr. de la Colombière (in N° 4 above) saying, "... I am as-tonished that out of a hundred thousand there are as many as *three* who are saved."

Chrysostom himself in another passage addresses priests in the following terms:

> In vain do I look for them and lament when I think how many perish of those who had been saved; how many brethren I lose, *to how small a number are reduced those who attain salvation, so that the greater part of the body of the Church is like to a body that is dead and motionless.* And if anyone should ask what relevance this has to us, I answer that it is highly relevant to you if you do not care for them, do not exhort them, do not help them with advice; if you do not impose obligation on them, drag them forci-bly, nor call them back from such irreversible carelessness. For we must

---

[231] *Commentarius in Evangelium Sancti Matthæi,* cap. VII, 13,14.

[232] *Pat. Græc.,* vol. LX, col. 189.

[233] This is the official theological course (in nine volumes) for the use of the Semi-nary of the archdiocese of Mechlin or Malines in Belgium. Originally written by Fr. Peter Dens (1690-1775), it has been substantially modified over the years under the guidance of the archbishops and their selected theologians. — Translator

[234] *De Deo,* n. 50.

[235] Cf. Van Steenkiste on Matthew, 3rd edition, vol. I, p. 385.

not only be useful to ourselves but also to many, as Christ shows by calling us the *salt*, the *leaven* and the *light*.[236]

Finally, in his work against the opponents of the monastic life, lib. I, Nº 8, he says: "Narrow is the gate and strait is the way that leadeth to life and few there are that find it." But if there are few that find it, there are certainly many fewer who can reach its end.

> And again he says that there are many called but few chosen. So since Christ says that those that perish comprise the greater part and declares that salvation, by contrast, is the lot of only a few, why do you contest my words? In doing so it is as if you were to complain that a sermon about the Flood of Noah should mention that all had perished save two or three men who escaped the chastisement — and you imagine that you can refute my statements with such reasoning, as though I should not find courage to announce the damnation of a vast number. Yet I am convinced that it is so and I have no intention of preferring that vast number to the truth. Nor are the events of our own days any less grave than those of that period, indeed they are much worse — so much the more so in that the threat of hellfire has been pronounced and even this does not suffice for men to desist from their vices.[237]

Behold then what a *Terrorist* Saint Chrysostom turns out to be, preaching hellfire and the fewness of the elect to the people to the great chagrin of the Progressives!

61. PHILO OF CARPASIA
(FL. 4ᵀᴴ CENTURY)

Commenting on the text of Canticles III, 1-2: *I sought him whom my soul loveth: I sought him, and found him not. I will rise, and will go about the city: in the streets and the broad ways I will seek him whom my soul loveth: I sought him, and I found him not*, he writes:

> Not even now, she says, did she find him, even though she has risen up … and by prayer has gone forth to him. Why once again she found him

---

[236] Vol. III, p. 158 of the 1721 Paris edition. On the text of Romans XII, 20: "But if thy enemy be hungry…".

[237] *Pat. Græc.*, vol. XLVII, col. 330.

not is explained in the same words: *I will rise, and will go about the city: in the streets and the broad ways*; i.e. amid the affairs of the world and in the street that leads to perdition. This is why she says that she did not find him, *for narrow is the gate and strait is the way that leadeth to life.*[238]

62. SAINT AMBROSE
DOCTOR OF THE CHURCH
(340-397)

Among other things, he bears witness that the worship of God is rarer among Catholics than the worship of this world, when he writes, on Psalm XL, 2, *The Lord will deliver him in the evil day*:

> The day seems bitter which condemns many to punishment. For the way of virtue is narrow, that of vice broad. Hence they who walk in virtue are fewer and they who dwell in shame are more numerous. *Hence it is that the number of them who are to receive reward for their merits is lower* than that of those whose grave sins will earn them an adverse sentence in judgement.[239]

Then, in his *Apology for David*, Chapter IX, he quotes Psalm XIV, 1: *Lord, who shall dwell in thy tabernacle? or who shall rest in thy holy hill?* And he answers in these words: "Not no one at all, I grant, but few."[240]

63. SAINT GREGORY NAZIANZEN
DOCTOR OF THE CHURCH
(C.325-390)

In his Farewell Oration (Discourse 42) to the to 150 Bishops of the Second Œcumenical Council of Constantinople (381 A.D.), N°s 7 and 8, he cites the text: *For if thy people, O Israel, shall be as the sand of the sea, a remnant of them shall be saved…*"[241] and then continues, "*But*

---

[238] *Enarrationes in Canticum Canticorum*, LXXIII; *Pat. Græc.*, vol. XI, col. 78.

[239] *Pat. Lat.*, vol. XIV, col. 1071.

[240] *Ibid.*, col. 868.

[241] Isaias X, 22 (Septuagint).

with most ... God was not well pleased.[242] You count the myriads, but God counts those who obtain salvation; you count the uncountable dust, but I the vessels of election."[243]

Those he refers to as *dust* are orthodox believers, not infidels, so nothing could be more clearly favourable to my case.

His meaning here is made clearer by a remark well worthy of note found in the *Scholia*:

> Hence we are taught that those who obtain salvation are few. But do not be disconcerted by the great number of those who are deemed to be pious *in name*. For the name of Christ is invoked among many, but in few is it corroborated by the evidence of good works.[244]

And in Discourse 27, which is the first against Eunomia, N° 8, he says:

> When you hear that there is one way and that this one way is *very narrow*, what do you think these words mean? The *one* way refers to the practice of the virtues and that it is called *narrow* is on account of the effort called for to follow it and because it is not in fact trodden by many, if you advert to the *multitude* of those who journey by the contrary path of the vices. This is how it appears to me.[245]

64. SAINT EPHRAEM[246] (C. 306-373)

The Syrian deacon states in three places the position defended in this work:

1. Such indeed did the Lord establish the way that leads to life: narrow and strait, as it is written, and few there are that go in thereby.[247]
2. Our Lord and Our God JESUS CHRIST says in the Gospels: *Strive to enter by the narrow gate.* Let us travel by this road, my brethren, in order to partake of the inheritance of eternal life. It is paved with

---

[242] I Corinthians X, 5.

[243] *Pat. Græc.*, vol. XXXVI, col. 467.

[244] Verschuren, *Arcta via*, p. 84.

[245] *Pat. Græc.*, vol. XXXVI, col. 22.

[246] Doctor of the Church, 1920. — Translator.

[247] *De Patientia*; *Opera*, Rome, 1743, vol. II, p. 331.

penance, fasting, prayer, compunction, watchings, humility, poverty of spirit, contempt of the flesh, care of the soul. These are the flagstones of the narrow gate and the strait way which has the kingdom of heaven for its blessed reward. But broad and spacious is the way that leads to perdition.[248]

3. The Lord of glory said: *Enter by the narrow gate.* What is the meaning of this narrow gate and strait way that leads to eternal life and of *the few there are that find it*? And who is it that finds it and makes known this way to us? It is all the Saints.[249]

65. SAINT BASIL THE GREAT
DOCTOR OF THE CHURCH
(329-379)

In his sermon *On the Renouncement of the World*, he addresses these words to a religious:

> Imitate those who live rightly and inscribe their actions on your heart. *Choose to be of the number of the few.* For what is good is rare; which is why *there are few that enter into the kingdom of heaven.* Take care not to think that all are saved who dwell in a cell, be they good or bad. For this is not so. Many indeed adopt a holy and devout mode of life, but few suffer its yoke. *For the kingdom of heaven suffereth violence and men of violence bear it away.* [Matthew XI, 12] These words are from the Gospel.[250]

66. PSEUDO-BASIL
[FL. 4ᵀᴴ CENTURY]

This anonymous author says in his *Commentary on Isaias*, cap. VIII, § 213:

> There are many who perish on account of the softness and broadness of their life, but *few* there are who reach the kingdom of heaven, because they will not bear the bitterness and labour entailed by the life based on the commandment of virtue.[251]

---

[248] *De Pænitentia, Ibid.*, vol. III, p. 398.
[249] *De Parænes., Ibid.*, vol. II, p. 175.
[250] *Pat. Græc.*, vol. XXXI, col. 646.
[251] *Pat. Græc.*, vol. XXX, col. 486.

And in the same work, cap. X, § 246, he writes:

Let no one be astonished to learn from this passage that so great a number of the people of Israel was reduced to so few. What matters is not the multitude of those who are called worshippers of God, for many are enrolled under the name of Christ, but *in few* is the dignity of Christian confirmed by the testimony of good works. *For if thy people, O Israel, shall be as the sand of the sea, a remnant of them shall be saved...*"[252] was indeed said of the former people, because salvation is not found in the multitude but in the remnant who, according to the election of grace, obtain salvation.[253]

67. SAINT HILARY
DOCTOR OF THE CHURCH
(†368)

In his *Treatise on the Psalms*, Psalm LXIV, 5: *Blessed is he whom thou hast chosen and taken to thee; he shall dwell in thy courts*, he follows the common interpretation of Our Lord's words, writing:

All flesh shall come, i.e. we shall be assembled from every kind of men, but blessed is he that shall be chosen, for *many*, in the Gospel, *are called, but few are chosen* (Matthew XXII, 14).[254]

And in his Commentary on Matthew XXII, 7, Hilary writes:

This man, therefore, is taken away and cast into outer darkness, for *many are called, but few are chosen*. So it is not the invited who are in short supply but the elect who are rare; for in the Inviter is found the kindness of popular goodness without exception; but among the invited, by a just judgement, election is made of uprightness.[255]

68. PSEUDO-ATHANASIUS
[FL. 5TH CENTURY]

In his first Letter to Castor, § 13, he writes:

---

[252] Isaias X, 22 (Septuagint).
[253] *Ibid.*, col. 551.
[254] *Pat. Lat.*, vol. IX, col. 415.
[255] *Ibid.*, col. 1044

According to the divine Scripture, if you come to serve God, prepare yourself, not for carelessness, not for sloth, but for temptations and tribulations.[256] For by many tribulations we must enter into the kingdom of Heaven[257] and *narrow is the gate and strait is the way that leadeth to life and few there are that find it.*[258]

Apply your mind therefore to those *few that are good* and arrange your life by their example, paying no attention to the slothful and the scornful no matter how numerous they may be. For He says that *many are called but few are chosen* and the flock is small to which it has pleased the Father to give a kingdom.[259, 260]

And the same writer, in his second *Dialogue against Macedonius* (First Confutation), writes:

Against those who think that what is true depends on how many people hold it. Have we not heard Our Lord saying: *Many are called but few are chosen?* Or again: *Narrow and strait is the way that leadeth to life and few there are that find it?* Who then, if he is of sound mind, would not prefer to be among the few who enter by that narrow way to salvation rather than of the many who hasten by the broad way to destruction?[261]

69. EUSEBIUS OF CÆSAREA (C. 260-C.340)

In his Commentary on Psalm LX he declares:

Paul lamented...: *Unhappy man that I am, who shall deliver me from the body of this death?* But he is troubled and almost despondent on account of his sense of humanity at the sight of so great a multitude of those that perish, for *broad and spacious is the way that leadeth to perdition.*[262]

---

[256] Ecclesiasticus II, 1 : *Son, when thou comest to the service of God, stand in justice and in fear, and prepare thy soul for temptation.*

[257] Cf. Acts XIV, 21.

[258] Matthew VII, 14.

[259] Cf. Luke XII, 32.

[260] *Pat. Græc.,* vol. XXVIII, col. 867.

[261] *Ibid.,* col. 1342.

[262] *Pat. Græc.,* vol. XXIII, col. 578.

70. LACTANTIUS (C. 250–C. 325)

This author discusses the *way of truth* and the *way of the vices* in his *Institutions*, lib. VI, capp. IV and VII, showing that the former leads to eternal goods and the latter to eternal evils, and he concludes that those who enter upon the way of virtue are fewer, for which reason it is stated to be narrow, from which it is only reasonable to conclude that fewer are saved.

> So as good things and evil are set before men, each of us ought to consider how preferable it is to undergo brief sufferings for perpetual benefits rather than to pay the price of perpetual sufferings for brief and short-lived goods.[263]
>
> But this way, which is the way of truth and of wisdom and of virtue and of justice ... is *narrow* because virtue is given to fewer; and *arduous* because there can be no reaching that good which is supreme and sublime save with the greatest difficulty and effort.[264]

71. ORIGEN (185–C. 253)

In his Commentary on Saint Matthew, concerning the parable of those invited to the wedding feast, he says:

> Because many are invited but are not worthy [of the heavenly banquet] at the end of the entire parable He adds: *for many are called*. And with reference to those who in fact entered the wedding feast, and, few in number, sat down at it, we read: *but few are chosen*.
>
> But if you first consider the numerous gatherings of the churches and then weigh how many truly lead a devout and upright life and are reformed in newness of mind against how many live slothfully and are conformed to this world,[265] you will realise why Our Saviour said: *Many are called but few are chosen*.

---

[263] *Pat. Lat.*, vol. VI, col. 646.

[264] *Ibid.*, col. 659.

[265] Cf. Romans XII, 2: *And be not conformed to this world; but be reformed in the newness of your mind, that you may prove what is the good, and the acceptable, and the perfect will of God.*

But elsewhere it is written: *Many shall seek to enter, and shall not be able, and Strive to enter by the narrow gate, for few there are that find it.*[266]

And in his Homily IV on Jeremias he teaches the diametrical opposite of Fr. Castelein's inventions:

If however we give weight to faith and truth rather than to numbers and we consider men's will, rather than how many of them there are, we see that *amid so great a number of churches it is hard to find faith.* Then were the faithful truly such, when martyrdom struck down its victims, when they returned to the Church sorrowful after attending such bloody rites of passage, when the whole assembly was in mourning, when catechumens utterly new to faith were led forth to undergo martyrdom, when girls and the weaker sex remained intrepid unto death. Then were there signs from the heaven and portents came forth from the earth, then were the faithful few but worthy of the name, entering upon the narrow and strait way that leads to life. But now that we are become so numerous, since it is hard for there to be many that are good — and Jesus does not lie when He says *Many are called but few are chosen* — of so many that profess the Christian faith few indeed are found that have faith and truth and *are worthy of beatitude.*[267]

72. TERTULLIAN (C.155–C.245)

In his work *On Flight in Persecution*, cap. 14, Tertullian says:

He that is afraid to suffer cannot belong to Him who suffered, but he that is not afraid to suffer, the same shall be perfect in love.… And hence there are *many called but few chosen.* He that is ready to follow the *broad* way is not sought for but he that is ready to follow the *narrow* way.[268]

73. SAINT IRENÆUS (†202)

In book IV of his *Contra Hæreses*, Chapter 15, we read:

And if certain persons, because of the disobedient and lost Israelites, assert that the Teacher of the Law was limited in power, they will find

---

[266] *Pat. Græc.*, vol. X, col. 848, and especially col. 952.

[267] *Pat. Græc.*, vol. XIII, col. 287, n. 3.

[268] *Pat. Lat.*, vol. II, col. 142.

that *in our calling, many are called, but few chosen*; and that there are those wear sheep's clothing outwardly but inwardly are wolves.[269]

And a little later, in Chapter 27:

> ... as, in the former case, God showed Himself not well pleased in many instances with those who sinned, so also in the latter, *many are called, but few are chosen*. As then the unrighteous, the idolaters, and fornicators perished, so also is it now, as the Lord Himself declares, that such persons are sent into eternal fire (Matthew XXV, 41) ....[270]

And finally in Chapter 36:

> For as in the former covenant, *with many of them was He not well pleased*,[271] so also is it the case here, that many are called, but few chosen.[272]

CONCLUSION

Now *therefore we also having so great a cloud of witnesses over our head*,[273] i.e. these seventy-three Fathers, Doctors and holy men of the Church, call in vain upon the gainsayers to name even a single Saint or Father who holds their position.

Fr. Castelein makes a vague attempt to do so, alleging in vague terms that, "two illustrious Doctors of the modern era, Saint Francis de Sales and Saint Alphonsus Liguori, *seem* to incline in favour of the opposite opinion" (*op. cit.*, p. 283). But the learned author ought to *read* the works of these Saints; he should seek out, find and quote, word for word, what they say. The topic is certainly well worthy of serious research.

The Rev. Victor Mauran has other ways of delivering himself from the burden of authority: "It must be admitted," he says, "that the Middle Ages, with their terrible combats against the Barbarians

---

[269] *Pat. Græc.*, vol. VII, col. 1014.

[270] *Ibid.*, col. 1060.

[271] I Corinthians X, 5.

[272] *Ibid.* col. 1096.

[273] Hebrews XII, 1.

from the North and against the Saracens in Spain and in the East and their struggles with the Jews did not provide a fertile soil for the growth of *liberal* ideas." (*Sic*, p. 239) This amounts to suggesting that Catholic doctrine, the truth of the Lord that abideth for ever, depend on whether we are at war or in peace.

But does Fr. Castelein display better sense when, to evade the unanimous consensus of the Fathers, he dares to write: "*A good many of the Fathers* believed that the number of the reprobate would be greater than the number of the elect?" (*op. cit.*, p. 283) He ought frankly to avow that *all* of the Fathers thought this, not just *a good many*, as though at least some of them held the opposing view. Nor should he say, "… but this opinion, *perhaps* motivated by their *conjectures* as to the history of the world, *as it was then known*, with its forty centuries of paganism cannot command assent." (*Ibid.*) For the Fathers do not base their teaching on conjectures of greater or lesser probability, but on proofs derived from Holy Scripture.

Indeed Pope Leo XIII expressly acclaims the Fathers "not only because they excel in their knowledge of revealed doctrine and in their acquaintance with many things which are useful in understanding the apostolic Books, but because they are men of eminent sanctity and of ardent zeal for the truth, on whom God has bestowed a more ample measure of His light."[274]

The Progressives forget this truth when they disregard the Fathers or when they adopt a critical approach to their writings, as if they were profane works, instead of reading them in a spirit of faith. "The expositor should make it his duty to follow their footsteps *with all reverence* …" says Pope Leo in the same passage.

But having taken the measure of this admirable patristic consensus, let us now draw some conclusions from it.

3. It is certain that the Progressives are mistaken in claiming that the doctrine according to which the greater part of mankind will not obtain eternal salvation is still a matter of free debate.

---

[274] Encyclical *Providentissimus Deus*, 18th Nov. 1893.

In reality this doctrine is the *mind of the Church*, since at every time and in every place all the Fathers and Doctors have transmitted it.

4. It is certain that those who prefer novelties based on no solidly credible argumentation to the unanimous doctrine of antiquity *err far from the truth and lead the people astray.*

5. It is certain that the Fathers with unanimous consent interpreted the celebrated texts of Scripture concerning the fewness of the saved in such a way as to infer from them this conclusion: *the way to heaven is narrow; it is found by few, the elect are few* in comparison with the reprobate.

6. The Fathers not only state, on the authority of Scripture, that the majority of the faithful will be damned, but they seek additional proof for it in the fact that so many live a life unbefitting a Christian and contrary to the example and teaching of our Redeemer.

7. The number and weight of the assembled testimonies of the Fathers further show that the doctrine of the fewness of the saved has been set before the faithful often and fearlessly. From which it follows that the Progressives are entirely deluded and are taking fright at the merest bugbear with their cackle about terrifying the faithful into dark despair if ever this truth were taught. Terrifying events do not happen because they are preached about; they are preached about because they happen. So if the holy and the wise thought it good in the early Church, as soon as the fervour of the golden centuries began to decline but while the Bride of Christ was still bedewed with the blood of martyrs, to warn the faithful not to tread the broad and common way, but to go with the few in order to ensure their election, why should this truth be held back in our own days when not only bad morals but also lax opinions are swelling the numbers of the damned?

8. Nor are the gainsayers entitled to claim that the Saints, since they were speaking as preachers, have exaggerated Christ's teaching by constant hyperbole. For many of the Saints not only taught the doctrine here defended in the fervour of the spoken word, but also consistently maintained the same truth in writings composed in calm and solitude. Moreover the Church never refuses the Fathers as witnesses to the apostolic tradition and as interpreters of Scripture, for they taught God's word with the utmost zeal.

9. Let us also bear in mind that the Saints were not hypocrites. What they feared for others, they also feared for themselves. As one of them said: "Have I written it? Can I delete it? If I delete it, I fear to be deleted. I could say nothing about it, but I fear to do so. I am forced to preach. I frighten others because I am frightened myself."[275] Indeed they were far from being hypocrites but like Paul, they practised what they preached: *But I chastize my body, and bring it into subjection: lest perhaps, when I have preached to others, I myself should become a castaway.*[276]

Let us hear and imitate the Saints as they themselves were hearers and imitators of Christ.

[275] The quotation is from Saint Augustine, Sermon XL, c. 3; *Pat. Lat.*, vol. XXXVIII, 246. — Translator.

[276] I Corinthians IX, 27.

CHAPTER FOUR

THE TEACHING OF THE SAINTS IS APPROVED BY THE THEOLOGIANS.

THE TEACHING OF THE SAINTS is also approved by the spiritual writers as common and true; indeed some say that it is *de fide*.

The gainsayers frankly admit that they are departing from the common teaching of the theologians. Thus Fr. Faber writes:

> In point of theologians the rigorous opinions regarding the whole mass of mankind have an *overwhelming* authority.
>
> The rigorous opinions concerning the damnation of the majority of adult Catholics have … numerically more theologians on their side than the milder view.[277]

These admissions are made by the pious Faber, who, as we shall see below, abstracts from discussion with regard to the entire human race.

Bougaud:

> Hence the opinion, *so general*, of the theologians concerning the fewness of the elect in humanity taken as a whole. Misgivings are inevitable when contradicting so widely-held an opinion.[278]

The Rev. Victor Mauran:

---

[277] *The Creator and the Creature*, 4th edition, p. 352.

[278] *Op. cit.*, 4th edition, vol. V, p. 365.

Alas it must be admitted that the great majority tell us, as Saint Thomas Aquinas does, that the saved are in the minority! — What a terrible doctrine. I admit that it has always shocked me. — Yet it is very painful to see such an opinion taught throughout the Middle Ages. In our own days those theological treatises that are *classics* in a great many Major Seminaries still teach the same opinion, notably the theological manuals of Vincent and Bonal. Cardinal Gousset also tells us that "the majority of men are lost." Yet a reaction against these deplorable doctrines is becoming established in men's minds.[279]

Fr. Castelein is not so absolute however: "I am only too well aware that several of my ideas are in disagreement with the opinion of *certain* theologians." (Introduction, p. X). But these theologians must surely be few in number, little known and of no great weight, for he immediately adds, with regard to *his own ideas*: "They are the fruit of a *profound* study ... of the teachings of *our greatest theologians.*" (*Ibid.*) In the light of the catalogue on which we are about to embark, however, the reader will be hard put to discover who these great theologians may be, especially as Fr. Castelein prudently refrains from naming a single one of them.

Let us recall the genuine teaching concerning the authority enjoyed by theologians and ascetic writers.

As everyone knows very well, just as the Holy Father succeeded the Apostles as Doctors of the Church, so the Holy Fathers were in turn replaced, albeit in a lesser degree of authority, by the scholastic theologians and the other more celebrated Catholic Doctors, who, while they teach what has been passed down by the Fathers, stand as it were in their stead.

The ascetic writers should also be added to the speculative-practical theologians, for ascetical theology is a part of practical or moral theology; it may be defined as *the science of sanctification* since its object is to lead man to perfect holiness.

Now in those things which concern the principles of faith or of morals, or undoubtedly follow therefrom, the authority of the

---

[279] *Élus et sauvés*, preface, pp. VIII and IX.

unanimous opinion of the Theologians is so great that to contradict it would appear to be at least proximate to heresy or to error.[280]

And as a matter of fact, such unanimity of judgement is indeed found among the Theologians with regard to the fewness of the saved out of the whole of mankind, while some divergence prevails as to the salvation of only a minority of Catholics.

I

THEOLOGIANS WHO CLEARLY TEACH THE FEWNESS OF THE SAVED

1. JOANNES TRITHEMIUS (1462-1516)

The pious and learned Abbot of Sponheim sets forth the unanimous teaching of the Saints in the following pious and well-chosen words:

> Truly the flock of them that are advancing towards eternal life is a little one, because there are few who strive to ascend by the narrow way to the heights of the virtues. For the narrow way consists in valiantly resisting vices and carnal desires, fearing no opposition from the ravening world and despising the blandishments of the present life by yearning for those that are eternal.
>
> Learn now in what the way of perdition and of death consists, for it is trodden daily by many. The broad way is to fulfil the pleasures and concupiscences of the flesh, to flee the shackles of the world.
>
> Now judge for yourself which of these two ways bears the greater number of travellers. Are there not more who love the world than who love God? Are there not many *who seek the things that are their own*, and few *who seek the things that are Jesus Christ's*.[281] Are not all, to use the words of the Prophet, *given to covetousness from the least of them even to the greatest*?[282] Are there not more proud than humble? More insolent than obedient?

---

[280] Schouppe, Francis-Xavier S.J. (1823-1904), *Elementa Theologiæ Dogmaticæ*, tr. 1, nn. 112, 34 and 116.

[281] Philippians II, 21.

[282] Jeremias VI, 13.

It is a little flock that advances along the steep path of the virtues, for *the kingdom of heaven suffereth violence and the violent bear it away.*[283] For there are two ways; the hard road that leads to life and the broad one that leads to death.

Few there are who tread the narrow way. They are those who have learnt to struggle against the inclinations of the flesh and to do violence to themselves, who prefer the love of God to all else, who flee worldliness and sin and guard their integrity with the utmost care.

But there are many who walk in the broad way. They are all those who love fleshly pleasures, take little notice of the love of God, love the things of this world and neglect purity of heart.

There is no third way available such that you may avoid choosing between the two and take a different route, for the way of the just leads to life and the way of the impious leads to death.

So the number of the saved is less. For many are called by faith but few are chosen by charity. But it is better to enter the heavenly Kingdom with the few than to go down into hell with the many.[284]

2. LANSPERGIUS (1489-1539)

Beloved of God and men, Fr. John Just of Landsberg, Just by name and by nature, expresses in the following terms the conviction defended in the present work:

Who is not frightened by the last words of Christ in this Gospel: *Many are called but few are chosen?* This is a hard and terrifying saying and is it wondrous that we do not think about it and ponder it more often. For Truth Himself has said it, Truth Who can neither lie nor impose on anyone. The elect are those who shall be placed at the right hand at the last Judgement, to hear *Come ye blessed of my Father ...*

And He says that they will be few. Yet all have been invited, as many as have received knowledge of the faith ...

Hence it is that of the many who are called, there will remain but few who are chosen, for almost all men love darkness rather than light and love vanities and worldly things rather than eternal things.

[283] Matthew XI, 12.
[284] Epistle 14.

Hence it is not surprising that *there are few elect*. Dearly beloved, we are all called. But how many of us shall be chosen, we know not.[285]

3. ALVAREZ DE PAZ S.J. (1560-1620)

This author's observations would make an exceedingly useful meditation for the Progressives concerning the ancient ways from the point of view of the confessor:

If we are all wayfarers and the way we must travel appears narrow to flesh and blood and is trodden by *very few* (for *narrow is the way that leadeth to life and few there are that go in by it*), let us seek the guide to this way, lest we carelessly go aside from the desired destination. *Thus saith the Lord* [Jeremias VI, 16]: *Stand ye on the ways, and see and ask for the old paths which is the good way, and walk ye in it: and you shall find refreshment for your souls.*[286]

Let not the folly of others withdraw us from our holy undertakings, *for we must live after the manner of the few* if we are to attain that dignity which is reached only by the select few, only by those who strive valiantly. "Consider yourself to be one of the few and the elect," says Cassian,[287] "and do not allow your fervour to abate on account of the example and the lukewarmness of the multitude; rather live as the few do in order that you may merit to be found among the few in the kingdom of God. *For many are called, but few are chosen.* And it is a little flock to which it has pleased the Father to give the inheritance [Luke XII, 32].[288]

4. LUDOVICUS CARBO A COSTACCIARO[289] (1430-1485)

They are fewer who are saved, because eternal beatitude exceeds the common state of nature, especially as it is deprived of grace owing to original sin. And in this the very great mercy of God is apparent, which raises some to that salvation which the majority fall short of.

---

[285] *Sermones de Tempore*, Septuagesima Sunday; Montreuil edition, vol. I, p. 144.

[286] *De Vita Spirituali*, lib. V, pars II, c. XII; ed. Vivès, vol. II, p. 360.

[287] *De Institutis Cœnobiorum.*, lib. 4, c. 38

[288] *Ibid.*, lib. IV, pars III, c. XXXVIII; *ed. cit.*, p. 276.

[289] Also known as Ludovico Carbone. — Translator.

These are the words of this academic's *Compendium Absolutissimum Totius Summæ D. Thomæ*, taken word for word from the teaching of the Angelic Doctor.[290]

5. FR. ALFONSO SALMERON S.J. (1515-1585)

Commenting on the parable of the wedding guests in Matthew XXII, he applies the words *Many are called but few are chosen*, saying:

A fate like that of the guest expelled from the wedding into exterior darkness will befall all those who, having once been invited to the wedding banquet, have rendered themselves unworthy of it; from which it is strictly exact to infer that *many are called* to the heavenly kingdom, but among them *few are chosen*, in comparison with the number of the called, as some indeed come but some are cast out.[291]

6. VEN. LOUIS OF GRENADA O.P. (1505-88)

To the same effect he writes:

Contemplate that region where Christianity is most widely professed and see in what state Christianity is to be found in our own most deplorable century and you will admit that in this mystical body *scarcely any sound member is to be found.* Take any one of our most famous cities in which at least some traces of doctrine remain, then scan the lesser towns, fortifications, villages and hamlets and you will find peoples to whom the words of Jeremias V are applicable: *Go about through the streets of Jerusalem, and see, and consider, and seek in the broad places thereof, if you can find a man that executeth judgement, and seeketh faith* [i.e. a truly just man] *: and I will be merciful unto it.*[292]

---

[290] On Part I, q. 23, a. 7 ; 1580 edition.

[291] Cited by Knabenbauer, *Commentarius in Evangelium secondum Matthæum*, p. 248.

[292] Vol. III, lib. I, p. 3, cap. 27.

7. ALPHONSUS DE MENDOZA O.S.A.
(† C. 1591)

This Professor of theology at Salamanca refutes at some length the error of the salvation of the greater number and concludes as follows:

> Moreover the greater part, and indeed the *very greatest part* of men, even of the faithful, in the absence of sickness or injury, entangle themselves without fear or scruple in various kinds of sin, so that there are *exceedingly few* of whom a fair and detailed examination of conscience would not bring to light at least one or two unforgiven mortal sins, whenever it was carried out except for a period of one or two days around Easter when they make some stumbling efforts to dispose themselves to receive the Sacraments.[293]

And this is confirmed by the daily experience of mission work.

8. LUIS DE MOLINA S.J. (1535–1600)

This theologian who has himself been called "as lax as can be found"[294] refutes the Progressive laxists with these words:

> For my part, although I see the efficacy of the Passion and the merits of Christ and of the Sacraments, yet when I consider the multitude of sinners, and how little trouble men take about their salvation and how casually, if not entirely without preparation, they approach the Sacraments, *I greatly fear that the majority of the faithful are of the reprobate rather than of the predestinate*, especially since a single mortal sin is enough for eternal damnation.[295]

9. GREGORY OF VALENCIA S.J. (C.1550–1603)

> *For many are called but few are chosen.* God reproves [for their sins] this great multitude of men, i.e. the majority of mankind.[296]

---

[293] *Quæstiones Quodlibetales*, q. 1, propositio 4.

[294] Verschuren, *op.cit.*, p. 110.

[295] Commentary on the *Summa Theologiæ* of Saint Thomas Aquinas, Part I, q. 33, a. 7.

[296] *Theologicæ Disputationes.*

10. GABRIEL VASQUEZ S.J. (1549-1604)

There are more reprobate than predestinate.

It is perfectly clear from Scripture that the number of the reproved and of those who are damned is absolutely greater than that of the predestined and of those who are saved. See Matthew VII: *Narrow is the gate and strait is the way, etc.* and many other passages.

But with regard to the faithful it is uncertain whether the majority are damned.

There are some who piously judge that more of the faithful are saved, since the greater part receive the sacraments before death and it is probable that the majority of these are saved. And this is corroborated by the parable of Matthew XII in which, out of all the guests invited to the wedding, and who represent the faithful, only one is found who has no wedding garment.

Others, however, think that the majority of the faithful are damned, an opinion favoured by Gregory, Augustine, etc. This is indicated by the parable of the sower in Luke VIII, where the seed sown was divided into four parts according to what happened to it, and only one of the four bore fruit. Since only one quarter yielded a harvest, this seems to indicate that fewer of the faithful are destined to be saved. Nicholas of Lyra and the Interlinear Gloss on this passage of Saint Matthew favour this view.[297]

11. FRANCISCO ZUMEL
MERCEDARIAN (C. 1540-1607)

This Professor of Sacred Theology and Superior-General of his order was a man of the most discriminating judgement and superior erudition, held, says Hürter, in the greatest esteem and respect.[298]

In the following passage on divine election and predestination, he explains his view of the text of Saint Matthew with striking candour:

Saint Augustine goes on to tells us what they were chosen *for*. "They were chosen to reign with Christ," and again, "He chose them to obtain

---

[297] *Commentarii ac Disputationes in I^{am} S. Thomæ*, q. 23, a. 7, disp. CI, cap. III; Antwerp, 1631, vol. I, p. 676.

[298] *Nomenclator Litterarius*, vol. I, p. 273.

his kingdom." It is therefore clear that Saint Augustine is speaking of election to glory, and this is the sense in which we must interpret a number of Scriptural texts which cannot be understood of any other election. For instance, there is the text of Saint Paul (Romans VII, 33) *Who shall accuse against the elect of God?* and the text of Matthew (XX, 16): *For many are called but few are chosen.*[299]

What could be more clearly said?

12. GULIELMUS ESTIUS[300] (1542-1613)

This theologian well deserved his sobriquet of *Doctor Fundatissimus.*[301] He writes:

> It is neither false nor rash, but all too true, that the number of the reprobate is far greater than of the elect, in terms of the entire human race.
>
> The reason is plain. For from the beginning of mankind to the time of Christ, very few in the whole world were worshippers of the true God, and not all of *them* were good. And although after the coming of Christ the true religion began to become widespread, yet in every period of every age up to our own there have been more unbelievers than believers.
>
> Furthermore, *even among the faithful,* Scripture and the authority of the Fathers bear witness that there are more bad than good, and hence more reprobate than elect .... *Nor is a single one of the Fathers to be found who ever wrote the contrary.* And if the Fathers thought this of the members of the Church there can be no doubt that overall, i.e. out of the whole human race, there are many more reprobate than elect.
>
> Saint Thomas proves this in this way: "Although the good that is proportionate to the common state of nature is to be found in the majority and is wanting in the minority, the good that exceeds the common state of nature is to be found in the minority, and is wanting in the majority."[302]
>
> To this reason another is subalternate, based on the difficulty of the good that leads to salvation. The cause of this difficulty is the propensity

---

[299] *Variarum Disputationum,* vol. I, p. 432.
[300] Also known as *Willem Hessels van Est.* — Translator.
[301] "Well-founded Doctor".
[302] *Summa Theologiæ,* I, q. 23, a. 7, reply to objection 3.

to evil and ignorance of good which found entry into the human race by the sin of our first parent.[303]

13. VEN. JOHN OF JESUS MARY[304] O.C.D. (1565-1615)

Outstanding for his prudence and learning, together with his uprightness and innocence, this man was held in high esteem by Pope Paul V and by Bellarmine.[305] He writes:

> From the teaching of the Gospel, *it is certain how very few* there are who are saved. ... For Divine Truth Himself has said: *Narrow is the way that leadeth to life and few there are that find it.* Now this statement of Our Lord Jesus Christ is of such authority and weight that I do not think any Christian could be found to contest it. ... Hence we may infer that there are very few Christians whose dispositions and attitude to God's Majesty are such that we may prudently judge them to be of the number of the elect.[306]

14. FRANCISCO SUAREZ S.J. (1548-1617)

Dubbed the *Doctor Eximius* ("Eminent Doctor"), Suárez addresses the question *Is the number of the predestinate greater than the number of the reprobate?*[307]

> Several comparisons are possible relative to this question.
> THE FIRST COMPARISON concerns the Angels alone. And the theologians commonly reply affirmatively in that case, with Saint Thomas, I, q. 63, a. 9 ad 1.

---

[303] *In IV^{tam} Lib. Sent.*, lib. I, dist. 30 § 24 ; p. 148 of the 1662 edition. He adds: "In IV Esdras, chapter VIII, we read: *For many are created but few shall be saved.* And more strongly still, in Chapter IX: *They are more which perish than that shall be saved as a flood is multiplied more greatly than a drop.* And in Chapter 10: *Because almost all are walking towards perdition.*

[304] Also known as Juan de San Pedro y Ustarroz. — Translator.

[305] Cf. Hürter, *Nomenclator Litterarius*, vol. I, p. 334.

[306] *Opera omnia, Ars Vivendi Spiritualiter*, Florence, 1772, vol. II, p. 150.

[307] *De Divina Prædestinatione et Reprobatione*, lib. VI, cap. 3.

THE SECOND COMPARISON concerns men, in absolute terms, embracing everyone that has lived or shall live from the beginning of the world to its end.

And in this case the common and true opinion is that the number of the reprobate is greater.

This is derived from the text of Matthew VII, 14 : *Narrow is the way that leadeth to life and few there are that find it.* This is why in Scripture the elect are often designated as *the few.* Many understand in this way Psalm XVII, 14 : *O Lord, divide them from the few of the earth,* and Ecclesiasticus VII, 34 : *For thy negligences purify thyself with a few.*

Hence IV Esdras VIII says : *The Most High has made this world for many but the world to come for few.* And more explicitly a little later : *Many indeed have been created but few shall be saved.* And although this book is not canonical is has great authority. It also states, by way of example : *As the earth gives much more material for earthenware to be made but little of which gold and silver made, so is the action of the present world.* It may be that the reason why Scripture calls the elect *golden vessels* and compares them to gems and precious stones is precisely on account of their rarity.

Then, it can easily be shown by an induction. For if we consider the state of men preceding the coming of Christ, knowledge of God was then rare and holiness too. And since the coming of Christ countless nations either have not yet heard the Gospel or do not believe it *and of those that believe, many are damned,* as I shall be saying shortly.

Hence, everything duly considered, the number of the reprobate is undoubtedly much greater.

And the reason for this is stated by Saint Thomas (I, q. 23, a. 7 and I-II, q. 72, a. 2, reply to the 3rd objection).

It is primarily due to the condition of human nature which is composed of appetites that are in a certain sense contrary, and the things we meet with that can incline to evil are more familiar and proportionate.

To this is added the disorder left by original sin on account of which I stated above that original sin is in a manner the cause or occasion of the damnation of many men.

Another reason may be derived from the elevation and excellence of the end which man is ordained to obtain by means that greatly exceed his natural powers especially in the fallen state.

From the human angle these explanations are very sound, but from the point of view of God this counsel of His wisdom is profound and we have nothing to say save that God wished in this way to show forth the excellence of His grace in the elect, as Paul indicates.

THE THIRD COMPARISON — THE FIRST OPINION.

This comparison concerns believers, or Christians: are more of them saved than damned, or the contrary? Some piously believe that more of the faithful are saved, e.g. Sylvester in his *Rosa Aurea* (Septuagesima Sunday, the end). It is also customary to appeal to the parable of the wedding feast in Matthew XXII in favour of this view. At the wedding feast only *one* guest was found not to have a wedding garment, whereas in Matthew XXI, of the ten virgins, five were foolish and five were wise. But harmonization is possible, for among Christians more die fortified by the sacraments whose power is quite able to justify them, so it is likely that the majority of them are saved.

But the contrary view is more commonly held, *viz.* that more Christians are reprobate than predestinate.

This is openly stated by Saint Gregory in Homily XIX *on the Gospel* and by Saint Augustine in Lib. 3, cap. 66, and Lib. 4, c. 53, *contra Cresconium*, in explaining the parable of the wheat and the chaff. For, as he says, the threshing floor symbolizes the Church and the chaff stands for the reprobate, but it is certain that there is a greater amount of chaff than of wheat.

The same is the view of Chrysostom, Hom. XL, *ad Populum* and *Hom. LXV on Matthew*, and of the Gloss and the commentators in general on the text found in Matthew XII and XXII: *Many are called but few are chosen* and on the parable of the sower, where only one fourth part of the seed bore fruit (Luke VIII).

Finally, Cajetan, in his explanation of the parable of the virgins says that even of those who *in the Church* live middlingly and *have some care for their conscience*, one half are damned; which is very rigorous. The reasons or signs of this excess are drawn from experience, from daily observation and from the propensity towards bad morals. For undoubtedly the greater number of Christians live badly and fail to persevere in the state of grace and it is very likely that they die as they live.

It is a doubtful matter and to my mind a distinction applies.

By *Christians* we may understand *all* those who claim to be followers of Christ, many of whom are heretics, apostates or schismatics. And in this general understanding of the term *Christian* I incline to think that the number of the reprobate is greater. And that is how I understand all that is adduced in favour of the second opinion.

This can be confirmed because heretics and apostates have always been exceedingly numerous and when added to the number of the faithful who die bad deaths they plainly exceed the number of those who die holily.

But if by Christians we understand only those who die within the Catholic Church, it seems to me *more likely* that more are saved under the law of grace.

The reason for this is that of those who die before adulthood the very great majority die with Baptism, while of adults, although the majority of men commit very frequent mortal sins, yet as often they return to grace and thus they pass their lives in a sequence of alternating falls and rises. Finally, there are few who are not prepared for death by the Sacraments and who do not grieve for their sins at least by attrition, which is sufficient at that time for their justification. And after this justification they usually persevere with ease without committing a new mortal sin for the short period that remains; so all things considered it is likely that the majority of these Christians are saved.

In our own days, unhappily, there are many thousands of Catholics so indifferent to all religious practice that the final argument advanced by Suárez has no relevance at all to their case.

Let us now summarize the teaching of the most learned Suárez:

1. He says that the opinion that the greater part of mankind as a whole are damned is *common* and *true*.

2. He says that it is the *commoner* view that the majority are also lost of the baptized as a whole, i.e. including heretics, schismatics and bad-living Catholics.

3. Among Catholics, to the strict exclusion of others, Suárez thinks it *likely* that more are saved.

Yet the teaching of Suárez is sometimes misrepresented by omitting this distinction.

15. VEN. LEONARD LESSIUS, S.J. (1554-1623)

This pious author gives an excellent explanation of why it is that the number of the saved is relatively small:

The lowness of this number is not due to its being predetermined; any number, albeit greater than the actual number, would be fitting and proportionate to the Kingdom of God. All may be stones in this palace, members of this body, citizens in this heavenly Jerusalem and guests at the eternal wedding-feast without danger that the palace may become outsized, the body disproportioned, the city overpopulated or the banquet insufficient. That this number will be so small is due to the carelessness and folly of men, who prefer to enjoy the comforts of this life and enter by the broad way that leads to perdition, rather than by the narrow way that leads to salvation. In the same way the guests invited to the heavenly wedding-feast make excuses, preferring human business, temporal profits or pleasures, as Our Lord expressly teaches in the Gospel.[308]

16. MARTIN BECANUS S.J. (1563-1624)

It is probable that there are more reprobate than predestinate, from Matthew VII, 14 : *Narrow is the way that leadeth to life and few there are that find it*; and Matthew XX, 16 : *Many are called but few are chosen.* Saint Gregory understands this of the faithful alone, so on the basis of Gregory's opinion it is to be said that even among Christians and the faithful the number of the reprobate is greater than the number of the predestinate.[309]

17. THEODORE SMISING O.S.F. Obs. (1580-1626)

This author edified Louvain with his mildness, piety and erudition. His virtue was mature and holiness seemed to radiate from him. His sole care was study and prayer.[310] Here is his admirable teaching on the question here examined in his *Disputationum theologicarum de Deo* :

Question : Has man in the wayfaring state been informed by divine revelation of the number of the elect and the reprobate as God foreknows them?

---

[308] *De Prædestinatione*, sect. 6, assert. 5, n. 160 ; Paris, 1878, p. 477.
[309] *Summa Theologiæ Scholasticæ*, tract. I, cap, 14 ; Rouen,1652, p. 95.
[310] Hürter, *Nomenclator Litterarius*, vol. I, p. 498.

I answer that it is certain from divine revelation that although the number of the elect is great — as emerges from Apocalypse VII and elsewhere — yet only a minority of men is elected to eternal life. This is clear from Matthew VII: *Narrow is the way that leadeth to life and few there are that find it*, and from Matthew XX, 16: *For many are called, but few chosen*. Hence this conclusion is of faith [*de fide*].

So if only those who observe faith and upright living until the end are to be saved, as is known from other Scriptures, it is certain that there are very few predestinate in comparison with the multitude of the reprobate.

The holy Fathers furthermore infer as probable that even among the faithful only a minority will be saved. … I say "as probable" as it is not certain, and doctors[311] can be found who think that the greater number of Christians will be saved, such as Silvester in his *Rosa Aurea*, orat. 2, on the Gospel for Septuagesima Sunday, in a question near the end; Franciscus de Christo (I dist 41, q. ult., concl. 3); Cartagena (*de Prædestinatione*), and Suárez (lib. 6, *de Prædestinatione*).

But I think the opinion of the Fathers more probable, whether we consider the signal corruption of the morals of Christians or the Scriptures adduced which seem to be referring to the faithful when they stress the fewness of the good.

And if anyone should wonder how it is that so many perish and fail to attain the end to which they are ordered, even though the efficacy of grace is greater than the efficacy of nature and nature is defective in achieving its end only in a minority of cases, Saint Thomas (*Summa Theologiæ*, I, q. 23. a. 7, ad 3, 1ᵃ and 2ᵃ; q. 71, a. 2, ad 3) makes the excellent answer that there are two reasons; (i) because the end in question is supernatural and disproportionate to unaided human power, which of itself is more inclined to the inferior goods and pursues them in preference to the supernatural end; (ii) it is connatural to man that there be a struggle in him between the sensitive and the rational appetite and in this struggle the sensitive appetite is so much the more powerful as bodily and sensible things are more like to man, not only because all natural knowledge begins from what falls under the senses and is continued with imagination of the same things, but also because human nature needs the use of bodily and sensible things for its consideration. And although the disproportion of the supernatural end is made good by grace and this re-

---

[311] Note that Smising does not say "Fathers".

bellion of the lower appetite is conquered by grace if the grace is efficacious, yet this efficacious grace is given to few since the fall of Adam. And the ultimate reason for this is naught else than the good pleasure of the divine will, showing mercy to whom it will and hardening whom it will and hence the fewness of the saved is to be attributed to the inscrutable divine will as to its root cause, with the Apostle in Romans IX.[312]

18. DIEGO RUIZ DE MONTOYA S.J. (1562-1632)

Hürter says that Ruiz de Montoya is to be counted as one of the stars among the Schoolmen.[313] This author bravely attacks the personal opinion of Suárez as to the salvation of the majority of Catholic adults, saying:

> This opinion is more attractive than convincing; it wins the adherence of its patrons *more by appeal to the will than by weight of argument or authority.* But as Saint Augustine says, the inclinations of human opinion have never saved anyone; their effect is rather, by flattering and comforting men, to encourage many to sleep on and be damned.[314]

19. JEREMIAS DREXEL S.J.[315] (1581-1638)

The following extract is from the final chapter of Fr. Drexel's *Christian Zodiac,* entitled *On the great scarcity of the predestinate:*

> We are all hastening towards the final goal, but, alas! how different are the paths by which go, we run, we perish! Narrow is the way of life, but smooth, broad and bestrewn with roses is the way of perdition; the former is steep and mountainous but the latter leads downwards towards the valleys. Easy is the descent to Avernus.[316]
>
> Truth cries out, admonishes and exhorts: *Enter by the narrow gate, for wide is the gate and broad the way that leadeth to perdition and many there are who go in thereat; how narrow is the gate and strait the way that leadeth to life*

---

[312] *Op. cit.,* vol. I, *De Deo Uno,* tract. III, disp. VI, *De Provid.,* nn. 803-805; Antwerp, 1626.

[313] *Nomenclator Litterarius,* vol. I, p. 518.

[314] *De Prædestinatione,* lib. IV, sect. I.

[315] Also know as Drexelius. — Translator.

[316] "Facilis descensus Averni." See *Æneid,* VI, 126.

and few there are that find it! Again He insists: *Strive to enter by the narrow gate, for many, I say to you, shall seek to enter and shall not be able.* Truly this path is narrow and it must be travelled one by one and without companions. Each of us will render his own account to God; each of us will bear his own burden; each of us will receive the proper reward of his own labour. And this is why Christ plaintively declares: *Many are called but few are chosen.* This one small word "few", like a uniquely terrifying thunderclap, roused a great part of the world from the lethargy of its vices; not a few were the men it drove forth from the cities into caves and horrid wildernesses or deserts; how many hundreds of thousands of Martyrs did it not spur on towards scaffold and the rack, towards wheel and fire, cross, the jaws of wild beasts or the armed hands of torturers? All were unanimous in their cry: It is easy for us to die, so long as we may live among those Few Elect; let the sword tickle our throats so long as we may be counted among those Few but Blessed ones. And which of them dared not say: If I who am one can bear a hundred crosses, I do not refuse; if I who am one can bow a hundred necks beneath the executioner's axe, I do not withdraw one of them; a hundred deaths will be a mere jest to me, and torments a refreshing bath so long as I shall be admitted to the company of the Few in paradise. Hence came the most generous words of the martyr Saint Ignatius: Let fire, cross, beasts and all the torments of the devil be mine if only I may possess Christ! This single thunderclap issuing from the mouth of Christ, this one small word "Few", has ushered so many men of impure life out of the pleasant meadowlands of licence and brought them together in the house of mourning and penance. They thought it better to be saved among few than to perish with many, for one does not perish one whit the less for perishing in a crowd. ... God cares for no number save the number of the good; the road to hell is not a long one for it can be travelled in the time it takes to draw a single breath: by a single mortal offence we become guilty of lèse-majesté and deserve the eternal flames. Thus it once happened that for a single sin of lust forty thousand Israelites and fifty thousand six hundred Benjamites were slain.[317] How many thousands of the Bethsamites, merely for gazing too curiously at the ark of the Lord, suffered the penalty of bloody death for this licence of the eyes....

Now count out for me the number of the Jews from Abraham until the last day of the world and you will see that the one hundred and

---

[317] See Judges XX. — Translator.

forty-four thousand which the Apocalypse mentions as the number of the saved among them comes to less than a thousandth of the whole number, so that taking the whole number together not one Jew in a thousand can be counted as predestinate. And what applies to the Israelites is rightly interpreted as applying, in due proportion, to all men together taken as a whole. For what Christ foretold to the Jews is also common to all others; it is not only of the Jews that only a few will tread the narrow path to life, for He declared without making any distinction: *Few there are that find it.*[318]

Thus Fr. Drexel had already long since refuted Fr. Castelein's notion that this exceedingly severe prediction of Christ related only to the Jews of Christ's day: "This passage would be very alarming if its sense was absolute and its scope universal. But the context clearly shows that it is restricted to the entrance of the Jews who were contemporary with Our Lord into the kingdom of the Messiah." (*Op. cit.*, p. 34)

20. JOHN OF SAINT THOMAS O.P. (1589-1644)

Concerning the quantity, or number, of the elect in comparison with the reprobate, some have wondered whether the number of the predestinate is greater than the number of the reprobate. Now this difficulty with regard to men (for in the case of the angels it seems more certain that the majority are saved) is easily solved in a general sense, to the effect that out of the whole human race there are fewer who are saved. *For many are called but few are chosen.* And again: *How narrow is the gate and strait is the way that leadeth to life and few there are that find it.* And the angel to Esdras (IV Esdras VIII).

It is certain however that the elect are described as few not in absolute terms but by comparison with the number of the reprobate.....

Some go further than this, descending to particulars so as to be able to measure the multitude of the elect in some way. But *who hath known the mind of the Lord?* So let us accept the sober verdict of Saint Thomas expressed here in Article VII, which joins the sentiment of the Church, in preferring to say that *the number of the elect to be placed in eternal happiness is*

---

[318] Antwerp, 1660, vol. I, p. 297.

known to God alone.[319] Do not seek reassurance for your carelessness and sloth in the thought that many are saved even by taking only mediocre pains, but rather be very solicitous to enter by the narrow gate, for many seek to enter and will not be able to, i.e. because even of those who have not entirely given up all effort and abandoned themselves to vice, but who still take some trouble to seek to enter heaven, some will not succeed in doing so. So let us put aside the anxious quest for information whereby to multiply the number of the elect and instead take pains to walk in the paths of the elect.[320]

21. JOHN PAUL NAZARIUS O.P.[321] (1556-1645)

If therefore a number of those to be saved were established by God, more would be saved than damned, for God wills all men to be saved, but the opposite is true as is shown from Matthew VII: *Broad is the way*, etc.[322]

22. GIULIO CESARE RECUPITO S.J. (1581-1647)

This distinguished Neapolitan professor of philosophy and of theology wrote two treatises *on the signs of predestination* and *on the number of the predestinate and of the reprobate*. In the latter he divides and resolves the question as follows:

1. It is *certain* that the greater part of *mankind* are reproved, if you include everyone, even infidels, and throughout all the ages of the world. Even today if you consider the Church of the faithful outside of which there is no salvation, it represents a very small part of mankind in comparison with the multitude of infidels — the Moslems, pagans and heretics — whose damnation is certain. So the whole controversy is reduced to the faithful.

---

[319] "Deus cui soli cognitus est numerus electorum in superna felicitate locandus..." From the Secret of the Mass for the living and the dead.

[320] *Cursus Theologicus in Summa D. Thomæ*, ed. Vivès, III, pp. 885 *et seqq.*4

[321] Also known as Giovanni Paolo Nazario.

[322] *Commentaria et Controversiæ in primam partem Summæ S. Thomæ*, q. 33, a. 7 (p. 696), and again in *Commentaria et Controversiæ in tertiam partem Summæ S. Thomæ* where he follows Saint Thomas.

2. It seems certain that the greater number of the faithful are of the elect if the number of children dying in the first seven years or so of life, before the use of reason, is included.... So the controversy is further reduced to the case of adult Catholics: are more of them reprobate than predestined?[323]

Then the author sets out the grounds of the opinion in favour of a greater number of elect and concludes: "This opinion is better adapted to wishful thinking than to truth; its verdict corresponds to desire rather than to hope.[324]

3. The contrary opinion *seems truer*, namely that the number of the predestined among adult Catholics is exceeded by the number of the reprobate.

And he goes on the demonstrate this at length from the Scriptures, the Fathers, the difficulty of the means of salvation, etc.

23. VINCENT CONTENSON O.P. (1641-74)

This pious author abounds in the sense of the Fathers and offers some remarks well worthy of being meditated on by priests and religious. Would that they, who are obliged to set an example to others, always themselves followed the narrow way of Christian edification instead of seeking some third way quite unknown to the Gospel!

Although it is not possible to pin down the exact number of those who are to be saved, yet from the Scriptures and the tradition of the Fathers *it is certain* that those who are saved will be few, and *much* fewer, than those who are lost (...)

Of Catholics, tell me pray, how many are they who tread the narrow way of salvation, lead their life according to the maxims of the Gospel, do not follow after the concupiscences, who keep their innocence, do serious penance after a fall, do not often relapse, do not love the world, who pursue holiness, without which no one shall see God? Rare indeed is such a man in this century of ours, for the lamentation of Salvian over his own times might more truly be applied to ours: *Apart from a very few,*

---

[323] Tract. II, cap. II; 1681 edition, p. 4.
[324] *Ibid.*, p. 8.

what else is almost the whole body of Christians save a cesspit of vices? A situation that calls rather for tears than proofs.[325]

Indeed in the ecclesiastical order itself how many Bishops and Priests are there who may be seen to imitate the Saints, how many successors of the Apostles' authority are also imitators of the their conduct? How many respect the way of life prescribed by the Fathers of the Fourth Council of Carthage and renewed by the Council of Trent in its Session 25, cap. 1, *de Reformatione* in words which the clergy ought to re-read each day and each day carry out in practice?

And what should I say of religious, I who, though all unworthy, am a religious by state and a priest by anointing? When we behold so many monasteries fallen away from their primitive observance, boasting ever more members who profess the regular life, but no greater inner joy? Indeed I would make my own the words of Saint Bernard in his *Apology to Abbot William*: *Who at the beginning, when the monastic order began, would have believed that monks would come to such slothfulness? Oh how far we are from those who were called monks in the days of Anthony! Was it thus that Macarius lived? that Basil taught? Was it this that Anthony laid down or thus that the Fathers of the Deserts of Egypt conducted themselves?* — What then would Bernard say today of so many religious house (I except those in which the Rule is observed to the letter, and we rejoice in the Lord that they are many) in which *the gold is become dim, the finest colour is changed and the stones of the sanctuary are scattered*[326] — those which Pope Clement VII so sadly despaired of reforming, as is reported by Prosper Fagnanus. Saint Augustine was right when he said he had seen no men better than those who advance in a monasteries and none worse than those who fail to do so: like the fig-trees of Jeremias, of which the good are very good and the bad are very bad. And of the true religious may rightly be said what Jerome said of Origen: "When he did well, better than any, when he did ill, worse than any."[327] — To him applies in all its force the philosophers' maxim: *Corruptio optimi pessima,*[328] or the everyday proverb that the finest wine makes the roughest vinegar.

You have heard, Reader, that there are very few elect. Here now the root of this truth. The reason why so many are lost eternally is that they

---

[325] *On Providence*, Book III.

[326] Lamentations IV, 1.

[327] "*Ubi bene, nemo melius; ubi male, nemo pejus.*"

[328] The corruption of the best is the worst.

convince themselves that there is a third way that the Gospel does not teach. The testimony of Truth Himself is that there is one broad way that leads to perdition and one narrow way that leads to life, and yet we seek a middle path: we do not consent to lead a life of enormous crimes but neither are we ready to embark on the narrow paths of holiness, so instead we enter on a path that is neither too broad nor too narrow. But surely it is just as perilous to imagine a third way as to suppose a third possible destination when for adults in the long run only two exist For it is written in Matthew XXV that the others shall go into eternal punishment but the just into eternal life. And this third track dreamed up by the lukewarm is the same we are warned of in Proverbs XIV: *There is a way that seemeth right to a man, but the ends thereof lead to death.*

They who embark on this third way are in so much the greater danger as they believe themselves to be in less, for they think themselves safe as they are not enslaved to the more atrocious sins. In point of fact it is quite rare for a man to be utterly abandoned in conscience, for, as Augustine says: *Just as there are few whose piety is really great, so too there are few whose godlessness is extreme.*[329]

But they are utterly, wretchedly mistaken. For whoever does not enter by the narrow way is marching in the broad way. Anyone who thinks otherwise is deceiving himself and is so much the more incurable as he is unconscious of his real state, for while he presumes that he is of the number of the elect he is in reality included among the vast number of the reprobate. Do not take my word for it; listen to the Fathers and learn from them wherein lies the narrow way: *The narrow way is the law of God*, says Augustine,[330] *which confines our passions.* And Ambrose[331] says: *There are two ways, the one of the just and the other of sinners; the one of equity and the other of iniquity; the way of the just is narrower and that of the unjust is broader; in the former is fasting and in the latter feasting; in the former joyful intemperance, in the latter perseverance of tears.* And Gregory the Great[332] says: *Does not the narrowness of this way consist in living in this world while a stranger to its concupiscences?* Whosoever journeys by this way will be numbered among the little flock of the elect. For as Saint Paulinus so admirably

---

[329] Sermon 30, *de Verbo Domini.*

[330] Commentary on Psalm I.

[331] *Ibid.*

[332] *Morals*, lib. 27, cap. 22.

puts it,[333] in commenting on the text *How broad is the way that leadeth to destruction*: "All that we do and all that we say is either of the broad or of the narrow way. If with the few we have found a certain narrow and finely traced path, we are journeying towards life, but if we are travellers on the way of the many, according to Our Lord's declaration, we are on our way to death. If we trample all our passions underfoot and seek only to be rich in virtues, we are advancing in the narrow way, for such is the conduct of the few and it is exceedingly rare and hard to find suitable fellow-travellers in this path."

This is why the holy Council of Trent so wisely warns that no one should allow himself any confidence of absolute certitude, though all of us should nourish the firmest *hope* in the divine assistance, for God, if we do not desert His grace, having begun a good work in us, will also bring it to completion it, operating both the will and the accomplishment.

Hence we live under this uncertainty, between hope and fear, and we work out our salvation with fear and trembling, in labours and watchings and almsgiving, in prayer, sacrifice, fasting, chastity, knowing that we are born again not yet to glory but to the *hope* of glory, especially as our struggle is against a threefold enemy before which human weakness very often succumbs; the fight is a daily one but victory is rare and can be sought only from God and hoped for from Him alone, for little or great it cannot be achieved without Him without whom nothing at all can be done.

This being so, who shall give a shower of tears to our eyes to bewail the state of Christians today reduced as it were to nothing at all? For this earth of ours, enriched by the counsels and examples of Christ and bedewed with His Blood, yet brings forth thorns and brambles in place of the proper harvest! Who would not tremble to hear this constant doctrine of the fewness of the elect? But the worst of all woes is hanging over him who experiences the effects of reprobation and suffers not. *Whosoever is such*, to borrow the worlds of Saint Gregory,[334] *is greatly to be sorrowed at because he has no sorrow.* And since, Reader, my sighs and groans interrupt me and prevent me from bewailing both your sins and mine together, I will here end my sermon.[335]

---

[333] Epistle 50.

[334] Homily 34, *On the Gospel.*

[335] *Theologia Mentis et Cordis*, lib. II, dis. VI, cap. II, spec. III; Cologne, 1687, vol. I, pp. 137-139.

In this text Contenson both proves the fewness of the saved and strives to deliver Religious from pharisaical presumption.

24. NICOLAS TURLOT[336] (C. 1590-1651)

This French counter-reformation theologian solidly teaches and proves that the majority of Catholic adults are damned. Against the objection of those who think that more are saved he states his judgement in the following terms:

> On the other hand both reason and authority solidly based on the Scriptures and the Holy Fathers appear to support the view that more Catholic adults are damned than are saved.
>
> The reason for this is that by far the greater number of Christians lives in the state of mortal sin, and according to Saint Augustine's principle, as a man has lived so does he die, so that it is rare for one who has lived a bad life to die well, and vice versa.[337]

In the same place Turlot extensively proves from the Scriptures and the Fathers the claim here made.

25. MATTHIAS FABER S.J. (1586-1653)

Throughout his first sermon for the nineteenth Sunday after Pentecost he shows that many are called but few are chosen. Having cited various authorities he continues:

> From them it is clear that the majority, even of Christians, live in the state of mortal sin. According to Saint Augustine's rule, he who lives well dies well and he who lives badly generally dies badly.

His sermon concludes as follows:

> This being so, listeners, who would not be afraid for himself? After all, if only a few thousand were to be damned out of the whole world, or just one person from our city, ought not everyone to fear? When the disciples heard the words "One of you is about to betray me,"[338] all of

---

[336] Also known as Turlotius.
[337] *Le Vrai Trésor de la Doctrine Chrétienne*, partie I, chap. 13, leçon 5.
[338] Matthew XXVI, 21.

them "were very much troubled, and began every one to say: Is it I, Lord?" So when we are told that not one out of twelve but *far more* are to be damned, who would not be yet more afraid? So let everyone examine himself to see in which direction he is headed; does he live with the few or rather with the many?[339]

26. JEAN-BAPTISTE SAINT-JURE S.J. (1588-1657)

As the number of those who give themselves up to their passions and their disorderly appetites and who transgress the commandments of God is beyond all comparison greater than the number of Christians who follow the guidance of reason and obey the laws of their Creator; as all, in the words of Jeremias (VI, 13), "from the least of them even to the greatest, all are given to covetousness: and from the prophet even to the priest, all are guilty of deceit," it is not surprising that the number of the damned is *incomparably* greater than that of the saved.[340]

If you ask me how it is possible for God, who loves men so greatly, who so yearns to save them all, who suffered so much for their salvation, to accept that *almost all* should be damned, I will answer that His love for them and His desire for their salvation is even greater than we may say or think...

Since the number of the reprobate is so great and that of the elect is so low, since so many are damned and so few are saved, which of us ought not to fear to be numbered among this prodigious multitude?[341]

27. HENRI ENGELGRAVE S.J. (1610-1670)

This pious and learned man, as he is called by de Backer, in his famous work entitled *Lux Evangelica*, under *Emblem 47*, says:

Many are called but few are chosen. (Matthew XXII) "Out of many perhaps there will be only one! — Few, by the fruit of good works, are predestined to eternal life.[342]

---

[339] *Opus Concionum Tripartitum, pars æstiva*, p. 904 of the 1650 edition.

[340] *De la Connoissance et de l'amour du fils de Dieu Nostre Seigneur Jésus-Christ*, livre III, chap. XXIII, § 2, vol. III, p. 139 of the 1847 Lyon edition.

[341] *Ibid.*, pp. 138 and 140. See the entire passage reproduced below at the end of Chapter VIII.

And in another publication:

> Out of millions, the sun of justice snatches away but very few, just as out of thousands sown scarcely does a single melon ripen. Now I invite you to consider, by a loftier flight of imagination, the entire world. Have not the immense kingdoms of Japan, Malacca and China been buried for six thousand years or more in the darkness of idolatry? You see too that Asia, Africa and America are a cesspit of paganism, heresy and every sort of wickedness. And of those who dwell, as Christians, in this small part of the world called Europe, is it not astonishing that so very few are to be counted among the elect? Terrifying indeed, yet most true, is the prophecy of the golden Orator [sc. Chrysostom] that even of orthodox believers scarcely one in a hundred is saved.

Then come two paragraphs, of which the first evaluates the fewness of the saved in comparison with infidels, heretics, etc. and the second concludes that among the faithful, i.e. Catholics, many more are damned than are saved.[343]

28. PHILIP OF THE BLESSED TRINITY O.C.D. (1603-1671)

Fr. Philip was superior-general of the Order of Discalced Carmelites and his life was as full of labour as of piety and reputation for holiness; he published several immortal works, according to Gonet, in which learning contends with piety.[344]

To the question "Whether the number of the predestined is greater than of the reprobate," he replies:

> *Conclusion.* I answer that with reference to the whole of mankind, the number of the reprobate is much greater than that of the predestined.
>
> If, however, we speak only of Christians, it remains more probable that the number of the reprobate is greater than the number of the predestined.[345]

---

[342] Cologne, 1655, p. 750.

[343] Antwerp, 1657, p. 276.

[344] Hürter, *Nomenclator Litterarius*, vol. II, p. 34.

[345] *Cursus theologicus juxta partes summæ D. Thom.*, Lyon, 1564, vol. I, p. 309.

29. GIOVANNI CARDINAL BONA (1609-1674)

A man who was outstanding not only for dignity but also for learning and holiness of living.[346]

In his celebrated work entitled *Principia et Documenta Vitæ Christianæ*,[347] he sets out the teaching of the Fathers on salvation with brevity, accuracy and force. Would that the Progressives, for the sake of their own eternal salvation and of others, would deign to study it!

The relevant chapter is entitled: *Many are called, few chosen*. Its eminently holy author opens as follows:

> There is no more powerful incentive to correct sinful behaviour and bring our life into conformity with the Gospel than the terrifying and awe-inspiring pronouncement, *Many are called but few are chosen*, at least if we penetrate its inner meaning.
>
> No man knows whether he is "called" in the sense in which it is written that "*whom he predestined, them he also called. And whom he called, them he also justified. And whom he justified, them he also glorified.*"[348] "*A man knoweth not whether he be worthy of love or hatred, but all things are kept uncertain for the time to come.*"[349]
>
> No one knows whether he is called in such a way that he will persevere to the end in his calling....
>
> Amid such doubt of salvation, therefore, and such uncertainty of perseverance, every Christian ought to be continually horror-struck, striving with fear and trembling to make certain his calling, so that by a life of faith working through love he may show by good works that he belongs to that small and most blessed number whom God in His mercy had chosen *before the foundation of the world*.[350]
>
> The number of the elect is small, and much less than the number of the reprobate, *even speaking only of those who hold the orthodox faith*, to the exclusion of children who die before the use of reason: this is shown by the

---

[346] Renaudot, *Liturgiarum orientalium collectio*, Præfatio.

[347] I.e. *Principles and Examples of the Christian Life.*

[348] Romans VIII, 30, 31.

[349] Ecclesiastes IX, 1.

[350] I Peter I, 20.

infallible testimony of the Scriptures and by many signs and reasons as well as by experience.

This is why Christ admonished His Disciples that it is very laborious and of the greatest difficulty to enter the path of salvation, to which access is gained only by the narrow gate. *Enter*, he says, *by the narrow gate...* Then, as though struck with astonishment, he adds: *How narrow is the gate*, etc.

Then the pious cardinal goes on to interpret the most celebrated passages of both Old and New Testaments.

Concerning the prefigurements found in the history of the Jews, he concludes: "These things befell them in figure, to show how small is the number of the elect in comparison with that of the reprobate."

And on the subject of the lesson of daily experience, he differs widely, and for good reason, from Suárez:

The same conclusion can be reached from the fewness of those who quit this life truly contrite. For although many appear to men to die well, yet when sorrow for sins arises from the fear of death, it is very difficult for it to attain true repentance.

For how can a sinner begin a good life when he has reached its end?

How shall he detest his sins above all things, and abominate the very delights that he has spent the whole course of his life intensely loving?

How shall he sincerely embrace that penance which he has always held in horror?

How shall he make an efficacious resolution to give up, if his life is spared, all that inveterate habit has made him accustomed to?

How shall the mind, amid the torments of illness and death, contemplate supernatural things, remote from the senses, which it has never seriously reflected on when its powers were undiminished?

How shall he overcome by contrary acts the habits of a lifetime while he is suffering so greatly and afflicted both by his bodily condition and by inner temptations?

Experience teaches us that hardly anyone is found who, when the danger passes, remains firm in his resolution. All relapse into their old habits and promptly forget the decisions that the fear of death, the exhortations of friends or worldly wisdom had convinced them to make; especially as, even on their deathbeds, there are very few who wholly give up the hope of living longer — a trick by which the demon lures many to perdition.

Add to all this the lethargy of the soul, fearing to leave the body, and the feebleness of all the faculties which scarcely allow a man to be in command of himself so that the words of those who surround him, suggesting acts of the virtues, strike him as no more than empty sounds devoid of meaning.

Granted it is permissible to *hope* for the salvation of those who have given signs of repentance at the close of life, but such signs give *no security* as is shown by the clear example of King Antiochus in II Machabees IX.

For when death was close he humbled himself beneath the hand of God, praying and promising that he would compensate the Jews for the losses he had inflicted on them, pledging to adorn the temple and to allow out of his revenues the charges pertaining to the sacrifices, to abjure paganism and become a Jew, indeed to travel throughout the whole world preaching the power of God.

Who would ask for greater and surer marks of repentance from a sinner?

Yet he did not merit pardon, as the Scripture says: "Then this wicked man prayed to the Lord, of whom he was not like to obtain mercy," — because his repentance, arising from the fear of death, was not sincere.

Then the most pious Cardinal concludes with these salutary words of warning which all of us ought to reflect on and put into practice:

Who would not take fear at the thought of these things?

Who would dare, amid so many difficulties and dangers, to promise himself sure salvation?

Who will not shudder at the thought that he knows not whether he is worthy of love or of hatred?

Therefore, because *the elect are few* **and perchance many fewer than we think**, we should withdraw from the multitude and live with the few that are holy, elect and innocent, so that each of us may at the end of his life with a clear conscience say to our all-just divine Judge: Render me the reward Thou hast promised, for I have done what Thou hast commanded.[351]

---

[351] Bona, *op. cit.*

30. THE VAN WALENBURCH BROTHERS
(ADRIAN 1609-1669 AND PETER 1610-1675)

Both were suffragan bishops, outstanding not only for their noble birth and honourable life but also for their theological learning. On the subject of justification, the general vocation to grace and the efficacious vocation to glory, they adduce the well-known text of Matthew XXII, 14, and observe:

> The words of the Apostle in Romans VIII, 28 are undoubtedly true: *We know that to them that love God, all things work together unto good, to such as, according to his purpose, are called to be saints.* From this it is clear that the Apostle is not referring to vocation in general, as in the text of Matthew XXII, 14: *Many are called but few are chosen*; he is speaking of vocation *according to purpose.*[352]

31. FR. FRANCISCUS BONÆ SPEI O.C.D.[353] (1617-1677)

He was long a lecturer in philosophy and theology at Louvain. In a work entitled *Commentarii tres in Universam Theologiam Scholasticam,*[354] he writes: "That the number of the reprobate is greater than the number of the predestined follows from the Gospel — Matthew VII: *Enter by the narrow gate,* and XX: *For many are called but few are chosen.*[355]

32.— BISHOP GUILLAUME HERINCKX[356]
O.F.M. REC. (1621-1678)

In absolute terms the number of the elect is great..., but in comparison with the number of the reprobate it is inconsiderable.... This is why the

---

[352] *Tractatus Speculativus de Controversiis fidei*, vol. II, tr. VII, *de Justificatione*, c. 90, pp. 525 and 535.

[353] Also known as François Crespin or Francis of Good Hope.

[354] I.e. *Three Commentaries on the Whole of Scholastic Theology.*

[355] *Commentarii tres in Universam Theologiam Scolasticam*, vol. I, disp. 18, dub. 2, p. 183, n. 23.

[356] Also known as Willem or Gulielmus Herinckx. — Translator.

election of those who are to be saved is compared to the casting of lots, since, as when lots are cast, the lot falls seldom and on few.

Indeed whether we heed the Scriptures as expounded by the Fathers or the great corruption of the behaviour of Christians or Catholics, it is all too likely that even of these the number of the elect is less.[357]

33. JEAN-BAPTISTE GONET O.P. (1616-1681)

It is a *certain and universally recognized fact* that, if we speak of all mankind together, the number of the reprobate is much greater than that of the predestined. For Christians are few in comparison with infidels and even among Christians many are heretics or schismatics.

He then quotes the well-known text from the fourth book of Esdras, before adding the following arguments:

Reason supports the same conclusion:

1. the predestinate are the friends of God and predestination is a special and unique friendship with God, but one of the conditions of friendship is that it should be among few, as is taught by Aristotle and Saint Thomas. Therefore the predestinate are few in comparison with the reprobate.

2. The predestinate are like Kings and Princes while the reprobate are as it were their servants and slaves. But every king has *many* servants and there are always *more* slaves and servants than princes and lords. Therefore there are more reprobate than elect.

3. Whatever is precious tends to be rare, not commonplace, as is shown by the example of precious stones. But Holy Scripture compares the predestinate to precious stones and the reprobate to dung and clay. Therefore the predestinate are few in comparison with the reprobate.[358]

This once established there remains the difficulty and debate among theologians as to whether, of those Christians who are truly such and live and die in the faith of Christ and in obedience to the Holy Roman Church, more are predestined than reprobate.

---

[357] *Summa Theologiæ Scolasticæ et Moralis* — disp. VIII; Antwerp, 1680, vol. I, p. 154.

[358] *Clypeus theologiæ thomisticæ contra novos ejus impugnatores*, tr. V, disp. IV. digress. 2; ed. Vivès, vol. II, p. 362.

An affirmative answer is given by Silvester, Suárez, Granada and Ruis, who think that the majority of Catholics are saved, and among them Ruis pays the devout sex the compliment of asserting that more women are predestined than men.

But the negative opinion is *more common* among theologians, as Suárez admits, and is taught by Cajetan (on Matthew XXV), Vasquez and Molina on Saint Thomas, *Summa Theologiæ*, I, *q. cit.*, a. 7, Alvarez, *de Auxiliis*, disp. 43, Philippus a S. Trinitate[359] in S. Th., *l.c.*, disp. 17, dub. 4 as well as by scriptural interpreters including Nicholas of Lyra, Maldonatus, Cornelius à Lapide, Carthusianus[360] and others.

I will now briefly show that the opinion holding that many more of the faithful are reprobate than elect agrees better with Scripture, the Holy Fathers and ecclesiastical history.

Then he expounds in the usual way the classic texts *Many are called but few are chosen*, and *Lord, are there many who are saved?*, as well as *Strive to enter*, etc. — an interpretation he confirms by quoting the Fathers, before adding:

Moreover in Isaias XVII and XXIV the number of the elect is compared to the very few ears left in the filed by the reapers and to the very rare bunches of olives that remain, when the olives have been shaken out, in the topmost branches, or to the handful of grapes that hang on the vine after the grape-harvest.

This can be confirmed from the epistle to the Colossians I, 12, where the Apostle says of the elect: *who hath made us worthy to be partakers of the lot* [Latin: *sors*] *of the saints*, and from Ephesians I, 11: *In whom we also are called by lot...*

In these passages the use of the word "lot" [Latin: *sors*] of the vocation of the saints indicates their fewness. For just as when a lot is cast, some thousands of men are eligible but only very few are in fact selected, so among the many thousands of men the lot of predestination falls only to very few.

---

[359] Also known as Fr. Philip of the Holy Trinity O.C.D. (1603-71). — Translator.
[360] Also known as Denis the Carthusian (1402-71). — Translator.

34. JOANNES BOSCO[361] (1613-1684)

This Scotist belonged to the Order of Friars Minor and was long *Lector Jubilatus*[362] of sacred theology in the University of Louvain. Hürter[363] calls him a most profound theologian. He was often consulted in matters of the greatest difficulty. In his *Theologia Spirituali, Scholastica et Morali*[364] he holds the common teaching of the Fathers on this subject quite as openly as the Thomists.

Conclusion: Written in the book of life are 1. the greater part of the Angels, 2. the lesser part of mankind, 3. the greater part of the faithful, but not of adults.

A minority of men are saved even though all are ordained to salvation and have sufficient help.

The discrepancy between men and Angels is due to the fact that the latter did not encounter so many and such great obstacles in the wayfaring state as men do.

And the greatest of these obstacles is the rebellion of the sensitive appetite, a difficulty which evidently does not apply to the Angels.

And so the second part of our conclusion [i.e. that only a minority of men are saved] does not conflict with the first part [viz. that the majority of the Angels were saved] as the first part does not imply the contrary of the second.

The second part is favoured by Holy Scripture: *Enter by the narrow gate,*[365] and *Many are called but few are chosen.*[366]

Hence the part of our conclusion which states that only a minority of men are found in the book of life is *de fide*. And Smising adds that it is confirmed by experience.

If the question is restricted to adult believers it is quite credible that there are more reprobate than predestined. And the way of life of the

---

[361] Not to be confused with Saint John Bosco (1815-88). — Translator.

[362] The highest professorial degree conferred among the Franciscans. — Translator.

[363] *Nomenclator Litterarius,* vol. II, p. 538,

[364] I.e. *Spiritual, Scholastic and Moral Theology.*

[365] Matthew VII, 13.

[366] Matthew XX, 16.

bulk of the faithful lends weight to this, as well as Matthew VII, 14: *Narrow is the way that leadeth to life and few there are that find it.*[367]

35. GERVASIUS BRISACENSIS[368] O.F.M. CAP. (1648-1717)

1. Speaking of all men, both the faithful and the infidels, it is certain that there are more reprobate than elect. This is expressly declared in Holy Scripture.

2. The only difficulty concerns Catholics, concerning whom there are two opinions. The first of these is that more of them are chosen.... In favour of which it is argued that a great many infants die after Baptism but before attaining the use of reason. If I am asked my own view I reply that in view of the goodness of God I find the former opinion preferable. Or rather, I find the whole subject quite uncertain.

But do thou, who by the mercy and grace of God art counted among the little flock, beware lest his grace be void in thee[369] and lest another receive thy bishopric.[370] Strive by good works to make sure your calling.[371] For whatever our speculations as to gratuitous election may be, it is certain by faith that the reward of eternal life is granted only to those who do good.[372]

36. THE SALMANTICENSES[373]
(FL. XVIITH CENTURY)

It may be enquired whether the number of the reprobate is greater than the number of the elect, and secondly whether *of the faithful* the majority are of the elect or of the reprobate.

---

[367] *Op. cit.*, vol. I, *De Providentia divina*, disp. III, sect. 3, conc. 8, p. 115.

[368] Also known as Gervasius of Breisach.

[369] Cf. I Corinthians XV, 10.

[370] Cf. Acts of the Apostles I, 20.

[371] Cf. II Peter I, 10.

[372] *Cursus Theologicus*, tr. 3, d. 3, n. 154-9; Cologne edition, 1716, vol. I, p. 266 *et seq.*

[373] This is the name used for the discalced Carmelites of Salamanca, Spain, as authors of their collectively-written works of theology and philosophy. — Translator.

To the first question it is *certain* that the number *is* greater from Matthew XX and VII and from Isaias XXIV in which the elect in comparison with the great number of the reprobate are likened to a few olives or to the bunches that remain after the grape harvest.

Concerning the second question, however, since it cannot be settled by certain reason or authority, Saint Thomas says that the matter is known to God alone so we will not make it the subject of a specific enquiry.[374]

37. FRANCESCO LORENZO CARDINAL BRANCATI DI LAURIA (1612-1693)

In the person of Cardinal Brancati we have a consultor of the Holy Office and of the Sacred Congregation of Rites and an Examiner of Bishops, held in the highest esteem both for his eminent virtue and his profound learning by Popes Alexander VII, Clement IX, Clement X and Innocent XI. In Chapter XIX of his study *On Predestination* he devotes a section to the subject of *Whether the number of the predestined is greater than the number of the reprobate*. He answers the question as follows:

Note that this enquiry may take three forms: 1. in the context of both the faithful and the infidels, 2. among the faithful only, and 3. between men and angels, in comparison with the infidels alone or with infidels and the demons.

I answer:

1. If we make the comparison only among the faithful or Christians, *the predestinate are fewer than the reprobate*. This is proved from the crystal-clear testimony of Christ in Matthew XXII, 16 and XX, 14: *Many are called*, etc. Nicholas of Lyra says that in its moral sense this parable means that from the beginning of the world men were called to faith: Adam, his sons, etc. Then at the time of Henoch etc., then Noah and his sons etc., and so on until Abraham and the others under the law of Moses, then finally all Christians under the law of Christ, and of all of these taken together, under which ever law they were called into the vineyard

---

[374] *Cursus Theologicus, De Prædestinatione*, disp. X, dub. II, ann. circa art. VII.

of the Lord, i.e. the Church or assembly of the faithful, the elect are few. Would it were not so! ...

In the second passage of Matthew ("Many are called..."), the Interlinear Gloss says "to the kingdom" and Nicholas of Lyra observes: "Many are called to the Catholic faith, but few are elected to glory, for they are few, comparatively speaking, with regard to those who are called to faith.

2. In the context of *the whole of mankind* the number of the reprobate is held to be greater than of the predestinate.

A. This is proved from several passages of Saint Augustine:

(i) In his letter 157 (alternatively numbered 190) to Optatus he writes, "The reason why, in creating, He willed so many to be born who He foreknew would not belong to His grace, was so that they would be incomparably more numerous than those whom He deigned to predestine to the glory of His kingdom as sons of the promise; so that the multitude of those rejected would show forth the utter irrelevance before divine Justice of the number of those justly damned."[375]

(ii) And in Book XXI, Chapter XII, of the *City of God*, he writes: "The closer man's companionship with God, the greater his wickedness in departing from Him, so that by destroying this good in himself he becomes worthy of eternal evil. This is why the whole mass of the human race was condemned: since the one who initially committed this sin was punished together with the whole progeny that was destined to take root from him in order that no one might be delivered from this punishment due in justice save by mercy and unmerited grace, and that the human race should be so divided that some might show forth the worth of merciful grace and the rest of just retribution. Neither justice nor mercy was to be manifested in all, for if all remained in the punishment of just damnation, the merciful grace of redemption would appear in none, while if all were transferred from darkness into light, none would bear witness to the severity of retribution. And that *there are many more under retribution than not* is to show what was due to all."[376]

B. It can be proved by historical fact.

Here is a synopsis of the learned Cardinal's explanation:

---

[375] *Pat. Lat.*, vol. XXXIII, col. 860, n.12.

[376] *Ibid.*, vol. XLI, col. 727. Cf. *Brev. Rom.*, Dom. Sept., second nocturn.

Before the Flood, there were few just God says that the whole human race misbehaves. Noah is said to have found grace before God. At the time of the Flood there were few saved.

After the Flood, we do not read of many just until the confusion of tongues, after which idolatry become widespread and generalized.

The author then concludes:

To return to the subject under discussion, it is clearly inferred that before the coming of Christ there were very few faithful and it is unlikely that countless, *indeed almost all*, of them were not reprobate, so in the context of all the nations the effect implies that *the predestinate were very few in number*.

And from the coming of Christ to our own times everyone knows the number and kind of nations that have been and now are faithful and among the faithful how many are wicked.

It must therefore be said that the reprobate are incomparably more numerous than the predestinate.

38. FR. PAOLO SEGNERI S.J. (1624-1694)

What the holy Doctors teach us with one accord must be accepted as the truth; but these holy Doctors are in agreement in holding that more Christians lose Paradise than gain it.[377]

39. LOUIS THOMASSIN (1619-1695)

Another reason why few are elect, few are predestined to be extracted from that mass of damnation unto glory, is so that realising that nothing in their destiny gave them a better right than those who are rejected, they are so much the more grateful to divine mercy and inclined to humility.[378]

---

[377] *Il Cristiano Istruito*, parte I, ragionamento 5, n. 3; Milan, 1854, vol. III, p. 51. See below, Chapter VI.

[378] *Theologiæ Dogmaticæ Compendium*, ed. Vivès, vol. II, p. 145.

40. THOMAS MUNIESSA S.J. (1627-1696)

Muniessa is called "a famous theologian" by Hürter[379]. He was chief professor of theology in the College of Barcelona, Rector of the College, Provincial of Aragon, Qualifier of the Holy Spanish Inquisition and synodal examiner for the dioceses of Barcelona and Saragossa, etc. The following extracts are taken from his rare and valuable work entitled *Disputationes scholasticæ de Providentia Dei.*[380]

Hilary wrote to Augustine about the inhabitants of Marseilles: "Likewise they do not accept that there should be a definite number of those that are chosen and to be accepted." Against them and any others of the same view we must hold it for certain that the number of the predestined and of the reprobate is certain to God, although to us it is uncertain and unknown and only knowable by divine revelation. This once granted, the theologians enquire whether the number of the predestinate is greater than that of the reprobate or the contrary. But here too we have nothing certain and can only speak subject to certain distinctions.

It seems that:

1. Taking *all men and angels* together, the number of the predestinate is greater.

2. Taking *all men together*, the number of the reprobate is greater. For it is certain that the number of unbelieving and barbarous nations on earth has almost always been much greater than of the faithful; so that in comparison we may indeed call the latter a *little flock*. This should be understood of those damned to *the pain of loss*, but not necessarily of those condemned to *the pain of loss and of sense*, on account of the huge multitude of the children in so many provinces of infidels who die with original sin alone and are condemned only to the pain of loss.

3. In the context of *all the faithful, including adults and children*, the number of the predestinate is greater. This is because among the faithful (and likewise even among heretics and schismatics having valid Baptism) there are almost as many baptized children who die, all of whom are saved, as adults, many of whom are certainly saved too, as Montoya's scholarly study of parochial registers (see below) has established....

[379] *Nomenclator Litterarius*, vol. II, p. 348.

[380] *De Reprobatione*, disp. XVI, sect. 4, p. 296.

4. With regard to the adult faithful, whether the number of the predestinate or of the reprobate is greater :

A. The pious view in favour of a majority of predestinate is followed by Suárez, lib. 6, cap. 3; Granadus,[381] tract. 12, disp. 3, cap. 5; Pallavicini, I, 2. disp. 2, q. 3.

B. But on the other hand in favour of a greater number of reprobate we find the common opinion of the Doctors, both scholastic and expositive, very strongly supported by Holy Scripture and the Holy Fathers and by weighty arguments furnished in abundance by the very learned Montoya in his *Disputatio 54* in which the fullest and most accurate information can be found on the subject for the use of both theology students and popular preachers. Hence I do not dare pronounce an opinion.

Note that Muniessa recognizes the opinion defended in these pages as *commonly held by the theologians*.

41. VENERABLE HENRI-MARIE BOUDON (1624-1702)

Here are the blunt words of the devout archdeacon of Évreux and Doctor of Sacred Theology :

It is not only the Fathers of the Church, nor only the prophets and the greatest saints who have taught us that there are few people who are saved; it is a God who has come from the other world, who knows all things and from whom nothing can be hidden who has revealed it to us....

No further doubt is possible. *It is an infallible matter and of the utmost certainty* that there are few who are saved. Everyone must agree with this and yet there are few who are thoroughly convinced of it!...

Although we ought to be persuaded beyond possible doubt — unless we mean to give the lie to God — that there will be but few who are saved, we live as though we had no grounds for fear and as though heaven had been guaranteed to us....

What a great and infinitely astonishing truth it is, but its certainty is infallible : there are few who are chosen. This truth inspired the greatest terror in the hearts of great saints and of saints who had never lost their baptismal innocence, in those who had always lived innocently, always

---

[381] I.e. Diego Granado S.J. (1571-1632).

in penance. What then must be the state of sinners, who spend their lives in the pleasures of the senses?[382]

42. LOUIS BOURDALOUE S.J. (1632-1704)

In Chapter I Bourdaloue was quoted saying explicitly: *It is well-established that the number of the elect will be smaller and that there will be incomparably more reprobate.* Let us now quote another passage from the "King of Preachers and Preacher of Kings":

Ah! What is more striking in the Gospel than the small number of the elect? What is there that the Saviour of the world has declared more authentically, has in his divine instructions repeated oftener, has given us to understand more clearly and more formally?[383]

43. THE JESUIT FATHERS OF WÜRTZBURG[384]

That the number of the elect...in comparison with the reprobate will be small is quite explicitly taught by Christ, agreed by the Fathers and confirmed by reason if we subdivide history into its different parts, for *before* Christ's birth almost the whole world was infidel, and *after* His birth the greater part of the world continues to wallow in unbelief: and among Christians there are many who are *heretics* or *schismatics* and among the faithful many who are depraved. Yet there are some who think that the majority of Christians are saved if those who die in childhood are counted as well as adults, but not even this much is at all sure.[385]

---

[382] *Dieu inconnu*, chap. V, Avignon, 1834, p. 113.

[383] *Pensées sur le salut*; "Petit nombre des élus"; Migne, *Orat. Sacr.*, vol. XVI, col. 617.

[384] Also known as the *Wirceburgenses*.

[385] *De Deo uno*, n. 224; Paris, 1853, vol. II, p. 323.

44. BOSSUET (1627-1704)

Fr. Hürter justly counts this sacred orator among the greatest theologians; the French take the greatest pride in him who, for his sublime genius, they call the "Eagle of Meaux".[386] Bossuet writes:

> The little flock is everywhere, and everywhere it is a part of the great Church.
>
> As the elect, *who are few*, are among the called, who are many, the strait way of the commandments and rigid virtue is also everywhere to be found; and although little frequented by the malice of men, it remains visible before them throughout the world. The small number of those who go in, although great in itself and small only in comparison with those who perish, heed the same Gospel by which they were called.[387]

And in his *Meditations on the Gospel* he eloquently sets forth his meaning:

> There are many called and few chosen. Jesus Christ has often warned us of it.
>
> This is true first of the Jews...
>
> But the Saviour does not speak only of the Jews in the part of the parable we are reading, for it is after representing to us the call of the Gentiles in the person of these blind and lame who are invited to the banquet that he says, in conclusion, that there are many called and few chosen. Let us strive therefore to enter by the narrow gate that leads to life, for the way that leads to death is very broad and many there are who go in thereat. How few there are, Our Saviour continues, who go in by the narrow way!
>
> So there are many called and few elect. But the condition of those who are called and fail to persevere in their calling is more terrible than the others, for they are the servants who knew the will of their lord but did it not and who will be more severely punished.[388] Tyre and Sidon[389] and the Ninivites[390] will rise up against them and the judgement of these ungrateful cities will be light in comparison with that which awaits Chris-

---

[386] *Nomenclator Litterarius*, vol. II, n° 381.

[387] *Seconde instruction pastorale sur les promesses de l'Église.*

[388] Cf. Luke XII, 47.

[389] Cf. Matthew XI, 21.

[390] Cf. Luke XI, 32.

tians who are unfaithful to the grace they have received. O Jesus, O Jesus, save me from the iniquity of a perverse people; save me for iniquity is multiplied[391] among the children of men and no saint[392] is seen. All is full of these who are called but will not even think of their calling *or remember that they are Christians.*

Let us not live like the majority. Let us not say: such and such people act thus and are suffered to do so; and let us not excuse ourselves be appealing to the multitude, for the multitude is itself inexcusable. If God had been susceptible to mere number He would not have consumed with fire these abominable cities nor drowned the entire world in the Flood.

Neither let us invoke custom, for Christ has said: "I am the truth," and there is no prescription against God. Every one shall bear his own burden[393] and we shall not be judged by the others.

Let us rather enrol ourselves among the small number of the elect whom the world does not know but "whose names are written in the book of life," and to whom the Saviour said, "Fear not little flock" — small in number and in lustre, the offscouring of this world,[394] which is hidden with Jesus Christ, but which will one day appear with Him.

O small number, however few you may be and wherever you may be hidden in the world, I unite with you in spirit and I wish to live in your shadow.[395]

45. FR. FRANCIS VERSCHUREN S.T.D. (1660-1723)

This author will be cited at greater length because he has treated *ex professo* the subject herein discussed in his 378-page work entitled *Via arcta cœli asserta, ubi contra Doctorem Steyaert demonstratur, plures e fidelibus adultis damnandos, quam salvandos,*[396] which appeared in 1706.

The preface to this book states its subject matter as follows:

---

[391] Cf. Psalm CXVIII, 69.

[392] Cf. Psalm XI, 2.

[393] Cf. Galatians VI, 5.

[394] Cf. I Corinthians IV, 13.

[395] *Méditations sur l'Évangile*, Dernière semaine du Sauveur, 34th day; Paris, *Œuvres complètes*, vol. V, p. 524.

[396] Second edition, corrected and expanded, Liège, 1706.

The question is therefore whether more adult Catholics are to be saved than lost or, to the contrary, those to be saved are more than those that will be damned.

The former answer is defended by F. Steyaert together with some Progressives.[397] For he thinks that the way to Heaven, which eternal Truth Himself has said is narrow and strait and found by few is nevertheless trodden wherever we may look by Catholics provided only they live as most others are commonly accustomed to live. For he says in his thesis defended 16th July 1695 that the *narrow gate* spoken of in Matthew VII *is the gate of the Christian religion even as observed by the bulk of the faithful (and not restricted to any more specific rigours).*

Which shows that in Dr Steyaert's view the majority of the faithful considered at random are saved.

This is a mild opinion indeed and one that the mass of the faithful will inevitably embrace with open arms since nothing could be more agreeable to their hearing than to be told to be sure of their salvation if only they observe the rule of the Christian religion as it is practised by most of those they rub shoulders with in daily life, especially if in addition those who hold the contrary view are derided as eccentrics who add arbitrary unknown rigours to what Christian living means.

And I should be the first to subscribe to the same view if it were as true as it is agreeable, for what Catholic would not be delighted to learn that the generality of the faithful were to attain salvation?

But in point of fact I have no intention of seeking what is more desirable but what is more true.

The fact that this or that writer thinks that more will be saved is not going to make it happen. On the contrary by rashly declaring salvation for all and sundry he is liable to make many slothful and remiss in performing good works so that in fact *fewer* are saved. For if the faithful were once convinced that most of them by simply living like everyone else will easily be saved, surely there will not be many to work violence on the kingdom of heaven.[398] They will simply live as they observe most people live — a way of life which is far removed from heaven! They will think themselves good Christians though they have little or nothing

---

[397] The champions of this theory are deservedly called Progressives or Novelty-mongers [*neoterici*] ; indeed before the dawn of Protestantism their opinion was held by no one at all.

[398] Cf. Matthew XI, 12.

of the spirit of Christ, but this will not justify them. Terrible indeed is the statement of the Spirit of Truth: "There is a way that seemeth just to a man but the ends thereof lead to death."[399]

Hence I have undertaken in these pages to refute the opinion of Dr Steyaert because I have no doubt that it is false and highly pernicious.

Dr Verschuren then offers the following wise warning against imprudent use of the position he defends.

Furthermore I now beg Catholics to be cautious in presenting the opinion here defended and the arguments adduced in its favour to the faithful.

Let them take care not to declare that only a certain number of men in such and such a village or town will be saved.

Let them not declare that more men than woman are to be saved, or vice versa.

Let them not state without qualification that few mortals are to be saved, for the saved will be all but countless.

Such predictions are in most cases utterly rash, false and odious, lending themselves to mockery and idle chatter as well as sometimes driving some listeners into a sort of despair.

Nor do those who make such claims have any right to cloak themselves in the example of a few words of Saint John Chrysostom, for what could prudently be said by that incomparable prelate, in whom outstanding holiness rivalled with his eloquence, ought not to be imitated by priests of no special standing who have little or nothing in common with so great a man.

I readily admit that statements not only from this outstanding Confessor but also of other great men whom I shall be citing should be understood mildly, not always in a strictly literal sense, although I believe that when understood in a natural and tolerable way they invariably prove what I contend is proved. This is why I have not even considered it appropriate to mention the various revelations as to the fewness of the saved — not even that which Saint Nilus alleged had been received by Saint Simon the Stylite to the effect that of ten thousand scarcely one soul was led to heaven by the hands of the Angels, as is reported by Baronius under the year 976. Nor even that which revealed that on the

[399] Proverbs XIV, 13.

day of Saint Bernard's death, out of thirty thousand men who died only five were saved.

The same goes for the allegation reported in Platus's[400] *de Statu Religioso*, book I, chapter 5, to the effect that of sixty thousand only three had reached salvation. I do not believe such things.

But in any event a truth that is already certain on other grounds has no need to be bolstered by appeal to doubtful revelations. Indeed these feeble arguments tend to cast doubt on what is already as solidly established as could be.

For this reason I maintain that instructions on this subject should be so couched as to teach the faithful to work out their salvation in fear and trembling instead of following the crowd to do evil[401] so that they strive to learn from and imitate the best models available.

On the contrary, if the Christian orator should notice that his listeners are struck with excessive fear he must endeavour to raise them up to hope in the divine mercy, even by emphasizing the great number of those whom God has always and everywhere saved for Himself and will continue to do so. For this purpose it will be found very useful to admonish Catholics with the words of Saint Augustine's *de Dono Perseverantiæ*, chapter 22: "So you must hope to obtain perseverance in obedience from the Father of lights, from whom cometh every best gift and every perfect gift, and you must ask for it in daily prayers, and in so doing you must trust that you are not strangers to the predestination of the people, for it is God Himself that grants you to do so.[402]

These remarks are in such close agreement with the words and teaching of our holy father Saint Alphonsus that I am delighted to make them my own.

46. DIONYSIUS WERLENSIS,[403] O.F.M. CAP. (1640-1709)

Fr. Dionysius was a devout and deeply-read Capuchin, says Hürter,[404] and exceedingly zealous for peace and concord. In his

---

[400] I.e. Fr. Girolamo Piatti S.J. (1545-91).

[401] Cf. Exodus XXIII, 2: "Thou shalt not follow the multitude to do evil: neither shalt thou yield in judgment, to the opinion of the most part, to stray from the truth."

[402] Verschuren, *op. cit.*, pp. 5-16.

[403] Also known as Dionysius von Werl. — Translator.

Pseudo-pœnitens, sive doctrina Ecclesiæ catholicæ, solemniorumque Doctorum de vera pœnitentia,[405] he writes:

> Very many are damned for receiving the sacraments badly. That Doctor of the whole world to whom when he was once labouring in the dead of night the Apostle Paul appeared; dictating into his ear what to write — I refer to Saint John Chrysostom of course — writes as follows: "I speak not with rashness but as I believe and feel: I do not think that there are many among priests who are saved, but many more that perish."[406] And elsewhere[407] he speaks in general, saying: "How many, think you, are there in this city of ours [viz. Constantinople] who will be saved? Distressing though it is to say, I will say it nonetheless: Among so many thousands there are not a hundred who will be saved, indeed I doubt whether there will be so many."

> Hence the commoner opinion of the Doctors is that, not only of the whole human race but even of Catholic adults alone, more are damned than are saved.[408]

47. FRANCISCUS HENNO O.F.M. (1662-1714)

> In comparison with those who perish there are few who are saved. But are more saved than lost of the true faithful? ... The more common opinion and the one which better agrees with the Fathers is that more are damned.[409]

48. CANON NICOLAS PAUWELS (1655-1713)

Professor of theology at Louvain this highly practical author first states the common opinion: "In the light of such clear passages from

---

[404] *Nomenclator Litterarius*, vol. II, p. 669.

[405] I.e. *The pseudo-penitent, or the teaching of the Catholic Church and of her weightier doctors on true penance.*

[406] 3rd Homily on the Acts of the Apostles.

[407] 40th Homily to the people of Antioch.

[408] Liège, 1692, cap. IX, p. 374.

[409] *Theologia Dogmatica ac Scholastica*, tract. I, disp. IX, quæst. 7; Douai edition; 1713, p. 302.

Holy Scripture *it is not lawful to doubt that there are many more reprobate than elect.*"

Then he enquires "why God has willed to permit the number of the reprobate to be greater than of the elect."

A question to which he adds, "Why indeed does God allow the reprobate to exist or live at all?"

In response to which he offers four reasons taken from Saint Augustine:

> 1. So that God may make manifest his justice;
> 2. To show how little free will can achieve unaided by His most omnipotent grace;
> 3. So that the elect will recognize God's mercy towards them in snatching them out of the mass;
> 4. So that the elect may be exercised by the reprobate and thus make greater progress in good. As the Apostle says, *For there must be also heresies: that they also who are approved may be made manifest among you.*[410]

But the right reply is surely that given by the same Saint Augustine in his Book II *contra Julianum*: "Many there are who *want* to know God's reason why there are more who perish than are saved, but very few indeed, if any at all, who in fact *do* know it."[411]

For the same reason no attempt is made in the present work *On the Fewness of the Saved* to penetrate the inscrutable counsels of the Most High: it proves simply the *fact* of this fewness.

49. ANTONIUS GINTHER (1655-1725)

Here is the beginning of his consideration On the small number of the saved and the elect:

> I reflect each day anew, without ever reaching a conclusion, how it is that Christian man, created by God for this end — to serve, praise and reverence his Lord and God here below in the present life and finally to obtain eternal salvation — notwithstanding this lives in such forgetful-

---

[410] I Corinthians XI, 19.
[411] *Theologia practica, de Fide et Symbolo*, cap. XIV, n. 46; Antwerp, 1824, p. 440.

ness of eternal salvation and of his last end and indeed each day hastens with broad strides towards damnation!

O people without counsel, and without wisdom![412]

Do not your ears ring in your heads when you hear from the mouth of Truth itself the most true and irrefutable declaration: *Enter by the narrow gate...* (Matthew VII, 13)? When Saint Luke (XIII, 24) has: *Strive to enter by the narrow gate*, and the Greek for strive is ἀγωνίζεσθε, i.e. use your utmost endeavours to be able to enter into life by this strait and narrow gate? And yet, alas! how few are the mortals that find it? Why, I ask, if this is the voice of eternal Truth and Wisdom do we not seriously set to work to save our souls?

Instead of which we suffer the same fate as often befalls trees in spring-time, when they put forth all but countless flowers but with the passage of time, whether through frost, hail or gales, they lose their flowers and when autumn arrives have barely one or two ripe fruit to yield.

This is indeed an image of those who are to be saved, for all are called to salvation, but few are chosen, since *few cooperate until the end with their vocation and the sufficient grace of God.*[413]

50. PIERRE COLLET (1693–1770)

All sacred ministers should carefully weigh this author's state-ment: "To the question, 'Is the number of the predestinate greater than the number of the reprobate?' the answer is that it is not, but rather the contrary."

After adducing texts of Holy Scripture, he indicates various rea-sons of the which the last is as follows: "Countless of the faithful, and even — I say it weeping — of the ministers of the altar, deny their faith by the sinfulness of their lives."[414]

51. FR. ZACHARIE LASELVE (FL. 1696)

In the analysis given in his sermon on *The Fewness of the Saved*, Fr. Laselve, a Religious of the Province of the Blessed Sacrament and

---

[412] Deuteronomy XXXII, 28.

[413] *Currus Israel et Auriga ejus*, 4th ed., vol. I, p.121.

[414] *Tractatus de Deo*, Cf. VIII, art. 7; Paris, 1757, vol. I, p. 238.

Professor of Theology ,writes : "It is *de fide* that the number of the elect and of the saved is small as Christ said that few are chosen."

In the body of the sermon he continues :

This is stated quite clearly in Holy Writ, lucidly explained by the Holy Fathers, taught by the theologians and proclaimed by natural reason itself.

1. Taking all men together there are few that are saved.

Since *he that doth not believe is already judged*,[415] it is plainly certain that if we take all men together, the elect and the saved are few, indeed very few, in comparison with the reprobate and the damned.... This must be believed, yet there are very few who in fact believe it. For if we firmly believed that the elect are few in comparison with the reprobate, who would not tremble? Who would not strive to live in holiness and piety? Who would not endeavour to enter by the narrow gate by which few go in?

2. Of all Christians, there are few elect.

What tears of blood we ought to shed at the thought! So great is the cunning of the devil, so great the perversity of the world, so great the malice of men, that even of Christians themselves few are saved. Not because grace fails them but because they fail grace ; not because the gate of heaven is not open to them but because they do not choose to enter by it ; not because they are not provided with the necessary means of salvation but because they refuse to make use of the means supplied.

3. Of all adult Catholics, few are elect.

If we speak of Catholic adults alone, I see that *more of them are damned than are saved*. In other words there are *few elect among Catholic adults* in comparison with the reprobate.

Reflect, says Louis of Grenada, on any of our more famous cities in which traces of true, pure and sincere religion still remain. I do not invite you to visit in imagination the taverns and public places devoted to lying, drunkenness and swindling, but the homes of townsfolk — and what execrations, oaths and blasphemies you will hear. Go if you will to the palaces and law-courts, the workshops, markets, barracks, meeting-places, ships, vehicles and private homes, and there you will observe boys ad girls, adolescents, men both old and young, engaged in perjury,

---

[415] John III, 18.

fraud, invective, hatred, drunkenness, lust and the other vices. Go into the very churches and shrines and note the sacrileges, profanations, acts of irreverence and other behaviour unworthy of the name of Christian. Wherever you turn, do you but examine the behaviour of Catholics *seriously* [and not through the rose-tinted spectacles of Fr. Castelein! — Author] you will see so many living in negligence indiscipline and sloth that you will have no doubt that even in the case of Catholics, the words of the Lord are true : *Many are called but few are chosen.*[416]

52. CAROLUS GISLENUS (CHARLES-GHISLAIN) DAELMAN[417] (1670-1731)

Let it be deeply impressed on our minds that many more perish than are saved, and this is why Our Saviour said that *many* are called, but *few* are chosen, and why He said that the way that leads to life is narrow and the way that leads to perdition is broad — a truth to which experience readily bears witness.

You may ask whether among *Catholics* more are saved than are damned, or the other way around. Who knows? The matter is quite uncertain.

Steyaert's opinion or conjecture that more Catholics are saved than damned is opposed, on the basis of many authorities, both scriptural and patristic, by Dr Verschuren and there is no denying that even now many join him in maintaining that the majority of Catholics are damned, rather than saved ; albeit the arguments by which they strive to demonstrate this are not so powerful as they suppose.[418]

53. FR. CLAUDE JUDDE S.J. (1661-1735)

In the second point of his meditation on the particular judgement the celebrated orator presents the supreme Judge answering in these terms the proffered excuse : "I lived like the crowd."

---

[416] Laselve, Zacharie, *Annus Apostolicus*, Conc. pro Dom. Sept. ; Liège, 1727, vol. I, p. 177 *et seqq.*

[417] Regius Professor of Theology in the University of Louvain.

[418] *Theologia seu observationes theologicæ in summam D. Thomæ*, vol. I, c. V, obs. viii ; Louvain, 1759, p. 308.

Was not this a reason for distrusting your conduct? What other more evident sign of reprobation had I given than that of going along with the crowd. "Wide is the gate and broad the way that leadeth to destruction."

There are few elect even in the religious life if the religious life is scarcely differentiated from the world and every effort is not made to enter by the narrow gate. *Strive to enter by the narrow gate... Many are called but few are chosen.*[419]

54. VINCENZO LUDOVICO CARDINAL GOTTI (1664-1742)

Following his master Saint Thomas, Cardinal Gotti replies affirmatively to the question "Is the number of the reprobate greater than the number of the predestinate?" After citing the classic biblical passages on the subject, he adds:

Among the people of Israel, how many idolaters and wicked men Scripture recounts!

After the coming of Christ, only a small minority worships Him, so that of the four quarters of the globe not one is thoroughly Christian.

Of Christians, a significant fraction are schismatics or heretics.

And of Catholics, if you examine them closely, how many are found to live badly and how few who faithfully keep the law of God, without the observance of which eternal life is not granted!

David expressed this of his own days in Psalm XIII, 3: "They are all gone aside, they are become unprofitable together: there is none that doth good, no not one."[420]

55. ANTONIO MAYR S.J. (1673-1749)

This religious and Professor of philosophy and theology at Ingoldstadt was eminent for learning, moderation and holiness of life. In his work *Theologia Scholastica* in discussing God's will for all men to be saved, he says:

---

[419] Paris, 1833, vol. I, p. 168.

[420] *Theologia Scholastico-Dogmatica*, tract. VI, *De Deo Provisore, quæst.* IV, *De Reprobatione*, dub. 3, n. XV; Venice, vol. I, p. 353.

It is certain that in the context of the entire human race more are destined to be reprobate than blessed. This is inferred from Christ's words in Matthew VII, 13 and again XX, 16. Of adult believers, Fr. Segneri maintains that more are damned than saved, in his *Cristiano instruito*, p.1, wherein he proves his opinion from the Fathers, Theologians and reason…. But irrespective of this, it is certain that of all men together the majority are damned.[421]

56. DANIEL CONCINA O.P. (1687-1756)

A theologian of the highest reputation, although justly taxed with Rigorism in morals, his outstanding zeal for virtue and piety won him the esteem of Pope Benedict XIV whom he served as adviser in various ecclesiastical affairs.

The title of Chapter VII of his *de Locis Theologicis*, lib. I, diss. II, is: "Demonstration by proofs of all kinds that the majority of Catholic adults are damned." In its pages he enquires: "Does the same apply to priests and religious?"[422]

It is agreed *by all* that the number of the reprobate is far greater if we include all men: Catholics, heretics, faithful and unbelievers together.

Our question therefore concerns only Catholic adults, sons of the Church, to the exclusion of small children.

Holy Writ, the Holy Fathers of the Church and the more recent theologians commonly teach that the majority of adult Catholics are damned, and the minority saved. This is the common teaching of the theologians of the last century.[423] To show which let it suffice that everyone agrees to this doctrine. We invite gainsayers to adduce a single Father of the Church who teaches that the number of the elect exceeds that of the reprobate.[424]

Then this learned and fervent author, incensed by zeal against the Progressives, writes words worthy of the closest attention on the part

---

[421] *De Deo*, tr. I, disp. IV, q. 2, a. 2, p. 140.
[422] Naples, 1776, vol. I, p. 304.
[423] *Ibid.*, p. 303.
[424] *Ibid.*, p. 313, n. X.

of the unhappy clerics who have been wretchedly deceived by reading the works of these radicals:

When on the one hand I hear the whole of the Scriptures and all the Holy Fathers inculcating the fewness of the saved and on the other I read authors who, unsupported by a single ancient Doctor, use such far-fetched and ridiculous interpretations to evade the natural sense of the revealed text that they seem to be jesting, I cannot truthfully claim to remain impassive.

All the Fathers discuss this tremendous question and all to a man teach the fewness of the predestinate since all the Scriptures, both in the literal and the figurative sense teach it.

And yet men are to be found in our own days who make up at whim the vainest distinctions in order to undermine the authority of the Scriptures and the Fathers and offer their miserable opinion in the vulgar tongue for the perusal of the unlearned! Meditating gravely on these things, I cry out with Christ: *How narrow is the gate... Few there are that find it. Beware of false prophets*, who see vain things and make sweet-sounding promises. Close your ears to such teachers and open them to the Doctors of the Church, whom we know to have been divinely enlightened.[425]

57. CHARLES RENE BILLUART O.P. (1685-1757)

In comparison with the reprobate *those who are saved are fewer than those who are damned*, as Augustine says in Book II of his uncompleted work against Julian, Chapter 142, relying on Matthew VII: *Many are called but few are chosen*.

And it is clear that there are fewer Christians than infidels, while even among Christians how many are heretics — cut off from the communion of the Church outside of which there is no salvation!

As to whether of Catholic Christians the number of the predestinate is less than of the reprobate, theologians differ and on either side base their case on debatable foundations, for which reason I leave the question unresolved.[426]

---

[425] *Ibid.*, p. 316. n. XIII.

[426] *De Deo*, diss. IX, art. VII, 1747 edition, vol. II, p. 459.

58. GIOVANNI LORENZO BERTI O.S.A. (1696-1766)

The number of the elect is great, but very small in comparison with the number of the damned.

This is shown first by Holy Scripture. In Matthew VII, 14 we read: *Narrow is the gate and strait is the way that leadeth to life and few there are that find it.* And in Luke XIII, 24 to an enquirer who asks, *Lord are they few that are saved?* Christ replies, *Strive to enter by the narrow gate, for many, I say to you, shall seek to enter, and shall not be able.* There is also Matthew XXII, 14: *Many are called but few are chosen.* And in chapters XVII and XXIV of Isaias the predestinate are compared to the ears that remain in the field after the harvest and to the grapes and bunches that remain on the branch after the grape-harvest Then again in the Gospel they are called *little flock*, not only on account of their humility but also, says Bede, on account of the greater number of the reprobate.

Secondly it is proved from the Fathers: Saint Augustine on Psalm XLVIII; Saint Gregory, Homily XIV; Saint Chrysostom, Discourse XIV.

Add to this the very clear evidence of reason: for the state of mankind is subdivided into three, namely of nature, the law and grace, i.e. from Adam to Moses, from Moses to Christ and from Christ to our own times and henceforth to the end of the world....

All of which establishes that in every state and for every kind of men the predestinate are indeed a *little flock*.[427]

59. GUILLAUME FRANÇOIS BERTHIER S.J. (1704-1782)

The prophet Isaias in Chapter LXVI says that the number of the damned will be very great, which is not difficult to conceive as *the number of the enemies of God surpasses almost infinitely the number of His servants.*[428]

---

[427] *De Theologicis Disciplinis*, lib. VI, c. XVII, p. 176.

[428] Quoted by Fr. Joseph Coppin C.SS.R. (1840-1915), *La question de l'evangile: Seigneur, y en aura-t-il peu de sauvés: ou, Considerations sur l'écrit du R.P. Castelein, intitulé: Le rigorisme et la question du nombre des élus*, p. 250.

60. PIER FRANCESCO FOGGINI (1703-1783)

Foggini was guardian of the Vatican Library and was admitted by Pope Benedict XIV to the Pontifical Academy of History established by that most learned pontiff.

In 1752 he published at Rome a quarto volume, reprinted at Paris in 1759 and translated into French in the following year under the title *Patrum Ecclesiae de paucitate adultorum fidelium salvandorum, si cum reprobandis fidelibus conferantur, mira consensio asserta et demonstrata* ["Assertion and demonstration of the extraordinary consensus of the Fathers of the Church as to the fewness of adult faithful saved in comparison with the faithful who are reproved"]. This study was provoked by a sermon of Alexander Borgia, Archbishop of Fermo, asserting that the number of the elect is small relative to the number of all men in the aggregate, but not of Christians.[429]

A critic of this work wrote:

> Foggini ought to have distinguished between the passages of the Fathers in which all Christians including heretics are concerned and other authorities which relate exclusively to Catholics; he ought also to have reproduced and explained other testimonies from the Fathers which appear to favour the contrary opinion for there can be no other way of reaching a safe judgement in favour of the alleged extraordinary consensus, which, if we restrict ourselves only to adults, does not seem to exist.[430]

All of this is easy to claim, but it must first be established whether (a) a *single* Father of the Church in discussing the fewness of the saved *ever* distinguished between Catholics and heretics, and (b) *ever* appeared to favour the contrary opinion. I for my part have certainly found none.

---

[429] "Die Zahl der Auserwählten sei klein im Verhältnis, nicht zur Zahl der Christen, sondern der Menschen überhaupt." [The number of the elect is small in comparison not with the number of Christians but of men overall. — Translator] (Reusch: *Der Index*, vol. II, p. 976). — Cf. also *Bulletin de N. D. de la Sainte Espérance*, May 1899, p. 262.

And Foggini is quite right when he says:

> It is quite uncontested by anyone that many more men are to be damned than saved if we consider the entire human race, since it is quite plain that the greater part of mankind does not belong to the one holy Catholic Church and that no one can be saved unless he remains in the bosom of the Catholic Church.
>
> What is of special interest to many is whether *of Catholic adults* there are more who are damned or who reach eternal salvation. This is a grave question and therefore not to be judged rashly, but rather on the basis of the mind of the Fathers, whom we must always consult in matters related to faith and morals.
>
> And the mind of the ancient Fathers on this subject is that *adult Catholics* will for the greater part be eternally damned, and no single Father can be found to have written otherwise.[431]
>
> But since days have arrived in which perversity of opinions and support for poisonous liberty are so great as never to have been greater, men have begun to call into doubt even this conviction of the ancient fathers notwithstanding their unanimity, granting it to be no more than *the more common opinion*, to which they have no qualms in announcing their preference for what they call a *milder* opinion as though it were in some way good, useful, more worthy of God and *better adapted to our times*. As though we ought to teach and believe not what is true but what is useful, or as though the mere belief or hope that the majority of believing adults will be saved could in fact make it happen![432]

61. VIATOR A COCALEO O.F.M. CAP. (1706-93)[433]

This author states the following proposition as a thesis:

> I am forced to my great regret to say that the number of the elect destined to be set in the heavenly fatherland is probably exceeded by the number of the reprobate, even of those who live within the Catholic Church.

---

[430] Arevalus cited by Hürter, *Nomenclator Litterarius*, vol. III, p. 356.

[431] *Op. cit.*, Præfatio, pp. 2 and 3.

[432] *Ibid.*, p. 3.

[433] Also known as Viatore da Coccaglio. — Translator.

N.B. The subject addressed is not the number of the reprobate who by defecting from the true faith or by heresy die as unbelievers or misbelievers outside the communion of the Church, for in their case there is nothing to discuss: *he that doth not believe, is already judged.*[434]

Proof of this proposition

Christ, in pronouncing on the number of the elect in Luke XIII says that they are *few.* ...

The reasons for these pronouncements are not hard to find. So great are ignorance, concupiscence and other difficulties among Catholics that the promises made in Baptism are not observed by a very great number; in the same way the laws of nature, God and the Church are not obeyed; in a word there are few who conform their life to Christ's.

Fr. Viator then addresses himself to the Progressives:

The adversaries of this thesis are untiring in digging up comparisons or parables which they think appear to favour the opposite view. They say, for instance, that of the wedding guests only one was excluded for not wearing a wedding garment; of the Apostles only Judas was damned, few adults doe without confession, etc. To all of which I reply that if we are to argue from figures and images the strongest certainly support my thesis. Only eight were saved in Noah's ark; only two out of so many thousands entered the promised land, etc. *But as a matter of fact the question ought rather to be determined by Tradition than by the interpretations of the moderns.* Would that our gainsayers were right, but I greatly fear the contrary for there is not a single passage of Holy Scripture which clearly favours their position, nor can they prove that it is the opinion of the Fathers.[435]

62. CLAUDE D'ARVISENET (1755-1831)

Canon d'Arvisenet is rightly counted among the theologians on account of his outstanding skill in ascetic theology and the science of the Saints, as is shown by his well-known works *Memoriale vitæ sacerdotalis* and *Sapientia christiana.*

---

[434] John III, 18.

[435] *Tentamina theologico-scolastica*, vol. II, dis. IX, cap. 13, prop. 2; p. 207 of the 1768 edition.

In Chapter v of the *Memoriale*, entitled *On the Fewness of the Elect*, Christ speaks as follows to the priest:

> My son, how few priests there are who follow the strait way! How few who enter by the narrow gate!
>
> How few elect! My son, let the fear of this truth penetrate your flesh.
>
> Fear, lest, if there are few of the sheep who are saved, there may be still fewer of the priests.
>
> Fear, for the priest passed by as did the Levite, and only the Samaritan was found worthy of praise.
>
> Fear my son, for many of the last shall be first and the first shall be last.
>
> Fear, for many shall come from afar and shall recline with Abraham, Isaac and Jacob in the kingdom of heaven while the children of the kingdom are cast into outer darkness.

And in his work entitled *Sapientia Christiana*, Part One, Chapter XXX, once again entitled *On the fewness of the elect*, the divine Redeemer gives this advice to a layman:

> I want all men to be saved, my beloved, and for this I died for all. Yet *few are saved*; many indeed are called, but few are chosen.
>
> Strive, yea strive, to enter by the narrow gate for many seek to enter and shall not be able.
>
> You see, my son, these are the words I spoke: weigh them carefully and tremble at that terrible prophecy, for, being pronounced by God Himself, it shall most certainly not return unto me void.
>
> *True it is that there are few who are saved*; true it is that there are many Christians and true that many of them shall perish.
>
> Truly there are many who hear and receive the doctrine of the faith and who frequent the sacraments of Holy Church and truly there are many nonetheless who shall go into eternal fire.
>
> Not that anything on my part has been wanting to them, for I have given them both faith and grace, but because they would not know my ways *by act* in order to enter into my rest.

This is the true and sound ascetic doctrine, most unlikely to find favour with our lax Progressives.

63. Pierre CARDINAL GIRAUD (1791–1850)

What motives of encouragement and confidence! What a joy to be able to say: I am called, I am on the way to heaven; the good God, tender Father that He is, who has set me in this way, undoubtedly wants me to arrive at its term; if I fail to do so the fault will be in my own malice and not in His Will which is all kindness and love.

But if it is sweet to consider that all are called, who can hear the following words of my text without shuddering: All are called but few are chosen: *Multi vocati, pauci vero electi.*

I hesitated, I admit, to share with you the terror that seizes my soul when I read this text: I fear to give needless alarm to timorous consciences or perhaps to discourage that which is yet weak in the law and in virtue; but I recalled that fear is the beginning of wisdom; I will not be more cautious or delicate than my divine Master who did not scruple to teach these truths and who commands us to teach them in His Name....

When I say that the number of the elect will be small in comparison with the multitude of the reprobate I have no need, in order to back up my claim, to expand the terms of the comparison to the whole of mankind. The truth I am preaching to you would be less alarming for us if its peremptory and absolute character concerned only pagans or the peoples whose malice, or a just punishment of God, have left astray in the ways of heresy and schism.

But I am speaking here of the children of the true Church: I say that within the bosom of the Catholic Church the number of the elect will be the lesser figure and I prove it from Scripture, the mind of the Saints and by reason itself when enlightened by the light of faith. [436]

64. FR. GIOACCHINO VENTURA DI RAULICA (1792–1861)

In his incisive condemnation of the vices of the age Fr. Venturi explicitly holds the doctrine herein championed:

Now when this life of sensuality softness and dissipation, in which all is for the body and nothing for the soul, all for the world and nothing for God, all for vice and naught for virtue, this life in which the omission of any good is aggravated by the commission of every evil, when this life, I say, has become the *common* life not only of the nobility but also of the middle classes, not only of the great but also among the masses, when the *immense majority of Christians* spend their days and years in a damnable inactivity as to their eternal salvation, in which so far are they from making the least sacrifice to be saved that their daily efforts tend rather towards their damnation, *is it astonishing that only a small number are saved?*

Herein lies the explanation of the terrible enigma by which Our Lord Jesus Christ concludes today's parable : *Many are called but few are chosen.* It means that the calling is for a large number, for all — it is the effect of the divine mercy whereas election is but for a small number — a number whose smallness is due to the malice of men. *Multi vocati pauci vero electi.*[437]

65. NICHOLAS CARDINAL WISEMAN (1802-1865)

The illustrious and learned cardinal preached a sermon in which he passes on the common doctrine concerning the smaller number of the elect.[438] It begins as follows :

THE Apostle, my brethren, compares the life of the Christian to a race in which all push forward to obtain an eternal crown ; but where, of many who start together, one only obtains the prize. ...

few persevere through every opposition, and finally reach the goal at which they have aimed. Such, my brethren, is the illustration given, by this faithful interpreter, of the awful words, which teach, that though many are called by God to the participation of His mercy and His glory, yet few are found worthy to be chosen for their enjoyment. ...

It is, then, folly to avert our eyes from this dreadful declaration.

The small number of the elect must, in spite of all our delusions, strike us, whenever we peruse the sacred page ; and the fearful consideration that those who are saved form only a happy exception to the bulk of mankind, must terrify us when we meditate on it....

---

[436] *Homélie du petit nombre des élus* ; *Œuvres complètes,* 1863 edition, p. 635.

[437] Homélie IX, *Les ouvriers de la Vigne.*

[438] Wiseman, Cardinal Nicholas, *Sermons on Moral Subjects,* Dublin, 1864 : Sermon XI, *On the Small Number of the Elect.*

The Cardinal then sets forth the mercy of God, who wills all to be saved and to this end leaves no stone unturned. Yet few are they who are saved, for there are few who cooperate with divine grace.

Had the doctrine that few will be saved, out of all that hope for salvation, been less clearly expressed in God's word, it might have been considered an ingenious device of pious men to terrify the wicked into repentance, and preserve the good from transgressing. But wherever we look at the history of God's providence, we find but too clearly that the number of those who can hope with reason for this eternal blessing are but a small remnant....

He proves his thesis from both Testaments of the Bible.

66. THOMAS CARDINAL GOUSSET (1792-1866)

Others hold that the reprobate are more numerous than the predestinate. In favour of this opinion appeal is made to Our Lord's words: "Many are called but few are chosen; Enter by the narrow gate," etc.

This third opinion is the commonest However, as the texts invoked in its support prove that most men are lost but do not determine whether there are more elect than reprobate among Catholics, this latter question remains doubtful as Suárez quite rightly observes.[439]

67. FR. PETER JULIAN EYMARD[440] (1811-1868)

There are few who are chosen, said Our Lord; of the two paths that lead, the one to life and the other to death, the first is little followed and the second is dense with travellers. *According to these words the majority of men are damned.*

Even if the Gospel did not give this to be understood, what we see before us would already given abundant grounds for fearing that it was so.[441]

---

[439] *Théologie Dogmatique*, tr. *Dieu*, partie III, chap. III, art. 3 ; Brussels, 1850, vol. II, p. 89.

[440] Beatified 1925. — Translator.

[441] *La divine Eucharistie*, 4ᵉ série ; 1884 edition, p. 232.

68. Dom Prosper Guéranger (1805-1875)

The great Dom Guéranger, Catholic to the bone, and restorer of the Roman liturgy holds the same view as prevailed in every preceding century.

Sin reigns and triumphs in the midst of Christianity. Undoubtedly, the just are more numerous than they were in the days of Noah; but then, what riches of grace has our Redeemer poured out on our degenerate race by the ministry of His bride the Church! Yes, there *are* faithful Christians to be found upon the earth, and the number of the elect is every day being added to; *but the multitude are living at enmity with God, and their actions are in contradiction to their faith.*[442]

69. Henricus de Blieck (1814-1877)

This practical theologian, in his *Expositio methodica et elementaris Theologiæ universæ* enquires:

Is the number of the elect greater than of the reprobate?

And he answers:

Of men, taking all from Adam to the end of the world, the number of the reprobate will be greater, for there are few who enter through the narrow gate.[443]

70. Theologia Mechliniensis[444]
(Petrus Dens, 1690-1775)

This extract is from the *Tractatus de Deo*, n° 50, on "The number of the damned":

1. Whether more men (in general) are to be damned than saved?

---

[442] *The Liturgical Year*, Tuesday in Sexagesima week.

[443] *Expositio methodica et elementaris Theologiæ universæ tum dogmaticæ tum moralis ex probatis auctoribus deprompta*, vol. I, p. 371.

[444] See footnote to p. 111.

Answer. Saint Thomas teaches that more are to be damned, in accordance with Matthew VII, 14 : *How narrow is the gate and strait is the way that leadeth to life and few there are that find it.*

The same is evidently proved by the incomparably greater number of infidels and heretics who die in infidelity or in heresy.

2. Whether *of Catholic adults* more are to be damned than saved?

Answer. Suárez and Steyaert think that more will be saved, since in James II, 13 it is said that *mercy exalteth itself above judgment* ; while in Matthew XXII, 13 only one is cast into outer darkness.

But nothing is proved from this parable any more than the parable of the ten virgins proves an equal number of saved and damned.

And the text taken from James can be fulfilled even with few saved by the mere fact that *some* of mankind are saved, even though the *whole* of mankind lay under the judgement of condemnation.

Gonet, A Lapidè, Fromondus, etc., say that more will be damned, an opinion a Lapidè proves with many arguments, authorities of the Fathers and examples in his commentary on the above passage from James.

However this opinion is clearly not proved by the words of Christ *Many are called by few are chosen*, (Matthew XX, 16), for these words may include unbelievers or at least heretics who are subject to the Church by Baptism, or they may be understood of those "called" who are indeed saved, but among whom few are "chosen" or "elect", i.e. outstanding.

After which the author adds the following practical conclusion :

Anyone wanting to choose the certain path amid the uncertainty of this question should conclude in practice that he must choose the narrower way, being firmly convinced that he who lives well dies well, but fearing lest, if he lives as most live, he may be damned with the majority.

71. FRANCIS-XAVIER SCHOUPPE S.J. (1823-1904)

"Many are called but few are chosen."
There are two admissible interpretations of this declaration depending on the meaning to be attributed to the word "chosen". If by *chosen* we understand the predestinate, i.e. those who are certainly to reach salva-

tion, the meaning is: Many are called to salvation, but few will in fact reach it and hence many will be damned.[445]

1. There are many sinners but few just.

2. There are many lukewarm but few fervent.

3. There are many hirelings but few who labour freely and out of love for the Lord.

4. Hence Christ has good reason for warning each of us to strive to be of the little flock of the elect, saying: *Enter by the narrow gate.* (Matthew VII, 13)[446]

With regard to mankind, if we take all, from Adam to the last man born, *the number of the reprobate is greater*, for few enter by the narrow gate.[447]

72. MGR. LOUIS-ADOLPHE PAQUET (1859-1942)

Here is the complete text of this celebrated Canadian theologian, dean of the faculty of theology of the University of Laval, taken from his *Commentarii in Summam Theologicam D. Thomæ* :[448]

It is thought more probably that:

(i) the number of the predestinate as composed of Angels and men together exceeds the number of the reprobate;

(ii) of the faithful who die in the Roman Church, many more are saved;

(iii) but out of all men together, fewer are saved.

(…)

Proof of statement (iii):

Note first that:

(a) The Congregation of the Index condemned in 1772 Chapter V of the work of Benedict Plazza on Paradise with commentary by J. M. Gravina. This chapter uses many arguments to defend the proposition that "It is probable that the elect among mankind are far more numerous than the reprobate."

---

[445] *Les évangiles des dimanches et des fêtes.*, vol. I, p. 236.

[446] *Ibid.*, p. 243.

[447] *Elementa Theologiæ Dogmaticæ*, vol. II, n. 285.

[448] *De Deo Uno et Trino*, disp. VI, q. 2, a. V, p. 390.

(b) Even though it may be maintained by Catholics, as it is in fact by some, that the number of the predestinate is equal to (Gener, Hürter) or even greater than (Bougaud) the number of the reprobate, nevertheless *the more probable and common opinion* (as Suárez says) holds that the reprobate are more numerous.

In favour of this opinion are:

from Holy Scripture itself: Matthew VII, 13, 14; Luke XIII, 23-4; Matthew XXII, 14; Ibid. XX, 16; I Peter IV, 18.

from the Fathers: Saint Augustine *de Correptione et Gratia*, cap. X; *contra Cresconium*, Lib. III, cap. 66.

From Saint Thomas: I, q. XXIII, a. 7 ad 3; LXIII, a. 9. ad 1^{am}; I-II, q. LXXI, a. 2 ad 3^{am}.

And the lamentable history of times and nations lends confirmation.

Would that the opinion of French writer Bougaud were more convincing, when he rejects the common teaching lest evil seem to triumph over good and over Christ Our Redeemer.

But:

(a) Good accomplished is to be weighed, not merely counted, and this applies especially to the good accomplished by grace, so that even if it achieved the salvation of only a single man an almost infinite degree of glory would result to God.

(b) Evil happens only to the exact extent that it is permitted by the supreme and most wise Providence of God.

(c) Finally, since for the elect "all things work together unto good,"[449] the works of Satan and his satellites are so disposed and ordered by the action of God that, like to triumphal spoils hanging from the chariot of the just, they concur to the greater glory of the divine empire.

73. GERARDUS MARTINUS JANSEN (1828-1900)

This highly-respected professor of dogmatic theology in the archdiocesan seminary of Rijsenburg in Holland writes as follows in his textbook of dogmatic theology:

On the subject of whether the number of the predestinate is greater than the number of the reprobate, the Fathers and theologians are in disagreement. Some think that the number of the predestinate is less than

---

[449] Cf. Romans VIII, 28.

of the reprobate, and in absolute terms, speaking of all men in the aggregate, *it is hardly possible to cast doubt on this.*[450]

74. MGR. JOSEPH-ÉLIE MÉRIC (1838-1905)

Mgr. Méric is a Doctor of Theology and Professor of Moral Theology at the Sorbonne. In his work *L'Autre Vie*, vol. II, chap. x, he discusses the number of the elect. After stating the doctrine of Fr. Faber he concludes by embracing the position of Suárez, namely that the greater part of the human race is damned but that of Catholics the majority are saved.

> If you re-read now the passages of the Gospel explaining them in the light of Suárez's apposite distinction, all difficulty vanishes. Many are called, for it is of divine faith that God wants the salvation of all men; *there will be few chosen, taking the human race as a whole,* including heretics, schismatics, pagans, etc. i.e. the aggregate of men that God would have saved.
>
> But if you consider only Catholics it is permissible to believe that the majority will be saved, as taught by Suárez.[451]

II

THEOLOGIANS WHO ARE ADDUCED
IN FAVOUR OF THE OPINION OF
FR. CASTELEIN

After perusing so long a list of the finest Theologians, surely everyone would agree with Suárez's conclusion: "So all things considered, the number of the reprobate is undoubtedly greater: this is the *common and true* opinion" And with Muniessa's statement that "the Doctors, both scholastic and expositive, hold this opinion, very strongly supported by Holy Scripture and the Holy Fathers."

---

[450] *Theologia Dogmatica Specialis*, Utrecht, 1879, vol. II, p. 144.
[451] 1882 edition, p. 307.

How is it possible then for Fr. Castelein to claim that his extraordinary ideas "are the fruit of a profound study of the teachings of our greatest theologians"?[452]

It is time for him to give us the names of these "greatest theologians", quite unknown to the present writer! For the authorities I find mentioned in his book entitled *La Science du Salut* bear names such as Aristotle, Plato, Pythagoras, Hesiod, Homer, Solon, Pindar, Æschylus, Sophocles, Euripides, Herodotus, Thucydides, Xenophon, Plutarch, Socrates, Anaxagoras, Xenophanes, Parmenides, Michel-Eugène Chevreul, Robert Mayer, Faraday, Cuvier, Élie de Beaumont, Geoffroy Saint Hilaire, Barrande, L. Agassiz, de Quatrefages, A. Ampère, Becquerel, Regnault, Wurtz, Hirn, Clausius, Jean-Baptiste Dumas, Cauchy, Foucault, Biot, Fresnel, Claude Bernard, Leverrier, Pasteur, François Arago, Darwin, Helmholtz, Virchow, Tyndall, Huxley, Paul Bert, Dubois-Raymond, Haeckel, Bertholet, Copernicus, Kepler, Galileo, Pascal, Descartes, Newton, Leibnitz, Linnæus, Huyghens, Euler, etc. But in vain do I seek the names of our holy Fathers and theologians in this "fruit of a profound study of the teachings of our greatest theologians"!

But although the learned author entirely fails to cite "our greatest theologians" his disciple "E.T." S.J. has undertaken to supply the omission, boldly announcing that Fr. Castelein "is in excellent company: Suárez, Cajetan, Saint Francis de Sales, Bergier, Lacordaire, Ravignan, Faber, Mgr. Besson, Fr. Monsabré, etc., etc."[453]

However, "E.T." does not seem to have much trust in his claims, for he does not give a single reference so that readers may verify them independently. I have therefore been obliged to do my best to locate and verify the relevant opinions of each of these authors and to quote their words accurately.

---

[452] Second edition, *Introduction*, p. X.

[453] Letter published in *Le Patriote*, 19th March 1899.

Fr. Castelein's thesis is, in summary, that *the greater part of the entire human race* will be saved (see above, p. 47). So let us now compare the teachings of the authorities he appeals to against this thesis.

1. FRANCISCO SUÁREZ

The second comparison concerns men, in absolute terms, embracing everyone that has lived or shall live from the beginning of the world to its end. *And in this case the* **common** *and* **true** *opinion is that the number of the reprobate is greater.* [See the full extract in context as quoted above, p. 131]

So Suárez considers Fr. Castelein's doctrine to be neither common nor true, in other words to be *singular* and *false;* hence he cannot fairly be adduced in its favour.

2. THOMAS CAJETAN

Suárez himself (*loc. cit.*) tells us of Cajetan that "in his exposition of the parable of the wise and foolish virgins he says that of those who live a mediocre life *in the Church* and *have some care for their conscience, one half* [i.e. 5 out of 10] *are damned.*" And Suárez adds in his own name, "which is very rigorous".

But if one half of those Catholics *who have some care for their consciences* are damned, what must be said of the great number of Catholics who entirely neglect such care? And what is to be said of Pagans, Mahometans, Protestants; schismatics, etc? For anyone who recognizes that most *Catholics* are damned *a fortiori* holds that most members *of the entire human race* are damned.

And yet we are told that Cajetan supports the doctrine of Fr. Castelein!

3. SAINT FRANCIS DE SALES

Where on earth has "E.T." located a single word in the voluminous writings of this holy Doctor in favour of Fr. Castelein's thesis?

Although I can find nowhere that Saint Francis discusses the subject directly and in detail I will nevertheless quote some relevant remarks that I *have* found:

> The statement that *there are many called but few chosen* is never considered enough. All those who are in the Church are *called*, but not all those who are in the Church are *chosen*, which is why the word *Church* does not mean election but convocation.[454]

> Anyone clear-sighted enough to see the outcome of the race run by men would see that the Church has good reason to cry out: *Many are called but few are chosen*, i.e. many are within the Church militant who will never be of the Church triumphant. How many are within who will be without, as Saint Anthony the Abbot foresaw of Arius and Saint Fulbert of Berengarius![455]

> On the day of judgement the virtues of the pagans will be a defence not so that they will be saved, but so that they will be less severely damned.[456]

In the light of which I cannot understand the effrontery of Fr. Castelein in claiming (p. 264) that...

> Saint Francis de Sales forbad even an unfavourable opinion as to the salvation of those who, after an evil life, die with no sign of repentance.... And to confirm this truth he used to recount what he had once heard a preacher say about the death of Luther: "Who knows whether at the hour of his death God may not have touched him with efficacious grace?"

But where, I enquire, did the Saint say this? To this pseudo-Francis dreamed up by Fr. Castelein and other Progressives, I oppose the true and authentic Bishop of Geneva, who dared to declare that many bishops and prelates are damned:

> But when should I have finished if I were now to begin to accumulate the names of so many bishops and prelates who, having once been le-

---

[454] *Des Controverses*, I, chap. 2, art. 2; Annecy, 1892, vol. I, p. 55.

[455] *Ibid.*, p. 60.

[456] *Traité de l'Amour de Dieu*, livre XI, chap. X; *Œuvres complètes*, Paris, 1839, vol. IV, p. 449.

gitimately placed in this office and dignity, later fell from their first grace and died heretics? ... Behold Origen ... suffer shipwreck and be lost in the very harbour of his own burial... What then? There he was at last, a heretic, excommunicated, outside the Ark, perishing in the deluge of his own opinion. So not only may a reprobate be *of* the Church, he may even be a *Pastor* of the Church.[457]

These are authentic words of the gentle Saint! Let Fr. Castelein now cite verifiable words from him in the opposite direction! In all probability he has never consulted the sources and his error has led astray "E.T." who in good faith swears by the words of his master, as well as leading astray a hundred thousand readers.

4. NICOLAS-SYLVESTRE BERGIER

This learned writer twice in his works discusses our question *ex professo*; but nowhere does he prove that the number of the elect is greater.

A. In a work entitled *Dictionnaire de Théologie* he speaks in these terms of the great argument of our learned adversary:

> If Christ does not in fact save the majority of souls, the conquest of Satan would be in its own order finer than that of his Divine Victor. Indeed would not Satan himself emerge the victor? [pp. 189, 190] ...

But the reader will perhaps be surprised to learn that Bergier then goes on to qualify this argument as "in all respects absurd"! (The entire passage is quoted below.)

Bergier then sets out to show that in the Gospel Parables the word *electi* ("chosen") never means *saved*, so that it is impossible to base an argument in favour of the fewness of the saved on the parables, which, according to his interpretation, rather suggest the contrary. But he does not positively solve the question, nor does he prove that the number of the saved is greater; indeed he avows that he does not intend to address that subject.

---

[457] *Op. cit.*, Annecy edition, vol. I, p. 54.

I will not enter into the question of which meaning (*faithful* or *predestinate*) of this word of Our Lord (Matthew XX, 16 and XXII, 14) should be adopted. There are authorities so numerous and respectable in favour of each that it is not easy to see which deserves to be preferred. I will therefore restrict myself to a few reflections.

A mature and well-instructed mind does not let itself be troubled over a problematic opinion concerning which the Church has not pronounced such as whether the number of the elect is great or small. *Even if the latter is correct*, it would only follow that the great majority would be of those who do not *want* to be saved, who resist the graces God sends them and who die in final impenitence.[458]

B. And in his *Traité de la vraie Religion*, in answer to an objection, he again says:

The question is whether the word *chosen* refers to those who are saved or only to those who are in the way of salvation: the faithful.

And he does not resolve this question but simply shows that it cannot be the basis of any argument against Christian hope.

Even assuming it were absolutely necessary to take the expression "few are chosen" in its most rigorous sense, what would follow? Only that the greater number is made up of those who have not wanted to be saved.[459]

So Bergier does no prove that the greater part of men are to be saved and it is in vain that he is invoked in favour of Fr. Castelein.

5. JEAN-BAPTISTE-HENRI DOMINIQUE LACORDAIRE O.P.

In his Lecture 71 On the Results of the Divine Government, he teaches:

It is towards eternity that we must cast our gaze if we wish to pronounce a definitive judgement on Providence, and it is there no doubt that you await my remarks, armed with the celebrated text: *Many are called but few are chosen.*

---

[458] *Dictionnaire de Théologie*, article "Élu", edited by Gousset, 1853; vol. II, p. 215.
[459] Part III, chapter XI, art. vii, objection 4; Tournai, 1827, vol. 10, p. 327.

I hasten to address the subject of your impatience, for I can calm it with a very simple statement: the fewness of the elect is not a dogma of faith but a question freely debated in the Church. Not only do I tell you that this is so, but if you so wish I will at once give you the proof of it.[460]

Fr. Lacordaire's proof consists in demonstrating that the scriptural passages invoked do not prove the fewness of the saved. Then he shows that one third of the human race dies before the use of reason and one half before puberty, so that one half is either saved or at least not damned.

I am well aware, gentlemen, that the inhabitants of limbo cannot be counted among the elect chosen for divine life, and indeed if they could the question of the number of the elect would be mathematically resolved, but without making any such claim it remains true that premature death renders service to God's clemency even though it does not entirely satisfy it.

But, argues the eloquent Preacher, women are saved for the most part, and the poor.

And what are the rest in comparison? What are the rest even though eternity did not harvest a single soul among them? But that is far from being the case. … Riches, learning and power are not abandoned to evil. Christ has repaired all, blessed all, conquered all, and he clasps the entire world in His generous hands. Whoever escapes them perishes by his own fault, and after what has just been said, *it is at least doubtful whether this unhappy fate awaits the greater number.*

He adds two further considerations:

First, many souls among these peoples [unbelievers] *may have been saved* by the providential ways pointed out in our previous lecture; and secondly, we know neither the extent of the ages which God has allotted in His divine thought to the action of Christianity, nor the degree of power and universality the Church may attain in the future…. It is quite as likely for this secret to fall on the side of good as of ill, *and thus the question remains veiled to the advantage of freedom.*

[460] *Conférences de Notre Dame,* year 1851, chapter 71; *Œuvres complètes,* Brussels edi-

In other words, it is not certain that the greater part of mankind is damned, so the rationalists have no right to reproach the Providence of God with the greater number of the damned as proof of its failure to attain its objective.

But how does this help Fr. Castelein's thesis?

6. GUSTAVE DELACROIX DE RAVIGNAN

In the writings of this preacher I have found no more than an eloquent and general recommendation of the divine mercy, but nowhere have I found where he discusses the issue before us. If there is such a passage, let those who deny our contention point it out.

7. FR. FREDERICK WILLIAM FABER

Two remarks should first be made about this author which show that he is appealed to in vain.

In his *Growth in Holiness* he emphasizes that he does not wish to examine the question of the eternal salvation *of the entire human race,* but only to discuss the salvation of *Catholics.*

> We are discussing a temptation of the Catholic spiritual life; and we may keep to what is strictly practical. Consequently we are dispensed from touching on the question of the fewness of the elect out of the whole number of mankind. We have nothing to do with curiosity about the future destinies of heathen and of heretics.[461]

And he declares the same restriction in his *The Creator and the Creature,* so there can be no grounds for appealing to him in favour of an opinion which he explicitly refuses to discuss.

And as to his doctrine of the salvation of the majority of Catholics, readers will surely be astonished to be informed that the author frankly admits the weakness of his own arguments, but it is so — here are his own words:

tion, 1854, volume IV, p. 121. This freedom is further discussed below.

[461] *Growth in Holiness,* 15th American edition, p. 393.

These are all *bad arguments*, taken simply, but collectively they establish a lawful benignant supposition.[462]

Now far be it from the present writer to deny that arguments which, taken separately, are not *demonstrative*, but nonetheless have some influence on the mind thanks to a certain *probability*, may give rise to a measure of conviction by mutual corroboration; but if they are frankly *bad arguments* to begin with, they have no force to add to one another and hence even taken collectively they can never amount to anything at all.

8. Fr. Louis Besson

I think I am right in saying that the allusion intended is to *L'Église, œuvre de l'homme-Dieu* by Fr. Besson, published at Paris,[463] Third Lecture: *Où va l'Église?* In its pages, Fr. Besson speaks of the principle "Outside the Church, no salvation", saying in summary:

1. Nothing is more certain than this maxim: it is founded on Scripture, the teaching of the Fathers and on the data of reason itself.

2. Nothing is more mysterious than the application of this maxim, as we are held back by: (i) the mystery of grace; (ii) the mystery of good faith, and (iii) the mystery of death.

Conclusion. Let us adore the justice of the God-Man, but let us not pass judgement on His mysteries.

In the final section we read these words: "Is Voltaire damned? I suppose so, says reason. I fear so, says piety. But the sole answer given by the Church is: I do not know." (p. 75)

But in vain do we seek anywhere in its pages any statement to the effect that *the greater part of mankind* attain salvation; so it is vain to adduce Fr. Besson as a patron of Fr. Castelein's opinion.

---

[462] *Ibid.*, p. 395.
[463] Second edition, Paris, 1865, p. 52 *et seqq.*

9. Fr. Jacques-Marie-Louis MONSABRÉ

If the reader refreshes his memory of what has already been said about this learned apologist's words and their meaning (p. 49 above) he will be aware that not only does Fr. Monsabré *not* hold Fr. Castelein's thesis, but he explicitly recognizes that, on the contrary, the greater part of the human race, alas! by its own fault incurs damnation.

10. CONCLUSION

As none of these theologians falsely invoked in fact holds the opinion herein opposed, the time has come to pass on to the names of those who do in reality teach the same as Fr. Castelein concerning the greater number of the saved and to show the futility of their reasoning. I have found none except Gravina, Bougaud and Mauran, and after analysing their case I shall be happy to leave them to Fr. Castelein and to "E.T."

III

THEOLOGIANS WHO REALLY *DO* FAVOUR THE OPINION OF FR. CASTELEIN

1. GIUSEPPE MARIA GRAVINA S.J.

Not only was this unhappy author condemned by the Holy See, but as a matter of fact, unlike Fr. Castelein, he never advanced his opinion as certain, but only as *probable*; indeed he admitted that the opposing view is *more probable*. Here are his words:

> I have no intention of depriving the contrary view of its probability. Indeed, to be generous, we grant to our adversaries that their opinion is *more probable* than ours, if they will but be kind enough in turn to recognize our view as probable. For I have elsewhere undertaken to show, in a

more copious work, that a *probable* opinion, faced with a *more probable* opinion, remains tenable.[464]

So Gravina considers Fr. Castelein's view to be probable and ours to be *more probable.*

It would be superfluous to demonstrate the feebleness of Gravina's arguments as our adversaries are the first to admit it: "... arguments that are un-theological, even puerile", says "E.T." in *Le Patriote* of 19th March 1899.

Gravina's arguments are concisely summarized by the learned editors[465] of the review *Bulletin de Notre Dame de la Sainte Espérance* (1899, p. 264):

> The will of God and of Jesus Christ for men's salvation provides our author with an inexhaustible arsenal. But he apparently finds this word *will* too weak, for he replaces it with the Latin word *studium* which he defines, following Cicero, as: *The assiduous application of the mind to an object towards which one is borne with ardour, with a strong will.* "Thus," he adds, "God and Jesus Christ are so busy — to use human terms — procuring the salvation of men that they want it assiduously, ardently, with fulness of heart." And to prove that in consequence the majority of men are saved, he invites us to note how God congratulates Himself, in Habacuc, on His very abundant catch: *He lifted them all up with his hook, he drew them in his drag, and gathered them into his net: for this he will be glad and rejoice. Therefore will he offer victims to his drag, and he will sacrifice to his net: because through them his portion is made fat....* (Habacuc I, 15, 16) What Fr. Gravina has overlooked is that the prophet is speaking here *not* of God but of the wicked and of the devil. (See Saint Jerome's Commentary, Migne, XXV, col. 1287.) Elsewhere he supposes that the number of the Angels who persevered in justice is twice as many as fell. And since God loves men more than angels, this implies, he concludes, that among men the elect are more numerous than the reprobate. But this argument is arbitrary and sophistical as well as *taking no account of original sin,* as indeed no account is taken of it anywhere in the remainder of his work.

---

[464] Page 676 of this condemned book.

[465] Chief among them being the saintly Fr. Emmanuel André (1826-1903). — Translator.

He maintains that from the beginning of Genesis to the end of the Apocalypse no single person is designated by name as lost (the Antichrist is the only person he admits to be certainly damned) whereas the names of a multitude of the elect are given. Therefore — the logic is admirable — there are more elect than reprobate.

He draws a similar conclusion from Our Lord's parables. In some of them (*The Prodigal Son, The Lost Sheep*, etc.) only the elect appear; in others (*The Wise and Foolish Virgins*) the elect and the reprobate are present in equal numbers. And finally in others, for a single lazy servant, you see two that are faithful and prudent. Therefore....

Our Lord Jesus Christ is the *Redeemer of all*. He would be misnamed and the devil could address insulting reproaches to Him if most men were not saved.

Every man has one or more guardian angels, especially unbelievers, as they have no other aid. But the angels have more power and wisdom to save than the devils to damn. Therefore....

The elect are like stars and they must be so much the greater in number to the reprobate *as the stars are more numerous than the comets.*

However, as though the author were astonished by his own position, he pretends to be struck to see the human race in ignorance of the true God, known almost exclusively in Judæa before the coming of Christ, and then the true Church enclosing but a small number of the nations in comparison with those who have not received the Gospel, and the deluge of vice which has in every age covered the face of the earth. He finds it therefore very difficult ("*maxime arduum*") for those who reach salvation to be so numerous as he thinks them to be. But Gravina takes courage from the thought of the Providence, power and wisdom of God.

Another source which he finds no less fertile in *conjectures* is the Fathers of the Church, whom he divides into several categories.

1. Some of them say, in speaking of the miraculous cures worked by Our Lord say that He healed souls before healing bodies. But the sick restored to health by Christ are countless — *innumeros sanavit*. Therefore....

2. A second class of Fathers comprises those who, in speaking of the wicked whom God punished during their lifetime, establish — he says — as a general rule, that God does not punish the same sins twice. So there are strong grounds for confidence that all the sinners who have undergone chastisement for their crimes in this world will be saved. The texts advanced concern the inhabitants of Sodom, consumed by fire

from heaven, the Egyptians submerged in the Red Sea, the Israelites struck dead in the desert, etc.

3. He attributes to other Fathers, those of his third category, the notion that many infidels were saved — some purely and simply on account of their *ignorance*, and others, such as Plato, Socrates and the Sibyls, because of their *wisdom*; in which respect he manifestly misapplies the texts he cites as they evoke the possibility of salvation in the latter cases only on the assumption that those concerned possessed explicit faith in Our Lord Jesus Christ.

Finally, to consolidate his thesis, the fragility of which he is conscious of, Gravina cites various visions, of varying authenticity, also tending to suggest that *whatever kind of life they have led*, God and His Saints use so many *stratagems* (his expression) to save sinners at the article of death that they usually "pull it off". And this advantage is not restricted to Catholic Christians: all the sects may enjoy it, be they Mahometans, heretics, schismatics, Jews or pagans — no one is excluded by professing a false religion as most of them do not realise that their religion is not the true one. They would embrace Christianity and join the Church if they were shown the need. They are *hidden Christians*. They are *infidels* only in name, for Gravina claims to admit no one but Catholic Christians to paradise. And for those who, despite so many explanations, still have difficulty in understanding how such people can belong to the Church as her children while remaining strangers to her creed and worship, he invites them not to be surprised as it is a Mystery — *mysterium dico vobis* — and it is proper to mysteries to be obscure.

2. FR. ÉMILE BOUGAUD

This author misquotes or truncates the words of Saint Alphonsus, Saint Francis de Sales, Fr. Ventura[466] and others, but I grant that he held Fr. Castelein's opinion, based on arguments such as: "Suppose that the world lasts many centuries yet, *thousands of centuries...*"; "suppose..., grant..., etc."[467] Even if I am mistaken,...[468] Etc., etc.

---

[466] *Op. cit.*, p. 365.
[467] *Ibid.*, p. 366.
[468] *Ibid.*, p. 382.

3. Fr. Victor Mauran

Here is a selection of the arguments advanced by this theologian:

The fact that Christ clearly states that few are chosen is precisely because their fewness is quite unrelated to the number of souls that are saved. (*Élus et Sauvés*, p. 16)

The wicked and the unbelieving who were struck in the days of Noah were saved in virtue of the Sacrifice of Christ and delivered from the prison in which divine justice held them captive — Peter III (*sic*). (p. 62)

It is a proven fact that the head of the executed man retains its vital heat for a certain time. The brain, which is a real calorific reservoir only cools down slowly and it is *not unlikely* that life should find a refuge in it and survive there for a time *perhaps* long enough for *the soul to be able to turn to God.* (p. 66)

Am I mistaken? Whether I am or not I believe that it is *preferable to err* and offer consolation and hope to souls rather than fear and despair. (p. 225)

I imagine that if God had consulted his elect before creating them, seeing themselves so few, they would have made the sacrifice of their eternal happiness to spare their brethren, the great mass of mankind, the torments of Hell. (p. 150)

If Gravina's arguments are *puerile*, what is to be said of these?

And Mauran has the effrontery to accuse Saint Thomas of begging the question (p. 239), though to have written such a thing he cannot realise what question-begging consists in, for the holy Doctor is not attempting to *prove* the fact that the elect are the minority, but to explain that fact, *admitted as certain*, and reconcile it with God's providence and mercy. How rightly has the Vicar of Christ said of those who neglect Saint Thomas:

Events already bear all too clear witness to the tendency, when Thomas is disregarded, for the resulting intellectual chaos to give rise to monstrous opinions.[469]

---

[469] Letter to the Minister-General of the Order of Friars Minor, 25th Nov. 1898. See page 75 above.

4. CONCLUSIONS

I am happy to leave Fr. Castelein with his theologians Gravina, Bougaud and Mauran to substantiate his claim that "these ideas are true and just They are the fruit of a profound study of *our greatest theologians*." (*Introduction*, p. X) I am happy to leave him "in excellent company," to borrow the words of his apologist "E.T."

But how preferable it would have been for him to cultivate familiarity with the theologians of his own Society, bearing such illustrious names as Frs. Peter Canisius, Robert Bellarmine, Ven. Leonard Lessius, Claude de la Colombière, Álvarez de Paz, Alfonso Salmerón, Gregory of Valentia, Francisco Suárez, Gabriel Vásquez, Martinus Becanus, Jeremias Drexelius, Paolo Segneri, Tomás Muniessa, Louis Bourdaloue, Jean-Baptiste de Saint-Jure, Claude Judde, Cornelius a Lapidè, Joseph Knabenbauer, the Würtzburg fathers and so many others!

By doing so he would have fulfilled the orders of Pope Leo XIII which I will now transcribe for the benefit of all readers, especially as they are not well enough known.

They are taken from the Apostolic Letter *Gravissime Nos* confirming the constitutions of the Society of Jesus as to the profession of the teaching of Saint Thomas Aquinas[470] and the contents of which "are to be and to be held by all throughout the Society of Jesus as a defined and perpetual law concerning the choice of doctrines" and "individual copies of which are to be given to each and every member who is or shall ever become a master of theology or of philosophy."[471]

The first point, well known to all, as the Society's illustrious founder decreed in many passages of its Constitutions, is that in, every discipline solid and sure doctrine must be followed, indeed *the surer and more ap-*

---

[470] *Gravissime nos*, 30th Dec. 1892; *Leonis XIII Acta*, Vatican edition, vol. XII, p. 366.

[471] *Ibid.*, p. 380.

proved :[472] a duty often duly reaffirmed by the decrees and orders of the congregations and superiors.

And he further commanded that the doctrine to be followed by the Society was to be one and the same for all and in the fulfilment of all offices:

"Let us all think the same thing and, insofar as possible, say the same thing, in accordance with the Apostle. Let different doctrines not be admitted, whether by words spoken in the pulpit or lecture-hall or written in books."

The same holds for the priests from the various nations delegated to revise the book concerning the nature of the studies [Ratio Studiorum], as they decided to give pride of place to their treatment of the choice of opinions and set forth as its foundation that the Society's doctrine must be uniform, sure and solid in accordance with the Constitutions. And it should not be thought that this command of doctrinal uniformity is limited only to those opinions that are common to all the schools, for it also applies more broadly to those opinions about which there is less agreement among Catholic doctors: *Care should also be taken that agreement should reign in the Society even on those matters concerning which Catholic doctors disagree or are in contradiction.*

The Society's Father, Ignatius, clearly saw that to attain the kind of agreement and charity which the Society required the commonly approved rule by which diverse opinions are tolerated in accordance with the dictum *in dubiis libertas* was by no means enough; it was necessary that there should be no such differing opinions in the Society and he specifically forbad them within it.

But lest this precept of uniform doctrine appear too harsh to anyone he also prudently advised that every member, before binding himself by the vows of religion, be asked whether he was ready to submit his own opinion and to adopt the view established in the Society, by which means free choice is made of what might seem scarcely tolerable if it were imposed by mere law.

Hence it would be entirely foreign to the nature and to the written laws of the Society for anyone to demand therein the same freedom of opinion enjoyed by most outside her. For even if the opinions in question were highly tenable and patronized by learned men, those who adopt them would indeed avoid the reproach of novelty, temerity or

---

[472] *Constitutiones*, pars IV, c. V, § 4.

error, but would utterly depart from that single form of doctrine so much desired and commended.[473]

<hr>

[473] *Leonis XIII Acta, ibid.,* pp. 368-70.

CHAPTER FIVE

<hr>

THE CERTAIN AND UNIVERSAL TEACHING OF THE
SAINTS ON THE FEWNESS OF THE SAVED IS CONFIRMED
BY THE SERIOUS INTERPRETERS OF HOLY SCRIPTURE.

<hr>

I

EXEGETES WHO EXPRESSLY TEACH THIS

1. LUDOLPH OF SAXONY (C. 1295-1378)

IN EXPLAINING the parable of the labourers in the vineyard, Ludolph warns his readers:

> Although you have heard in the parable that all received a penny, do not think that all those who are called to the faith are to receive eternal life. This is why a further, fear-inspiring statement is added: *for many are called*, at the first, third, sixth, ninth or last hours, to faith and to merit, but of them all *few are chosen* for the reward and reign of beatitude. Many belong to the Church militant who shall not belong to the Church triumphant. In which He shows that those who are saved are few in comparison with those who are called at each of the hours..., *for wide is the gate, and broad is the way, that leadeth to destruction, and many there are who go in thereat*, etc.[474]

---

[474] *Vita Jesu Christi*, part II, cap. XIX ; ed. Palmé, p. 446, col. 2.

2. NICHOLAS OF LYRA (C. 1270-1349)

Commenting on Matthew VII, *Wide is the gate and broad is the way,* etc., he says:

> For many are found to be defective, in accordance with what is written in Ecclesiastes I: *The number of fools in infinite,* and very few are found to be virtuous, which is why the text goes on to say: *How narrow is the gate, and strait is the way that leadeth to life: and few there are that find it !*[475]

And in his commentary on Matthew XX:

> Many are called to the Catholic faith, but few are chosen, i.e. to glory; for they are few, i.e. in comparison with those who are called to faith.[476]

3. TOSTATUS ABULENSIS[477] (C. 1400-1455)

In explaining Matthew XX, this bishop of Ávila observes (Question 69 on verse 14): "Many are called to faith, i.e. are converted to it, yet few are chosen, since few from among Christians are saved."

4. JOANNES GAGNEIUS (†1549)[478]

Gagneius was theologian, chaplain and almoner to King François I of France. Writing on the text of Matthew VII, 15 he says:

> By the narrow gate and the straight way he refers to the path of virtue which is difficult from the start and *very rarely* trodden by the masses. The broad gate and the spacious way is the path of sensual gratification into which almost all cast themselves. So Christ does not want those who belong to Him to tread the broad way of pleasure with the masses and the many, for it leads to death; He wants them to enter by the narrow gate of virtue and to follow the strait path of the few who live virtuously.[479]

And commenting on Luke XIII, 32, he says:

---

[475] *Glossa Ordinaria et Postilla Litteralis,* Antwerp, 1634, col. 150.

[476] *Ibid.,* col. 367.

[477] Also known as Alonso Fernández de Madrigal, bishop of Ávila. — Translator.

[478] Also known as Jean de Gaigny or de Gagny. — Translator.

[479] *Scholia in Evang.* Ed. Paris. *1552.* fol. 16. recto.

Christ exhorts His hearers to seek only how to be saved and reache eternal salvation, which can be reached only by the narrow gate... But many try to enter by it and cannot for their efforts are not serious but perfunctory and negligent.[480]

5. JANSENIUS GANDAVENSIS[481] (1510-1576)

Commenting on the words *Enter by the narrow gate*:

Because the very absolute mode of life hitherto prescribed by Him is narrow, strait and rare, lest His listeners be revolted and alienated both by the vexations and difficulties of this life and by the fewness of those who follow it, He exhorts them rather to embrace this narrow way than the broad way of the wicked, for the latter leads to Hell, while the former leads to life....

Note that there are various senses in which it is possible to understand this statement that the way of virtue is strait and narrow. First, because it is trodden by *few*, if compared with the number of those who travel the path of wickedness, which for this reason is called *broad*....

It should also be noted from Jerome how carefully the Lord differentiates the two ways. For He says that many *tread* the broad way, while few *find* the narrow way. For we do not seek the broad way, nor is there any need to find it as it confronts us willy-nilly. But not all find the narrow path, nor do all who find it at once enter by it, or else they do not all persevere in it, for many, having once found the way of truth, being ensnared by the pleasures of the world, turn back midway. Rightly then is it said *Few there are that find it*, implying also that there are *fewer still* who travel by it.

So the Lord taught us by this parable of the two ways to take no notice of how the masses behave but rather to become imitators of those that are fewer.[482]

---

[480] *Ibid.*, fol. 138 verso.

[481] Also known as Cornelius Jansen the Elder, Bishop of Ghent. He should not be confused with Cornelius Jansen, Bishop of Ypres, who originated the Jansenist errors, although he died before their condemnation. — Translator.

[482] *Commentarius in Concordiam et Totam Historiam Evangelicam*, cap. XLIII; Lyon, 1684, p. 324.

And commenting on the words: *And a certain man said to him: Lord, are they few that are saved? But he said to them: Strive to enter by the narrow gate...* (Luke XIII, 23-4), he says:

> The Lord seizes the opportunity provided by the question He is asked to teach how salvation is to be reached, and at the same time His response satisfies the question by indicating that there will be few who attain salvation: *For many shall seek to enter and shall not be able.*[483]

6. ALFONSO SALMERÓN S.J. (1515-1585)

On the text of Matthew XXII, 13 concerning the heavenly wedding feast he concludes:

> The guest expelled from the feast is the model of all those who having first been invited to the wedding have made themselves unworthy; it follows that the literal sense is that many are called to the fellowship of the heavenly kingdom, and among these many, there are few — in comparison with those called — that are chosen by God, as among them some do not come and others are rejected as unworthy.[484]

7. THOMAS STAPLETON (1535-1598)

> *For many are called but few are chosen.* This is a moral text concerning the fewness of the saved, useful for arousing fear.... This entire passage, so salutary for maintaining us in fearfulness derives almost its entire force from the contrast between the immense multitude of Christians called and the immense fewness of those that are chosen. Hence the Prophet Isaias says in Chapter IX: *Thou hast multiplied the nation, and hast not increased the joy* — but rather fear and sorrow seeing that amid the multitude of peoples who throughout the whole world confess Christ with their lips there are so few that believe with the heart and show forth their faith by good works....
>
> Foreseeing this fewness and wishing to forewarn us of it, Christ said: *And yet the Son of Man when He cometh, shall he find, think you, faith on earth?...* And for the same reason Christ warns us to enter by the narrow

---

[483] *Ibid.*, cap. XC, p. 636.
[484] Quoted by Knabenbauer, *op. cit.*, p. 348.

gate, *for strait is the way that leadeth to life* — not the way of faith but of morals, the way of charity and of the observation of the commandments of God, which is trodden by few; and hence there are few that reach the goal of this way which is heavenly bliss.[485]

8. SEBASTIANUS BARRADIUS S.J.[486] (1532-1615)

The number of the elect is small if compared with the multitude of the damned.[487]

And commenting on the text of the Vulgate, *Many are called but few are chosen* he accumulates the opinions of the ancients:

Saint Gregory: *What follows is very terrible, since many come to faith and few are led on to the heavenly kingdom.* Bede's interpretation is the same. Haymo says: *Many are called through faith, but few are chosen through action.* And the Interlinear Gloss: *Many are called to faith, but few to glory.*[488]

9. FRANCISCUS LUCAS BRUGENSIS[489] (1548-1619)

On Matthew XX:

And lest anyone should object at the last being first and at the exclusion from eternal life of some who have been worshippers and servants of God, He says: Many in every age have been called and shall be called by God to come to His knowledge and worship just as that householder called labourers at any hour of the day to come to serve him in cultivating his vineyard; but few of them are chosen by God for eternal life, i.e. so enriched with the grace of God as to attain to everlasting bliss; just as not all were acceptable to the householder in the parable for him to pour forth his gratuitous generosity upon all.

---

[485] *Promptuarium Morale super Evangelium*, XIXth Sunday after Pentecost; Antwerp, 1593, p. 513.

[486] Also known as Sebastián or Sebastião Barradas. — Translator.

[487] *Itinerarium filiorum Israel ex Ægypto*; Lyon, 1620, vol. V, col. 628.

[488] *Commentaria in Concordiam et Historiam Evangelicam*, lib. I, cap. 17; vol. I, p. 350, col. 1.

[489] Also known as Franz Lucas of Bruges. — Translator.

Moreover Jesus does not only reply that not *all* those who are called are chosen; He says that *few* are. This introduces the consideration of the terrible judgement of God whereby not only from among men in general but specifically from among the called, i.e. upon those who at one time were endowed with right faith in God — whether Christians, Israelites, or those who had faith even before these dispensations — *few are chosen* in comparison with the reprobate of the same dispensation.[490]

10. FRANCISCUS HARÆUS (1555-1632])

This exceedingly learned Doctor of the University of Louvain, write sin his expositions on Matthew XX, 16; following Saint Gregory the Great:

For many indeed come to faith, but to the kingdom of heaven few are led for the greater number seek God in words but shun Him by their deeds.

11. JACOBUS TIRINUS S.J. (1580-1636)

On Matthew XX, 16: *Many are called*, etc.

On the part of God and of Christ, all are called. Matthew XI, 28: *Come unto me, all...*; and in fact many indeed follow that call to faith and to justice.

But *few* are *chosen* unto eternal glory, for *by far the greater part* do not obey the call and refuse to come, while of those who *do* come many again turn back; hence it is that *very many, in comparison with those that perish*, shall be found at the end of time to have been selected for heavenly glory.[491]

12. CORNELIUS A LAPIDÈ S.J.[492] (1567-1637)

This learned exegete is praised in the following terms by the Pope Benedict XIV, himself both learned and judicious, for his treatment of the question before us: "Above all he handles the issue with con-

---

[490] *Commentarius in Sacrosancta Quattuor Jesu Christ Evangelia*; Antwerp, 1712, vol. I, p. 306.

[491] Antwerp, 1688, p. 952.

[492] Also known as Cornelis Cornelissen van den Steen. — Translator.

siderable erudition and relies on the authority of many Fathers to defend the opinion he sets forth."[493] My compatriot Cornelius proved the common opinion of the Fathers and the theologians in more than one place, of which the most celebrated is his commentary on Numbers XIV, 30. But I deliberately refrain from appealing to it, because Fr. Castelein demands a *learned* reply: "I shall have no difficulty in replying to my contradictors. I only want their attack to be *learned* and precise." (*Introduction*, p. XI) And the passage in question does not appear to be sufficiently learned for my adversary. "Whoever consults, for instance, the commentary of Fr. Cornelius a Lapidè on Numbers XIV, 30 will find alleged revelations quite unworthy of credence; the author is undeniably a learned and worthy exegete, but from time to time in his immense labour of compilation his critical sense lets him down. And even admitting the authenticity of the visions he relates, they could *perhaps* be understood of the small number of souls who rise straight to heaven immediately after death." (Footnote to p. 285)

I therefore cite a passage above all criticism, having been praised by Benedict XIV, putting aside the revelations which the critical learning of the Progressives holds in such contempt.

So, on James II, 13: *And mercy exalteth itself above judgment*, Cornelius offers the following illuminating dissertation:

> Some authors, quoted by Bede, explain this passage as meaning, "More are saved by the mercy of God — i.e. those who have themselves shown mercy — than are damned by judgement; there are more elect than reprobate.
>
> With regard to the Angels, this is true....
>
> But of men it is false, *for it is certain* that by far the majority of men are damned, if all men together are included, even pagans, Saracens and heretics.
>
> And both reason and authority seem strongly to suggest that more adult Christians are damned than are saved.

---

[493] *Institutiones Ecclesiasticæ*, XXVII, n. XVIII.

The case based on reason is that by far the greater part of Christians live in mortal sin, and according to the rule of Saint Augustine, a man dies as he has lived so that it is rare for one who has lived badly to die well, and vice versa.

To the objection that all receive the sacraments at the end of life, I reply: not all do, for many die without the sacraments in battles, aboard ship, in mountains or remote villages [to whom in our own day we may add the wicked whose attachment to money and the world keeps them from the sacraments even at the end of their lives, a tribe unknown to Cornelius — Author.]

Moreover, of those who do receive the sacraments, many receive them badly and hence do not expiate their sins, for many labour under crass ignorance of the articles of faith which they are bound to know and believe explicitly, as well as of the sacraments, especially not realising that to be capable of absolution the efficacious purpose of abstaining from sins is required: they have no notion of the strength and constancy of the resolution required for the purpose to be deemed absolute and efficacious.

Others again, although they know what is required for salvation, yet live in carelessness of that salvation, entirely devoted to accumulating riches and honours so that seldom or never do they think of God and eternal life or of their conscience, except at Eastertide, and then only because they are obliged by the precept of the Church to confess and communicate; as soon as Easter is over, they rush back to worldly affairs and immerse, indeed submerge, themselves therein. [Not to mention the thousands who do not even communicate at Easter! For in our day the proportion who respect this precept at Brussels and in other places of little piety is, of women, a quarter and of men just five percent, including practically no public school-masters – and what is to become thereafter of the pupils taught by such men? — Author]

Some are held back by sins of usury or simony or by unjustly acquired goods that they refuse to restore.

Others have mistresses or are so embroiled in obscene loves that they cannot free themselves for they have no serious wish to be so freed.

Others again foment quarrels, fights and undying enmities.

Many again, although they know that an efficacious purpose is required for absolution, yet make no effort to obtain and maintain such a purpose, but pretend to have it and may even deceive themselves into believing that they have it.

For this serious purpose is a demanding, lofty and difficult affair, whereas many refuse to do violence to themselves and to strive with all their strength for something so arduous, especially in sickness and at the hour of death, when a man's reason, judgement, senses and strength are weakened and sedated so that the habit of so many years makes the resolution they make at death no better than they made each Easter, namely superficial, merely verbal and quite without force.

This is the very opposite of the notion of those "good deaths" prepared for by empty faith, of which Fr. Castelein exclaims: "Ah, how pleasing is such faith to God! How many good deaths it prepares, notwithstanding the infidelities of life!" (p. 62)

I have no idea where anyone will find, among senior missionaries and pastors of souls, that priest who "has thousands of times witnessed these good deaths." (*Ibid.*) Daily experience confirms the doctrine of the pious and learned Cornelius and the well known proverb "*Qualis vita, finis ita*" — as life, so death.

But let us return to Cornelius, who continues as follows:

For the just chastisement that befalls the sinner is that he who in life was forgetful of God is himself forgotten in death, say Saint Gregory and Saint Augustine (book III, *de Libero Arbitrio*). It is the just punishment of sin that he who *would* not act rightly when he *could* should find that he *cannot* when he *would*.

There are various signs from which it can be inferred that many lack this firm purpose.

The first is that they elicit their resolution casually, but once a year, at Paschaltide in order to accomplish the confession they are obliged to; so that their purpose is rather a matter of constraint and necessity than free and spontaneous. Hence they swiftly return after their Easter confession to their avarice, vices and sins, as many also return to them after a confession made in danger of death if they escape the danger and get better — and this relapse is a sign that the purpose of amendment was forced and wrenched from a reluctant heart rather than sincere and serious.

The second sign is that many have bad habits, such as drunkenness, fornication etc., which they refuse to give up. Or even if they want to give them up they do not use the remedies needed to rid themselves of vices so deeply-rooted. And beyond all other vices, lust and pride everywhere dominate in men and between them these two most powerful vices fill hell.

And the third is that many hold principles of a political or vicious nature which are directly opposed to this firm purpose and in which they have been raised from infancy, have grown up and continue to live, e.g. the supposed duty to avenge wrongs suffered by oneself or one's family, under pain of disgrace and infamy; to accept a duel if challenged, rather than be dishonoured; to drink, on social occasions, as many draughts as one's companion, thereby becoming intoxicated; to look after one's prospects and those of one's children and family, making every endeavour to keep intact or increase one's condition and honour, taking no account of the laws of God or His Church if they stand in the way; to protect one's life and fortune against all comers irrespective of God's commandments; not to bear insult, calumnies or blows without returning like for like. Such dictates and principles as these are very often in their thoughts and renewed in their intentions, never being put aside even in the confessional, for if they are explicitly asked about them by the confessor they reply that they mean to persist in them, for where honour, money or convenience are involved they care neither for conscience nor for God nor for hell.

But these intentions, habitually and even virtually remaining in their souls, are diametrically opposed to the serious purpose of avoiding all sins and obeying God's laws in all things.

The following words are worthy of special attention on the part of certain modern writers and preachers:

Often preachers fail to teach, explain and inculcate these things; they content themselves with recommending to sinners the Passion of Christ, the mercy of God, generous almsgiving and devotion to Our Lady who will not let her devotees perish, but they do not address in detail the specific vices of this or that place so as to denounce them and eradicate them, which is why cities and peoples remain in the same evil laws, customs, intentions and vices and gain little or no fruit from all the sermons they hear.

Fourthly, albeit some of those who confess when dying elicit a true purpose of amendment, yet if they are spared for a few days after confession, as often happens, the memory of their past evil desires returns and solicits the soul which of old used to wallow in them to relapse in intention, consenting to evil thoughts and morose delectation concerning the illicit pleasures of their past lives to which they had been accustomed; especially as the devil habitually chooses that moment to present such thoughts to the mind and to reawaken the old attachment, attacking a man most grievously during the final battle right up to the final tearing apart of soul and body, all of which is permitted by a just judgement of God to punish the sins and neglect of those who took no trouble to mortify such inclinations when they were hale and hearty, rather indulging them as the horse and the mule, and this causes many to succumb and perish as is shown by many undeniable examples.

Fifthly, virtue, salvation and heavenly glory are sublime and arduous, far above all our natural powers, whereas human nature is corrupted by sin and utterly cast down to earthly things so keen are its earthly affections and desires for riches, honours, conveniences and pleasures that it can scarcely apprehend or grasp heavenly things, much less lift itself towards them and strive with all its strength to rise to them.

For although man is aided by the grace of God, yet this grace in fallen man is like to medicine in a man that is sick and prostrated and hence is scarcely able to raise him up, and if it does raise him he easily collapses and falls again. For which reason, in the general corruption of nature, it is easy for anyone amid so many occasions and temptations of the flesh, the world and the devil, to fall into some mortal sin, but to rise again from it by penance and an efficacious purpose of amendment is arduous and exceedingly difficult. But these are two causes and as it were two poles around which turns the nub of this issue, viz. the great number of the damned and the fewness of the saved. There is much truth in Saint Justin's pithy reflection: "The soul is hard to recall to good things from which it has fallen away, neither is it easily extricated from the evils to which it has become accustomed."

In truth it was the weight of these reasons and their own experience which moved such wise men as our own Benedictus Justinianus[494] to change their minds, so that having originally taken the view that the majority of Christians are saved, he modified his position on this subject, judging that more are damned.

At Rome I have heard many take the same view and among them a certain celebrated teacher and preacher recently declared everywhere

---

[494] Benedetto Cardinal Giustiniani S.J. (1554-1621), author of several biblical commentaries. — Translator.

that confessions made by sinners when close to death after a bad life are worse than those made in the whole of their previous life.

Indeed Saint Augustine also, in his Sermon 57 *de Tempore*, says, "Nor let him nourish the hope of seeking repentance at the very end of his life when he can no longer do penance. Such a persuasion is in vain." And a little later: "So the penance sought by a sick man is sickly and the penance asked for by a dying man is itself, I fear, liable to die. This is why, dearly beloved, whoever would find the mercy of God must do penance in the present world while he is in health so that he may be in health in the world to come." and again in Homily 41 of 50: "He who does penance and is reconciled, if he then quits this life feeling confident, I am not confident for him." And he explains that, "If you wish to do penance when you can sin no more, it is not you who have abandoned your sins but your sins that have abandoned you. Choose what is sure, therefore, and reject what is unsure." His doctrine is the same in Sermon 24 *de Verbis Domini secundum Lucam*: "Live well, lest you die ill."

And Cornelius adds:

The same reasons convince me that although in some towns and places and where the people are of good character and education,[495] i.e. where there are outstanding schoolmasters, pastors, confessors, senators and governors who assiduously instruct, nurture and encourage the people in faith and piety from their earliest years, we may well believe that more are saved, yet in many others, where all this is wanting, i.e. where bad native character is nurtured and strengthened by *bad education* or company, I would opine or fear that more are damned than saved.

Next comes the voice of authority. He cites first the fourth Book of Esdras, adduced also by Suárez and Gonet, in which it is expressly stated that "Many indeed have been created, but few shall be saved." And he notes that "this book, although not canonical, yet has its authority."

After which he moves on to the well-known arguments from the Scriptures and the Fathers, before citing Alphonsus Mendoza who, using much the same reasoning, abundantly proves that the number

---

[495] A highly relevant precision in the light of the socialist education dispensed in the "neutral" schools of Belgium. — Author.

of the predestinate is exceeded by that of the reprobate. And then, in his customary way, this pious and learned interpreter offers a moral, i.e. a conclusion of practical spirituality:

These arguments and this judgement ought to inspire each of us with a lively fear and holy dread as to his own salvation, so that he may, as the Apostle says, work out his salvation with fear and trembling; let each one of us also seriously search his conscience and if he should find therein principles and dictates opposed to salvation let him thoroughly cast them aside and withdraw himself in word and deed from the excessive love of riches and honours, generously resist his inclinations, attach himself entirely to the Lord and to the Law of God, preferring rather to suffer all than to lose all, and preferring a thousand times to die than to offend Him or to lose His grace and friendship.

For when so many, even of Christians, are damned and so few saved, who would not fear, who would not strive to be among the few, who would not make every effort to avoid the perils to salvation and to secure that salvation by every means?

For we have but one soul, not several. Whosoever you may be that read this, think on these things. Live for God and live for eternity.[496]

13. Cornelius Jansenius[497] of Leerdam
Bishop of Ypres (1585–1638)

Enter by the narrow gate. — By the strait and narrow way is understood the path of virtue, first because it is prescribed by the terms of the divine law and especially of the Christian law hitherto passed down, so that it does not allow a man to wander astray whether to left or to right in order to satisfy any disorderly inclination, and secondly because it is hard to follow — not of itself, for it is highly adapted to our nature — but because of the proneness of corrupt nature towards all that is sensible, from which it is difficult to hold it back, and also because there is only *one* such way, from which it is not permitted to depart by so much as a hairsbreadth.

But because all our inclinations over the whole range of vices tend to become corrupted whether by excess or by defect, it is said that *wide is*

---

[496] Cornelius a Lapidè: *Commentary* on James II, 13.

[497] Also known as Corneille Janssens. — Translator.

the gate and broad is the way that leadeth to destruction, i.e. the way of iniquity, *and many there are that go in thereat*, and thereby advance in the direction of eternal damnation. For the majority of men are bewitched by ease and are readier to do what they enjoy than what they ought.

Hence it is that our Saviour adds, in a tone of astonishment, *How narrow is the gate and strait is the way that leadeth to life and few there are that find it*; yea and fewer still who tread it and very few indeed who persevere on it to the end, as Jerome remarks both in commenting on this passage and in Book II of his dialogue against the Pelagians. For no Philosophers, heretics, Turks or Pagans find it, no bad Catholics enter by it and few that are good reach its end. By contrast the broad way is exceedingly easy, for no guide is needed save error itself and departure from the strait way, which may occur in countless ways. The very pagans saw this same truth by the light of nature ....

Since Christ has said that the right way is hard to find and in fact is found by few, so that some guide ought to be sought, He adds very appropriately that guidance ought not to be indiscriminately sought from anyone: *Beware of false prophets*, ...[498]

What Jansenius teaches here is perfectly Catholic and approved.

14. LIBERTUS FROMONDUS[499] (1587-1653)

It is certain that out of the entire human race more are damned than saved. And if we count even apostates and heretics among Christians, though they falsely bear that name, far more Christians will be damned than saved.

Among the true faithful who die in the Catholic Church and faith, Saint Augustine and other holy Fathers infer from various scriptural passages that more are damned than saved.

And although it is perhaps true that the majority of the faithful do not die without the Sacrament of Penance the greater part of the worldly do not receive the fruit of this Sacrament for they lack the sincere detestation of their sins and the efficacious purpose of amendment necessary for justification; for a very great grace of God is needed for men long attached to riches, honours, pleasures and the other things of this world suddenly to rise from such an abyss to the sublime heights of penance —

[498] Mechlin, 1825, vol. I, p. 106.
[499] Also known as Libert Froidmont. — Translator.

as is well and abundantly proved against Suárez by Cornelius a Lapidè in his commentary on this passage, wherein he mentions that even in Rome he had heard several theologians say the same thing on account of the general corruption of morals and laxity of living.[500]

15. Joannes Stephanus Menochius[501] S.J. (1575–1655)

Commenting on Matthew XXII, 14, he says:

This conclusion *For many are called but few are chosen*, is to be referred to the whole of the preceding parable in which we see that many were in fact called, *but few came*, and of those that came *not all were chosen*.

16. Nicolas Talon S.J. (1605–91)

Here is an extract taken from Fr. Talon's *L'Histoire Sainte du Nouveau Testament*:[502]

Enter by the narrow gate, for wide is the gate and broad is the way that leadeth to perdition and many there are that go in thereat. (Matthew VII, 13)
Tauler,[503] whose virtue gave no cause for disquiet, could hardly ever think of these words without shuddering, and when one day he had to preach on them he began his sermon by shedding tears ... and thereby bore witness to his inward conviction of the fewness of those who tread the path of virtue...

Talon then evokes various symbols representing the narrow gate of paradise, before concluding:

All these things are figures of the fewness of the saved, of which we find yet more explicit prophecies in Isaias.

---

[500] *Commentarius in Omnes Epistolas Pauli Apostoli et Septem Catholicas*, on James II, 13; Louvain, 1678, p. 473, 2.
[501] Also known as Giovanni Stefano Menochio. — Translator.
[502] Vol. I (*Vie agissante de Jésus-Christ*), cap. LII: "L'assurance du Salut dans la voie etroite," p. 243.
[503] John Tauler, c. 1300–1361, a German Dominican and one of the greatest mystics of the Middle Ages. — Translator.

After citing various scriptural passages and the gravest testimony of several Fathers, he observes: "This is the belief of all the Fathers of the Church."

17. BERNARDINUS A PICONIO[504] O.F.M. CAP. (1633–1709)

Many are called to salvation, for there is no one that is not so called, but few are found worthy to be numbered among the elect.[505]

Few are chosen, because the rest refused the invitation.[506]

For many are called, indeed all, but few are chosen, i.e. few are those who being once called comply with their calling and persevere holily therein.[507]

And commenting on Matthew VII, 13 and 14: *Enter ye in at the narrow gate: for wide is the gate, and broad is the way that leadeth to destruction, and many there are who go in thereat. How narrow is the gate, and strait is the way that leadeth to life: and few there are that find it!* He says:

Enter by the narrow gate; choose to advance *with the few* towards this happiness; avoid the path which leads, *with the many*, to eternal perdition.

Broad is the way that leadeth to destruction, and many there are who go in thereat. This is the way of the multitude who follow the character and customs of the world as their rule of life, giving free rein to the lusts of corrupt nature.

How narrow is the gate and strait is the way …! These seemingly astonished words show that no one can widen this narrow way which alone leadeth to heavenly glory.

Finally in commenting on Luke XIII, 24, Fr. Bernardin answers in advance the objection of our Progressives who claim that Christ's exhortation *Strive to enter by the narrow gate* concerns only the Jews of

---

[504] Also known as Bernardin de Picquigny. — Translator.

[505] *Triplex expositio in Sacrosancta Domini Nostri Jesu Christi Evangelia*, on Matthew XX, 6.

[506] *Ibid.*, note.

[507] *Ibid.*, XXII, 14, paraph.

the time of the Messiah and has no connection with the Christians of later centuries:

> This most unhappy lot foretold to the Jews by Christ is a prophetic warning of future eternal woe made to Christians who refuse to lead a life in conformity with the Gospel.

18. NATALIS ALEXANDER O.P. (1639-1724)[508]

In his Exposition of the Literal Sense of Matthew VII, he says:

> This narrow way is found or followed by few, for they do not judge rightly as to the ends of things and the ways to attain those ends, nor do they make the efforts needed to be able to judge these matters rightly, for their power of right judgement is depraved by their perverse affections and unbridled concupiscence.

Then, speaking of the wide gate and broad way, he continues:

> Many there are who go in thereat and thus advance towards damnation. For the majority of men are seduced by their perverse inclinations, the customs pomps and evil examples of the world [notwithstanding Fr. Castelein's denial!] and the temptations of the devils [which Fr. Castelein seems to have overlooked!] and choose this path.[509]

On Matthew XX, For many are called but few are chosen, he comments:

> Many are called to faith and charity from without by the preaching of the Gospel and from within by the action of grace, but few of them are chosen to reign with Christ.[510]

And on Matthew XXII:

> Many are called in the sense that they indeed obey the voice that calls and come to the wedding feast, but few are chosen to take part in that feast and be counted among the friends of the Groom.[511]

And on Like XIII:

---

[508] Also known as Noël Alexandre. — Translator.

[509] Expositio Sancti Evangelii secundum Mattheum, 1703, col. 166-167.

[510] *Ibid.* col. 553.

[511] *Ibid.* col. 590.

There are few who are saved in comparison with the many who shall perish.[512]

19. ANTOINE AUGUSTIN CALMET O.S.B. (1672-1757)

Dom Calmet follows the common understanding of the Holy Fathers in interpreting the text whose meaning the Progressives are so keen to alter:

> It has always been a great question whether the number of the saved is great. But in the whole Gospel Our Lord Jesus Christ shows that the number of the elect is small and that the door of heaven is narrow and found by very few, while the path that leads to it is strait and arduous so that not many follow it to the end.[513]

20. FRANÇOIS DE LIGNY S.J. (1709-89)

On Matthew VII, 13:

> Our Lord Jesus Christ formally declares that the majority will be prevaricators and that *the number of faithful observers will be incomparably smaller;* that thus His law must be heard and observed to the letter, or, to explain in practical terms, it is only in the *practice of the small number* that the true meaning should be sought.[514]

And on Matthew XX, 16:

> It is as if Christ said: you seem astonished to hear me say that the first shall be sent back to the lowest rank, but how much more astonished ought you to be at the fact that among this great number of men who have been, or are yet to be, called, *very few* will receive the reward.[515]+

---

[512] *Ibid.* col. 1086.

[513] *La Bible en Latin et en Français, avec un Commentaire littéral et critique,* on Luke XIII, 23.

[514] *Histoire de la Vie de Jésus-Christ,* 1824, vol. I, p. 226.

[515] *Ibid.,* vol. II, p. 300, note.

21. LOUIS-CLAUDE FILLION (1843-1927)

Wide is the gate and broad is the way... Here we have a double figure symbolizing the ease, freedom and pleasantness obtained by an unbridled life given up to the passions and to sin. No inconvenient obstacle obstructs the entrance to this path.

... that leadeth to destruction.... But once a man has entered by this gate and followed this easy downward path, where does it lead him? To eternal ruin. And what is sad indeed is that most men nonchalantly or even enthusiastically hasten in this direction : *and many there are who go in thereat!*

How narrow is the gate... This is a symbol of the pains and sacrifices imposed by Christian uprightness well practised... But what is the reward that awaits those who courageously surmount these obstacles? *...that leadeth to life* : eternal life within the bosom of God wherein to rest from their labours. But alas : *few there are that find it.* These words must have been uttered in a tone of deep sadness. In our own days as at the time of Christ and in every era, mankind is divided into two categories : the majority follows the broad way with no thought of the abyss which lies at its end, and the few laboriously ascend the narrow path, taking comfort from the prospect of future joys. *The Fathers and Doctors rightly saw in this passage an argument favouring the view that the number of the elect will be relatively small.*[516]

22. FERNANDUS JOANNES PETRUS GREGORIUS VAN ETTEN O.S.A. (1830-1909)

Fr. van Etten taught Holy Scripture for 25 years in the Society of Jesus. In his exceedingly learned work : *Het Leven van Onzen Goddelijken Verlosser,*[517] he holds as manifest and unquestionable that the number of the elect, although great in itself, is yet less, in comparative terms, than the number of the reprobate.

Here are his words :[518]

---

[516] *Évangile selon Saint Matthieu,* VII, 13 and 14 ; 1878, p. 146.

[517] I.e. *The Life of our Divine Redeemer.*

[518] Fr. Godts, a Fleming writing in Belgium, quotes Fr. Van Etten in the original Flemish. — Translator.

Few are they who find it! By this statement Jesus certainly does not indicate that the number of those who will be saved, taken absolutely, is small. No! He is here speaking in comparative terms, as appears from the contrast: *Broad is the way that leadeth to destruction, and many there are that go in thereat.* His meaning is that the number of those who walk the path of renunciation and live accordingly, although in itself not small, must nevertheless rightly be considered small in comparison with the large crowd that is complacently advancing along the path whose destination is everlasting destruction.[519]

And he repeats this when commenting on Matthew XXII, 16: *Many are called,* etc.[520]

23. FR. HENRY JAMES COLERIDGE S.J.[521] (1822–1893)

On Matthew VII, 14:

This doctrine which naturally emerges from Our Lord's words, that the majority of men follow the path of perdition may seem harsh and discouraging; there is no shortage of thoughtful minds who strive to escape the conclusions which appear to flow from it.[522] ... Our Lord tells us that the immense influence of the majority of the men we live among is added to out own weakness and to our evil inclinations to lead us on. We shall always have the crowd against us: the example of the crowd has always held back, and continues to hold back, many souls in the pursuit of perfection. It is the example of the multitude among Catholics which ever provides a pretext for those outside her fold not to enter it. It is the example of the multitude of so-called Christians that closes the hearts of millions of unbelievers to the evidence of the Gospel.[523]

And speaking of the monasteries this pious author adds:

---

[519] Part II, p. 94.

[520] *Ibid.*, p. 239.

[521] The distinguished and learned English convert priest Fr. Coleridge is the author of what is perhaps the most detailed life of Our Lord in existence in the many volumes of his *Life of Our Life.* — Translator.

[522] *La Vie de notre Vie,* vol. VII, p. 300. The quotation has been retranslated into English from the French version used by Fr. Godts.— Translator.

[523] *Ibid.*, p. 306.

Yes, there too the example of the multitude sometimes becomes in-imical to perfection.... These neglects in so high a vocation ... suppose a want of fidelity and of correspondence with grace of which it is impossi-ble to foresee all the consequences.[524]

And on Luke XIII, 24 he writes:

The meaning assuredly seems to be that those who enter by the nar-row gate are few in number while the majority follow the broad way which leads to destruction. [525]

24. CANON FRANÇOIS CORNELIUS CEULEMANS S.T.D. (1856-1918)

This solid Professor of Sacred Scripture in the Seminary of Mech-lin comments as follows on Matthew VII, 14: *Few there are that find it.*

The broad way is ever to hand, but the narrow way must be diligently sought out: it is the way that leads to eternal life, but there are few who find it and follow it. From these words of Christ it may be inferred that the number of the reprobate will be much greater than that of the saved, at least in the context of the whole of mankind. The proportion of the saved among Christians or Catholics alone is more doubtful. [526]

25. JOSEPH KNABENBAUER S.J. (1839-1911)

The gainsayers are not slow to proclaim loudly that this most celebrated and learned interpreter stands for the opinion that the majority are chosen.[527] Let the reader judge for himself of the credi-bility of this claim.

---

[524] *Ibid.*, p. 307.

[525] *Ibid.*, vol. XIII, p. 158.

[526] *Op. cit.*, p. 82.

[527] "It is strange that both the most learned exegetes of the present century, Mgr. Beelen and Fr. Knabenbauer, had no suspicion of this...." (Fr. Castelein, 2nd edi-tion, p. 64); "The commentaries of *a certain number* of Holy Fathers did not place any constraint on the two most erudite exegetes of the century, Mgr. Beelen and Fr. Knabenbauer, for they adopted quite a different interpretation." (Fr. Castelein, letter to *Le Patriote*, March 1899); "The objections, which I grant to be very nu-merous, drawn from the writings of the Fathers ... did not prevent our century's

First, writing on the text of Matthew VII, *Few there are that find it*, he speaks of the fewness of those that obtain salvation:

The difficulty of this affair is also shown by the fact that *there are few that find it*. Hence it must be sought solicitously, i.e. salvation must be worked out with fear and trembling.

And when He says *few there are*, Chrysostom says that He is manifesting the sloth of the many, and instructing His listeners to pay no attention to the prosperity of the crowd, but rather to heed the labours of the few: do not attend to the multitude nor be troubled by them, but imitate the few.

Hence what matters is not to travel in company but to choose the right destination. If you consider the time when Christ was speaking indeed there were not many out of the whole of mankind who carefully respected the law of nature written on their souls and kept themselves from illicit pleasures and other vices and sins. Among the Jews themselves the Pharisees and Scribes, despite their ostensible zeal for the law, were polluted with many sins (cf. Matthew XXIII, 3 et seqq.). And what of the others such as the Sadducees and Herodians who rejected the law to take the side of foreigners? And what of the masses? See Matthew XI, 21 *et seq.*; XXIII, 37; Luke XIII, 2-5, etc. So it is truly said "*Few there are…*" And what of our own days? What of the whole course of the centuries? The words of Saint Jerome remain true: "The broad way is the pleasure of the world which men are attracted to; many tread the broad way while few find the narrow way; the broad way is not sought and does not need to be found as it spontaneously confronts all and is the way of those who go astray. But not all find the narrow way, neither do those who find it at once enter on it, for many, having once found the way of truth, yet being ensnared by the pleasures of the world, turn back in mid-journey." Christ teaches: if thou wilt enter into life, keep the commandments.[528] For they are the narrow gate and way, but it is hard

---

two most learned exegetes, Mgr. Beelen and Fr. Knabenhauer S.J., from interpreting the famous text ['Many are called but few are chosen'] quite differently from how it was interpreted over long centuries." (Fr. Castelein, letter to the *XXe Siècle*, March 1899); and the same claim is made by his champion "E.T." in his letter to *Le Patriote* of 19th March 1899. It is true that Fr. Knabenbauer is here interpreting Matthew VII and not XX or XXII, but his opinion is nonetheless clearly contrary to that of Fr. Castelein and he certainly does not depart from the common opinion of the Saints.

[528] Cf. Matthew XIX, 17.

for a carnal man to walk in complete fidelity to the divine commandments (Salmerón), and how many, think you, of the whole human race embark with constancy upon that path? Is it not few?

Such is the teaching of Knabenbauer.[529]

26. JOSEPH FRANZ ALLIOLI (1793-1873)

Fr. Allioli lectured in oriental languages and held the chair of exegesis and archaeology as well as producing a German version of Holy Scripture with initial notes. Commenting on Matthew XX, 16, *Many are called but few are chosen*, he remarks:

> Many, indeed all, are called by God to His kingdom, but only a small number reach eternal happiness. This pronouncement of divine Wisdom "Many are called but few are chosen," may be set alongside this other, "And thus the last shall be first and the first shall be last." There is nothing surprising in the idea that first shall be last and last first, as the Parable continually inculcates, for it happens even that some who are not at all received, are nothing at all, for many do not correspond with their vocation or do not cooperate faithfully with it, from which it follows that there are relatively few who reach beatitude. (Suárez).

And on Matthew XXII, 14, he says:

> In consequence we may say that in general, considering mankind as a whole, the number of those that are chosen for everlasting bliss is small.[530]

27. JEAN-ALOIS VAN STEENKISTE (1830-1913)

The relevant work of this celebrated exegete and Professor of Sacred Scripture in the Seminary of Bruges is entitled *Sanctum Jesu Christi Evangelium secundum Matthæum*.[531]

---

[529] 1892 edition, p. 298.

[530] 1855 edition, p. 135 *et seqq.*

[531] I.e. *The Holy Gospel of Our Lord Jesus Christ According to Matthew*, third edition, carefully revised and doubled in size, 1880, nn. 267 and 268.

The passage of Matthew VII, 13-14 concerning the narrow gate and the strait way provides this celebrated author with the opportunity to examine in detail what he calls "the scriptural question *concerning the number of the elect*". "On the present occasion," he says, "the general topic will be addressed: What is taught in Holy Writ, and especially in the Gospel, concerning the *small* or *smaller* number of the elect?

He poses the question from various angles and adduces various texts:

> 1. It is twice stated that *many are called but few are chosen.*
> Granted the context is favourable to the opinion of those[532] who think that in both places the reference is to election to faith and grace, *but* other statements of Christ taken together suggest that *election to glory*, or *predestination to heaven* is included. And *although* Christ *adapts His statement to the Jews of His day*, yet we understand the words to be of general application, for a declaration which specifically concerns a certain group may at the same time express a general truth.

This is a question, gentle Reader, that we shall soon be examining.

> 2. On two occasions mention is made of the *narrow gate that leadeth to life* and of *the few* that *go in thereat*: Matthew VII, 14 and Luke XIII, 24. While Luke attests that these words of Our Lord Jesus Christ are *adapted* to the Jews of His time, yet the *very broad* meaning that the same words bear in Matthew *is not thereby excluded.*
> 3. In the Parable of the Sower, *only one quarter* of the grain bear fruit, which suggests that even after the coming of Christ and under the New Testament *the good will be fewer*. Hence the words of I John V, 19 will always be true, even to the end of time: *The whole world is seated in wickedness.*

The author then makes various other comparisons between those *who are saved by Christ* and those *who on account of original sin are cast into hell...*

> Finally, in speaking of those *who are disciples of Christ*, he continues:

---

[532] I.e. of the adversaries of what is maintained in the present study. — Author.

4. In several of the parables the Church is described so as to make the good seem more numerous than the bad ....

And the author goes on in this way to treat of the proportion of the elect *among all Catholics, among all adult Catholics, to the exclusion of heretics*. Then finally he speaks of the opinion that the number of the elect is small *in absolute terms*, as Massillon argued:

5. However it may be, I have no intention of reducing the number of the elect, among truly Catholic adults, so far as Massillon did in his famous sermon *On the Fewness of the Elect*.

Having thus posed what he terms the *general question*, he states no positive conclusion about what is taught in Holy Scripture as to the small, or smaller, number of the elect, contenting himself with the statement that "We know nothing," before adding:

I conclude therefore that we know little and that it is not in our interests to know. For there is one thing that really matters, namely, however narrow the gate may be, at least to strive to enter by it.

He had already said on the preceding page:

From the words of Christ it may be concluded *as certain* that at the end of the word the multitude of the reprobate will be denser than the happy flock of the elect. This is the common and true opinion, as Suárez says.[533]

Now let us turn to the specific passage of Q. 458 to which the Author refers his readers to clarify *what is known*, granted that "we do not know much". There he clearly explains himself with regard to the remarks made under N° 1 above and explicitly poses this question: "Is it possible to conclude *as certain* from the words *Many are called, few are chosen,* that the number of the Saints in heaven is less than the number of the damned?" To which he replies:

On this subject I have already made some remarks above in Questions 267 and 268 [quoted above]. The reply *on the basis of the interpretation here adopted* is that it is right to conclude that *the number of the elect or of the*

---

[533] *Loc. cit.*, p. 386. q. 267.

blessed is inferior. The objection is made, of course, that this opinion does not fit in with the two parables which close with the statement *Many are called but few are chosen*. To which I answer that the first of these parables is intended to show that the labourers of the eleventh hour, i.e. the Gentiles, are better off in the kingdom of Heaven from which many Jews are excluded. And in the second, while only one is *cast out*, there are many who do not enter in the first place. [534]

In this context allow me to say as clearly as possible that I fully grant that the *primary intention* of these texts and the *specific lesson* they aim to teach is not *strictly demonstrative* in favour of my position, while fully agreeing with Van Steenkiste that their *secondary meaning*, also truly intended, makes this position at least *completely certain*. It is therefore right to conclude that "we know little…," while going on to add that *we can conclude with certainty* that the number of the Saints in heaven is less than of the damned. So speak John of Saint Thomas and many others.

It is worth observing too how this author understands the interpretation of the celebrated Mgr. Beelen, [535] not concerning the first passage — Matthew XX, 16 — but the other, to wit Matthew XXII, 14, for his words fully confirm what I have said about that Louvain Doctor.

What is the meaning of the closing words of the parable, *Many are called but few are chosen*? It is replied that Lucas Brugensis, [536] Klofutar and Beelen refer them to the last part of the parable, making them mean that among the Gentiles called to the faith few will be *chosen* (or *elect*) in the strict sense, i.e. will be admitted to heaven, and therefore *even among Catholics* belonging to the true Church of Christ *the number of the blessed will be less than of the damned.* [537]

---

[534] *Ibid.*, pp. 740-742.

[535] See below for more information about this distinguished exegete.

[536] Also known as François-Luc de Bruges (1552-1619). — Translator.

[537] *Sanctum Jesu Christi Evangelium secundum Matthæum*; 3rd edition, 1880, p. 799.

Van Steenkiste rounds off his presentation on this subject by asking what was Christ's intention in proposing this parable. He answers:

> R. It seems to me that His primary aim is to teach that *the Jews* are to be excluded from Christian salvation for their obstinacy and indeed severely punished, the Gentiles being substituted for them. But His *secondary aim* lies in the closing part of the parable, by which it is signified that not all who embrace the Faith and enter the Church will be saved, for in addition to faith, the state of grace, i.e. a holy life, is required for salvation.[538]

28. LEONARDUS KLOFUTAR[539] (1819-1901)

This Doctor of Sacred Theology and public and ordinary Professor of New Testament Biblical Studies in the Ljubljana diocesan Institute of Studies, adviser to the episcopal consistory and synodal examiner, has made use of the best sources and resources, i.e. of the works on Holy Scripture that have emerged from the presses of Germany *in our own times*, e.g. those of August von Berlepsch, François-Xavier Patrizi, Peter Schegg, August Bisping, Wilhelm Reischl, Joseph Langen, Joseph Franz Allioli, Johann Hyacinth Kistemaker, Franz Xaver Massl, Adalbert Maier, Jordan Bucher, Christian Gottlieb Kühnöl, Wilhelm de Wette, Ernst Friedrich Karl Rosenmüller, Karl Wieseler, Josef Heinrich Friedlieb, etc.

Fr. Klofutar is therefore far from ignorant of modern exegetes and has carefully studied their methods of interpretation, giving us the mind of the moderns in a nutshell. And if the reader will kindly read what he has to say on the subject we are studying, in commenting on Matthew XX, 16 and XXII, 14 and Luke XIII, 23, he will see that it fully confirms the case made in the present book. First come his words on the text *Many are called but few are chosen*.

---

[538] *Ibid.*, p. 800.

[539] Also known as Leonhard Klofutar S.T.D., mitred provost of the cathedral of Ljubljana in present-day Slovenia. — Translator.

These words are usually explained as meaning that many are called to eternal happiness but not chosen for it because they fail to follow the call. But this explanation is unacceptable. The *chosen* in this passage means the most excellent and outstanding among the called. The fact that the same words, *Many are called but few are chosen*, later occur (XXII, 14) in another sense does not conflict with my explanation because the context is different.

When he comes to comment on this other passage (Matthew XXII, 14): *Many are called but few are chosen*, Fr. Klofutar interprets as follows:

Many are called to the kingdom of the Messiah, i.e. to salvation, yet will be condemned, for there are few who are chosen by God's decree to be truly participants of that salvation in the next life. The reason for what is stated in the first half of this sentence is divine charity which wills the salvation of all; the reason for the second half lies in God's infallible foreknowledge that many will spurn the salvation that is offered them. But when Christ says that *many* are called it would be wrong to infer that not all are called to His kingdom (i.e. to eternal happiness). *All* the called are here referred to as *many* in opposition to the *few* who in fact enjoy that happiness, i.e. they are *many* when compared with the few. Christ's intention here is to stress the great number of the called.

Let us now turn to Fr. Klofutar on the text of Luke (XIII, 23):

Lord, if there are few that are saved?[540] I.e., Lord, are there few who shall obtain eternal happiness, or who shall have part in the consummated reign of the Messiah? For the word σώζω in Scripture is used to refer ... to *salvation by the Messiah in the consummated Messianic Kingdom*, i.e. in eternal happiness. The questioner was undoubtedly a follower of Christ, perhaps moved by the *severity* of what Christ had required of His followers, or by the *reluctance* of men to accept His teaching.

The Greek particle εἰ in a direct question has the same force as the word πότερον, corresponding to Latin *an*, or *num*. To the question posed, Christ replies in this way in order (indirectly) to reveal the *reason*

---

[540] In Greek: εἶπεν δέ τις αὐτῷ, Κύριε, εἰ ὀλίγοι οἱ σωζόμενοι;

why many will not attain salvation and at the same time to *exhort all* to strive by every means to become partakers of this salvation.[541]

II
AN OUTSTANDING MODERN EXEGETE TO WHOM FR. CASTELEIN WRONGLY LAYS CLAIM

We have seen Fr. Castelein twice cite in his favour of his opinion "the two most learned exegetes of our century, Mgr. Beelen and Fr. Knabenbauer S.J."

As to Fr. Knabenbauer, we have already seen[542] his teaching concerning the *fewness* of those who enter the narrow way, so it remains for us to say a word about the celebrated Mgr. Beelen.[543]

The reader is invited to bear in mind in reading what follows that the words "Many are called but few are chosen" appear twice in Saint Matthew's Gospel (XX, 16 and XXII, 14)

On the first passage (XX, 16), the authenticity of which has sometimes been rather adventurously challenged but which should certainly be retained, Mgr. Beelen's exegesis is hesitant and tentative in accepting the explanation of this text as specifically referring to the greater or lesser degree of holiness which Fr. Castelein roundly declares to be its meaning. But he explicitly observes that the second occurrence of the same formula "Many are called but few are cho-

---

[541] *Commentarius in Evangelia Sanctorum Matthæi, Marci, Lucæ et Joannis, concinnatus per Leonardum Klofutar*, Vienna and Ljubljana, 1894.

[542] See N° 25 in the list of exegetes quoted above in the present chapter.

[543] The reference is to Mgr. Ian Theodor Beelen, exegete and orientalist, (1807-1884). After a brilliant course of studies at Rome, crowned by the Doctorate of Theology he was in 1836 appointed Professor of Sacred Scripture and Oriental Languages in the recently reorganized Catholic University of Louvain. This position he held till 1876, when he resigned his place to his pupil, Prof. T. J. Lamy. *The Tablet* (5th April 1884) remarked in reporting his death: "None of those who had the privilege of attending his lectures will ever forget the perfectly Ciceronian Latin which flowed with the grace of a born orator from his lips, combined with the remarkable profundity of interpretation and clearness of explanation which made him one of the foremost expounders of Holy Scripture." — Translator.

sen" in Saint Matthew has a different meaning. Here are his words [originally in Flemish]:

> *Many are called but few are chosen.* This confirms what immediately precedes: *So shall the last be first, and the first last* And its meaning, in this place, seems to be ["de zin is *dunkt mij* deze"] that in general terms among those who are called earlier or later there will be but a few who are chosen or outstanding, i.e. who can be called pre-eminent [in holiness]. But the same statement occurs a second time in chapter XXII, verse 14, *and in that place its meaning is different.* ["In Hoofdst XXII, 14 komt dit gezegde nog eens voor, maar op die plaats heeft het eenen anderen zin."]

And when we turn to Beelen's explanation of what this different meaning of the same words in the second passage is, we find quite simply the common understanding according to which the words *Many are called but few are chosen* apply, in Our Lord's intention, not to the Jews or to those who are to occupy the foremost seats in Heaven, but to those of all kinds who are called to faith and to salvation and to those among them who shall fail to receive the reward at the last judgement:

> *Many are called but few are chosen.* This declaration does not concern the parable [of the guests invited to the wedding banquet] as a whole, but only to verses 9-13 and it is intended to explain Christ's words that *There shall be weeping and gnashing of teeth.*
>
> Now in this part of the parable the subject is the calling of all without distinction, including the Gentiles, to the joys of grace and eternal salvation. The coming of the king symbolizes the general judgement while the man who is cast out represents those who, *although they have been called* to faith and salvation, are yet found without sanctifying grace and ... *shall perish forever.*

Thus the *second* meaning of the formula *Many are called but few are chosen* identified by the celebrated Louvain exegete is quite clear. In Matthew XX, 16 the meaning in his view is that *many are called* ["velen geroepenen"], but *few are of exceptional virtue* ["weinigen uitgelezenen, dat is uitmuntenden"]; but when it appears in Matthew XXII, 14 the same words retain their natural sense: *Many are called,* ["velen zijn geroepenen"], *but few are **elect*** ["*weinigen zijn **uitverkorenen***"].

Moreover in Mgr. Beelen's view these words *Many are called but few are chosen*, when they are connected with the immediately preceding words of Our Lord — *there shall be weeping and grinding of teeth* — state the *reason* for these shrieking throngs. He repeats this point: "This statement, which does not refer to the whole parable, but only to verses 9-13, gives the reason for the words just uttered: *there shall be weeping....*"[544] But could such great bewailing be adequately accounted for by the ejection of a single wedding-guest? Whereas if those who are to perish are seen to be a huge multitude, in comparison with which the others may readily be termed *few*, such lamentations and groanings are easily understood.

From all this the reader will be well able to judge in all gravity and integrity whether Fr. Castelein is really entitled to boast as he does of Beelen's interpretation of the first passage in Matthew when the same celebrated exegete explicitly rejects Fr. Castelein's interpretation with regard to the second, more authentic passage, preferring the common opinion defended in the present work. Note too that this doctrine of Mgr. Beelen's squares perfectly with what he says in his commentary on the Epistles and Gospels for every Sunday of the year. Under Septuagesima Sunday, on I Corinthians IX, 24-X, 5, he warns, with Saint Paul, that to avoid eternal damnation and exclusion from beatitude, religious confession is not enough, for a Christian life holily conducted is also necessary, and he joins forces with all who hold the stricter view by adducing as an example of this the temporal perdition of the people of Israel in the desert, in which the greater part failed to please God and were therefore excluded from the promised land.

And to confirm this truth, he points them now to Israel's ancestors who, although God's people ... nonetheless, for the most part were re-

---

[544] "Deze uitspraak, welke niet op de gansche parabel slaat, maar alleen op v. 9-13, geeft de reden van het *zoo* even gezegde: *daar zal geween zijn.*"

jected and punished God on account of their sins,... All, without exception , enjoyed God's special blessings ; and yet in most of them God had no pleasure ...[545]

What emerges is that Fr. Castelein's appeal to the authority of Knabenbauer and Beelen is cut from the same cloth as his invocation of Saint Alphonsus and Saint Francis de Sales and his assertion that his ideas are "the fruit of a profound study of Holy Scripture and of the teachings of our greatest theologians".[546]

Yes, indeed, this is the Fr. Castelein whose panegyrist "E.T." in all seriousness assures us that "its author evinces great understanding of the Scripture and a solid exegetical learning — an advantage which gives him the right to interpretations which a less well-armed mind would shy away from but whose *wise audacity* is founded on motives which carry conviction to the informed and unprejudiced reader."[547]

[545] Cf. I Corinthians X, 5.
[546] Second edition, Introduction, p. X.
[547] Letter to *Le Patriote*, 19th March 1899.

CHAPTER SIX

EXAMINATION OF THE RESPECT SHOWN BY THE
PROGRESSIVES
TOWARDS THE HOLY FATHERS AND DOCTORS
AND OF
THEIR WAY OF INTERPRETING HOLY SCRIPTURE

HAVING NOW ACQUAINTED OURSELVES with the common opinion of the Fathers, Doctors and Theologians of the Church concerning the fewness of the saved we are equipped to rebut the sophisms of the Progressives.

This task will be divided into two parts for the sake of order, the first and most important of which relates to the authority of the Fathers and the interpretation of Holy Scripture and will be covered in depth in the present Chapter, while the remainder will be addressed more concisely in Chapter VII.

The reader should not suppose, however, that even this orderly two-part analysis will suffice to exhaust all the fallacies of the Progressives. Only the main ones will be refuted while those of lesser importance will be disregarded.

However some other doctrines advanced by Fr. Castelein of a less than edifying character will be highlighted in Chapter VIII and immediately contrasted with authoritative teaching, generally taken from the writings of the Saints.

(1)

The writers of the opposing party with gratuitous and intolerable impudence accuse all the Doctors, Fathers, Theologians and Exegetes of the Church who teach the common doctrine of the fewness of the saved of "Rigorism", "Terrorism", "Pessimism", "Residual Jansenism" and the like.

Here is a collection of extracts evincing this polemical tactic:

"This ancient legacy of Jansenism..." (Fr. Castelein, 2nd edition, p. X) — "A Rigorism that spreads narrow ideas and disquieting prejudices..." (p. 10) — "Away then, you Rigorists, away with your gossamer balances. God has no time for them. We shall need sturdier scales to weigh your Rigoristic, pessimistic, intolerant and despairing arguments." (p. 53) — "The theory of Rigorism holds up only thanks to incredible *confusion* in the order of principles and incredible *exaggeration* in the order of facts." (p. 155) — "Further to such truly inconceivable *confusion* and *exaggerations*, I charge the Rigorists with an omission that is even less admissible on the part of theologians: the omission of the causes of salvation as God has revealed them to us." (p. 157) — "Terrorism which finds no justification in the Gospel..." (p. 304) — "The Rigorism and terrorism that some would impose on us..." (p. 308) — "The Islamic terrorism which all too often seems to inspire our Rigorists... This terrorism, less worthy of God and of man, which does too great violence to our mind and will..." (p. 322) — "Brethren gone astray in the false theories of Rigorism and terrorism ... you prevent the love of Christ from being a *popular* love within His Church. Such is the evil wrought ... by your unhappy doctrine." (p. 352-3)

To whom are these felicitous descriptions applied? Who are these wicked Rigorists and terrorists with their gossamer balances, narrow minds and timorous consciences? Who are these Islam-inspired extremists who sow confusion and exaggeration in their teaching, whose incredible negligence leads them to overlook the very causes of salvation as God has revealed them, who laboriously build up a doctrine of despair and a system of odium which they are unable to prove, etc? These ignorant men are quite simply ... all the Fathers and Doctors of the Church, together with all the theologians and exegetes so extensively and concordantly quoted in the foregoing chapters.

And since we have such warriors in our ranks, let us once more challenge the defenders of the lax opinion to name a single canonized saint who held their view!

There are even some among the gainsayers who claim, believe it or not, that this "Rigorism" of the Saints was invented by the *worldly*! "This doctrine of the fewness of the elect does not result from the severities of the Gospel but of the world. The world sees only evil and the damned on every hand."[548] But if the world is so scrupulous and tender of conscience, why did our Divine Master say: *Woe to the world because of scandals?* (Matthew XVII, 7)

To dismiss these unfounded claims suffice it to say that the Church, *the pillar and ground of truth*, having no truck with either Rigorism or with the spirit of the world, has nevertheless given the fullest approval to the common teaching of the saints and continues to approve it in our own days.

(2)
Does modern exegesis represent great theological progress?

Had the shadows cast by the words *Many are called but few are chosen*, at that time misunderstood owing to still imperfect exegesis, not darkened the penetration of these illustrious doctors… (p. 273)

The solution contrary to our own long prevailed among the doctors owing to a defective interpretation of this celebrated text, now explained quite differently thanks to the *progress* of exegesis. (p. 283)

It is *our* task to make good an immense lacuna! (p. 157)

Brethren gone astray in the false theories of Rigorism and terrorism … *I* do not want you to spoil our Gospel. (p. 352)

Now as a matter of fact I freely admit the existence of *scientific* progress in sacred exegesis in our days, especially thanks to the decipherment of the inscriptions and other antiquities of Nineve, Babylon and ancient Egypt.

---

[548] Bougaud, *op. cit.*, p. 376.

But I am slower to hail *theological* progress in the field of exegesis and I certainly do not think that any of it will come from the Progressive camp, for I am mindful of the words of Leo XIII in the encyclical *Providentissimus Deus* (18th November 1893) concerning scriptural studies:

> The valuable work of the scholastics in Holy Scripture is seen in their theological treatises and in their Scripture commentaries; and in this respect the greatest name among them all is Saint Thomas of Aquin. ... The Professor of Holy Scripture, therefore, amongst other recommendations, must be well acquainted with the whole circle of Theology and deeply read in the commentaries of the Holy Fathers and Doctors, and other interpreters of mark. ... Wherefore the expositor should make it his duty to follow their footsteps with all reverence, and to use their labours with intelligent appreciation.

Sound interpretation of Scripture therefore invariably demands that the greatest respect be shown to venerable Catholic antiquity and wariness of the newfangled interpretations of the Progressives.

But far different is the attitude of the gainsayers, for they think that the ancients were quite unaware of the true interpretation of Holy Writ, were deceived or failed to get to the bottom of the issue – defects they think it is reserved to "*us*" to supply!

> It is *our* task to make good an immense lacuna! (p. 57) *I* do not want you to spoil our Gospel. (p. 352) *For our* part, however, we are no longer shackled by so defective an interpretation. (p. 190) Etc.

I should also like more information about the "exegetical principles currently adopted" — utterly different from the ancient ones — and to know who are the "best exegetes" referred to in the following passage:

> The *true* meaning which *we* have established in the light of the exegetical principles *currently* adopted by the *best exegetes*. (p. 190)

For Leo XIII warns us not to "attach too much weight to certain *new* opinions which ought rather to be *feared*, not because they are new but because for the most part they lead those who embrace them astray, by the appearance and simulation of truth."[549]

Yet Fr. Mauran makes open profession of this very novelty in biblical interpretation.

> A reaction set in against these lamentable doctrines [i.e. those of the entire Middle Ages! — Author].
>
> No doubt our age has its defects, but we must admit that it has its qualities too — I would even say its virtues. Human intelligence appears today to embrace a vaster horizon.
>
> A truer idea and love of the good, the happiness of all, and a more exact notion of eternal justice are taking possession of mankind.
>
> Thus great Christian orators are combating with skill the odious doctrine which abandons the majority of human beings to the abyss of reprobation. Their voice has found an echo on the part of a great many writers and preachers.
>
> I come to take my humble place among them.
>
> True enough my own *thesis*, as I am going to expound it, has some distinctive traits which set it apart. In several respects my treatment adopts a new standpoint.[550]

The Progressives are so blinded by this itch for novelty that they are prompt to oppose the moderns to the ancients, recent scholars to the Doctors of the Church, Saint Alphonsus and Saint Francis de Sales to the ancient Fathers, Lacordaire and Monsabré to our canonized preachers, Beelen and Knabenbauer to the interpreters of centuries gone by, etc. We have already seen how little founded in reality are such alleged oppositions, but they press on, wasting their time in vain hopes, for the unanimous consensus of the Fathers concerning the fewness of the saved brings to naught all the labours of the Progressives.

---

[549] *Breve ad Fratres Minores*, 25th November 1896; Cf. *Nouvelle revue théologique*, vol. XXXI, p. 73.

[550] *Op. cit.*, Introduction, pp. IX and X.

(3)

To believe the moderns, all the texts traditionally used for so many centuries to demonstrate the fewness of the elect in fact prove nothing of the kind.

Although, in days when exegesis was still in its infancy and the use of contexts and parallelisms to reach *the true meaning* of certain elliptical texts was unknown, theologians felt obliged to take the famous proverb *Many are called but few are chosen* in an absolute sense, at least they did not erect this interpretation into a *theological certainty.*

Having no *suspicion* [!] of the *true* meaning which we have established in the light of the exegetical principles [?] currently adopted by the best exegetes, they refrained, for the most part, from a *thorough* treatment of the question. (p. 190)

In other words, the Fathers and Doctors erred in determining the true meaning of these texts!

But how a theologian can dare to advance such things I have no idea. For it has been plainly shown that the consensus of the Fathers and Doctors is unanimous in affirming the fewness of the saved. Anyone who peruses the texts cited above must at once observe that the Fathers base their doctrine, presented as certain and evident, on the interpretation of these very scriptural passages.

In fact the Council of Trent decreed "in order to restrain petulant spirits, that no one, relying on his own skill, shall, in matters of faith, and of morals pertaining to the edification of Christian doctrine, wresting the Sacred Scripture to his own senses, presume to interpret the said Sacred Scripture contrary to ... the unanimous consent of the Fathers..." (Session IV, Decree Concerning the Publication and the Use of the Sacred Books) The same warning was given by Leo XIII in the encyclical *Providentissimus Deus.*

The conclusion is evident and undeniable.

Indeed if what Fr. Castelein says here be once admitted the authority of the Fathers in the interpretation of Holy Writ is over, for anyone may henceforth dismiss their interpretation on the grounds that they did not know the rules of authentic exegesis.

In order to vindicate the authority of the Fathers in interpreting these scriptural passages let us now examine them one by one.

<h1 style="text-align:center">I</h1>

THE NARROW WAY AND THE FEW THAT FIND IT
(MATTHEW VII, 13-14 AND LUKE XIII, 23-24)

Fr. Castelein begins by citing the passage from Saint Matthew, but he immediately adds:

> This passage is reproduced by Saint Luke with a slight variant and an addition at the beginning and at the end. Let us cite the text in Saint Luke's version in order to take full advantage of the light it sheds. (p. 33)

In reality, however, the passage from Saint Luke is *not a reproduction* of the passage from Matthew; the words of Our Lord are indeed *almost the same*, but they were uttered *on a different occasion and under different circumstances*. Thus Fr. Castelein deceives himself and his readers by having recourse exclusively to Saint Luke for the meaning of the passage in Saint Matthew.

<h2 style="text-align:center">(A)</h2>

So let us first take the words of the first Gospel — Matthew VII, 13-14 — in text and context.

The Sermon on the Mount is drawing to its close. This Sermon is a brief presentation of the legislation of the Messianic Kingdom or Church to be founded by Christ And the legislation in question is the perfecting of the legislation of the former Kingdom of Jehovah. *Do not think that I am come to destroy the law, or the prophets. I am not come to destroy, but to fulfil.*[551] It is therefore a more perfect law (Matthew V, 21-48) to be observed in a more perfect way (VI, 1-18) by, among other things, eschewing excessive solicitude for things foreign to the kingdom of God; (19-34) eschewing untimely or misguided concern of the salvation of others (VII, 1-6) and above all by prayer. (7-11) And before passing on to His final exhortations the divine Orator, returning to the opening of the Sermon (V, 17), encapsulates all these

---

[551] Matthew V, 17.

things in a single golden rule: *All things therefore whatsoever you would that men should do to you, do you also to them. For this is the law and the prophets.* (VII, 12)

It is difficult, however, for men such as ourselves, prone as we are to evil, attracted by the blandishments of vice and seduced by so many bad examples, to practise such perfection:

> Nor does Christ deny this; indeed in figurative terms He calls the kind of life He prescribes *a strait way*, as it is hemmed in on both sides by the divine commandments which do not suffer a man to go astray, and *a narrow gate*, which a man cannot enter at except by restraining his nature and pruning back his perverse inclinations. Hence there are few who find and follow it. By contrast the way that leads to eternal perdition is broad; its gate is wide and many are they who go in thereat. But Christ earnestly exhorts His listeners [this is the first part of His closing exhortations — VII, 13] to march energetically along this way, albeit narrow and little-trodden, and manfully to strive to enter by this gate despite its straitness, for it is the one and only entrance to eternal life.[552]

Van Steenkiste poses the pertinent question: "Can it be inferred with certainty from [the texts we are discussing] that the number of those who are predestined to heavenly glory is small?" To which he replies:

> Catholic interpreters, following the Fathers of the Church, rightly teach that these words were not spoken exclusively of Christ's contemporaries but of the entire human race through all the ages of the world, from which they legitimately conclude that the number of those who enter heaven is small in comparison with the multitude who are damned in hell.[553]

---

[552] Liagre, Canon A-J., *Commentarius in Libros Historicos Novi Testamenti, ad locum.* Among the numerous authors who take the same view are Beelen and Knabenbauer: "the two most learned exegetes of our century" according to Fr. Castelein (footnote to p. 64).

[553] *Sanctum Jesu Christi Evangelium Secundum Matthæum,* 3rd edition, p. 385, q. 267, reply to objection 3.

And the same writer, speaking of the interpretation defended in the present pages, though he does not otherwise dwell on it,[554] says that "it would be temerarious to forsake it, on account of the unanimous consensus of the Fathers."

Notwithstanding which, Fr. Castelein teaches:

> This passage[555] would be alarming indeed if its meaning were absolute and its scope universal. But the context clearly proves *that it concerns only the entrance of the Jews of His day into the kingdom of the Messiah.* (p. 34)

To understand this statement it must be noted that the author distinguishes between (i) the "visible kingdom of the Messiah" (footnote to p. 27; p. 35) i.e. the Church, (ii) the "eternal kingdom of the Messiah" (p. 34), by which he understands heaven, and (iii) the "kingdom of the Messiah in its fullest sense" (p. 25) meaning both the Church *and* heaven; but sometimes he simply says "kingdom of the Messiah" (p. 25, footnote to p. 27, p. 34) in which case his meaning must be inferred from the context. In the present case the context shows that heaven is meant. He continues:

> It cannot be maintained, that this image of the narrow way … refers to the Catholic Church and to the faithful. Our Lord Jesus Christ is here depicting the unhappy state of the Jewish people to whom He was preaching His Gospel. This state was one of decadence. The doctors of the law with their vain formalism and inveterate vices were leading the multitude to perdition. They claimed that their dignity of children of Abraham alone sufficed to ensure their entrance into the *eternal kingdom of the Messiah* and that they would be led there via the way and the gate … through which every vice may pass. (p. 34)

---

[554] *Ibid.,* reply to objection 1: "The direct and proper meaning intended [by Our Lord] is entry into the kingdom of God, i.e. the Church; but on another level the reference is to obtaining eternal life in heaven, which is the perfect life, to which *perdition* is strictly opposed." The difference between this explanation and that given above is due, I think, to the fact that the author is giving a united explanation of Matthew and Luke.

[555] Strictly speaking the reference is to Luke X, 23-4, but as he confounds the two passages his words must also be understood to apply to Matthew VII, 13-4 as is clear to any reader of his work.

But surely this restrictive interpretation is not only *temerarious* as it is judged to be by Van Steenkiste, but also *false* and *intolerable*?

In the first place it is *false* and by no means "indicated by every detail of the text and context of Saint Matthew". (p. 34) For it is the *text*, i.e. the words themselves, which indicate the way to eternal life and the opposite way leading to hell or perdition. Concerning the former, Our Lord on another occasion says: *If thou wilt enter into life, keep the commandments*, (Matthew XIX, 17) and "*It is better for thee to go into life maimed or lame, than having two hands or two feet, to be cast into everlasting fire.* (Matthew XVIII, 8) Moreover He does not say in the present passage "many there are *among you* that go in thereby" or "few *of you* there are that find it." He is words are simple and universal: *many*; *few*. Neither does the context suggest such a restriction, any more than the text itself. It is a commonplace among the Fathers and interpreters to call the Sermon on the Mount a brief legislation or the chief heads of the law of the Kingdom of the Messiah (the Church) — a kingdom already preached from the time of John and *borne away* by *violence*,[556] indeed which had already been *borne away* by the new Apostles and other disciples among Christ's listeners. Our Lord is teaching them and all who wish to enter the Church the way in which they are obliged to walk until the end if they will build the house of their salvation upon foundations of rock and enter into the kingdom of heaven. (Matthew VII, 21, 24) This is perfectly evident throughout the Sermon and nothing therein suggests that our Lord's words exhorting men to follow this way despite its difficulty and the fewness of those that tread it should or even could be restricted to His contemporaries.

Turning now to the words of Matthew VII, 15-16 (*Beware of false prophets, who come to you in the clothing of sheep, but inwardly they are ravening wolves. By their fruits you shall know them*), if we are to believe Fr. Castelein these are the only words in the whole Sermon on the Mount which are connected with verses 13-14: (*Enter ye in at the nar-*

---

[556] Cf. *And from the days of John the Baptist until now, the kingdom of heaven suffereth violence, and the violent bear it away.* (Matthew XI, 12)

row gate: for wide is the gate, and broad is the way that leadeth to destruction, and many there are who go in thereat. How narrow is the gate, and strait is the way that leadeth to life: and few there are that find it.)

Hence in the text of Saint Matthew, after saying that there are few that find the true way, He *at once* adds: 'Beware of false prophets, who come to you in the clothing of sheep...' Plainly the Master is here referring to the Pharisees of whom He had said in Matthew V, 20 'For I tell you, that unless your justice abound more than that of the scribes and Pharisees, you shall not enter into the kingdom of heaven.' (p. 35)

But the connection is not so close as the words "He *at once* adds" suggest The words *Beware of false prophets*, etc. relate not so much to the immediately preceding two verses as to the entire discourse to which they constitute a new hortatory epilogue. Let Fr. Knabebauer explain them to us:

In verse 15 Christ points out a further grave danger: *Beware of false prophets...*; since in this Sermon He is expounding the justice of His kingdom and hence speaking not only to His contemporaries but also to the faithful of every age, He is rightly understood here to allude not only to the Pharisees and Scribes (as is held by the Protestant Weiss) but to all those who over the centuries to come shall endeavour to deceive the minds of the faithful and lead them into error.

Next, I have described Fr. Castelein's restriction as *intolerable*. For what is to become of all the moral teachings preached by Our Lord throughout His public life in Palestine, what indeed is to become of the whole of Christian morality, if the words spoken by Christ and the sacred writers are to be understood as restricted exclusively to those to whom they were immediately addressed? As Christ in the Last Supper prayed *not for them only ... but for them also who through their word shall believe in me*, (John XVII, 20) did He not, when teaching, intend His doctrine generally, if not always, for these future believers? Indeed His statements of a moral character are made *directly* for our instruction, not to be philosophized about so that we may merely draw from them consequences of a more or less practical nature which, depending on our whim, may or may not be relevant to us.

No argument against this can be based on the fact that Our Lord in His discourses sometimes addresses Himself directly to the persons present, adapts His teaching specifically to them or develops it according to time, place and other circumstances, for all we preachers surely do the same, without for a moment intending our teaching to be particularized so as to be true only for our immediate listeners.

(B)

We must now examine the remaining passage: Luke XIII, 23-24: *And a certain man said to him: Lord, are they few that are saved? But he said to them: Strive to enter by the narrow gate; for many, I say to you, shall seek to enter, and shall not be able.*

Fr. Castelein informs us that: "The Gospel of Saint Luke places before this forceful declaration [Matthew VII, 13-14] an enquiry which seems to define its meaning and scope: '*Lord, are they few that are saved?*'" (p. 33) But he never in fact explains precisely *how* this question, which in the third Gospel precedes Our Lord's words, determines more clearly their meaning and scope. And in the same way, having promised to set forth all the light shed by this passage, he entirely neglects certain other means ideally adapted to this objective in the present pericope. All of which gives grounds for fear that the explanation of Our Lord's reply provided by the Reverend Father may be the fruit rather of his own wishful thinking than of any scientific process. Let us supply his omissions.

"There is little point in enquiring whence came the question asked by this 'certain man'," says Knabenbauer, "for the Evangelist is silent on the subject." But there is every point in enquiring what the question *means*, despite the declaration of the Rev. Victor Mauran that: "Jesus is right not to answer the naïve enquirer, and His readiness to affirm under different circumstances that *few are chosen* is precisely because the fewness of these 'chosen' is quite unrelated to the number of the saved."[557] In our view, to the contrary, a relation must certainly exist between the question posed to Our Lord and the reply He makes to it, albeit indirect, obscure and incomplete. Fillion explains that the Latin term *qui salvantur* here used is synonymous with the *qui salvi fiunt* so that both are rightly translated "those that are saved" as found in I Corinthians I, 18 and II Corinthians II, 15 (cf. also Acts II, 47), in opposition to *pereuntes* — *those that perish* found in the same passages. And Liagre[558] observes with simplicity: "*Are they few that are saved?* If the question is about salvation, according to the principle stated above, the answer must concern the same salvation."

And indeed the words of the first part of Our Lord's reply must be understood to relate to this salvation as is plain from the parallel with Matthew VII, 13 explained above: *Strive* [Greek: ἀγωνίζεσθε] *to enter by the narrow gate*, is a more striking way of saying *Enter by the narrow gate*. Indeed according to the judicious Bellarmine, the remainder of verse 24, which expresses the reason for this instruction: *for many ... shall seek to enter, and shall not be able*, means the same as the words *and few there are that find it* in Matthew VII, 14 — i.e. that few are saved:

> For what the Lord says in Matthew and Luke concerning the narrow way and gate that leads to life and through which few enter in, and the broad way and gate leading to destruction at which many go in *is common to the Israelites and the Christians*; for the man who asked Our Lord if few were saved did not ask if few *Jews* were saved, but simply *Are they few that are saved?* And Our Lord does not reply "Narrow is the way that leadeth to life and few are *the Jews* that find it," but absolutely — "few there are that find it."[559]

---

[557] *Op. cit.*, p. 16. This author opens his very lightweight book by an early reference to the difficulty this passage presents for his thesis. "An imprudent question: who was the man who one day posed this indiscrete question to Jesus: 'Lord, are they few that are saved?' The Gospel refers to him simply as *quidam* — *a certain man*. Why such anonymity? We should have liked to know his identity. (pp. 13 and 14.)

[558] See footnote to p. 253 above.

[559] *De Gemitu Columbae*, lib. I, cap. VI; ed. Vivès, vol. VIII, p. 405.

Very different is the interpretation of these words suggested by Fr. Mauran in his wisdom: "Does Christ not wish to say to us discreetly, in a confidential aside: 'Have confidence! Do not worry about the destiny of mankind!'" (p. 18) As though Supreme Truth, which speaks openly to the whole world[560] would have one thing on His tongue and another hidden in His breast!

And the same writer joins Fr. Castelein in boldly declaring: "Let us not forget that only the contemporaries of Christ are concerned. The word 'many' concerns only them. This is clearly proved by the texts that follow." (p. 17)

Let us therefore press on to what follows and examine the subsequent text (verses 25-30) which contributes to the context. Our Lord goes on to declare that many shall seek to enter but shall not be able. "Under a vivid allegory," says Fillion, of which the main elements have already been met in Saint Matthew (Matthew XXV, 10-12; VII, 21-23; XXV, 41; VIII, 11-12; XIX, 28-30), "Christ paints a terrifying picture of the end of times."

Note how Our Lord there speaks directly to the Jews who were listening to Him, refers his preaching to them, mentions their forefathers and prophets and contrasts them with the nations. Does it really follow from this, that "the terrible passage about the narrow way and the few that find it concerns a specific and exceptional situation — the state of decadence and corruption which characterized the Jewish people at the coming of the Messiah"? (p. 35)

Certainly not. On the contrary, as Van Steenkiste expresses it: "The declaration concerning the fewness of the saved is first stated as general in verses 23-4, as in Saint Matthew, then (verses 25-30) individually transferred to the Jews contemporary with Our Lord (indeed to the whole rejected people)."[561] And it is plain from their commentaries that other great exegetes such as Beelen and Knabenbauer take the same view.

---

[560] Cf. John XVIII, 20.
[561] Van Steenkiste, *op. cit.*, p. 385, q. 267, *in fine*.

If however the context so far impinged on the sense of the earlier words (verses 23-4) as to make them particular, could not "an assertion specifically relating to certain persons yet at the same time enunciate a general truth"?[562] Moreover, even if the words of Our Lord in Luke were to be understood only of the Jews, "this would not exclude the very broad application the same words have in Saint Matthew."[563]

II
"MANY ARE CALLED BUT FEW ARE CHOSEN."
(MATTHEW XX, 1-16 and XXII, 1-14=

The words whose meaning we are seeking in the second passage are called by Fr. Castelein "the celebrated text in which Rigorism entrenches itself as in a citadel." (Footnote to p. 64) The accuracy of this label is to some extent confirmed by the earlier chapters of the present work which have shown us those whom Fr. Castelein attacks as "Rigorists" making extensive use of these words of Our Lord in stating their case. As to what they mean, he says:

> It seems that we should see in them a proverb in popular use, but for a different order of application… On the two occasions when Our Lord uses it, it is by way of conclusion to a parable which does not lend itself to the apparent meaning of the proverb. (p. 34)

Although Our Lord spoke them twice, "nothing is less clear than the meaning of these words." (p. 24) The only basis advanced for this claim is that: "It is obvious that this proverb, to apply to the [first] parable, cannot have the meaning commonly attributed to it. On the contrary… If the parable concerned the salvation of all mankind, we should have to conclude that all are saved." (p. 25) And "If the [second parable] proved anything about the relative number of the saved and the reprobate the conclusion would have to be that the latter comprise but an infinitesimal minority. (p. 30) Elsewhere he explains what these words *"may perchance mean"*.

---

[562] *Ibid.*, p. 386, q. 268, r. 10.
[563] *Ibid.*, p. 386, q. 268, r. 20,

Let us now address both parables separately, beginning with the second which is the clearer of the two.

(A)

Our Lord's parables are commonly divided into three categories according to the period of His public life and the progress of the preaching and founding of His Kingdom to which they correspond. The parable of the wedding feast belongs to the third class, which comprises those belonging to the final period of the life of Our Lord which treat of the consummation of the messianic kingdom, i.e. of the reprobation of the Jews and of the last judgement. And in fact examination reveals that both of these features are found in Matthew XXII, 2-14, for from verses 2 to 10 the rejection of the chosen people and the adoption of the Gentiles in their place are clearly described, while in the following verses, 11-13, the final judgement is symbolized. The union of Christ with His Church, or mankind, to be perfected in heaven, are the nuptials of the Lamb, to which the Jews were first invited and then, after the reprobation of the Jews, all the nations. These guests are assembled in the Church as being the antechamber to the heavenly banquet-hall to which, of all those gathered, only those are admitted who are worthy, i.e. those who are *wearing a wedding garment*.

The interpretation of this parable seems to me quite certain and I am astonished to find the Reverend author doubtful in his exposition of its first part: "It is very *probable* that this second parable ... has in view the rejection of the Jewish people ... from the Church," and wrong, or at best obscure, in explaining the second part: "... a guest is expelled ... : an allusion to the Gentiles who are to enter *the Church but not all of whom will remain therein*." (pp. 27-8)

The next question of course is to what precisely the conclusion of the parable in verse 14 relates: *For many are called, but few are chosen*. Some say to the whole story, others to the second half only and others again, Fr. Castelein among them, only to the first half. He tentatively argues in favour of this view on the grounds that Saint Luke, "the Evangelist of mercy and of the Gentiles," recounts the same parable (Luke XIV, 16-24), but without mentioning the expulsion and punishment of the guest who has no wedding garment or adding the proverb *Many are called but few are chosen*. Hence, "By not citing the proverb, Saint Luke … *seems* to indicate that this proverb did not apply to the Gentiles, for whom he was writing." (Footnote to pp. 28-9) — He overlooks the fact that this argument is hardly compatible with his earlier claim that the expulsion and punishment of the wedding guest is "an allusion to the Gentiles who are to enter the Church but not all of whom will stay therein." — But all hesitation vanishes when he goes on to declare the meaning of the words of the much-debated conclusion: for Fr. Castelein it is that many *Jews* are called to the *visible Church of Christ*, but few are chosen for her — "… in the second parable this proverb *must* be so interpreted." (Footnote to p. 27)

So the reference is either to the final part of the parable or to the whole of it — it makes little difference to the meaning. For those who take the words *Many are called but few are chosen* to be the conclusion of the whole narrative understand them to mean: many are called, i.e. all, both Jews and Gentiles, but few are chosen, strictly speaking, "for some are unwilling to come and some have not the nuptial garment." (Saint Thomas) Others, however, disregard those who are invited but refuse to come, as being certainly not of the elect ("chosen"), and seek the elect ("chosen") only among the Gentiles. For the Jews neither are nor ever will be numerous enough, between their reprobation and the end of the world, for their inclusion or exclusion to make a significant difference to the overall proportion of the elect, especially as the reprobation of the Jews relates to the people as a whole rather than to its individual members.

In favour of the first opinion is the fact that the parables of the Gospel tend to close with a concluding phrase, for it should be noted that Matthew XX, 1-16 comprises a single, complete narrative. In favour of the second opinion is the fact that the words *Many are called but few are chosen* are immediately subjoined after the final part of the parable. See on the subject of this connection Beelen's explanation above.[564]

To this Fr. Castelein objects:

> If Our Saviour had wished to teach us by this parable that the majority of those called to replace the Jewish people are reprobate, He would obviously have modified the closing remark of His parable. He would have shown us the greater number of the new arrivals representing the mass of the Gentiles in the same state as the man expelled for not being fittingly dressed. (p. 30)

To which the answer is that Our Lord did not in this precise passage intend to teach *how many* of the called would not be chosen but *which*, i.e. those who at the coming of the Son of Man shall be found without sanctifying grace. The rule for the interpretation of the parables is that every last detail does not to be explained for some matters have no symbolic significance in themselves and are included, as Augustine says, for the sake of coherence with what has. Such details, therefore, are disregarded in explaining the parables, or at least not pressed too far. Hence just as we should be wrong to conclude from the first part of the parable that *all* the Jews refused the invitation, neither do verses 11-13 entitle us to conclude that only one or very few are damned, for the contrary is clear from what follows: the man expelled for want of a wedding garment represents the whole multitude of the faithful who show themselves unworthy of admission to the heavenly banquet.

---

[564] Page 243. It is there shown that is wrong to attribute to Mgr. Beelen the view that the interpretation of the Fathers left the matter free, or that there was no need to refute an objection based on the interpretation of the Fathers. (Footnote to page 64) It is also astonishing to find Fr. Castelein daring to call his opinion "the interpretation of the moderns" after citing *five* modern authors of whom *at least three* share *this* writer's view. No notice need be taken of the appeal to "a learned exegete" in the absence of any verifiable reference, but it should be observed that in the footnote to page 37 the Reverend author does not say whether he is referring to Matthew XX, 16 or Matthew XXII, 14.

(B)

The parable of the labourers in the vineyard (Matthew XX, 1-16) is harder to interpret. Many place it in the same category as Matthew XXII, 2-14. Fr. Castelein explains it as follows:

> I therefore believe, along with authorized interpreters, that this parable, taken as a whole, applies to the successive entrance of the peoples into the kingdom of the Messiah and that the aim of our divine Master in narrating it was to quash on this point a pretension of the Jews, particularly of the Doctors of the law… This leads to certain conclusions: God will treat the last called as the first He will call *the multitude* to Himself…, but in this multitude the élite which the entire Jewish people flattered itself it would represent will in fact comprise only a few. In other words, the Jewish race are to have no further privilege and will no longer be the élite of the human race. The Saints, who form this élite, in each century comprise but a small number among the multitude of the faithful. (pp. 25-6)

Apart from the appeal to authority — "along with authorized interpreters", though we are never told who they are — his only argument can be summarized as: *Saint Matthew, the evangelist of the Jews, is the only one who recounts this parable and my explanation is logical and clear.* But he is not entirely sure of this last point all the same as he adds in a footnote (p. 27) that the words *Many are called but few are chosen* may also in this passage mean the same as they did above in the parable of the wedding garment.

The difficulty involved in explaining this passage is due to the fact that if every tiny detail therein is pressed, it leads to contradiction and error. Some points must therefore be disregarded as embellishments of lesser importance, but which are they? The interpreters readily agree that the householder represents God, the labourers are men called to obtain salvation, the market-place is the world, the vineyard is the Church in which salvation is wrought, the steward is Christ, to whom all judgement is given and the distribution of payment is the judgement. But there is disagreement as to what the *penny* and the *hours* symbolize. Saint Augustine says that the penny "is eternal life." But to this there are two objections: (a) *all* receive the penny, even the murmurers, and hence all are saved, whereas for Saint Gregory "no murmurer receives the kingdom of heaven and no one who receives it can murmur;" and (b) all receive *the same* penny, neither more nor less — so in what sense are the first last and the last first; in what sense are there few who are chosen out of many who are called — indeed where are those who are *not* chosen?

Scholars of the calibre of Knabenbauer, Klofutar and others in fact think that all whom this parable concerns and who receive the penny are saved and that their murmuring is to be disregarded as being simply a mechanism to enable the householder to give his reply: they receive in fact equal reward for equal merit, their labour being reckoned equal insofar as the latecomers, despite the shorter time, are enabled by more abundant grace to furnish more meritorious work than the others.

But surely more importance than this must be attached to the ending of the parable in which the householder's sharp rebuke and indignation towards the first labourers is much too clear and vehement to be disregarded and is hard to apply to the saved. Moreover, in the absence of any overwhelming argument to the contrary, the ending of this parable being the same as the ending of the parable of the wedding, which is very similar in general meaning to the present parable, ought to be explained in the same way — see above.

Thus the first-called, having received a merely sufficient remuneration which they murmur at and are rebuked for ought to be considered not to have been rewarded but rather punished and rejected, just as in Matthew V, 19 "shall be called the least in the kingdom of heaven" means "shall not *even* be the least…": for the remainder, the *penny* is an inaccurate representation of beatitude, for as Saint Augustine remarks: "All the Saints shall reign for ever, although not all shall reign with the same eminence, just as it is common to all the stars to shine perpetually, although some sparkle more brightly than others."

To understand what is meant by the earliness or lateness of the different *hours* of the working day, we must remember the occasion when Our Lord proposed this parable. After He had expounded the difficulty of the salvation of the rich, Saint Peter asked Our Lord about the reward awaiting the disciples who had left all to follow Him. The Master's answer is a most generous promise, to which, however, He attaches a solemn warning: *Many, however* [note the antithesis], *that are first, shall be last: and the last shall be first* (Matthew XIX, 30) The parable of the labourers in the vineyard is in fact an amplification of this warning, which Our Lord repeats after it, adding a motive intended to forestall any lukewarmness which a sense of false security might arouse on the part of His disciples and to stimulate them to fervour. Their having left all does not mean that they are now sure of salvation and their reward; what they have done hitherto has been the gift of God: *All men take not this word, but they to whom it is given* (Matthew XIX, 11), and *You have not chosen me: but I have chosen you* (John XV, 16). They are the *first* in respect of the origin, time and dignity of their vocation and promise; yet one of their number shall be the very last: *Judas Iscariot, the son of Simon: for this same was about to betray him, whereas he was one of the twelve.* (John VI, 72)

But this warning is more general than the above application to the Apostles, as is plain from the words used and this application itself, for it includes every kind of priority in calling, whether of earlier time or of greater dignity or any other origin, and whether this priority relates to individuals or to nations. Hence it is true that this parable contains a prediction, albeit veiled, of the rejection of the Jewish people. See Fillion on this passage.

Once Matthew XIX, 30 and the first half of XX, 16 ["… *so shall the last be first, and the first last…*"] have been understood as shown above, it is not only possible but obligatory to understand the second half of XX, 16 in the same way as at the end of the previous parable, i.e. in the traditional and patristic sense. For why else will some of the first be last and will the publicans and harlots go before them into the kingdom of heaven, not entering it themselves, if not because "many are called but few are chosen"?

Now on the subject of this traditional, patristic meaning, Fr. Castelein's words must be quoted verbatim:

For the interpretation of the Fathers to fix the meaning of a scriptural text it is necessary for this interpretation to be morally unanimous in favour of a specific meaning which the Fathers declare to be what the revealed words are actually intended to mean. An opinion *in discussing* a text is not always the same thing as an interpretation *of* that text.[565]

But what follows from this of course is that even if we grant that there is no common interpretation of this *gnome* among the Fathers and that the reasoning and proofs of its meaning just expounded are unconvincing, the morally unanimous doctrine of the Fathers as to the fewness of the saved, expressed by them both when discussing this *gnome* and elsewhere remains in full force. And it is this *doctrine* which Fr. Castelein contradicts: he refuses the Fathers' interpretation of *many are called but few are chosen,* **because** he will not accept their doctrine of the fewness of the saved. But for its doctrinal content he would have no objection to their interpretation at all.

I shall not be commenting on the other parables appealed to by Fr. Castelein in favour of his explanations: it is enough to examine their scope in the light of the ordinary rules of hermeneutics for the value of their confirmation to become immediately apparent.

III
"THE KINGDOM OF HEAVEN SUFFERETH VIOLENCE AND THE VIOLENT BEAR IT AWAY."
(MATTHEW XI, 12)

This text must be explained, says Fr. Castelein, in the light of its context and of the parallel in Luke XVI, 16.

> So Our Lord is here comparing the two religions... This first religion ... had been entrusted to the Jewish people alone... From John the Baptist, says the Gospel, the kingdom of heaven, i.e. the true religion ... is preached. And preached for all. It is no longer a privilege in anyone's favour: no one at all is excluded from it. This is why Christ compares it to *a booty in wartime which everyone may seize.* The terms *violent* and *violence* are not there to signify how much effort is needed for salvation, as though effort had not been needed before. On the contrary, salvation

---

[565] *Op. cit.,* note to p. 64.

has been made easier. The objective of this metaphor is simply to correct the error of the Jews, who believed that the kingdom of heaven was theirs by right of birth, and to the exclusion of the rest of mankind. (p. 43)

Thus "in [his] own way" and "albeit imperfectly", as for the parable of the labourers in the vineyard, he sets out a certain opinion about this scriptural passage, before adding:

> I am here taking the passage in its traditional meaning, but the great exegete of our own days, Fr. Knabenbauer S.J., reprising Dom Calmet's explanation, has established by analysis of the Greek words used an entirely different meaning, viz. that the kingdom of heaven is *persecuted* and that men of violence — viz. the Pharisees — wish to destroy it.[566] In which case the objection falls away in any event. (p. 44)

Concerning this linguistic explanation proposed by Fr. Knabenbauer suffice it to quote his own admission:

> I am aware that this interpretation has few patrons, other than Calmet, Wilke (*Lexicon Graeco-Latinum in libros Novi Testamenti*) and the *Protestants* Cremer, Hilgenfeld and with regard to Luke XVI, 16, in addition to Calmet, also Louis de Dieu.[567]

This interpretation is therefore suspect for all who love to follow the interpretations of the Saints and it is morally certain that it was not intended by Christ, in other words that it is not the meaning of Holy Srcipture.

Castelein makes no mention of a third interpretation, stated by Fr. Bainvel to be "certainly false" and he goes on to admit the logical consistency of the commonly held opinion[568] to which Fr. Knabenbauer recognizes that it is related and almost universally added.

---

[566] "Bear it away," i.e., says Knabenbauer, carry it off and snatch it from those who wish to enter it.

[567] *Commentarius in Quatuor Evangelia*, I, p. 437. It is extraordinary that no Father or Greek interpreter can be cited in its favour.

[568] *Les Contresens Bibliques des Prédicateurs*, p. 220 *et seqq.*

Indeed Canon Van Steenkiste prefers this opinion and cites Allioli and Bisping in its favour.[569] Here it is in his own words:

> Since John began to preach until our own day there has never been, and still is not, any other way of reaching heaven than to take it by assault: men must do holy violence to themselves if they are to enter.

But there is no need for patrons of the more demanding doctrine to adopt this latter explanation for Matthew XI, 12 to argue in their favour; it is sufficient for them to follow the excellent, commoner view which does no violence to the words used, fits the context and is supported by the authority of those of the Fathers who have best exposed the literal meaning.[570]

Let us therefore now set it out in accordance with the context and parallel.

In this passage of the Gospel Our Lord proves the dignity of John the Baptist who is *more than a prophet*: for he is himself foretold by the prophets (v. X), he not only foretells the coming Messiah but points to Him with his finger (vv. XI-XIII), he goes before Christ in the spirit of Elias (v. XIV).

The first motive of John's excellence and the second in part (i.e. Matthew XI, 10-11) are also found in Luke VII, 27-8; the second motive appears in Luke XVI, 16: *The law and the prophets were* [teaching the kingdom of God] *until John; from that time the kingdom of God is preached* [by John and by Christ Himself], *and every one useth violence towards it.*

Making the necessary transposition in its words from the parallel text of Luke, as authorized by the connection between its verses 12 and 13, gives us for the meaning of Matthew:

> The prophets, the greatest men of the Old Testament, Moses himself and his law, all had the task of prophesying the reign of the Messiah to come, and were able to see it from far off and greet it (Hebrews XI), but John is the herald of the Messiah *as present* and the first preacher of His reign; from the beginning of his preaching until the present day men

---

[569] *Op cit.*, q. 341.

[570] Bainvel, *op. cit.*

have already been entering His kingdom — not the Scribes and Phari-sees, who ought to have been the first to go in, but the humble and poor, publicans and sinners, i.e. those to whom entry seemed to be closed; this kingdom suffers violence, and *those who are violent, not so much to the king-dom as to themselves, by doing penance and leading a better life*, bear it off.

In confirmation of this explanation see: Matthew III, 5-6; VIII, 10; XXI, 32; XXIII, 13; Luke III, 10-14, etc., but especially Luke VII, 29-3, which are the words of Christ, and what follows in VII, 27-29.

At this point Our Lord is not making a law in virtue of which all must perish who fail to do penance and live holily by doing violence to themselves: he is recording the fact that those who do this in fact win the kingdom of heaven. But "if salvation can be taken by assault and those whose birthright it was fail to reach it by not correspond-ing with grace, it follows that we must labour and make every effort to enter heaven just as we must labour and take trouble to win the prize in any contest."[571] Compare this passage with Our Lord's teaching on the narrow way and the strait gate.

That this explanation involves a transition from the kingdom of the Messiah to the kingdom of the blessed (Knabenbauer, *loc. cit.*) is evidently not a difficulty.

And as for the final assertion of our Reverend adversary "on the contrary salvation is rendered easier", let him turn to Saint Thomas and study the question *Whether the new law is heavier than the old?* pay-ing special attention to the statement that "with regard to the works of the virtues in interior acts, precepts of the new law are heavier than those of the old law." Or, as Saint Augustine puts it: "What is not burdensome to one who loves is yet burdensome indeed to one who does not."[572]

---

[571] Bainvel, *op. cit.*
[572] *Summa Theologiæ*, I-II, q. 107, a. 4, body.

IV

"A RICH MAN SHALL HARDLY ENTER INTO THE KINGDOM OF HEAVEN."
(MATTHEW XIX, 23-26; MARK X, 23-27; LUKE XVIII, 24-27)

Let us begin by three important observations:

(i) This text is not used by those Fr. Castelein calls *Rigorists* and *Terrorists* to prove the fewness in absolute terms of the saved but simply to show that *the rich are with difficulty saved.*

(ii) Moreover none of the Saints ever taught that the legitimate ownership and use of wealth was a sin, but only that it was an occasion of sin and a hindrance to salvation. All of them agreed with Saint Ambrose: "Let the rich learn that that the crime lies not in wealth but in not knowing how to use it. For just as riches are a hindrance to the wicked so in the good they are helps to virtue."[573] The Saints were also well aware of the others discourses of Our Lord Jesus Christ against riches, such as the parable of the Sower, in which He teaches that riches are thorns[574] which choke the word of God and hence render salvation harder; they well knew that terrible cry: *Woe to you rich, for you have had your reward*; they knew the account of the sad fate of the rich glutton, and the parable of the rich man who pulled down his barns to build greater in which a man is called a fool because "he ... layeth up treasure for himself, and is not rich towards God,"[575] etc.

(iii) We are well aware that the Gospel presents several rich and noble men that were called by God and beloved of Christ, such as Zachæus, *the chief of the publicans, and he was rich,*[576] Joseph of Arimathea, *a rich man,*[577] Nicodemus, *a ruler of the Jews,*[578] Lazarus, Martha and Mary, a respected family of standing, Joanna, the wife of Chusa,

---

[573] On Luke XIX, 2; Cf. Van Steenkiste *ad locum.*
[574] Cf. Matthew XIII, 7.
[575] Cf. Luke XII, 21.
[576] Luke XIX, 2.
[577] Matthew XXVII, 57.
[578] John III, 1.

Herod's steward,[579] etc. But the poor and ordinary folk were preferentially chosen by the God who had Himself chosen to be poor.

There could therefore by no point in Fr. Castelein's undertaking to "go to this passage and endeavour anew to dissipate the blindness of prejudice by an examination dedicated exclusively to the truth,"[580] except in the context of his Chapter IV on *The Human Obstacles to Salvation* in which these words of Our Lord are far from helpful to his thesis. Instead of which our author closes his remarks on this subject by promising "later on [to] expand on this beautiful [!] doctrine with evidence from faith and reason," (p. 40), but when we reach Chapter IV we find him announcing: "I can be briefer here, for I have already indicated the meaning and scope [?] of the celebrated text which condemns the wicked rich... I have already explained myself on this subject in Chapter One." (pp. 256-8)

1. But with no authority from any Father or Doctor, he dismisses it as no more than a specific warning by which Christ applies the general doctrine of salvation:

> This text provides no new argument in favour of the theory of Rigorism. It highlights an impediment to salvation which no Christian can doubt for it belongs to the general doctrine that it is impossible to be saved while preferring a created good to the Creator. (p. 38)

It was not thus that the Saints spoke. "Mighty is the tyranny of wealth," says Saint John Chrysostom...

> ...for though we may cultivate the other virtues, it alone undermines whatever else is good in us. Rightly therefore does Paul say that *the desire of money is the root of all evils*, for those who wish to become rich fall into temptation and into the snare of the devil and many useless and harmful desires which drown men in ruin and perdition.

A heavy burden is laid on the shoulders of innocence, says Saint Hilary, when it is preoccupied by an increase in wealth. For riches foment and arouse pride, gluttony, lust and other vices. Hence, as man's nature is inclined to evil, wealth aggravates the danger.

---

[579] Luke VIII, 3.
[580] Page 36.

Our Lord three times emphasizes the difficulty of salvation for the rich.

In Matthew XIX He uses the solemn introduction *Amen, I say to you*, to stress what follows: *that a rich man shall hardly enter into the kingdom of heaven.* And in Mark X He exclaims with force **How hardly** *shall they that have riches, enter into the kingdom of God!* And when His disciples are astonished, He repeats the exclamation: *Children, how hard it is…* before using a popular simile for matters of difficulty: *It is easier for a camel to pass through the eye of a needle, than for a rich man to enter into the kingdom of God.*

The lesson in summary, as Maldonatus says, is that it is very difficult for a rich man to enter the kingdom of heaven. And to anyone who may be wondering why so much emphasis is placed on the dangers of wealth rather than of ambition, lust vengeance, etc., Maldonatus answers that although there are some who are more greatly affected by these other things, yet for most men they present a lesser hindrance, for almost all are held back by riches.

To which we may add that riches act as a stimulus to all the other concupiscences.[581]

2. The Reverend author is thus mistaken in thinking that "this text provides no new argument…" And he promptly adds a further error by qualifying the allusion to the rich with the words "while preferring a created good to the Creator", for thus he does not admit the danger of damnation found in riches except for the wicked rich or those too given up to avarice: "This notion taken in the absolute, as it is expressed in absolute terms, signifies complete attachment of the heart, attached to wealth as to its supreme good and ready to sacrifice all for its sake." (p. 37) "… the rich … [who are] disposed and determined to sacrifice the law of God and the blessings of heaven to [earthly goods] … A passion pushed to such an extremity." (p. 38) etc.

---

[581] Knabenbauer, *ad locum*, I, p. 160.

But in reality the proximate danger of eternal damnation applies also to those rich who are not so vehemently attached to their wealth nor yet properly detached from it, but who seek *a third way*; "men whose danger is so much the greater as they think themselves safer and who believe themselves out of danger in so far as they do not utterly abandon themselves to the more atrocious vices. For rarely are men found to be utterly without conscience."[582] Even with moderation wealth exposes its owners to strong temptations of pride, gluttony, lust, etc.

3. He also errs in thinking that it is rare for the rich to be bad, continuing to use the word "rich" in his own special meaning the better to convince himself and his readers.

> "No, most men are not ready to sell their soul for a fistful of gold, and the ownership of this gold does not render them so harsh and inhuman as to refuse to relieve their neighbour's misery... Take a hundred rich men at random — I am intimately convinced that the majority of them, and in Christian lands the great majority of them, are upright and charitable." (p. 258)

I am not claiming that all the rich are in the state of mortal sin, but that all are *exposed to grave danger*, to which most of them succumb, especially when it is borne in mind how few live a Christian life. I am only too willing to grant that the particular wealthy persons frequented by our learned Jesuit are all exemplary Christians. But there is another member of his Society, himself descended from a noble and opulent family, Cardinal Bellarmine, who writes:

> But it may be objected that Our Lord uses the word 'rich' to designate those who love riches and possess them for the sake of their own enjoyment rather than to be laid out generously in favour of necessary and pious causes. ... This is quite so, but how few are the rich of the latter kind! Hence, at least on account of its rarity, the comparison of the salvation of the rich with a miracle is justified.[583]

---

[582] See Contenson's remarks, p. 146 above :.

[583] *De gemitu columbæ*, lib. II, cap. VIII; *Opera*, ed. Vivès, vol. VIII, p. 444, col. 2.

And Bellarmine was perfectly familiar with the rich of his own day and country, who were certainly better than our own.

4. Fr. Castelein further errs in exaggerating the salvific value of almsgiving:

> Where charity is found, selfishness and avarice are free of this absolute and exclusive character that is incompatible with the conditions of salvation. (p. 258)
>
> Against the rigour of these judgements [of God] we have an easy and magnificent compensation in works of charity. (p. 55)
>
> I find that this sentence [of the Last Judgement] in which the great role of charity is placed in such vivid relief, together with the efficacious remedy it contains against our failures in the other virtues, is reassuring against the troubles sown by Rigorism. (p. 57)

No indeed, Father! Charity, I grant, gives security to those who have loved God with their *whole heart* and their neighbour for His sake, but that it affords safety to those who habitually live without charity towards God, I deny.

Saint Thomas Aquinas treats expressly of the power of the works of mercy to deliver from eternal damnation. There he states as an Objection to the correct position: "It would seem that all who perform works of mercy will not be punished eternally, but only those who neglect those works." He then replies:

> **On the contrary,** It is written: "Neither fornicators … nor adulterers," etc. "shall possess the kingdom of God."[584] Yet there are many such who practise works of mercy. Therefore the merciful will not all come to the eternal kingdom: and consequently some of them will be punished eternally.
>
> Further, it is written: "Whosoever shall keep the whole law, but offend in one point, is become guilty of all."[585] Therefore whoever keeps the law as regards the works of mercy and omits other works, is guilty of transgressing the law, and consequently will be punished eternally.
>
> (…)

---

[584] I Corinthians VI, 9-10.
[585] James II, 10.

Reply to Objection 1: Those will obtain mercy who show mercy in an ordinate manner. But those who while merciful to others are neglectful of themselves do not show mercy ordinately, rather do they strike at themselves by their evil actions. Wherefore such persons *will not obtain the mercy that acquits altogether*, even if they obtain that mercy which rebates somewhat their due punishment.[586]

5. Finally with regard to the final words of the text of Matthew on this subject, *With men this is impossible: but with God all things are possible*,[587] Fr. Castelein takes the gravest liberties, making unfounded promises of efficacious grace so as to reduce Christ's terrible threat to futility:

> Thus this passage which is at first sight the most frightening in the Gospel contains in fact *its most consoling and reassuring principle.*
>
> Man is weak. ... Of himself he is unable to break his chains, but God can break them; He can always break them.
>
> And will He use this power?
>
> Our Lord *clearly implies that He will*, by using a formula which admits *neither limit nor exception.* The power of God will not allow itself to be defeated by the weakness of men. (p. 39)

Blessed are the rich! For after their earthly reign, Fr. Castelein promises them the kingdom of heaven!

Serious and genuine scriptural interpreters do not endorse this conclusion, however: "Christ's meaning," says Van Steenkiste, "is that...

> ...according to the commonplace, customary behaviour of men, such things do not happen, but *it can happen* thanks to *a singular and extraordinary* help of God; in a nutshell, it is something *rare* and *exceedingly difficult*... By a special grace of God it may be obtained and brought about. Thus Zachæus *who was rich* was converted to Christ.[588]

And Knabenbauer says:

---

[586] *Summa Theologiæ*, Supplement, q. 99, a. 5.

[587] Matthew XIX, 26.

[588] *Op. cit.*, q. 453-4.

The lesson given is to fly to God as helper. For God will give us a new heart and will place a new spirit within us. In this way a man's soul is wrenched free of earthly things so that he may say with Saint Paul "And I live, now not I; but Christ liveth in me. [Galatians II, 20]"[589]

V

CHRISTIAN RENUNCIATION
(MATTHEW X, 37-39)

Says Fr. Castelein:

The second text liable to be brought forward against us concerns the doctrine of renunciation. Evidently to earn salvation, one must practise renunciation. But let us see if, in its threefold object of family, earthly goods and life, it is really so awful or so rare. (p. 44)

He then quotes Matthew X, 37: *He that loveth father or mother more than me, is not worthy of me*, explaining — allegedly to refute his "Rigorists" and "Terrorists" — that the "hatred" here referred to means ... exactly what everyone, including all his adversaries, agrees that it means. To the same end, he demonstrates — what no one denies — that the perfect renunciation proposed by Our Lord to the young man in Matthew XIX, 17 is required only of those who are invited to the loftier vocation while the only renunciation required of others is...

... spiritual renunciation — the inward disposition of not wanting to obtain, dispose of, or enjoy these goods in such a way as to violate the divine law in grave matter. And who will claim that this disposition is troublesome or rare among Christians? It is even false to say that the tendency of opinion and behaviour on this point is opposed to the Gospel. (p. 46)

After this our adversary passes on to the subject of renunciation of life itself for Christ, the occasion of which he says is "exceptionally rare", and is accompanied by "exceptional graces whereby to triumph". He adds:

---

[589] *Ibid.*, pp. 161-2.

The conflict between salvation and the enjoyments of life is frequent. That is where human weakness is so often displayed, but we shall shortly prove that here the divine mercy is incomparably more generous in succour and in forgiveness than the Rigorists suppose. (p. 47)

For the complete meaning of this passage from Matthew X, 37-9 let us consult an exegete much respected by Fr. Castelein: Fr. Joseph Knabenbauer S.J., who concludes:

> These verses set forth the greatness of the strength of soul needed to adhere energetically to Christ, for which reason *it is again illustrated in VII, 14 by the narrow way and the strait gate.* At the same time they explain why *many are destined to be strangers to salvation.*[590]

But for Fr. Castelein, there are *many* who find the narrow way and enter by the strait gate, so universal, in his view, is evangelical self-denial.

VI
EVANGELICAL HUMILITY
(MATTHEW XVIII, 3)

One ploy of the adversaries of the common doctrine of the fewness of the saved, faced with Gospel texts inconvenient to their thesis, is to restrict their application to the Jews, the Pharisees, Our Lord's contemporaries, the pagan world, etc. Thus in their eyes Christ's warning *Unless you become as little children, you shall not enter into the kingdom of heaven*, occasioned by an ambitious contention among the Apostles, concerns the Apostles alone or at most those of the faithful who are invited by a special vocation to "the summits of virtue to which God destined the continuers of His work and the leaders of His Church." (p. 46) Of others no more is required than that humility "which is the avowal of our nothingness before God and faith in the divinity and teaching of Jesus Christ... Now thanks to our Christian upbringing and so many graces received, these conditions ... have been made much easier for us than they were for the Apostles." (p. 48)

---

[590] *Commentarius in Evangelium Sancti Matthæi*, pars I, p. 408.

I deny and utterly reject this lax interpretation. Humility is no mere evangelical counsel like voluntary poverty, celibacy and religious obedience: it is a fundamental Christian virtue which is absolutely necessary for each of us — such is the teaching of all the Saints. The specific obligations of the Apostles are clearly distinguished by virtue of their special calling to the Apostolate to which they are directed as means necessary to a particular end.

VII

The Opposition Between Christ and the World

What is to be said of the opposition between Christ and the spirit of the world?

This is what the Rigorists quite misunderstand.

The world that we must give up in order not be lost is ... the world that hates, combats and persecutes Jesus Christ... What right have these Rigorists to declare that the world so defined is ... the public society among Christians peoples? Is the milieu, the public society amid which we live no different then from in the days of paganism? ... Is it conceivable for a theologian to commit such a confusion, concluding from the use of the same word — *world* — that the two societies, pagan and Christian, are identical? (pp. 49-50)

As Fr. Coppin very well observes,[591] this is not a historical issue but a matter of morals. Christ did not condemn any particular society of His day, but rather the evil principles by which men are commonly led. Fr. Monsabré explains:

The *world* as it is to be understood here is not human beings in the aggregate, it is not the earth that bears us, it is not mankind, *nor is it this or that civilized society in which the good and the bad are mixed together*: the world is all that, in mankind, sides with a destructive Spirit whose life is devoted to hindering the plans of God... The world, in the meaning of the Gospel, is whatever, by thought word or deed, protests against God, His law, His grace, the higher life that He communicates to us, the hopes He gives us, the destinies He has allotted us. Christ has pointed out this world to us and disclosed its tendencies, its maxims and its vices... If you

___

[591] *Op. cit.*, p. 35.

have understood me, gentlemen, this curse of our Saviour falls rather on a set of maxims and works of iniquity than on a set of individuals.[592]

And these worldly principles are at the opposite pole to Christian principles.

> The world is corrupt in its maxims, corrupt in its works, which are but the public and despairing confirmation of those maxims... What are the maxims of the world concerning the service of God, the dignity of man, the purpose of life, social relations, etc? ... Corrupt works: possessions, power, public esteem — such is man's real dignity according to the maxims of the world, so every effort must be made to achieve it...[593]

All this is explained clearly and eloquently in the pages of Monsabré which are accessible to all. How then, we may well ask in our turn, is it conceivable for a theologian to commit such a confusion?

VIII
THE ACCOUNT TO BE RENDERED FOR EVERY IDLE WORD
(MATTHEW XII, 36)

The severity of the Judgement of God is declared in this passage:

> *But I say unto you, that every idle word that men shall speak, they shall render an account for it in the day of judgment.*

And there is no substance in Fr. Castelein's unblushing response:

> The Divine Master will be indulgent towards women, and many men, *among whom I very humbly count myself,* may count on the same indulgence. (First edition, p. 49)

I far prefer to join the Saints in calling the Judgement of God "*tremendum judicium*" — a judgement to be trembled at — and to sing with Holy Church

Dies iræ, dies illa...	Day of wrath and doom impending...
Quantus tremor est futurus, Quando Judex est venturus,	Oh, what fear man's bosom rendeth,

---

[592] *Retraite Pascale*, 1877; *Le Monde*, pp. 43 and 73.
[593] *Ibid.*, pp. 48 and 58.

Cuncta stricte discussurus!

When from heaven the Judge descendeth,
On whose sentence all dependeth.

Judex ergo cum sedebit,
Quidquid latet apparebit:
Nil inultum remanebit.

When the Judge his seat attaineth,
And each hidden deed arraigneth,
Nothing unavenged remaineth.

Quid sum miser tunc dicturus?
Quem patronum rogaturus,
Cum vix justus sit securus?

What shall I, frail man, be pleading?
Who for me be interceding,
When the just are mercy needing?

Ingemisco, tamquam reus:
Culpa rubet vultus meus:
Supplicanti parce, Deus.

Guilty, now I pour my moaning,
All my shame with anguish owning;
Spare, O God, Thy suppliant groaning!

Peccavi nimis in vita mea.
Commissa mea pavesco, et ante te
erubesco…

I have sinned too much in my life. I do much fear my misdeeds, and before thee I do blush…

Peccantem me quotidie et non me
pœnitentem, timor mortis conturbat
me. Quia in inferno nulla est
redemptio…

The fear of death doth trouble me, sinning daily, and not repenting: for that in hell there is no redemption…

Domine, secundum actum meum
noli me judicare; nihil dignum in
conspectu tuo egi.

Judge me not, O Lord, according to my deeds, for I have done nothing worthy in Thy sight.[594]

(4)

The Progressives endeavour to attenuate the events of the Old Testament by which the fewness of the saved is indicated and seem to reject their symbolic meaning.

First a short note on the "typical sense" or symbolic meaning. Holy Scripture contains passages which typify or symbolize something beyond the literal truth which they primarily express. This is agreed by (i) the ancient synagogue, its judgement being confirmed

[594] Mass and Office of the dead.

by Our Lord and His Apostles who expound various passages of the Old Testament in a mystical way, (ii) all Catholic interpreters, and (iii) the chief Protestant exegetes, whose differences on this topic are semantic rather than real. Indeed the learned Jesuit commentator Fr. Cornely S.J. holds, with Molina, Bañez, Vasquez and no few others that: "it is definitely of faith that types are found in Holy Scripture, in such a way that what is said of the types *must at the same time be understood of the antitypes* [or, in other words, what is said of the symbolic person or object is also true of that which he, she or it represents]."[595]

This meaning of Holy Scripture and its probative power must therefore be admitted as true quite as much as the literal sense whenever and to whatever extent it is sufficiently established that the Holy Ghost *intended* some persons or things to stand for others. And this certainty is abundantly established, of course, when one of the sacred writers themselves explicitly or implicitly attests its presence, for this gives us the authentic declaration of the Holy Ghost as to His intended meaning.

In addition to this rule about the mystical meaning, the recognized specialists in sacred hermeneutics are united in affirming another: If it is already certain that some person or thing of the Old Testament is a type of some other person or thing of the New Testament, we are entitled to prolong this special mystical meaning in particular circumstances affecting that person of thing as often as the fittingness of the type to the antitype emerges as certain and obvious. For it is not to be supposed that either Sacred Scripture or Tradition has exhausted the mystery of each equivalence of type and antitype; in doing so we follow the example set by the Fathers of the Church and her approved interpreters.

Against this background, omitting so many others, let me now advance just three types or symbols from the Old Testament that are most certainly such and have more than once been very justifiably invoked to prove the fewness of the saved. I cannot tell whether Fr.

---

[595] Cornely, K.J.R., S.J., *Introductionis in S. Scripturae libros compendium, De S. S. Interpretatione*, cap. I, *de S. S. Sensibus*, p. 534.

Castelein is deliberately ignoring or merely failing to understand these types and their typical or symbolic value when he first misrepresents the argument his adversaries base on them and then replies to them so inadequately. Here, first, is how he himself couches the case of his pet "Rigorists":

> That chastisement of the deluge which buried beneath its waters, in the eternal abyss, the entire human race save one privileged family, the rain of fire which consumed the five cities of the Pentapolis[596] except only the family of Lot ... the numerous and vast chastisements which struck the Jewish people ... all these comprise poignant and terrible objections against the doctrine of salvation as you explain it. (p. 65)

And to this self-serving misrepresentation he replies:

> Well, no, these objections are neither so poignant nor so terrible as they are believe to be at first sight. I hope to dissipate the objections drawn from the Old Testament as I have dissipated those from the New testament. (p. 66)

Fr. Castelein has two methods of dissipating the objections he refers to: (i) he argues from reason so as to reduce to a minimum the number of those who in fact perished in these divine chastisements, and (ii) at the same time he increases as greatly as possible the number of those whom the secret mercies of God brought to repentance and salvation.

But these attempts show only that Fr. Castelein has failed to understand the argument he purports to be refuting. No doubt in any general reckoning of the number of the damned over the centuries the horrifying spectacle presented in Holy Scripture by Divine Justice to *pierce our flesh with fear*[597] ought not to be disregarded, irrespective of Fr. Castelein's view, even in their status of simple historical facts. But more importantly they also furnish those Fr. Castelein calls "Rigorists" with another argument, namely that derived from these facts *considered as a figure of future events*. Let us now explain these two

---

[596] The word *Pentapolis* (Greek for "five cities"), found in Wisdom X, 6, designates the five cities of Sodom, Gomorrha, Segor, Adama and Seboim. — Translator.
[597] Cf. Psalm CXVIII, 120.

arguments and see what probative value they have in the context of the present controversy.

I

THE FLOOD
(GENESIS VI-VIII)

(A)

I am inclined to think that *fewer* men perished in the Flood than currently die every day. Readers wondering where I find the evidence in favour of this *admittedly rather daring and novel opinion* may rest reassured that it is in the pages of my Bible, carefully studied and evaluated. (p. 70)

And of this evidence Fr. Castelein goes on to add, in a footnote:

As no exegete to my knowledge has considered this subject I can only address it by means of the arguments invoked. They are enough *to justify my hypothesis* against which *I have been unable to locate* any plausible proof.

This evidence is as follows:

1. The period when the Flood took place. The author of Genesis indicates it by the words *after that men began to be multiplied upon the earth*. But, says Fr. Castelein, "... clearly these words cannot refer to a very large population." However in reality the formula quoted refers not to the time of the Flood itself but to the time of the initial divine decree to punish mankind, and the Latin words *cumque cœpissent multiplicari* ought not to be translated by *were beginning to be multiplied*,[598] but rather by **had begun** *to be multiplied*; moreover the Vulgate here uses a Hebraism which presents that which already existed as beginning to exist such tenuous arguments do not call for heavy artillery by way of refutation!

2. The cause of the Flood is "... a crime of the same kind, a collective moral disorder. But the propagation or the contagion of a single disorder supposes that the members of the human race are close enough neighbours to form still a moral unity." (p. 70) The reader

---

[598] Fr. Castelein quotes in French "*commençaient à se multiplier*" in opposition to "*eurent commencé à se multiplier*". — Translator.

will form his own judgement as to the force of this argument and as to the use of the word "collective", where "universal" would be more appropriate, for Genesis VI, 11 indicates the cause of the Flood by the words *And **the earth** was corrupted before God, and **was filled** with iniquity*.

3. Fr. Castelein's calculation of the number of men living at that time: "a few hundred tribes or patriarchal families, each itself composed of a few hundred members and spread over the valleys and mountains of Armenia. Such *in all probability* was mankind at the time." (p. 72) Since this calculation is idiosyncratic and gratuitous and no certainty is to be had as to the number of persons living at the time of the Flood, I should be happy to leave the claim undisputed, but its author cannot be allowed to bolster his claiming by adding: "*There are no grounds* for supposing that God would have unduly favoured the fertility of a race *He had resolved to destroy*." (Footnote to p. 71) For the Divine mandate to *Increase and multiply* (Genesis I, 28) indeed entitles us to suppose great fertility, and it is not permissible to suppose that God deprived the primæval human race of this greater fertility because its destruction was decreed.

Fr. Castelein continues his comments on the Flood in the following vein:

> In addition, we know from a passage of Saint Peter's first epistle (III, 19-20) that a certain number of its victims benefited from such pardons … although we do not know whether they were many or few… God … willed to engrave upon the memory of humanity … a lesson of stern morality … mitigated in its execution by a *relatively restricted* number of victims… (p. 74)

Now in fact no patron of the stricter doctrine on the number of the saved asserts that all the victims of the Flood were damned, but it is entirely justified to conclude from II Peter II, 4-5[599] that a *relatively*

---

[599] "For if God spared not the angels that sinned, but delivered them, drawn down by infernal ropes to the lower hell, unto torments, to be reserved unto judgment: and spared not the original world, but preserved Noah, the eighth person, the preacher of justice, bringing in the flood upon the world of the ungodly."

great number of them were cast down to the lower hell with the fallen angels.

(B)

We learn from the words of I Peter III, 19-21 adduced above by our Reverend adversary that the account of the Flood presented in Genesis VI-VIII contains, in addition to the literal and historical meaning a further, mystical sense. This typical sense is explained as follows by the learned Fr. Recupito of the Society of Jesus:

> He [Peter] says that the ark in which Noah with a few others was saved by water was a figure of the Church, in which the faithful are saved by baptism. Attention is drawn to the fact that *a few, that is eight souls*, were saved in the ark, to show forth the fewness of the predestinate in the Church. Although no comparison is here made bearing on the faithful among themselves, yet when it is said that *few* are saved in the Church just as *few*, i.e. eight souls, were saved in the ark in comparison with the whole of the rest of mankind that perished in the Flood, it is sufficiently shown that the fewness of those destined to be saved in the Church is such as to include, apart from children, the greater part of adults; for the eight saved in the ark are utterly insignificant in comparison with the rest of men. But the Flood is said here to be a figure of the Last Judgement... From this Flood, few shall be saved in the Church, although many are within the ark. Hence in the same place Saint Peter adds: *Whereunto baptism being of the like form, now saveth you also: not the putting away of the filth of the flesh, but the examination of a good conscience towards God.* In pondering which, Augustine says[600] that men baptized in Catholic unity who renounce the world in words but not in deeds do not belong to this mystery of the ark, for they have no "examination of good conscience". This same figure of the ark is also brought forward by Saint John Chrysostom [see above, p. 110] to show the fewness of the elect. In which respect it should also be borne in mind that the upper deck of the ark was very narrow while its main deck was very broad, to signify that in the ark of the Church *few rise to the heights* while many sink to the depths. This point is noted by Origen who exclaims: "How few are the saved. And in the ark built by Noah, its measurements revealed

---

[600] Lib. V, *De Baptismo contra Donatistas*, cap. 18.

from on high, the dimensions of its lower parts are stated to be 100 cubits long by 50 broad, while its topmost parts are no wider that a single cubit.[601]

So too Saint Gregory the Great says: "The ark was broad where it held beasts, but narrow where it held men... Many are called, but few are chosen." (See above, p. 99)

In a nutshell: just as in the days of Noah a minority of the animals and just eight human souls were saved from the waters of the Flood and from bodily death, so now in the Church, outside of which there is no salvation, only a minority of men enter and but a very small proportion of those that enter are saved from eternal damnation.

II

THE DESTRUCTION OF SODOM
(GENESIS XVIII, 16 to XIX, 39)

(A)

A few centuries after the Flood a corner of Palestine was struck by a chastisement that, although less extensive[602] took a more terrifying shape. Fire from heaven, *perhaps due to a volcanic explosion* produced by the laws of nature in harmony pre-established by God with the laws and designs of the moral order, destroyed *Sodom and the neighbouring villages.* Why? For unheard of crimes... *This time the chastisement seems to have been limited to a few thousand victims.* (pp. 75-6)

Such is Fr. Castelein's account of the event described as follows by the Holy Ghost: *And the Lord rained upon Sodom and Gomorrha brimstone and fire from the Lord out of heaven. And he destroyed these cities, and all the country about, all the inhabitants of the cities, and all things that spring from the earth.* (Genesis XIX, 24-5) He then continues:

But here too the mercy of God transcends His justice to restrain its outburst Who does not recall how this divine mercy ... condescended to the prayer of Abraham by accepting, to offset the balance weighed down

---

[601] *Tractatus de numero prædestinatorum et reproborum,* cap. III, § viii.

[602] Remember that Fr. Castelein has already reduced the victims of the Flood to a few hundred patriarchal families.— Author.

by all the sins of Sodom, only the merits of ten just men. (p. 75) … He [God] willed this chastisement less to avenge Himself on this multitude of sinners — for He would have spared them…, still less to damn them all, since He offered free pardon to each of them [see below p. 291 concerning this highly questionable assertion], than to cleanse mankind and offer it … a new warning… (p. 76)

Concerning which let us note:

1. I freely recognize God's intention of inspiring us with salutary fear, but I suggest that God's primary intention was precisely the punishment of the wicked: *And the Lord said: The cry of Sodom and Gomorrha is multiplied, and their sin is become exceedingly grievous. I will go down and see whether they have done according to the cry that is come to me.*[603] See too Deuteronomy XXIX, 23; Wisdom X, 69, II Peter II, 6-9 and Jude 7.

2. Although not a word can be cited from Holy Writ or from the Fathers stating or suggesting that a single one of the wicked who dwelled in the five cities were delivered by the temporal fire from the eternal fire, I will not declare that absolutely all were damned, but who can doubt that in the mass they incurred the punishment of eternal fire? *And reducing the cities of the Sodomites, and of the Gomorrhites, into ashes,* [God] *condemned them … And delivered just Lot, oppressed by the injustice and lewd conversation of the wicked. … The Lord knoweth how to deliver the godly from temptation,* **but to reserve the unjust unto the day of judgment to be tormented.**[604]

3. Whatever may be said of the number of those incinerated by this chastisement — a number which Fr. Castelein does all in his power in the above-quoted account to reduce as far as possible — there can be no denying that it increases the number of the damned and comprises a serious historically-based objection to the thesis of the gainsayers. Just as with the Flood, their reaction is to take cover from the destruction of Sodom and the other cities behind the fact that on a different occasion, under different circumstances, the city of

---

[603] Genesis XVIII, 20 *et seqq*.
[604] II Peter II, 6-9.

Nineve — also threatened by a well-merited chastisement — did penance and was spared:

> While the Rigorists enjoy appealing to the chastisement of the Flood — misunderstood and ill-explained [?] — as a terrifying example of divine justice, we are happy to oppose to them as a consoling example of divine mercy the miracle of the conversion of Nineve, in which a number of men perhaps twenty times as great[605] obtained full forgiveness. (p. 140)

But unless the deliverance of the Ninivites from the threatened temporal chastisement demonstrates their eternal salvation at the same time, this incident proves nothing relevant. We all admire God's mercy in pardoning the Ninivites and in His readiness to heed the prayer of Abraham by accepting that the merits of just ten just men would suffice to offset the accumulated crimes of Sodom and obtain deliverance for the five cities, but we must also wonder at the perversity of men seeing that among so many thousands these ten just men could not be found. And knowing that God's justice, like His mercy, is infinite, we see nothing to wonder at in the fact that the number of the damned is greater than the number of the saved.

4. Neither can I allow Fr. Castelein's naturalistic explanation of the rain of sulphur and fire to pass without a brief remark, when the sacred text tells us that *"**the Lord** rained upon Sodom and Gomorrha brimstone and fire from the Lord out of heaven."* (Genesis XIX, 24) "On this point the sacred text admits no doubt;" remarks Fr. Crelier[606] on this passage: "it clearly sets before us an *immediate* intervention of the Divinity, *a miracle*."

---

[605] Fr. Coppin pointedly remarks in refuting Fr. Castelein's estimate of the global population at the time of the Flood: "His figures are less conservative when he comes to his Trojan Horse in the 'rigorist' camp: 'Ninive', 'repentant Ninive', 'forgiven Ninive'; he assigns two million inhabitants to this city whereas authors of the highest competence estimate its population at no more than half a million." (*Op. cit.*, p. 72.)

[606] Crelier, Henri-Joseph (1816-89): *La Sainte Bible, Texte de la Vulgate ... avec commentaires, La Genèse et Introduction au Pentateuque.*

(B)

The typical, or symbolic, meaning of this event is made known to us by the Epistle of Saint Jude, verse 7, which says that: "… Sodom and Gomorrha, and the neighbouring cities … were made an example, suffering the punishment of *eternal* fire." Similarly Saint Peter (II, II, 6): "And reducing the cities of the Sodomites, and of the Gomorrhites, into ashes, condemned them to be overthrown, making them an example to those that should after act wickedly." As Estius remarks in his commentary on this passage, "Saint Peter sees God's punishment of these cities not as a commonplace deterrent example, as public execution sets an example to others not to commit similar crimes, but as a *typical example*, in accordance with Saint Paul's words: *Now all these things happened to them in figure* (I Corinthians X, 11). For this terrible, but temporal, punishment serves as a symbolic example, typifying the eternal punishment, far more terrible yet, which awaits wicked men and especially the masters of wickedness." And the same author goes on, when explaining a syntactical doubt affecting the text of Jude 7: "It is uncertain whether the genitive *ignis æterni* ('of eternal fire') depends on *exemplum* ('example') or *pœnam* ('punishment'). If the latter, the meaning will be that these cities, by undergoing the punishment recounted in Genesis, i.e. of fire and brimstone, *are intended as an example of eternal fire*, i.e. of the punishment of the wicked in eternal fire. For the appalling punishment inflicted on these cities was a conspicuous figure of hell… This meaning and construction better fits the words used by the Apostle Peter." The same is said by Calmet and Beelen in their commentaries on Jude and among more recent exegetes by Van de Putte, on Genesis, and others.

And while all the inhabitants of the five cities who perish represent those who are damned to everlasting fire, on the testimony of Saint Isidore of Seville in his *Allegoriæ quædam Sacræ Scripturæ*, Lot and his family, as the only ones delivered from the flame of fire, "represent the Saints who at the end of the world will be delivered from the fire of the wicked,"[607] *when the Lord*, as Holy Church sings, *shall come to judge the world by fire*.

III
THE ENTRY OF ONLY TWO INTO THE PROMISED LAND

We come now to the third historical event of the Old Testament which the Progressives attenuate and of which they reject the spiritual meaning as adduced by the Fathers to prove the fewness of the elect.

Reversing the approach hitherto observed I propose in this case to discuss the typical or symbolic meaning first, before going on to address the event in itself as interpreted by one particular adversary.

(A)

The Apostle expounds the symbolism in the following terms in I Corinthians X, 1-6 and 11-12:

> For I would not have you ignorant, brethren, that our fathers were all under the cloud, and all passed through the sea. And all in Moses were baptized, in the cloud, and in the sea: and did all eat the same spiritual food, and all drank the same spiritual drink... But with most of them God was not well pleased: for they were overthrown in the desert. Now these things were done in a figure of us... (...) Now all these things happened to them in figure: and they are written for our correction, upon whom the ends of the world are come. Wherefore he that thinketh himself to stand, let him take heed lest he fall.

To grasp the nature of the symbolism involved, note how Saint Paul uses it. After narrating the historical event, he exhorts the Corinthians to apply the lesson it contains, for to obtain salvation it is not enough simply to be Christians, it is essential for them to labour with all their strength to make certain that salvation.

This exhortation comprises two parts:

(i) the comparison with a race, in which the prize is won only by him who competes with great energy;

---

[607] Recupito, *op. cit.*, p. 18.

(ii) the confirmation of this doctrine by the *typical* or *symbolic* explanation of the exodus from Egypt.

Thus he begins by saying (I Corinthians IX, 27): *I chastize my body, and bring it into subjection: lest perhaps, when I have preached to others, I myself should become a castaway.* Saint Paul's purpose here is to prevent the Corinthian neophytes from thinking that such fear is vain and futile and to incite them to take appropriate measures in their own interest Then to confirm this he adduces the example of the Israelites, all of whom received the same benefits in leaving the land of Egypt, but very few of whom — to wit only Josue and Caleb — reached the promised land.

"Thus," says Cornely:

> ...he sets out in the first place the great benefits conferred by God on the Israelites who left Egypt, to show how they prefigured the far sublimer graces that are granted under the New Testament to all who quit Egypt (i.e. the world).
>
> Then, reminding his addressees that most of the Israelites died in the desert, he teaches that their sins and the punishments that befell them *are real prophecies of what happens to Christians.* Then, passing on the exhortation proper, he calls all to vigilance, at the same time assuring them that God will assist all who do not voluntarily expose themselves to temptations.
>
> There are two supreme benefits conferred on Christians: Baptism, in water and the Holy Ghost, by which man is born again to new life, and the Eucharist, by which the new life is nourished... A *figure* of each of these benefits was also vouchsafed to all the Israelites, for all those who went out of Egypt received the typical, or symbolic, Baptism and all who left Egypt were nourished with the typical food and drink.[608]

In the preceding section, addressing himself to the Greeks, as himself a Greek of sorts, the Apostle had drawn an illustration from their sports, reminding them that of all those who run in the stadium, but one received the prize. Now, speaking to the Jews, as himself a Jew of sorts, he draws on the history of the Jewish people for his illustrations: of some six hundred thousand who went forth from the land of Egypt, not counting women and children, only two entered the promised land.

All of the Israelites who went out of Egypt therefore received the same spiritual benefits from God, *but with most of them God was not well pleased*. Saint Paul here makes a double use of understatement, for the Latin says *"non in pluribus eorum beneplacitum est Deo"*, i.e., literally, God was not *very well pleased* with *several* of them, but the meaning intended is that God was not *at all pleased* with *the great majority* of them; on the contrary nearly all offended Him and hence *they were overthrown in the desert*. As Cornely continues:

> By their continual unbelief and contumacy, by their continual murmuring and sins, *the whole people* so far provoked the divine wrath that all of those who were counted at the departure from Egypt being aged upwards of twenty years forfeited the right to enter the promised land; all of them died of various plagues and other causes and their bodies were left behind in the desert, while just two, Josue and Caleb, out of more than six hundred thousand adult males [603 550 is the figure given in Numbers I, 46] entered Palestine.

Now all these things happened to them in figure: and they are written for our correction,[609] so that we may not set our hearts on evil as they did. Cornely continues:

> By His admirable providence God willed so to order the affairs of this ancient people that they would prefigure and predict what was to befall the new Church.

> Hence just as the Apostle sees in the spiritual benefits conferred on the chosen people at their emergence from Egypt prophetic figures of the much greater benefits that God was to confer on Christians, so too does he see, in the fate of this entire people cut off in the desert for their sins, *a figure of the much greater punishments* with which God will punish Christians if they should commit similar sins. For, as Chrysostom says, just as the gifts are figures [i.e. symbols], so too are the punishments; first Baptism and the Eucharist are symbolized, then what follows recounts how those who proved themselves unworthy of the great gifts that symbol-

---

[608] Cornely, *op. cit., ad locum*, pp. 370-371.
[609] Cf. I Corinthians X, 11.

ized them were put to death, in order to warn us to be more cautious and temperate. For just as in the case of the benefits the types came first and the *reality* followed, so in the case of the punishments the reality must inexorably follow the symbol. This means not only that those who are unworthy of Baptism and the Eucharist *actually received* will be punished, but that they will suffer *heavier* punishments than those who proved unworthy of the types that prefigured them. For the reality must exceed the symbol which foreshadows it, in punishments as well as in gifts.

In order to explain in conformity with Saint Thomas these last words, which imply that the type differs from its antitype just as the shadow differs from the object whose shadow it is, it should be noted that just as in the case of good things that which is prefigured is *far better* than its figure or symbol, e.g. the Kingdom of Heaven is far better than the promised land, so too in bad things, that which is prefigured is *far worse* than the symbol which represents it. And according to Augustine the sufferings undergone at that time by the Israelites *were a figure of hell,* which is greater than any other punishment.

The other older interpreters are of the same view, says Cornely,[610] no mean exegete himself, and no whit inferior to Fr Knabenbauer whom Fr. Castelein holds in such well-deserved esteem.

(B)

What our adversary goes on to write about so great a type (or symbol), disregarding the ancient exegetes and relying solely on his imaginary "profound study of Holy Scripture" and "the rules of exegesis currently adopted by the best exegetes", simply beggars belief:

Massillon, to prove that the elect are rare in every period of human history, pints to Josue and Caleb, who alone of all the 600 000 Israelites gained entrance to the promised land. But does this fact imply that all these Israelites, including Moses and Aaron, are damned? Obviously not. Moses is everywhere praised in the Holy Scriptures as a Saint and a prophet. God *may have* refused the others and Moss himself the supreme reward of entrance into the promised land, for *even a slight* failure of faith

---

[610] *Op. cit.,* p. 278.

or of fidelity to His law. But in any event was it not inevitable that during forty years of exhausting travelling in the desert under the scorching Arabian sun the great majority of these thousands of Israelites who had come out of Egypt should die a natural death? (p. 143)

Here there as many errors as words, whereby to deceive "even the most instructed of the laity". (Fr. Castelein, *op. cit.*, p. 9)

1. On the subject of Massillon, here are the opening words of his celebrated sermon:

> If my purpose was to alarm you rather than to instruct you it would be enough for me to set before you simply the most terrible passages of Holy Writ bearing on this great truth and to run through the history of the just, century by century, to show you that in every period the elect have been very rare... Josue and Caleb, etc... Such frightening *figures* (i.e. symbols) would have been followed by the utterances of the prophets... The Gospel would have added new details to the horror of these *images*...[611]

Nowhere, then, does Massillon say or suppose that the six hundred thousand Israelites were all damned. He simply joins Saint Paul and all the Fathers in seeing in them *a type* of the fewness of the saved: *figures, images, symbols.*

2. God *may have* refused the others and Moses himself the supreme reward of entrance into the promised land, for *even a slight* failure of faith or of fidelity to His law.

With regard to this alleged *slightness* of the sins of the Israelites, Saint Paul, in explaining the type we are discussing lists three specific sins which have in common the factor of being directly against God: for he never lost sight of his aim of withdrawing the Corinthians from idolatrous practices. These three sins are:
Idolatry: Neither become ye idolaters, as some of them. (v. 7)
Temptation of Christ: Neither let us tempt Christ: as some of them tempted, and perished by the serpents. (v. 9) But yet all the men that have seen my majesty, and the signs that I have done in Egypt, and in

---

[611] Migne, *Collection intégrale et universelle des orateurs sacrés*, vol. XLII, col. 705.

the wilderness, and have tempted me now ten times, and have not obeyed my voice. (Numbers XIV, 22)
Murmuring against God: Neither do you murmur: as some of them murmured, and were destroyed by the destroyer. (v. 10)

To these may be added a fourth sin: *Neither let us commit fornication, as some of them committed fornication, and there fell in one day three and twenty thousand.* (v. 8)

Is it then of these three sins against God, or of fornication, that Fr. Castelein dares to write of: "*even a slight* failure of faith or of fidelity to His law"?

> 3. …Was it not inevitable that during forty years … the great majority of these thousands of Israelites who had come out of Egypt should die a natural death?

Whatever may be said of the great majority, it was far from inevitable that *all* of the 603,550 should have died in that period, including the youngest of them — who must have died before the age of sixty — with only *two* exceptions. Into the promised land there entered only *twenty-three thousand males from one month old and upward,* including not a single one of those who had been counted in the desert. For the Lord *had foretold* that *all* should die in the desert, and none in fact remained save Caleb and Josue.[612]

> 4.…[W]as it not inevitable that … [they] … should die *a natural death*?

I suggest to my learned contradictor that a logically prior question is *why* God made His people, His *numerous* people, wander in the desert for forty years. A direct journey from Egypt to the Jordan required no such period. Has Fr. Castelein never read these terrifying words from the book of Numbers:

> And the Lord spoke to Moses and Aaron, saying: How long doth this wicked multitude murmur against me? I have heard the murmurings of the children of Israel. Say therefore to them: As I live, saith the Lord: According as you have spoken in my hearing, so will I do to you. In the wilderness shall your carcasses lie. All you that were numbered from

---

[612] Numbers I, 46; XIV, 21-24; XXVI, 62-65.

twenty years old and upward, and have murmured against me, shall not enter into the land … except Caleb the son of Jephone, and Josue the son of Nun. … Your carcasses shall lie in the wilderness. Your children shall wander in the desert forty years, and shall bear your fornication, until the carcasses of their fathers be consumed in the desert. According to the number of the forty days wherein you viewed the land, a year shall be counted for a day. And forty years you shall receive your iniquities, *and shall know my revenge*: for as I have spoken, so will I do to all this wicked multitude that hath risen up together against me: in this wilderness shall it faint away and die.[613]

And the Lord being angry against Israel, led them about through the desert forty years, *until the whole generation that had done evil in his sight was consumed.*[614]

Undoubtedly then their death, no matter how natural in itself, was decreed as a punishment for sin.

Moreover, what was the nature of this *natural* death? Moses himself, an eyewitness, towards the end of his life, in speaking to God of those who died in the desert says: *In thy wrath we have fainted away. … The days of our years … are threescore and ten years. But if in the strong they be fourscore years: and what is more of them is labour and sorrow.*[615]

And for the benefit of those who find this interpretation unsatisfactory because they refuse to accept that this Psalm was in fact written by Moses despite its explicit opening: *A prayer of Moses the man of God*, I observe, with the judicious Fr. de Hummelauer:

Those who were then little more than twenty years old were all to die before the completion of their sixtieth year, *which was certainly an extraordinary rate of mortality*, especially at a time when old men of eighty or even a hundred do not seem to have been rare. That a people having a fixed dwelling in the land of Egypt should be condemned to a nomadic life beneath the desert sun for forty years might perchance be expected to lead to a somewhat greater mortality even according to the laws of nature, but the *universal* mortality evoked in this passage was something

[613] *Ibid.*, XIV, 27-35
[614] *Ibid.*, XXXII, 13.
[615] Psalm LXXXIX, 9-10.

entirely extraordinary. *In the wilderness shall your carcasses lie. You shall not return into Egypt.*[616]

And the sacred text adds that when Moses announced this sentence of death *to all the children of Israel, … the people mourned exceedingly* — as well they might.[617]

In addition to these three typical figures or symbols several others are advanced by the Fathers to confirm the fewness of the saved. These include: the destruction of the city of Jericho, except only the house of Rahab; the three hundred soldiers who alone were chosen out of the 32,000 in the army of Gedeon; the symbol or figure of Ezechiel IX where a single angel is deputed to mark the letter Tau[618] on *the foreheads of the men that sigh and mourn for all the abominations that are committed in the midst thereof,* while *six* angels are ordered to strike and destroy all the others, beginning with the sanctuary; the passage in Apocalypse XX which refers to just *one* book of life whereas there are *several* books of death, i.e. registers of the reprobate; the Probatic pool, with its five porches, in which *lay a great multitude of sick, of blind, of lame, of withered; waiting for the moving of the water,* and of this great multitude, when the angel descended, only *one* was healed;[619] the grain in the parable of the Sower in which just one part in four fell on good ground; Saint Paul's comparison of the elect to vessels of gold and silver, which are rarer, while the reprobate are compared to vessels of wood or earthenware, which are commonplace, etc.[620]

---

[616] Hummelauer, Franz von (1842-1914), *Commentarius in Numeros*, XIV, 31, p. 117.

[617] Numbers XIV, 39.

[618] Shaped like a cross in the ancient Hebrew alphabet. — Translator.

[619] John V, 1-4.

[620] 2. Cf. Recupito, *op. cit.*, part II, chapter III; Cardinal Wiseman, *op. cit.*, Sermon XI, *On the Small Number of the Elect*: "Wherever we look at the history of God's providence, we find but too clearly that the number of those who can hope with reason for this eternal blessing, are but a small remnant; to use the figure of Isaias, like the few grapes which are left upon the vine by the gatherers, like the few ears which may be gleaned from the field after the harvest. Abraham alone is called forth from the land of idolaters to be rescued from perdition; only seven thousand men, who had not bent the knee to Baal, form the remains of God's religious

But these other types and symbols are less certain than the three mystical passages that have been examined in detail above and whose prefigurative character is indicated in the New Testament: those three are quite sufficient. On their strength we may now leave Fr. Castelein to glory in having refuted all the arguments of the Fathers of the Church by his vaunted knowledge of Holy Scripture and of tradition!

(5)

"The arguments from Holy Scripture and from theology are incomparably more favourable to a greater number of the elect."

Immediately after his futile demonstration, Fr. Castelein writes:

> The arguments drawn from Holy Scripture and from Catholic theology are incomparably more expressive in favour of a high number of the elect.
>
> The number, variety and clarity of the texts I have gathered together must dissipate *any doubt* on the subject. (p. 266)

What then is this incomparable evidence, overlooked by Saint Thomas and so many other theologians and which not one single Saint has ever noticed? Which are these scriptural texts — so numerous, varied and clear — whose light dissipates every doubt on the subject before us and which the greatest theologians all failed to spot? As my confrère Fr. Coppin well remarks: "It would seem that they [i.e. the Saints] were all wrong despite the brightness of the light which Fr. Castelein's work claims to reveal to the world!"[621]

kingdom in Israel. Tobias alone of the twelve tribes goes up to Jerusalem to worship God; Daniel alone at the court of Babylon observes the stated hours of prayer, when its practice becomes dangerous; the three young men alone refuse, of all the satraps, to fall before the golden statue of the king. In the gospel, the same disproportion of numbers is foretold of the true followers of Christ. They were reminded that in the days of Elias there were many widows in Israel, but that only the one of Sarepta was saved from famine; that in the days of Eliseus there were many lepers, but none were cleansed except Naaman the Syrian."

[621] Coppin, *op. cit.*, p. 100.

But in fact Fr. Castelein does not cite a single scriptural text or theological argument by way of direct proof of his teaching on the number of the saved. Instead, he accumulates such passages as teach the infinite mercy of God and the universality of the Redemption in favour of all *insofar as depends on God*, as though this sufficed to show that almost everyone is in fact saved.

> From all these teachings Fr. Castelein concludes in favour of a very great number of the elect, and leaves his readers the distinct impression that if he were not restrained by the decrees of the Church he would cheerfully announce that everyone without exception is really saved!
>
> For the good Father overwhelms his adversaries beneath an avalanche of *all*s and *every*s; he quotes copiously from both Testaments, whenever the word "all" or the word "every" appears, taking pains always to put these words *in italics* so that the typographer may join forces with the inspired writers to ensure that even the most dim-witted reader is convinced.[622]

The Reverend author first hits on "the teaching, both clear and consoling," expressed in chapters XI and XII of the Book of Wisdom. In these chapters we are told that God "has mercy upon all"; He "overlooks the sins of men for the sake of repentance"; He "loves all things that are, and hates none of the things which [He] has made"; He "spares all: because they are [His]," and He "loves souls".[623] Fr. Castelein then puts this teaching of the book of Wisdom to work in order "to explain correctly the chastisements presented as objections to us by Rigorism," (p. 66) as we have seen above. Then on p. 69 he repeats it, saying: "Let us never tire of opposing these very clear words to all the Rigorists, present and future."

But our author's use of this passage cannot pass without some remarks, for in fact he passes on only a part of the doctrine presented in it and omits its application to specific cases, namely the very punishments presented by "Rigorists" as an objection to his thesis.

In Wisdom IX-XII (Father Castelein seems to have started reading at Chapter XI and stopped at verse 21 of Chapter XII), the author of

---

[622] *Ibid.*

the book of Wisdom is demonstrating the value of wisdom from history. He states that: *By wisdom they were healed* [=saved], *whosoever have pleased thee, O Lord, from the beginning.* (IX, 19) whereas: *When the unjust went away from her in his anger, he perished* (X, 3). The unjust perish thus at the hand of the Lord on account of their iniquity who thereby punishes them, but He does not act in the same way towards His sons and towards the enemies of His servants. The distinction is brought out clearly in XII, 22 where the former praise God because *Thou chastisest us ... to the end that when we judge we may think on thy goodness: and when we are judged, we may hope for thy mercy,* whereas *Thou scourgest our enemies very many ways.* To the former He shows mercy "because Thou canst do all things, and overlookest the sins of men for the sake of repentance" (XI, 24). Hence *Thou chastisest them that err, by little and little,* (XII, 2) but *Thou shewest thy power, when men will not believe thee to be absolute in power, and thou convincest the boldness of them that know Thee not.* (v. 17) *But they that were not amended by mockeries and reprehensions, experienced the worthy judgment of God. ... for which cause the end also of their condemnation* [i.e. "ultimate damnation, destruction and extermination"[624]] *came upon them.* (vv. 26-27) In other words, according to the commentary of Jansenius of Ghent, they were punished with outright and complete condemnation temporally and with eternal punishment because they died in their obstinacy.[625]

As has been said, in setting forth this doctrine the wise man alludes various events from the annals of the Israelites: he briefly evokes the "end of the condemnation" or "ultimate condemnation" of the wicked human race by the Flood: *when water destroyed the earth,* (X, 4); he also refers in a few words to the destruction of Sodom, calling its inhabitants *the wicked that were perishing* (v. 6), but above all he treats of the punishment inflicted on the Canaanites (Chapter XII) concerning which Fr. Castelein says: "It is in this way [i.e. partially and in

---

[623] Wisdom XI, 24, 25, 27.

[624] Cornelius a Lapidè, *Commentary, ad locum.*

[625] Migne, *Scripturæ Sacræ Cursus Completus,* vol. XVII, col. 526.

accordance with his false interpretation] that we must envisage the chastisements inflicted very reluctantly on the Canaanite peoples." (p. 76)

How then can it be relevant or convincing for our adversary to declare: "So these collective public chastisements, the narration of which in the Bible seems so terrifying, do not of their nature imply the loss of eternal salvation." (p. 69) Such a claim is surely not compatible with the "ultimate condemnation" referred to in Wisdom XII, 27.

I will now press on to examine some of the other scriptural passages cited by the gainsayers:

> Let us begin with the Old Testament. We immediately find in its pages two utterly striking testimonies, in *the two celebrated visions of God* granted to Moses and to Elias, the one representing the Law and the other Prophecy.
>
> These two visions, the first recounted in Exodus XXXIV and the second in III Kings XIX, concern the divine attributes as God has resolved to manifest them and glorify them among men. (p. 161)

From the first vision, after an incomplete account of it, Fr. Castelein emphasizes the following words:

> "O the Lord, the Lord God, merciful and gracious, patient and of much compassion, and true, who keepest mercy unto thousands: who takest away iniquity, and wickedness, and sin."
>
> It is true that Moses adds:
>
> "… Who renderest the iniquity of the fathers to the children, and to the grandchildren, unto the third and fourth generation."
>
> As can be seen, God's mercy is declared first and expressed in absolute and unlimited terms. Then, by way of corrective, Moses adds a mention of the divine chastisements. But the superiority of mercy over justice is marked by the difference in the symbolic numbers.

Note that this vision concerns the establishment of the covenant by God with Moses, in which Moses receives the two new tablets of the law, the previous ones having been broken. The words cited by Fr. Castelein are attributed in the Hebrew version with its interwoven prayer not to Moses but to God Himself, describing *Himself as*

He enters this covenant with the Israelites. They are explained as follows by Fr. Hummelauer S.J.:

> First God proclaims His essence in three words: *Dominator, Domine, Deus* — *the Lord, the Lord God...* Then He declares the perfection which most shines forth in this covenant: *merciful and gracious.* Then He extols His *patience* or *longsuffering* — *patient and of much compassion,* a perfection first exercised towards those who are not grateful for mercies previously received. Then He adds: *and true.* The [Hebrew] word used here chiefly means truthfulness with regard to promises, and indeed to threats, i.e. faithfulness. *Who keepest mercy unto thousands* — i.e. unto a thousand generations. As the Hebrew term mainly refers to keeping an agreement or covenant, it here expresses faithful respect of *promised* mercy. Then mercy is manifested by the remission of sin: *who takest away iniquity, and wickedness, and sin.* ... But because this mercy is wholly tempered by fidelity, i.e. entails no failure in justice, *no man of himself is innocent before thee.* The Hebrew says *But in justifying He shall not justify,* i.e. God does not always justify and forgive indiscriminately, indeed He punishes severely and perseveringly: *Who renderest the iniquity of the fathers to the children, and to the grandchildren, unto the third and fourth generation.*[626]

This explanation is incompatible with Fr. Castelein's French translation and his explanations; it is also incompatible with the what Fr. Castelein alleges to be the meaning and intention of the vision itself: "These two visions ... concern the divine attributes as God has resolved to manifest them and glorify them among men. ... God therefore wishes especially to draw glory from His mercy." (pp. 161, 164)

And the second vision shows no clearer sign of this intention. Its meaning, as expounded by Fr. Clair,[627] is as follows:

> The Lord is in none of these phenomena, i.e. His justices proceed from Him, go before Him and bear witness to Him, but do not enable Him to be known in His essence. On the contrary His presence is rather manifested in the *whistling of a gentle air* which accompanies the peace that fol-

---

[626] *Commentarius in Exodum et Leviticum,* p. 329,

[627] Fr. Clair, of the diocese of Autun (1839-81), biblical commentator. — Translator.

lows the storm… The God of Israel proves that, in His power, He can chastise and annihilate those who despise Him, but that in His nature and essence He is the grace and love that give life; that although His people have broken the pact of the Covenant, *He* observes it faithfully as He has promised.[628]

Whereas Fr. Castelein exclaims: "Who does not admire the magnificent teaching which emerges from this double vision of God? Who does not grasp its *universal scope*?" (p. 166) He forgets, however, to remark, as does his confrère Fr. Bainvel, that, "It is almost always amid streaks of lightning and claps of thunder that Jehovah shows Himself, and the earth trembles at His presence."[629]

He confirms his conclusion from other passages of the Old Testament which teach the mercy of God — which we are all agreed is infinite. Among them, however, he cites Psalm CXLIV, 9, concerning which Fr. Bainvel specifically says: "This text should not be cited to prove that mercy is, as it were, the dominant attribute of God, surpassing all the others,"[630] which is precisely what Fr. Castelein does.

From there Fr. Castelein moves on to the New Testament, citing passages such as the following:

(i) … *There shall be joy in heaven upon one sinner that doth penance, more than upon ninety-nine just who need not penance.*[631] A citation which gives him the opportunity to compare the present writer — together with the Saints of every century — to the Pharisees: "Against whom is this teaching aimed? Against the Rigorists of those days — the Pharisees. (p. 173)

(ii) *They that are in health need not a physician, but they that are ill. Go then and learn what this meaneth, I will have mercy and not sacrifice. For I am not come to call the just, but sinners.*[632] "What could be imagined more touching or consoling than these words?" (p. 174)

(iii)   The parable of the prodigal son, etc. (*Ibid.*)

---

[628] *Commentarius in Exodum et Leviticum*, p. 345.

[629] *Les Contresens Bibliques des Prédicateurs*, p. 69.

[630] *Ibid.*, p. 98.

[631] Luke XV, 7.

[632] Matthew IX, 12-13.

(iv)   The birth of Christ, which the Angel calls *good tidings of great joy, that shall be to **all** the people.*[633] And Christ's own invitation to all to come to Him: *Come to me, all you that labour, and are burdened...*[634] (p. 176)

(v) The words of Saint Peter: *God is not a respecter of persons. But in **every** nation, he that feareth him, and worketh justice, is acceptable to him.*[635] (p. 179)

(vi)   The words of Saint Paul: *For there is no respect of persons with God.*[636] — *There is neither Gentile nor Jew, circumcision nor uncircumcision, Barbarian nor Scythian, bond nor free. But Christ is all, and in all.*[637] — *There is neither Jew nor Greek: there is neither bond nor free: there is neither male nor female. For you are all one in Christ Jesus.*[638] — *Who gave himself a redemption for all.*[639] — *And Christ died for all.*[640] (p. 180)

(vii)   *The words of Saint John: But if any man sin, we have an advocate with the Father, Jesus Christ the just: And he is the propitiation for our sins: and not for ours only, but also for those of **the whole world**.*[641] Etc. (p. 185)

One is left wondering whether these passages, in which the ideas of mercy and the word "all" (or "every") are continually encountered, do not in Fr. Castelein's view prove the salvation of *all* Christians! It is an insufficient defence of his approach to say that he intends only to demonstrate the greatness of God's mercy and the universality of the Redemption as made available to men by God — all of which his texts do indeed prove — for Fr. Castelein's overriding objective in multiplying such quotations is to convince his read-

---

[633] Luke II, 10.

[634] Matthew XI, 28.

[635] Acts X, 35.

[636] Romans II, 11.

[637] Colossians, III, 11.

[638] Galatians III, 28.

[639] I Timothy II, 6.

[640] II Corinthians V, 15.

[641] I John II, 1.

ers that most men are saved, a conclusion which is false and based on spurious logic, for a conclusion cannot be broader than the premises it flows from.

Moreover Fr. Castelein seems to be out to hoodwink his simpler readers, for the most part layfolk. For right from his Prologue, although explicitly admitting that his doctrine is new and unusual, he claims that it is the fruit of a most diligent study of Holy Writ, and at the beginning of his Chapter V "Final Considerations — Theoretical Conclusions" he makes the statement already quoted above: "The arguments drawn from Holy Scripture ... are incomparably more expressive in favour of a high number of the elect. The number, variety and clarity of the texts I have gathered together must dissipate any doubt on the subject." (p. 266) And further on he adds: "In opposition to all these very explicit texts in favour of Jesus Christ and the souls saved by Him, nothing comparable can be found in the entire Bible in favour of Satan and of evil." (p. 287) And to crown these and similar remarks, he issues on p. 189 the triumphant challenge: "How, in the light of such texts, could the Rigorists maintain their *despair-spreading* doctrine of the fewness of the saved?" (p. 189) Do not such remarks inevitably give the reader the impression that the author has provided positive, direct scriptural evidence of his main thesis? Do they not suggest to him that the texts actually quoted by Fr. Castelein genuinely fall into that category?

I note too, with regard to the expression "despair-spreading doctrine" ["*doctrine désespérante*"], that no one claims that men's hope is frustrated by any act *on God's part*. Our doctrine is that of Saint Thomas: "The fact that some who have hope fail to obtain beatitude is due to defect in their free will which sets in place the obstacle of sin, not to any defect in the divine power or mercy that hope is based on."[642] By contrast it can be argued that Fr. Castelein's own doctrine, by diminishing fervour and zeal for eternal salvation, itself undermines one of the foundations of hope and sows in its place presump-

---

[642] *Summa Theologiæ*, q. 18. a. 4, reply to objection 3.

tion, the vice which sins against true hope by excess and thereby stroys it quite as surely as does despair.

In the same vein I note that Fr. Bougaud follows the example of Bishop Camus[643] by pressing into service the text *There is now therefore no condemnation to them that are in Christ Jesus.*[644] Forsooth! But this is a *truncated* quotation, for the whole reads: *There is now therefore no condemnation to them that are in Christ Jesus,* **who walk not according to the flesh**. And would that this qualifying clause applied to the Christians of our day a great deal more generally than in fact we observe it to!

Progressives of this school, who glory in the modern interpretations of biblical texts which *hitherto* were invariably taken to assert the difficulty of salvation and the fewness of the saved, need to be reminded of the following warnings from the Vicar of Christ:

(i) In the interpretation of Holy Scripture, "every effort must be made to avoid transgressing by pride or even by levity or imprudence."[645] Yet what else is it to call the ancient and approved Interpreters "Rigorists" and to reject their common interpretation as erroneous and contrary to the Spirit of Christ, except to "transgress by pride, by levity *and* by imprudence"?

(ii) The pope continues: "In the first place too much weight should not be attached to certain *new* opinions which ought rather to be feared, not because they are new, but because for the most part *they lead those who embrace them astray, by the appearance and simulation of truth.* Here and there a fondness has sprung up, even in quarters where it ought least to be expected, for a method of interpretation which is too bold and takes excessive liberties."[646] Yet we see the Progressives admit that their opinion is "novel" and cheerfully hailing it as the fruit of exegetical *progress*; they are indeed *too bold* and *take excessive liberties*. Hence *fondness* for their deceptive teaching has

---

[643] *Op. cit.*, p. 373.

[644] Romans VIII, 1.

[645] Pope Leo XIII: *Breve ad Fratres Minores*, 25th November 1898.

[646] *Ibid.*

sprung up and it is preached "with admirable [sic] bravado,"[647] *even in quarters where it ought least to be expected.*

> Let all those who treat of the divine books understand and seriously consider this; let them also bear in mind that the simple key to safety in these studies is to heed the Church as they ought. Nor shall we pass over in silence ... the fact that no Catholic is entitled to neglect the precepts and documents of the supreme Pontiff.[648]

The Progressives stand in need of these words, but will they act on them? One may well wonder when one reads Fr. Mauran admitting that learned theologians had told him, on the subject of his work *Élus et Sauvés*, that: "The author explains certain texts of Holy Scripture in conformity with his thesis whereas *there is no evidence that this is really what the texts mean.*" To which, he tranquilly declares: "I replied that nothing prevents me from explaining in *my* sense obscure passages of the Bible which conceal hidden meanings and the real sense of which has never been officially given by the Church."[649]

Such an exegetical approach makes it easy indeed to prove that the number of the elect is the greater, in the face of the unanimous consensus of the Saints and the ancient interpretation of Holy Scripture.

And yet the same Fr. Mauran is seriously cited in the article on "The Elect" in Vigouroux's substantial *Dictionnaire de la Bible* (col. 1711) as an authority, immediately after Knabenbauer in favour of the thesis of the Progressives! And the article's author, Fr. Lesêtre, adds: "Among the moderns there is a marked tendency to interpret in a broader way the sentence which completes the two Gospel parables."

This completes this Chapter on the respect shown by the Progressives towards the Saints, the Doctors and the Fathers of the Church and the traditional interpretation of Holy Scripture which the reader will now be well able to judge for himself. The time has now come

---

[647] "E.T.", letter to "Le patriote" — 19th March, 1899.

[648] *Ibid.*

[649] Preface, p. 1, Author's Note.

to embark on the examination of the other sophistries of the Progressives.

CHAPTER SEVEN

Other Sophistries of the Progressives

HAVING EXAMINED how little respect the gainsayers display towards the Fathers and Holy Scripture I shall now embark on the rebuttal of the long series of their vain arguments which for the sake of good order I have classified as follows:

I. The general sophistry concerning the freedom of controversy as to the salvation of the greater part of mankind.

II. Specific sophistries relating to the honour of God.

III. Specific sophistries relating to faith and the Church.

IV. Specific sophistries relating to original sin and to the wounds it gives rise to.

V. Specific sophistries relating to lust.

VI. Various sophistries which fail to prove the thesis because they are irrelevant.

I

GENERAL SOPHISTRY

1

"The opinion that most men are saved is a matter of free discussion in the Catholic Church."

1. Weighing on the one side the countless authorities of the Fathers, Saints and Theologians and on the other the futile sophistries opposed to the common, indeed unanimous, judgement of the Saints, in the scales of sound theology, it is quite impossible to admit that the opinion *that incomparably more are saved* is entirely free among faithful Catholics.

Hence Fr. Castelein and other writers commit a grave error and lead their readers into it when they contend that the doctrine of the greater number of the saved is entirely free because the opposite has yet to be defined by the Church, as though the obligation of admitting a proposition could arise for the faithful only as the result of a *decision* of the infallible Magisterium.

> The Catholic Church, which constantly advances in its understanding of the revealed doctrine, leaves this question *free*. (p. 285)
> On the subject of the number of the elect, which is *freely debated* within the theological schools, we may *in all liberty of spirit* adopt the solution supported by the powerful arguments elaborated in these pages. (p. 190).
> The Catholic Church leaves the subject of this book *free*. (p. 283)
> The question of authority fully studied and resolved in favour of the *liberty* of the theologian… (p. 286)
> The question remains *free*. (Letters to *Le Patriote, le* XXe *Siècle*, etc.)

The same error is committed by Bougaud:

> We expect to be allowed to make use of that freedom which has always been granted to all in doubtful matters. *In dubiis libertas.* The judgement of the Church is not like that of men. She has the intuitions of a mother. (*Op. cit.*, p. 363)

And by Mauran:

> Let us be quite clear about this: the point at issue is not a doctrine taught by the Church... It is an opinion that is *private, free* and that it is permissible to combat and to reject. (*Op. cit.*, p. VIII)

This provides another occasion to remind ourselves in passing of the wise counsel of Saint Ignatius who "in many places in the Constitutions [of the Society of Jesus] stipulated that solid and sound doctrine was to be followed, *indeed the sounder and more approved doctrine.*"[650] And it was of this very counsel that Our Holy Father Pope Leo XIII reminded the Fathers of the Society of Jesus in his letter *On the Profession of the Teaching of Saint Thomas*, while pointing out to them the danger to be avoided: *a lust for novelty ... under the pretence of doctrinal progress.*[651]

2. It will therefore be worth our while to examine in greater depth the subject of the rules by which Holy Church governs sound theology and the teaching to be transmitted to the faithful. The object of this enquiry will be to establish on what principles Fr. Castelein and his allies could have based a legitimate judgement that his doctrine is a free opinion.

According to principles admitted by all, a proposition may be called *free* if:

(i) it is neither of faith nor contrary to faith;

(ii) it is not opposed to good morals;

(iii) it is openly defended in the Catholic academic world by many theologians in good standing.

Examples of free doctrines are: the various opinions concerning whether predestination is or is not consequent upon foreseen merits; middle knowledge (*scientia media*); whether the Incarnation would or would not have taken place in the absence of human sin; what makes grace efficacious, etc.[652]

---

[650] Pope Leo XIII, *Acta*, vol. XII, p. 368, Vatican edition.

[651] *Ibid.*

[652] Cf. Schouppe, *Elementa Theologiæ Dogmaticæ*, tr. I, n. 159; 6th edition, p. 50.

This being so, I submit that the doctrine of the fewness of the saved *relative to mankind as a whole* is by no means free. I reason as follows:

With regard to point (i) above:

(a) According to some theologians such as Laselve, Smising and Bosco, it is *de fide* (i.e. of faith); according to others, such as Suárez, Estius, Gonet and many others, it is *true, more than true* and *certain* — and no single Father is to be found to contradict it.

(b) Albeit not evidently *de fide* (for it is not certain with absolute clarity from divine revelation and the meaning of Holy Scripture, though clear enough, has not been infallibly declared to be such by the Church), I suggest that a doctrine can be called contrary to the integrity of the faith when it exposes the consensus of the Fathers and theologians to great danger, indeed to actual disrespect.

I further suggest that a proposition may be called temerarious when, in matters theological or in any way connected with theology, it is boldly advanced as new, arbitrarily, imprudently and rashly supported by defences which neglect or oppose right reason, and is commended chiefly on the grounds that it *is* new. I refer to an opinion which opposes — as has often been said — the common teaching of the Saints, Fathers and Doctors, not to mention the censure of the theological faculty of the Sorbonne against Marmontel's *Bélisaire*,[653] and the constant opinion of the greatest Theologians and biblical exegetes, as well as the very gravest reasons — contradicting them all without the slightest foundation in authority or reason.[654]

With regard to point (ii):

Although from a purely speculative point of view the opinion of the gainsayers is not directly opposed to good morals, the fact remains that it cannot be approved and defended without recourse to arguments which I have no hesitation in calling immoral and scan-

---

[653] Cf. *Bulletin de Notre Dame de la Sainte Espérance*, May 1899.
[654] Cf. Schouppe, *op. cit.*, n. 168, p. 52.

dalous. For I suggest that in reality, as expounded, a doctrine is opposed to Christian morality when:

(a) it undermines love and respect for the Catholic faith and the Catholic Church by teaching that salvation is easy even outside the Church;

(b) it fails to distinguish clearly between the supernatural and the natural order, speaking as though it were, under present conditions, sufficient for salvation to observe *natural* religion;

(c) it diminishes reverence and docility towards the Doctors and Pastors by alleging that they erred for so many centuries in expounding Catholic doctrine concerning matters necessary to salvation;

(d) it diminishes the horror of sin by taking into account only acts of the most appalling wickedness, all but disregarding "ordinary" mortal sins and in particular by palliating the malice of sins of the flesh;

(e) it diminishes the vigilance of Christians in what affects their salvation by attaching less importance to the danger arising from the triple concupiscence and all but denying the dangers due to the world and to evil example;

(f) it diminishes the fervour of the faithful in working out their salvation by good works, prayer and frequenting the sacraments, adopting a minimalism in this matter;

(g) by all these mains it easily beguiles the faithful into presumptuous foolhardiness.

With regard to point (iii):

Is Fr. Castelein's opinion *in fact* openly communicated in the Catholic academic world by *many* theologians in good standing? Certainly one or two Apologists may be found who, in replying to unbelievers, troubled souls or persons far from friendly to religion, have conceded that *the proportion of the elect is not a dogma of the Catholic faith* that all must believe; but no theologian can be found who teaches Fr. Castelein's opinion to the faithful or who passes it on to undergraduate students in the *Catholic academic world*. Hence it is not lawful to call it *free*.

3. What, then, do the words *the Catholic Church leaves this subject free* mean?

Does the Church then leave everyone free, according to his own judgement, to despise her decisions as manifested by the Sacred Congregations and to violate the laws by which Sacred Theology identified Catholic teachings?

This rhetorical question arises because as a matter of fact:

(i) A declaration of the Sacred Congregation of the Index exists on this subject, which calls for the pious and filial submission of faithful Catholics.[655]

Here are the words of Pope Pius IX directly corresponding to such decisions and theological truths:

> But, in the case of the submission obliging in conscience all those Catholic who pursue study of the speculative sciences so as to render new services to the Church by their writings, the members of this Congress must recognize that it is not sufficient for learned Catholics to accept and respect the dogmas of the Church as mentioned above: they must, also, submit both to doctrinal decisions issued by the Pontifical Congregations and to those points of doctrine which, with common and constant consent, are held by Catholics as theological truths and conclusions so certain that opinions opposed to them, though they cannot be termed heretical, yet merit some other theological censure.[656]

(ii) There are rules to be observed in Catholic theology, and the Church surely does not leave each one free to violate or respect these rules as he chooses. In particular, in addition to Sacred Scripture and Patristic Tradition (sources whose meaning must be regulated in accordance with our reasoning process in cases when, though certain enough, it falls short of being actually evident) there is the *sensus catholicus* or Catholic instinct which may not be

---

[655] Cf. *Regulæ Indicis*; Scheeben, Fr. Matthias, *Handbuch der katholischen Dogmatik*, vol. I, p. 396.

contradicted without the greatest rashness. As the renowned Scheeben observes:

> Even in the immediate present a kind of rule of faith is conceivable, even a living rule, providing direction with regard to juridical decisions. I refer to the unanimous mind of the faithful and of the teachers in so far as it is the echo of a previous ecclesiastical proposition or the testimony of the Holy Ghost acting in the whole Church.[657]

(iii)   There exist rules that are strictly theological upon which the Church bases her theological qualifications and wishes the doctrine transmitted to the faithful to be based on:

Beyond that truth which is Catholic in the strict sense, there is another truth which is also Catholic, an *ecclesiastical* truth, a theology in the broad sense, which a true Catholic must accept with respectful trust and which he cannot deny without offending the Catholic instinct, and which further restricts the field of free opinion.[658]

Relevant here is the statement of Melchior Cano that a unanimous consensus of all the Saints and Fathers furnishes the theologian with utterly certain evidence in favour of their assertions as such a consensus is the very mind of the Holy Ghost — or, as Duplessis d'Argentré puts it, of the Apostles. And that there exists a unanimous consensus of the Fathers in favour of the doctrine here maintained is declared by Estius: "Nor is a single one of the Fathers to be found who has written otherwise."[659]

As Fr. Vacant writes:

> There is an obligation to respect, or even to admit, on pain of *temerity*, a teaching of the holy Fathers or of the theologians which comes close to displaying unanimous agreement.[660]

---

[656] Apostolic Letter *Tuas libenter*, 21st December 1863, to the Archbishop of Munich, Denzinger 1679.

[657] *Op. cit.*, vol. I, p. 287, n. 114,

[658] *Ibid.*, p. 29S *n°* «7.

[659] See above, p. 134.

[660] Vacant, Fr. Jean Michel Alfred, Professor of the Major Seminary of Nancy, *Le Magistère Ordinaire de l'Église et ses Organes*, part IV.

Fr. Castelein's claim that whether the majority of men are saved or only a minority is a matter of free debate in holy Church is thus shown to be entirely unfounded.

II
SPECIFIC SOPHISTRIES CONCERNING THE GLORY OF GOD

2
"The doctrine of the fewness of the saved cannot be reconciled with the doctrine of the universality of the Redemption."

Fr. Castelein:

> The theory of the fewness of the elect is irreconcilable with the doctrine of the Redemption studied in its divine causes, its supernatural character and its universal object." (*Op. cit.*, p. 301)

So none of the Fathers, the Saints, the Doctors of the Church, neither Augustine, nor Thomas, nor Anselm, nor Alphonsus has ever understood the fundamental doctrine of the entire Christian religion! They were unaware of the causes of the Redemption, its supernatural characters and the universality of its object.

O happy twentieth century in which at last we have been delivered from such ignorance!

And upon what basis does Fr. Castelein make this gratuitous assertion?

Ought the Redemption to have dragged men into heaven even against their own will and compelled them to observe the commandments of God despite themselves? Ought the efficacious grace of the Redemption to be so powerful as to destroy man's free will?

Here is another argument to the same effect. It is the common teaching of theologians, in agreement with Tradition and Scripture, that Christ offered the price of the Redemption even for children who die without Baptism. But this by no means implies that the Redemption can be considered less universal because as a matter of fact these children do not receive its fruit. In the same way, therefore, the common opinion of theologians, in conformity with Tradition and

Scripture, that most men — and even most Catholics — are damned is not opposed to the universality of the Redemption.

In his efforts to boost the number of the elect the Rev. Victor Mauran goes so far as to invoke the eternal salvation of the inhabitants of other galaxies; here are the moving, though hardly theological, terms in which he couches his argument as to the universality of the Redemption:

> The Saviour never ceases calling Himself the Son of Man. Hence the unknown inhabitants of the planetary spheres make no attempt to snatch from us what is our own: our good, our gift, our crucified Jesus…
>
> What is there to gain by presenting the Redemption as a failed rescue mission, since mankind's ultimate lot remains that of Sodom and Gomorrha?
>
> What could me more ironic than to imagine our earth, consecrated by the human life of a God, united to Him by the flesh, soaked with His Blood — a Blood infinite in worth — then finishing its history by damnation and supreme despair while other worlds, oblivious to this immense catastrophe, proceeded towards their everlasting joys! (*Op. cit.*, p. 159)

Surely the irony lies rather in the thought that such ludicrous arguments could be seriously put forward.

3

"If the number of the saved is not greater than the number of the damned then Christ has not triumphed over the devil but the devil has triumphed over Christ."

1. Christ must gain a brilliant victory over Satan … yet it is alleged that He will not manage to win back one half of the souls Satan snatched from His heavenly Father!

If this were so Satan's conquest would be, in its order, finer than that of His vanquisher!

If Christ does not in fact saved the great majority of souls … *I cannot understand* how His triumph could be worthy of Him. (Castelein, *op. cit.*, p. 180)

Is it credible that His persevering efforts to save the souls He has created should not in fact succeed in saving half of them?

Once again, in this case would not Satan be the victor and the conqueror?

Away with so awful an image, such a loathsome assumption! (p. 190)

I could not believe it. On the contrary, *I* am convinced that, quite to the contrary, the bleeding embrace of Christ will carry before His Father's throne incomparably more souls than He will suffer to be snatched from His grasp. It is not only Christ's love for men that requires this but also His honour. (p. 267)

Christ's conquest *out of the whole of mankind* will be far greater than that of Satan. *I* am even intimately convinced that for the glory of His mercy and His merits He will succeed in winning *from every race and background* more elect than He will leave of reprobate. (p. 301)

Bougaud advances the same argument:

It cannot be that God should be defeated outright. The battle must be won. God cannot close the epic of His creation by allowing Himself to be defeated on every front! Otherwise, I repeat, what was the point of creating in the first place? Why enter battle at all? In such a hypothesis the battle plan must have been ill-conceived, the troops ill-equipped and graces quite insufficient. This immense and magnificent creation would in fact have been but the scene of an immense rout, a gigantic victory of evil over good and of Satan over God! *For my part* I do not believe it. No indeed, *I could not comprehend it.* I should see therein the divine wisdom, power and goodness fatally compromised.

It would appear *to me…* etc. (p. 364)

And the Rev. Victor Mauran:

If the majority of souls were to belong forever to the demon in Hell, to the great enemy of God, where then would be the victory of Jesus-Christ?

Since when is it permitted for a king who loses three quarters of his soldiers and his kingdom on the battlefield to call himself victorious?[661]

This argument, to which the Progressives attach such weight, is advanced as irrefutable in the heretical Dialogue *De amplitudine beati*

---

[661] *Op. cit.*, p. 19.

regni Dei,[662] praised by Gravina and not seldom presented by unbelievers as an objection against divine providence, as we shall shortly be seeing.

2. And yet the argument is quite preposterous. The authors quoted speak of Christ and Lucifer as though they were two equal gods, much as in the Manichaean error two supreme principles are admitted, the one good and the other evil.

"If Christ does not defeat Lucifer He will Himself be defeated by His adversary!" Indeed! It is true that Saint Ignatius compares Satan to a military leader in his *Meditation on the Two Standards*, but he is far from putting him on equal footing with the Son of God.

I reply as follows:

Without any exception Christ has always conquered, does conquer and will ever conquer the devil. He shall reign for ever and ever. His enemies are His footstool. Therefore even those who adhere to Lucifer are subject to Christ in His triumph, together with their leader and his angels. Bergier judiciously writes:

> The triumph attributed by Bayle to the devil over Christ on the day of the Final Judgement as a consequence of the great number of the damned is *in every respect absurd*.
>
> (a) It assumes that devil's role in the reprobation of the wicked is comparable to that of Jesus Christ in the eternal salvation of the saints, and that the former are lost because the devil was the stronger and Christ the weaker — an idea combining impiety with sheer insanity. They are damned not on account of the malice of the demon but on account of their own malice, since God did not allow the devil to tempt them beyond their strength and with the help of His grace it depended on them alone to overcome the enemy of their salvation. (b) Another absurdity is to imagine the destiny of the good and the wicked as a sort of combat between Christ and the devil in which Christ does all He can to save a soul, but does not succeed, as though salvation in turn depended exclusively on the power of the Saviour, leaving no

---

[662] By Italian renaissance humanist and neo-Arian Celio Secondo Curione (1503-1569). — Translator.

place for man's free cooperation. Has the devil then more power than it pleases God to grant him?

(c) It implies that the loss of a soul deprives Our Lord of some part of His happiness or His glory, and that He is saddened by it as the devil is embittered by his failure to pervert a just soul; that He has miscalculated as Satan's ambitions have miscarried — a parallel of sheer insanity! Jesus Christ, as God, has known from all eternity the number of the elect and of the reprobate; even if every human soul were to perish, Christ would lose nothing for Himself and the devil would be no less miserable for eternity.

No: the victory of Christ over the devil does not consist in preventing men from culpably compassing their own damnation, and if it were so virtue would have no merit and salvation would no longer be a reward. It consists in the fact that mankind, utterly banished from heaven by the sin of Adam, recovered by the Redemption, the power of entering there, while each individual receives, by the merits of Jesus Christ, all the graces needed to be saved, so that he is inexcusable if he is lost.[663]

I further reply that justice is just as much a divine attribute as mercy, and both are to be glorified. While the blessed in heaven glorify God in His mercy for ages without end, so do the damned, albeit unwillingly, glorify the infinite justice of God *so that in the name of Jesus every knee should bow, of those that are in heaven, on earth, and under the earth.*[664] The glory of God cannot be decreased by a hairsbreadth owing to the greater number of the damned. The pious and learned Ven. Fr. Lessius S.J. expounds this truth with wisdom:

God permitted a countless multitude of men to precipitate themselves into eternal damnation. For even though He foreknew that such great evil would follow from the withdrawal of original justice and the initial providence, He did not alter His project, as though He found such wholesale perdition of souls of little moment in punishing the sin. Just as when a prince, in punishing the misdeed of some powerful subject, refuses to remit any of the punishment even if he should see that in conse-

---

[663] Bergier, Nicolas-Sylvestre, *Dictionnaire de Theologie*, art. "Élu".
[664] Philippians II, 10.

quence the whole of His kingdom would become a wilderness and the greater part of his subjects die in civil war.[665]

And he addresses the following words to God Himself:

Again didst Thou show forth the same justice when on account of the sin of our first parents Thou didst despoil the whole human race of original justice and the happiness of their first state and subject them to countless miseries and death. By which punishment Thou didst already foresee that a countless multitude of men would be damned and barely one in a hundred would obtain salvation.[666]

Also worth attention are the words of Monsabré:

Would you argue, gentlemen, that the number of the elect, no matter how great, is less than that of the reprobate? What does it matter? You cannot now accuse the divine government of having failed in its providential action. God willed the salvation of all, to all He offered His helps and graces; no one is damned save those who did not choose to be saved. To every complaint uttered by the victims of His eternal justice, God can reply: You damned yourself: *perditio tua ex te*. No, the wretchedness of the reprobate does not dishonour Him any more than the execution of evildoers dishonours a great king. Not having obtained the triumph of His mercy over these rebels, He is assured of the triumph of His justice and can, with greater right, use the words spoken by the greatest, wisest and best of masters: the glory of my government is to be good and merciful towards those who submit to my sacred will, and forever to combat the froward — *parcere subjectis et debellare superbos*.[667]

And thirdly I reply with Mgr. Paquet: "Good done is to be weighed, not merely counted, especially in the order of grace,"[668] —

---

[665] *De Perfectionibus Moribusque Divinis, De Justitia et Ira Dei*, Cap. V; *De Secundo Opere Justitiæ Divinæ*, cap. 4.

[666] *Ibid.*, cap. 31.

[667] *Conférences de Notre Dame*, 1889, *Le Nombre des Élus*, p. 266. "Parcere subjectis et debellare superbos" means "to spare the humble but reduce the proud" and is taken from the prophecy of the mission of Rome found in Book VI of Virgil's *Æneid*. — Translator.

[668] Paquet, Mgr. Louis-Adolphe (1859-1942), *Commentarii in Summam Theologicam D. Thomæ, De Deo Uno et Trino*, p. 392.

and indeed of glory. Thus the Immaculate Mother of God alone renders greater glory to the adorable Trinity than all the damned could have done if they had been of the number of the elect. Such is the teaching of Blessed Clement-Mary Hofbauer.[669]

And Fr. Monsabré well illustrates this reply:

> No matter how great their number, these proud reprobates can never hold in check the vast army of the elect. A single saved soul is a masterpiece in which all the divine perfections play their part, in concert with human freedom; a single creature glorified and admitted to the beatific vision is a marvel of beauty more astonishing and ravishing than all the wonders of the heavens and the earth together. Yet attempts are made to dishonour the Artisan of this wonder by reproaching Him with the numerical quantity of the wretched creatures who have deformed themselves by abusing the divine gifts and their freedom. As well might one argue that there is no true artistic genius to be found among mankind because masterpieces are fewer in number than the stunted failures with which mediocrity has flooded the world. In such matters, Gentlemen, we must weigh as well as count: *non numeranda sed ponderanda*. The least of the elect weighs more in the balance of divine glory than the whole of Hell.

4. Having now refuted the arguments of the gainsayers, I take the opportunity to criticize the reasoning process of these Progressives. For all too often in the present debate we encounter, instead of solid arguments, remarks such as: "*I* do not understand," — the implicit syllogism being that "What *I* do not understand cannot be so," in the present case, therefore, "It is *not* so."

The reader will recall the examples recently cited on p. 308 above.

What all such arguments overlook is that there are many things that we do not understand but must nevertheless believe. Unbelievers reason along exactly the same lines even with regard to the mysteries of faith: "I do not understand the transmission of the sin of Adam or how a brief instant of carnal pleasure can merit eternal pun-

---

[669] "Were there but a single man who benefited from the merits of the Saviour, the devil would be racked with bitter envy for all eternity." *Vie,* by Fr. Michel Haringer, Tournai, 1887, p. 212.

ishment, therefore I will not believe them and in consequence thee things cannot in fact be so."

5. No better answer can be made to the bleeding-heart sentimentalists of our own day than was made of old by Saint Augustine concerning the "merciful" then rampant:

> If this opinion is good and true because it displays mercy, how much better and truer will it be when it shows yet greater mercy. Let its disciples therefore broaden and deepen the fountain of their *mercy* to include the fallen angels, by declaring that they are to be delivered from damnation at least after however many centuries. For why should the tide of mercy flow so copiously towards every member of the human race only to dry up at the first mention of the angels? The answer is that they dare not press their mercy to its logical conclusion by embracing the deliverance of the devil himself. But whoever does so will surpass them in their own "mercy"; yet each will be erring the more grotesquely and perversely against the words of the most just God the more he seems to himself to be overflowing with the milk of human kindness.[670]

And indeed, as Father Emmanuel writes of the gainsayers: "Their reasoning invariably comes down to this: God must save the majority of men because that *seems* fitting to *my* reason."[671]

The simple reason why Saints Augustine and Thomas and countless other exceedingly learned Saints did not hold the same position as our Progressives is that they humbly submitted their reason to divine revelation and tradition: *Narrow is the way … and few there are that find it.*

It is also perfectly fair to apply to the Progressives de Maistre's reply to Fleury when the latter wrote, "I believe that appeal may be made from the Pope to a Council." De Maistre remarked:

> Such recourse to the word "I" is unlikely to disquiet the Catholic Church… The sight of Fleury refuted by Mosheim and by Bossuet and about to be set back on the straight path by the Centuriators of Magdeburg shows where the taste for the first person singular leads. "I": it is terrifying to encounter this pronoun in theology.

---

[670] *City of God*, book 21, chapter 17; Migne, *Pat. Lat.*, vol. XLI, col. 732.

[671] *Bulletin de Notre Dame de la Sainte Espérance*, October 1898, p. 151.

4

***"Since the number of the good Angels is greater, by the same token the
number of the saved among men must also be greater."***

Let us now seek to shed new light on the solution to the problem we
are addressing, by using an analogical argument drawn from the angelic
nature… (Fr. Castelein, *op. cit.*, p. 272)

Just as the great Suárez, considering only the laws of creation, concluded that in the angelic nature benediction would far exceed maledic-
tion, so *I*, considering these same laws,… Etc. (*Ibid.*, p. 273)

Once again Saint Thomas Aquinas replies, not to Suárez — for
Suárez never drew any such inept conclusion — but to Fr. Castelein.
In his article devoted to whether the angels who sinned were as numerous as those who remained firm, he presents against his own position the following objection: "It would seem that more angels sinned
than stood firm. For, as the Philosopher says: 'Evil is in many, but
good is in few.'"[672]

To this argument he replies:

The Philosopher is speaking with regard to men, in whom evil comes
to pass from seeking after sensible pleasures, which are known to most
men, and from forsaking the good of reason, which good is known to
fewer. In the angels, however, there is only an intellectual nature; hence
comparison between the two cases is unjustified.[673]

He also rejects this "analogical argument drawn from the angelic
nature" on other grounds also, for he says:

Since Happiness surpasses every created nature, no pure creature can
becomingly gain Happiness without the movement of operation,
whereby it tends thereto. But the angel, who is above man in the natural
order, obtained it, according to the order of Divine wisdom, by one
movement of a meritorious work, as was explained in Part I, Q. 62, A. 5,
whereas man obtains it by many movements of works, which are called
merits.[674]

---

[672] *Nicomachean Ethics* II, 6.

[673] *Summa Theologiæ*, I, q. 63, a. 9, objection 1 and reply to objection 1.

[674] *Ibid.*, I-II, q. 5, a. 7 *in corpore.*

This is a second reason why the two cases are dissimilar.

5
"The Doctors who recognize that the majority of Angels are saved may be invoked in favour of the salvation of the majority of men, even though they expressly state the contrary, for they have misunderstood Holy Scripture."

If the shadows cast by the "few are chosen" text, misunderstood by an exegetical science still in its infancy, had not darkened the gaze of these illustrious doctors [Saint Thomas and Suárez] they would *without doubt* have reached the same conclusion as to the final salvation of human nature as they did concerning the angelic nature. I may therefore take shelter behind their authority. (p. 273)

Here is wisdom indeed! An appeal in favour of the salvation of the greater number of men to Saint Thomas and Suárez who, as we have seen, expressly teach that the majority of men are damned and certainly do not base their opinion exclusively on the celebrated biblical text of which the Progressives convince themselves they have finally, after nineteen centuries of confusion, discovered the genuine meaning.

6
"On this subject God's greater glory is better served even by error than by the despair-spreading doctrine of the fewness of the saved."

I am reassured by the intimate conviction that these ideas are true and exact. They are the fruit of a deep study of Holy Scripture and of the teachings of our greatest theologians. (p. X)

A doctrine understood according to the sound traditions of Catholic theology. (p. 355)

To the theologians too narrow or too timorous to share our views, we may oppose the great doctors of the schools. (p. 114)

No doubt these testimonials vouchsafed by Fr. Castelein in favour of his own belief bear witness to his good faith. But it is harder to pay the same compliment to those Progressives who overtly admit that their position is unreliable, indeed probably erroneous, yet continue to prefer it to the common and certain teaching.

For we find Bougaud writing:

> No doubt there is a *considerable element of conjecture* involved here. Fr. Faber does not deny this. "But", he says, "speaking of *what we do not know* … it is at least allowable to put all these considerations in opposition to those which … give us hard … thoughts of God. They are not doctrines. They are not certainties. They are inferences, they are hopes, they are speculations..."[675, 676]

Faber himself avows: "These are all *bad arguments*, taken simply..."[677]

But the Rev. Victor Mauran outstrips them all by blandly announcing:

> I am going to say an impossible thing.
>
> In my mind's eye I imagine that if God had consulted his elect, *before creating them*, they would, seeing themselves so few, have made the sacrifice of their eternal happiness in order to spare their brethren — the great mass of men — the torments of Hell.
>
> I beg the reader's forbearance for this whimsy. These few words suffice to show... Etc."[678]

But so great is the affection of the gainsayers for their own opinion that they think it would be good and useful even it were false!

> *Even if we are wrong* … we shall be better men for having tried to think such thoughts of God as get Him more honour among men, and more love from ourselves.[679]

---

[675] Faber, Fr. F. W., Cong. Orat., *The Creator and the Creature*, 4th edition, p. 392 and note to p. 369. — Translator.

[676] Bougaud, *op. cit.*, p. 382.

[677] *Growth in Holiness*, 15th American edition, p. 395.

[678] *Op. cit.*, p. 150.

Mgr. Charles Gay displays no less flippancy when he writes: "In any event we know nothing about it [the fewness of the saved] and it is wrong to appeal to the Gospel in this grave matter... Nothing clear or certain is to be found on the subject in the Gospel." (*Instructions pour les Personnes du Monde*, Paris, 1892, p. 385)

[679] Bougaud, *op. cit.*, p. 382 ; Faber, *The Creator and the Creature*, p. 392.

While Fr. Mauran frankly declares:

> But, who knows? May not this thesis be a sophistry and our hope an illusion? Am I not mistaken? Well, even so, I think it better to be wrong while offering comfort and hope to souls rather than fear and despair.[680]

There are three answers to such a claim.

1. While the intention stated is indeed a very good one, it is entirely futile. For a doctrine which represents God as not only good and merciful but as so forgetful of His own honour and rights as to cast the pearls of grace and of glory before swine and to allow hope and even certainty of salvation for those who err from the single path of truth or who devote their whole life to lust can have no possible good effect. Its obvious result would be to encourage men to conclude that the means of salvation such as frequentation of the sacraments, fleeing the occasions of sin, hatred of the world, bodily mortification, obedience and prayer are not so important as they have been represented as being by the Fathers and by the Church. Why should we set such burdens on our shoulders, men will say, for we shall be sanctified without them! God is *so prompt to forgive the sin of lust* "Come therefore, and let us enjoy the good things that are present, and let us speedily use the creatures as in youth. Let us fill ourselves with costly wine, and ointments: and let not the flower of the time pass by us. Let us crown ourselves with roses, before they be withered: let no meadow escape our riot. Let none of us go without his part in luxury: let us everywhere leave tokens of joy: for this is our portion, and this our lot."[681]

In his thoroughly excellent book *La question de l'Évangile...,*[682] Fr. Coppin, as we have seen, admirably demonstrates the pernicious character of Fr. Castelein's work.

---

[680] *Op. cit.,* p. 225.

[681] Wisdom II, 6-9.

[682] Coppin, Fr. Joseph C. SS. R. (1840-1915), *La Question de l'Évangile: Seigneur, y en aura-t-il peu de sauvés: ou, Considérations sur l'écrit du R.P. Castelein, intitulé: Le rigorisme et la question du nombre des élus.*

(i) Its first natural and necessary fruit will be to weaken in a host of minds respect and docility towards preachers and religious writers past, present and future.

(ii) Another baneful effect will be to weaken the horror of sin in many souls.

(iii)   Baneful again will it prove for lowering the true notion of the Christian life;

(iv)   And because it will strengthen and increase the spirit of worldliness in souls.

(v) Finally it will lessen the idea we should have of the Catholic Church and diminish our esteem for the favour of belonging to her by the true faith.[683]

The author goes on to expound each of these points lucidly and eloquently: his presentation would be too long to quote here but is earnestly recommended to the reader.

But surely no none can deny that these consequences flow logically enough. And even if the inferences were not strictly logical it cannot be denied that it is what in practice a great many readers *will* infer very readily. The scale of the damage thus done is as plain as a pikestaff.

The Progressives hope to spread the love of God among the people, but what kind of love is it that can co-exist with the spirit of this world — vain, proud and sensual as it is? The spirit that is appalled only by such sins as are exceptionally monstrous and obstinately voluntary? How can what decreases horror of sin increase love of God?

They hope to enkindle hope, but they engender presumption:

> What sturdy support Fr. Castelein's work will furnish to souls inclined to deadly presumption, with its generous estimates of the average suburbs of Brussels, its rhapsodies on sins of weakness, its unremitting refrain of the preponderance of grace, with its secret ways, its apparitions of Our Lord to souls on the threshold of eternity to pluck them heavenwards with a final victorious swipe, its countless multitudes of souls

---

[683] Coppin, *op. cit.*, p. 308 *et seq.*; see also above, p. 28.

transplanted into paradise without having ever lifted a finger to merit such a destiny![684]

Compare this doctrine with the Gospel warning: *By their fruits shall ye know them*.[685] Can such a doctrine, destined as it is to be a stumbling block to many, as is already proved beyond cavil by experience, be said to be *scandal-free*?

2. It is asserted gratuitously and impudently that the teaching of the Fathers of the Church is a hindrance to the love of God and to Christian hope. This is a grave accusation indeed against all the Catholic teachers who hold and preach this doctrine and against the ecclesiastical authority which has hitherto tolerated this doctrine. For to hinder hope and divine love is to hinder salvation itself which is the very opposite of the Church's goal. But such an accusation in fact betrays only the temerity of its authors. The Saints have always preached the true love of God, which abhors every sin and every danger of sin and therefore requires great renunciation and constant endeavours against the triple concupiscence. It is because the masses take no heed of such renunciation that the love of God is not widespread. We have seen that the Progressives are prompt to make such renunciation easier by attenuating it, but in doing so they are championing a renunciation essentially different from that demanded in the Gospel, and without which true love of God cannot exist The Saints have always preached Christian hope, based on God's promises and mercies, while opposing presumption and rashness. Never have they preached that the means of salvation are lacking to one who does what he can.[686] It is therefore clean impossible that anyone could ever have committed despair as a result of hearing a proper explanation of the teaching of the Saints on this subject.

3. "Even if we are wrong…!"

It is not lawful to preach error even if good were accidentally to arise from doing so. For it is not lawful to do evil that there may

---

[684] Coppin, *op. cit.*, p. 330.
[685] Matthew VII, 16.
[686] "Facienti quod est in se Deus non denegat gratiam."

come good.[687] It is written: *The truth shall make you free* — not error, which, no matter how sweet and salutary it may seem *to us* is invariably as baneful as it is false.

How much more in accordance with the spirit of the divine Saviour of souls are the words of that zealous apostle of Italy, the great Fr. Segneri S.J.:

> If I were like those doctors who prefer their patients to die rather than to be distressed I should break off my sermon at this point, for I know how upsetting some listeners will find what I am about to say. But whom would such silence really serve? By failing to speak out I should be doing the work of the devil, for as Eusebius bears witness, he encourages souls to remain untroubled as they are more easily damned. So we must press on. Saint Helen, the mother of Constantine had high towers built, on top of which fires were lit at night to show pilgrims from Constantinople to Jerusalem the safe path and save them from going astray. Our Lord has acted in the same way in His Church. From time to time He has raised up robust souls, like so many towers, whom He enlightened with more brilliant light so that they might shine out in favour of travellers who are striving to reach the holy city of paradise. Hence we should embrace as the truth, by whose light we may be guided in our perilous journey from this world towards the next, what the holy Doctors have taught us with one accord. And as a matter of fact these Doctors hold by common agreement that *there are more Christians who lose paradise than who reach it.* If then we are to advance with prudence and not go astray, let us put this opinion into practice in organizing our daily life.[688]

III

SOPHISTRIES CONCERNING FAITH AND THE CHURCH

Readers surprised to find that so many and such gross sophistries should be uttered on such a subject by an author in other respects pious and learned should bear in mind Fr. Castelein's own stated goal. Nothing was further from his mind in writing than to recall souls to penance, to the narrow way, to the fear of God, to flight

---

[687] Cf. Romans III, 8.

[688] *Il Cristiano Istruito*, parte I, ragionamento 5, n. 3; Milan, 1854, vol. III, p. 51.

from the world and from occasions of sin, to prayer or to frequentation of the sacraments. His battle cry was simply: "Beware of preachers infected with rigorism, terrorism or Jansenism!"

This is why the reader should note that:

(i) He writes unprovoked, in the absence of any existing controversy,[689] on a highly abstract topic, in the vernacular, in a secular periodical addressed to the laity, in order to reconcile their faith with reason!

(ii) With regard to Catholics, he holds that most of them are saved even if they live ill.

(iii) With regard to non-Catholics, he unduly enlarges the "soul of the Church" the better to smuggle pagans, Mahometans and Jews into heaven by good faith.

He would have done far better to follow the following warning of his holy father Ignatius:

> It befalls all too often that excessive preaching on and praise of faith, without proper distinctions and explanations, provides a pretext for the people to become lukewarm in the performance of good works, which precede and follow faith vivified by the bond of charity.[690]

7

"In our day faith must be reconciled with the requirements of natural reason and the demands of the heart."

I propose to examine, in the *Revue Générale*, some religious subjects about which even the most instructed laity generally have but confused and incomplete ideas instead of the clear, sharp and much fuller notions they need to harmonize their faith with the requirements of their reason. *These requirements of reason* must be satisfied. The more the mind is cultured the more the faith must be enlightened. Simple faith is commendable only in the simple: it cannot be an ideal for the educated classes.[691]

---

[689] "Note that it was without the slightest reason that Fr. Castelein wrote his book." (Coppin, *op. cit.*, p. 311.)

[690] *Spiritual Exercises, Rules for Thinking with the Church*, Rule XVI.

[691] *Le Rigorisme et la Question des Élus, Revue Générale*, 1898, vol. I, p. 40.

Whereupon, the better to harmonize faith with natural reason "and with the needs of their hearts" (p. 9), Fr. Castelein force-feeds them with his singular doctrine, entirely unknown to the Saints and the Fathers, and endeavours to support it with countless sophistries.[692]

1. Of course Fr. Castelein is not a rationalist: his *intention* is not to diminish or weaken faith or to enthral it to natural reason. He has the best of intentions — to win souls for Christ, especially those he refers to as "the educated classes, the enlightened laity"— and to compass this goal he hopes to show that the terrible doctrine of the fewness of the saved is no longer tenable in our days thanks to the progress of science, and has in fact already been rejected by recent Doctors of the Church and by the best modern scriptural interpreters.

Hence albeit unwittingly he appears to want to reconcile faith with the demands of reason of the learned laity and with the requirements of their hearts.

Nor am I alone in so understanding the purpose of the learned Jesuit, for last April Fr. Emmanuel, abbot of the Olivetan abbey of Notre Dame de la Sainte Espérance at Mesnil-Saint-Loup, wrote of Fr. Castelein's work in much the same terms as I have.

> The language of the Jesuit Father is distinctly reminiscent of expressions found in Marmontel's *Bélisaire*. In its pages the deist philosopher of the XVIIIth century declares: "God has given us two guides which must agree together, that of faith and that of sentiment or feeling. What natural and irresistible sentiment assures us of cannot be contradicted by faith... The same voice is heard both from the height of heaven and in the depth of my soul. It cannot contradict itself. If on the one hand I am

---

[692] Other Progressives also adulate our own age to the detriment of sound doctrine. "I undertake to write a new exposition of Christianity, from the point of view of the present day," writes Bougaud. "No age, perhaps, has received greater gifts... This age, great in its genius, noble in its hopes..." Etc. (*Le Christianisme et les Temps Présents*, Introduction) While the Rev. Victor Mauran says:"Our age has its qualities, I will even say its virtues. A truer instinct and love for the good, for the happiness of all and a more exact notion of Eternal Justice is taking possession of mankind... The syllabus of the Faculty of Theology for 1895 proves that this work is opportune." Etc. (*Élus et sauvés*, Preface, pp. X-XI)

informed that the just man who does good is dear to the Divinity, I cannot be told on the other that its vengeance awaits him. ... *Need there really be so many reprobate?*[693]

Let us beware of the Progressive tendency to want faith to come to terms with reason, described with admirable accuracy by Fr. Tournebize, S.J.:

> In the first place it is in the name of *Progress* that the Church is adjured to modify her teaching on the chastisements of the afterlife. She is told: *Everything in the Universe is evolving, constant transformations are taking place at every level in nature. How then could religious dogma remain immoveable?* Nor does the siren-song stop there: this development is required, it is alleged, by the nature of God and of man's mind. So the doctrine of the torments of Hell, docilely accepted in the Middle Ages, is no longer appropriate to our days. New formulæ must be found better adapted to current attitudes.[694]

In our days more than ever preachers must proclaim, with Saint Paul, that *the weapons of our warfare are ... mighty to God unto ... destroying counsels and every height that exhalteth itself against the knowledge of God, and bringing into captivity every understanding unto the obedience of Christ.*[695]

And to the faithful who believe themselves to be learned must be repeated again and again this Canon of the Vatican Council:

> If anyone should say that it is sometimes possible, as a result of *the progress of science* [or *knowledge*], for a meaning to be attributed to the dogmas proposed by the Church which differs from that which the Church has understood and does understand, let him be anathema.[696]

2. As for the "requirements of the heart", especially as they affect devout ladies (!), clearly they are to be submitted to the true and traditional teaching of holy Church. The consequences of failure to respect this are illustrated by a case I encountered personally.

---

[693] *Bulletin de Notre Dame de la Sainte Espérance*, April 1899, p. 258.

[694] *Opinions du jour sur les peines d'outre-tombe*, pp. 10-11.

[695] II Corinthians X, 5.

[696] Canons on Faith and Reason, Canon 3, Denzinger 1818.

The lady involved was of noble stock and exceedingly learned, recently converted from the Anglican heresy. Because of the "necessities of her heart" she refused to admit the eternity of the pains of Hell.

"How could I ever be happy in heaven," she demanded, "at the sight of my father and mother suffering in Hell, whom God Himself commands me to love?"

And when I showed her the explicit teaching of Holy Scripture on the subject she insisted that the texts threatening sinners with damnation were not absolute but conditional, like the decree of the destruction of Nineveh. She insisted that after the passage of a few of the centuries of eternity, at the prayers of Our Blessed Lady and of the Saints and Angels, God would surely revoke His original decree, remit the punishment due to the damned and admit them to Heaven where great joy would accompany the fulfilment of the prophecy that *then there will be one fold and one shepherd.*[697]

Such was the "requirement of her heart", and nothing could ever cure her of it save the imperative requirement of absolute faith.

This pious matron belonged unwittingly to the ranks of those "merciful" souls discussed by Saint Augustine in his *City of God*, Book 21, Chapter 18, i.e. "those who think that at the last judgement the intercession of the saints will ensure that no one is in fact damned," and whom he refutes in Chapters 23 and 24.

3. "Simple faith is only praiseworthy — or rather tolerable — in the simple. Let us never represent it as the ideal for the educated classes." In reality, the laity, no matter how learned they may be, have no need of a theological solution concerning rigorism and the number of the elect. Fr. Castelein's wish to take account of the social conditions of our own days is praiseworthy, but he undoubtedly falls victim to a double illusion: (a) in imagining that the laity of our day are troubled about the number of the elect, and (b) in the solution he offers to a problem that does not exist For if in fact some layfolk experience difficulties connected with this topic, no better or truer way

---

[697] Cf. John X, 16.

can be found to resolve them than that indicated by Bourdaloue, i.e. by declaring frankly that Holy Scripture and the Fathers affirm the fewness of the saved and then explaining the reasons for this fewness, so that the faithful may be dissuaded from following the same path and may energetically work out their salvation.[698]

Even for the most learned, this explanation suffices, for in Bourdaloue's day the laity knew their religion much better than today's laity, even those best informed in profane matters. How many of the learned laity are to be found who are thoroughly familiar with all the articles of faith and grasp their theological meaning. It would be far more useful to dissipate their ignorance in necessary matters than to conduct theological debates in their presence on secondary matters which only feed their vanity and presumption.

8

"The Christian people in general have living faith."

Most Christians must necessarily be saved, for:

> Simple and humble faith is far from rare. The Christian people taken as a whole believe in Jesus Christ with a faith that is simple, humble and lively.
>
> Whatever their weakness in their struggle against the vices, at the sight of the Cross, they *feel* that they love their Saviour.
>
> Ah, how this faith pleases God!
>
> And how many good deaths it prepares, notwithstanding the sad inconsistencies and deplorable failings of life!
>
> What priest grown grey in the ministry of souls has not witnessed, hundreds or thousands of times, such good deaths? (p. 62)

In fact, however, there is no such thing as a lively faith that hardly ever operates through charity. For faith without works is dead,[699] and hence cannot be called *lively*. Moreover, is it not a fact that in general the bulk of the people live habitually in mortal sin? "When we arrive in a place," wrote Saint Alphonsus to his missionaries, "we find the

---

[698] See above, p. 34.
[699] James II, 17, 20.

greater part of its inhabitants held fast by sin far from the grace of God."[700] And he wrote those words with reference to the Catholic villages of the very pious kingdom of Naples in the eighteenth century. What would he have said of our modern Sodoms and Gomorrhas? Surely Fr. Hoppenot is right to say: "Our dilettante Christians daintily choose the morsels of religion which suit them, sinfully rejecting what they find disagreeable. They accept the Gospel of charity, but not that of chastity; they applaud the command to love one another, but not that of bearing one's cross, doing violence to oneself and hating the world. They call themselves believers, but they no longer really practise."[701]

2. In the celebrated work of piety *Sapientia Christiana* by Canon Claude Arvisenet the faithful soul is represented addressing to Christ the following argument on the subject of the fewness of the saved:

> It is true, Lord, that it is so written; but it is also written that he that believeth and is baptized shall be saved. And there are many who believe and have been baptized.

To which the divine Commander replies:

> It is so, my son, but this faith of which it is written that together with baptism it works salvation is no simple knowledge of the mysteries or adherence to their truth. For thus far the demons themselves believe and yet they remain damned and under torture.
>
> Only that faith saves which dutifully carries out the works prescribed by the doctrine believed. Only to them have I promised heavenly beatitude who have done what is ordered. Only to him who has kept the commandments is it said: *Thou shalt live.*[702]

For, as we read in the Roman Breviary:

> Let no one promise himself eternal life on account of faith that is without works and dead… There shall therefore be eternal conflagration

---

[700] Circular Letter, 29th June 1774.
[701] Joseph Hoppenot S.J., *Le Crucifix*, 2nd edition, Introduction, p. XIII.
[702] *Op. cit.*, part I, chapter XXX, N° 4.

as of fire, and Truth has said that they shall go into it who have been de-clared to lack not faith but good works.[703]

"It would be a greater miracle," said Saint Vincent Ferrer, for evil-livers to make a good end than for the dead to rise."[704]

And in his most salutary work entitled *Preparation for Death* Saint Alphonsus repeatedly teaches that it is rash for a sinner to hope to make a good death after a sinful life, even if he has faith. It is well worth reading, among the other parts of this book, Consideration VI, *On the Death of the Sinner*, in which the Holy Doctor shows that "At his death the sinner will seek God and will not find Him." And as we still read in the Roman Breviary, "Shall the death of Christ deliver from eternal death those who live badly until death?"[705]

3. The common position concerning the putting off of repentance until tomorrow and the fruitfulness of the Sacraments received at the last moment of life is very well stated by the illustrious preacher Fr. Bourdaloue of the Society of Jesus:

> To the argument that in the final analysis it is death that decides men's eternal destinies, so that all depends on dying in Christian dispositions, I would reply: this is true, but one can hardly hope to die in Christian dispositions without having lived in them. And since very few live in them, I would conclude that there are very few who die in them.
>
> It would be easy for me to destroy the false opinion of the worldlings who convince themselves that to make a good end nothing is needed except to receive the last Sacraments of Holy Church in the last stages of illness, giving some signs of repentance.
>
> Ah, how many illusions flourish on this subject! I hardly dare say all that I think.
>
> It is not enough to receive the most holy Sacraments; they must also be received holily, in other words with true conversion of heart, but therein lies the rub.

---

[703] Monday following the first Sunday in Lent, 2nd Nocturn, from the Homily of Saint Augustine *On Faith and Works*, chapter 15.

[704] Sermon I, on the Nativity of Our Blessed Lady.

[705] From the Sermon of Saint Bernard found in the IVth Lesson of the Office of the Sepulchre of Our Lord Jesus Christ.

Knowing as I do what most of these deathbed conversions are worth — precipitate conversions, half-baked conversions, conversions wrought in a few moments in souls hardly aware of what they are doing, conversions that would be as many miracles if they were good and true — and aware as I am of the motives of strategy, worldly-wisdom, ceremony, human respect, soft-heartedness towards friends and relations, servile and natural fear and of half-measure Christianity that so often underpin them, I adhere to the verdict of Saint Augustine, indeed of all the Fathers, that as a rule *it is greatly to be feared that the repentance of the dying who repent only when dying should die with them and prove a reprobate repentance.*

And to this countless number of false penitents of the deathbed I would add the very substantial number of those carried off by sudden death, who die without the sacraments, without help, unconscious, with no thought of God.

And from all this I would unhesitatingly draw, after our Saviour, this terrifying conclusion : *Many are called but few are chosen.*[706]

9

"The visible Church is only the most effective and safest means of saving souls, an immense number of which are saved by the invisible soul of the Church."

1. Seeing that the greater part of mankind cannot reach eternal salvation unless the majority of non-Catholics, Mahometans, Jews and pagans, are also saved, Fr. Castelein leaves no stone unturned in his efforts to locate among these unbelievers a vast number, nay, huge multitudes, who err in good faith and thus belong to the soul of Christ's Church — as Gravina also held.

It is fitting at this point to quote at some length from the author's copious efforts to demonstrate the purity of the religion of many adherents of popular forms of paganism.

The reader should bear in mind that Fr. Castelein champions the *utility* of the Christian revelation for the salvation of individuals and what might be called its *social* necessity for raising whole peoples and

---

[706] *Pensées sur le salut, Petit nombre des élus* ; Migne, *Collection Intégrale et Universelle des Orateurs Sacrés*, vol. XVI, col. 622.

nations to the height of civilization. "It is certainly quite something to live in the *normal* conditions of the spiritual life and at the source of all human progress." (p. 224)

Note too that for Fr. Castelein the visible Catholic Church is an institution by which salvation is *safer and easier*: "It is certainly quite something to enjoy these more efficacious lights and helps which make salvation *surer* and the merits of the elect *more abundant*." (p. 224) "Salvation being *much easier* for members of the visible Church." (p. 289)

In the same vein he observes:

> For the exclusion [of the Jews] from the visible Church of Christ to entail necessarily their exclusion from this invisible Church and their eternal damnation it would have to be shown that this "blindfold of unbelief" could be explained only by bad faith pressed to the point of mortal sin… And is it claimed that we have the right to conclude that all these ignorant crowds are in bad faith? (p. 153)

> In any event, for all those who cannot receive the sacrament of Penance, be they Christians *or not*, return to God is accessible for all mankind by the act of *perfect* contrition or by the regret and purpose inspired by the love of God. (p. 22)

> Let us nourish the hope that among these *vast hosts* blinded by the prejudice of religious errors and thereby kept far from the Catholic Church the brightness of revelation, albeit diminished, may yet, thanks to the ever active, ever efficacious power of the Redemption, *save multitudes of souls.*

> What I say of dissident Christians I say too, though with some difference, of *non-Christians*…

> How can it be believed that God will make them expiate in the tortures of eternal damnation the fatal errors of which they are the unwitting victims?

> Away with such *cruel* theories! They have nothing in common with the Gospel and Catholic theory. (p. 223)

Further to which Fr. Castelein utters the following enormity which I submit to the judgement of all theologians: "To belong to the *soul* of the Church each one must practise the truth and tend to one's last end as it is known to him." (p. 214) Note that Fr. Castelein does not require sanctifying grace, charity, or even the lowest degree of *supernatural* faith for someone to belong to the soul of the Church!

Fr. Mauran labours under the same delusion:

> Our Lord teaches us that it is enough for salvation to observe the natural law, i.e. in accordance with the knowledge and possibilities of each, as no one is bound to the impossible. (*Op. cit.*, p. 114)

He then magnifies the soul of the Church in the following terms:

> Not a single human being will ever escape the action of the Church. It is true that as a visible and organized society ... she remains confined within narrow limits. But *her soul — that* cannot be held captive. *The soul of the Church!* What an admirable and profound expression. A soul is stopped by nothing. It knows no uncrossable frontier or inaccessible continent... And why should we not believe that that the souls conquered by grace outside the Church represent *the vast majority* of mankind? ... Jesus Christ is *the true light that enlighteneth every man that cometh into this world.*[707] It is true that souls *saved* outside the Church's *social body* are deprived of precious and exceptional graces. Their merits and virtues are for this reason far inferior to those of the *elect*. But what matter? The divine plan includes a secondary and *auxiliary* design. The Creator established it in favour of these inferior souls, whose countless host exceeds the irrevocably fixed number of the elect. (pp. 207-9)

And Bougaud writes:

> It is easy to say that outside the Church there is no salvation and the ignorant are quicker still to conclude that anyone, be he pagan, heretic or schismatic, who is not a part of the Church is infallibly damned. But if this were so where would God's justice be? (p. 366)

2. To refute these sophistries of the Progressive Sentimentalists let us carefully distinguish the *body* and the *soul* of the Church.

The *Body* of the Church denotes the *visible* society of the baptized who profess the true faith and live within the communion and obedience of the Roman Pontiff. Entrance to this society is gained by Baptism; those once in it are separated from it by a grave external sin against faith (heresy) or against obedience (schism), or by sentence of

---

[707] John I, 9.

excommunication inflicted by authority. Hence infidels, heretics, schismatics and excommunicates do not belong to the body of the Church. In this visible society Christ has established the *ordinary* means of salvation; therein lie the *ordinary* channels by which grace is communicated to men in the present order of Providence, i.e. the Word of God and the Sacraments.

With regard to the *soul* of the Church, note that:

> The soul of the Church (i) is indistinguishable from *the spiritual, internal and supernatural life*; while (ii) it is begun, advanced and completed by the same means and to the same extent as the supernatural life is begun, advanced and completed, for the soul of the Church is precisely coterminous with the spiritual life. Moreover whatever disposes and prepares for justification disposes and prepares for participation in the soul of the Church…
>
> In its essence it is perfected by justification and grows by various degrees which lead up to eternal beatitude. Hence the just, who are living the supernatural life, belong *immediately, formally and per se* to the soul of the Church; while all those who possess some gift of inward grace disposing them towards the habitual life of grace belong to it as it were inchoatively and in a second degree.[708]

The soul of the Church therefore comprises or embraces the invisible society of the just who enjoy sanctifying grace and the other supernatural gifts. Many *may* enjoy these gifts without belonging to the visible body of the Church. Nevertheless it must be admitted that — and this is what the Progressives forget — in the present order of Providence these graces granted outside the Church more commonly tend to lead unbelievers to the Church and only much more rarely to justify them "outside the Church". However this *can* happen, for although the grace of God is usually and ordinarily communicated through the means established by Christ, it can also be dispensed otherwise; but it is quite absurd to think this extraordinary way so common that far the greater part of men who are saved reach salvation otherwise than by the public means established by God, for this would transform the exception into the general rule, which is re-

---

[708] Hürter, *Theologiæ Dogmaticæ Compendium*, tract. III, thesis 37, n. 230, vol. p. 207.

pugnant to the wisdom and providence of God in establishing His visible Church.

For someone to be saved, therefore, outside the visible body of the Church, he must belong to her soul, i.e. be justified by sanctifying grace. Without the wedding garment no one is admitted to the banquet.

Let us now consider upon what terms those who are outside the body of the Church can achieve salvation. Beginning with…

3. *The Salvation of Unbelievers.* The Sentimentalists are loud in their praise for many Philosophers who, thanks to their well-cultivated reason, have come to know the true God from His creatures and, though lacking supernatural or revealed faith, have modelled their life in apparent conformity to uprightness — men, they claim, such as Socrates, Plato, Aristotle, Seneca, Trajan, Confucius, etc. For they observed the natural law, we are told, whereupon the Sentimentalists challenge the "Terrorists" to dare say that they are damned.

They pay special honours to Plato:

> Platonism constitutes an *eminently* moralizing religious doctrine. … beneath these principal virtues [faith, respect, trust in *the inferior gods*], which are the keystone of the religious and moral order and which Plato identifies with *piety*, lie the virtues to be exercised towards oneself and one's neighbour. These virtues come down to *interior justice*, wisdom, fortitude and temperance, with *exterior justice*, i.e. justice properly so called *doubled with charity*. (p. 125)

And of pagans in general he asserts:

> The worship of Jupiter, with some additions and corrections which reason and grace *could* have suggested to upright souls, *might* easily have been transformed into the worship of the true God. (p. 81) The pagans *could* have attained a sufficiently pure idea of the godhead. (p. 83)

And after explaining all this at length the learned Professor concludes: "In harmony with this design of *general and public* providence, God has a *special and private* providence for the salvation of all souls." (p. 131) A claim which he buttresses, as does Fr. Mauran, by appealing to the celebrated text of Saint John:

This doctrine sheds admirable light on the universal scope of the statement that *the true light that enlighteneth every man that cometh into this world*. Never, then can the darkness in which a man is born so darken his conscience as to prevent his knowing this true light, at least at the decisive moments of his life. (p. 135)

Along the same lines Bougaud says:

The pagans received little. They had only the natural law. The natural law taught them that there is but one God, creator and saviour of all men. This much was written in their hearts and they had to believe it. But when, how and in what manner is this Saviour-God to save souls? They are not required to know *explicitly* the answer to this. "Whoever thou art who didst make men, I entrust myself to thee; thou wilt save them as thou knowest best I am ready to use the means of salvation thou shalt make known to me or that shall be made known to me as coming from thee." This is enough. This *implicit faith*, this *baptism of desire*, is sufficient, according to the weightiest theologians, to put them on the path to heaven. (p. 367)

And in fact Fr. Mauran considers Baptism of desire to be in reality a more universal means than the Sacrament of Baptism for the salvation of the multitude. "In fact, are there not countless souls — and why should they not be the majority — who must content themselves with baptism of desire?" (p. 212) "For I stress that I have no intention of maintaining that salvation can be had outside the true religion and the Church." (p. 208)

4. Two distinctions will suffice to overturn all this: (i) the necessity of *supernatural religion* and (ii) the distinction between *negative and positive infidels*.

A. Natural religion is of itself powerless to save anyone.

Everyone should clearly understand that in the present order of providence the end of man is a *supernatural good* which can only be attained by *supernatural means*; hence *natural religion*, though it may bring a man to the *threshold* of the supernatural order, *can go no further and cannot by any means save him*. The gratuitous intervention of God is necessary to raise a man by faith and grace to the supernatural order.

A condition essentially necessary for salvation, by necessity of means, is sanctifying grace with its inseparable virtues, viz. faith, hope and charity. Whoever possesses them belongs to the soul of the Church and will be saved, but whoever lacks them, whether culpably or otherwise, cannot in the present order of Providence by any means be saved.

Now the *children* of infidels who die before the use of reason, as by far the greater number do, *cannot* be justified and hence are excluded from the beatific vision and cannot be numbered among the elect.

And *adults* do not attain justification except by faith — supernatural faith — which cannot by any means be acquired by the forces of nature, as the Council of Trent teaches:

> If anyone says that without the prevenient inspiration of the Holy Ghost and without His help man can believe, hope, love, or be penitent, as he ought, so that the grace of justification may be bestowed upon him, let him be anathema.[709]

> But without faith it is impossible to please God. For he that cometh to God, must believe that he is, and is a rewarder to them that seek him.[710]

> The faith to which the Apostle promises salvation *is supernatural and divine*, being *the substance of things to be hoped for* and *the evidence*, conviction or demonstration, *of things that appear not.*[711] Reason demonstrates that God is the author of nature, but reason does not declare that God is the giver of grace and of glory, for these are things *that appear not.* ... That God requires this faith of the nations is denied by no one save by such naturalists as are themselves unworthy of the grace of faith.[712]

5. This is true Catholic doctrine, expressed in the following terms by Cardinal Mazella S.J.:

> The faith which is said to be *necessary*, by necessity of means, for salvation is:

---

[709] Session VI, *On Justification*, Canon 3.
[710] Hebrews XI, 6.
[711] Hebrews XI, 1.
[712] Cf. the Jesuit Fathers of Würzburg (known as the *Wirceburgenses*), *op. cit.*, p. 47.

(i) *supernatural* faith, founded on divine authority and *revelation*;

(ii) both as to habit and, especially in adults to be justified, as to act;

(iii) the distinction between *in reality* and *in desire* is not applicable here: this actual, supernatural faith is *always and absolutely necessary in reality*.[713]

Concerning the two first of the four articles necessary by necessity of means for eternal salvation, the same Cardinal teaches:

(i) *Explicit* faith in the existence of God is necessary by necessity of means for salvation.[714]

(ii) *Explicit* and *supernatural* faith in God as rewarder is necessary by necessity of means.[715]

(iii) With regard to the mysteries of the Trinity and of the Incarnation, which are included together because, as Saint Thomas says, the mystery of the Incarnation of Christ cannot be explicitly believed without faith in the Trinity:[716]

a. All are agreed that in the law of the Gospel, after its sufficient promulgation, *explicit* faith in Christ is necessary *for all* by necessity of *precept*;

b. With regard to the necessity of means, there are four different opinions of theologians.[717]

End of quotation from Mazzella.

6. It must be carefully noted that this faith, to be supernatural, must be based on a supernatural motive, to wit the supernatural truthfulness of God revealing. Hence when a philosopher admits a dogma, for instance the existence of God, because it can be demonstrated by his reason, he does not go beyond the natural order, nor has he the faith that justifies, unless he believes it on account of the authority of God revealing.

[713] *De virtutibus infusis*, Disp. III, X, § 2; Rome, 1879, p. 444.

[714] *Ibid.*, p. 454

[715] *Ibid.*, p. 455. And Franzelin says that it is a *less* probable opinion that some are saved by supernatural faith in truths of the primitive (patriarchal or pre-Mosaic) revelation than in truths made known to them by private revelation (*De Traditione et Scriptura, in fine*).

[716] *Summa Theologiæ*, q. 2, a. 8.

[717] Mazzella, *loc. cit.*, p. 458.

Of course if heathens, having come to know God by natural intelligence from His creatures, then glorify Him by faithfully observing the natural law and earnestly seeking His aid, God who is rich unto all who invoke Him will not deny, to those who do what they can,[718] fuller graces such as internal enlightenment and external preaching by which to attain this supernatural faith.[719]

> If any of them had done what they could, the Lord would have provided for them according to His mercy, by sending them a preacher of faith as He sent Peter to Cornelius (Acts X) and Paul to the Macedonians (Acts XVI), but this very action by which some persons do what is in their power them by converting themselves to God, itself comes from God who moves their hearts to good.[720]

> If anyone raised in the wilderness or among brute animals were to follow the lead of reason in pursuing good and fleeing evil it is most certainly to be held that God would either reveal to him by internal inspiration [i.e. the *extraordinary* way] those things that are necessary to be believed or else would direct some preacher of the faith to him [enabling him to come to the faith by the *ordinary* way] as He sent Peter to Cornelius.[721]

7. Cardinal de Lugo rightly observes:

> But as Fr. Molina S.J.[722] astutely points out, seldom or never is anyone converted to the faith without the intervention of human preachers, for anyone who has never encountered information about the faith is *unlikely* to do what is in his power and hence it *very seldom* happens that God needs to propose the objects of belief by an angel or by direct divine intervention.[723]

But when an infidel is enlightened by grace, whether in the ordinary or in an extraordinary way, and explicitly believes, on the authority of God revealing, what must be believed by necessity of

---

[718] "Facienti quod est in se Deus non denegabit gratiam."

[719] Wirceburgenses, *op. cit.*, p. 47.

[720] Saint Thomas Aquinas, *In Epistulam ad Romanos*, X, 18.

[721] *De veritate*, Q. 14, A. 11, ad 1.

[722] *Concordia liberi arbitrii*, q. XIV, a. 3, d. ix.

[723] De Lugo, *De virtute fidei*, disp. XIII, s. 3, n. 36.

means, by that very fact he implicitly believes whatever else is contained in the deposit of faith, he is raised to hope of his supernatural end and enkindled with love for that end; charity thereupon expels sin and operates justification.

Such is the infidel who belongs to the soul of the Church.

8. This raises the question what the gainsayers mean when they present the alleged purity of pagan religion or the good faith of Mahometans as arguments against us. For even if these claims were true, they would be insufficient of themselves for salvation, for the reasons we have just seen.

But let us hear what the gentle Saint Francis de Sales has to say about the virtues of the pagans in his *Treatise on the Love of God* in a chapter entitled *A Digression Upon the Imperfection of the Virtues of the Pagans*:

> I earnestly ask you, Theotimus, what virtues could those people have, who voluntarily, and of set purpose, overthrew all the laws of religion?
>
> …
>
> As to the virtues that refer to our neighbour, they trod under foot, and most shamefully, by their very laws, the chief of them, which is piety. For Aristotle, the greatest intellect amongst them, pronounced this horrible and most pitiless sentence. "As to the question of exposing, that is, abandoning children, or of bringing them up, let this be the law: that nothing is to be kept that is deprived of any member. And as to other children, if the laws and customs of the city do not allow the abandoning of them, and the number of any one's children so increase on him that he has more by half than he can keep, he is to be beforehand, and procure abortion."
>
> Seneca, so praised as a wise man, says: "We kill monsters:[724] and if our children are defective, weakly, imperfect, or monstrous, we cast them off, and abandon them." So that it is not without cause that Tertullian reproaches the Romans with exposing their children to the mercy of the waters, to cold, to famine, to dogs; and this not by the force of poverty, for, as he says, the very chief men and magistrates practised this cruelty.
>
> Good God! Theotimus, what kind of virtuous men were these? (…)

---

[724] I.e. those affected by gross congenital malformations. — Translator.

Indeed if the pagans practised some virtues, it was generally for the sake of worldly glory, and consequently they had nothing of virtue but the action, and not the motive and intention: now virtue is not true unless it has a right intention.

"The virtues of pagans," says Saint Augustine, "were not true, but only resembled true ones, because they were not done for a proper end, but for transitory ends. (…)

So that the virtue of the pagans will, at the day of judgment, be a kind of defence to them; not such as that they may be saved thereby, but such as that they may be less condemned." (…)

For, even so, those pagan virtues are only virtues in comparison with vices, but in comparison with the virtues of true Christians, are quite unworthy of the name of virtues.[725]

9. As the Progressives are so fond of extolling the value of the natural virtues of the Pagans, Jews, Mahometans and others it will be worthwhile to remind them of the following very recent teaching of the supreme Magisterium of Holy Church concerning the rarity of such virtues and their worthlessness for eternal salvation. Here are the words of Pope Leo XIII in his letter on Americanism addressed to Cardinal Gibbons on 22nd January 1899:

> … [T]hose who are fond of novelty attach unwarranted importance to the natural virtues… [A]lthough outstanding acts of the natural virtues may sometimes be admired, how seldom does anyone *habitually* exercise the natural virtues. … While even the *individual acts* will frequently upon a closer investigation be found to exhibit the *appearance rather than the reality* of virtue. And even granting their existence, unless we would "run in vain" and forget that eternal bliss which a good God in his mercy has destined for us, of what avail are natural virtues unless seconded by the gift of divine grace? Hence Saint Augustine well says: "Wonderful is this man's strength, and swiftly does he run, but *outside the true path*."

10. Moreover with regard to worth of Platonism in particular we have a witness whose authority is for present purposes beyond question, for it is Fr. Castelein himself, writing on the subject in another work:

---

[725] *Treatise on the Love of God*, book XI, chapter X.

Even the best systems of pure philosophy, constructed by the finest minds without the light of Christian revelation, include highly regrettable aberrations concerning truths of the religious and moral order. To mention but a few significant examples:

Plato, one of the most powerful, rounded and complete geniuses that have ever lived, notwithstanding his extensive use of foreign sources to avoid error, emerges as *the father of communism, the champion of promiscuity and the patron of slavery*, as well as the bigoted, systematic adversary of the arts and of civil and political freedoms. He admits the pre-existence of souls with the hypothesis of faults committed by each of us in a former life, from which he concludes that we are all in an anti-natural state and that there lies in each of us *a disorder and positive vices over which our freedom is powerless*. In addition to which he cripples the sanction of eternal life by the chimera of metempsychosis [or reincarnation] and mingles with his theodicy a pantheistic theory which cannot stand up to firm and penetrating examination.[726]

Out of thy own mouth I judge thee![727]

11. On the subject of the good faith of Mahometans Fr. Castelein writes:

What I have said of dissident Christians I also say, though with some difference, of non-Christians.

Travel through Mahometan countries, for instance, and see the reverence and faith of these poor misguided souls in invoking the true God, "Allah". See their courage in undergoing the trials of Ramadan. How can it be believed that God will make them expiate in the tortures of eternal damnation the fatal errors of which they are the unwitting victims? *Away with such cruel theories!* They have nothing in common with the Gospel and Catholic theory. (p. 223)

I believe that the Mahometan populations respect in good faith and conscience the moral law of the Koran. (p. 253)

Far different is the teaching of the Saints and Theologians:

---

[726] Castelein, Auguste S.J., *La morale rationaliste et la morale chrétienne, Réponse au système moral de M. Denis*, Brussels, 1895, p. 13.

[727] Cf. Luke XIX, 22.

For Saint Alphonsus, the Koran "grants every licence to the flesh";[728] "approves every worship in which a single God is adored";[729] "embraces dogmas that are frivolous, ridiculous and contradictory";[730] "promises a heaven unseemly even for beasts";[731] "excuses infractions of the natural law on grounds of fear", etc.

Moreover, as explorers are well aware, the polygamy of Mahometans makes it lawful and even commonplace for them to practise such appalling sins as Onanism, abortion, infanticide and indeed the violent elimination of concubines who no longer please their masters.

Their fasting in Ramadan, pilgrimages, courage in warfare against Christians, etc., are due not to faith but to fanaticism and are of no avail for eternal salvation.

Fr. Ottiger S.J. pertinently writes:

> The teaching of Mahomet is *utterly opposed to sound reason* in that he teaches that everything happens by absolute decree of God so that it cannot happen otherwise and thus deprives man of his free will, replacing it with unavoidable necessity or fate. Hence he declares that God created some men for hell."[732]

His teaching allows concubinage and the law of talion at least for murder:

> He established laws on repudiation which grossly violate natural justice, he allows fornication with servants and inferiors, he order "unbelievers" to be slaughtered.[733]

In short it is a wonder indeed for Mahometans to be in good faith in opposition to the principles of the natural law — a wonder that can surely make very little difference to the numbers of the elect.

---

[728] "… accorde toute licence à la chair pendant cette vie, et ne promet qu'une licence plus grande encore et du même genre dans la vie future." *Œuvres Dogmatiques*, French translation by Jacques, vol. I, p. 238.

[729] *Ibid.*, p. 282.

[730] *Ibid.*, p. 425.

[731] *Ibid.*, p. 484.

[732] Ottiger, Ignaz S.J. (1822-1891), *Theologia Fundamentalis*, vol. I, p. 918.

[733] Herrmann, Jean C.SS.R. (1849-1927), *Institutiones Theologiæ Dogmaticæ*, Appendix to vol. I, n. 149.

B. What has been said hitherto of heathens can also be applied to all non-Catholics who are outside the body of the Church.

It is true that the latter can more easily obtain salvation since for the most part they accept the fundamental dogmas of religion and sometimes retain Baptism or even other sacraments and means of salvation.

But a crucial distinction must be made among all these unbelievers — one which must be especially applied to heretics, schismatics and the unbelievers of our regions, i.e. rationalists and infidels of the same kidney. The faithless — a term by which I denote all who are outside Catholic faith and unity — must be divided into *positive* and *negative*.

Negative unbelievers are all those who do not accept the Catholic faith or any specific dogma, or who are outside the unity of the Church because these things have not been sufficiently intimated to them, i.e. because in *good faith* they do not perceive the truth or necessity of these points.

Positive unbelievers, however, are those who dissent *in bad faith* from Catholic faith or unity. This includes not only those who know the Catholic truth and yet reject or oppose it out of malice and contumacy, but also those who labour under true ignorance but whose very ignorance is imputed as a vice because they have neglected or made ill use of the means of discovering the truths proposed by God.

For this reason it is not enough to inquire whether unbelievers and the heterodox carefully observe their religion and do nothing opposed to the supreme laws of nature; it is also imperative to inquire whether their error is imputable or not. If they are morally responsible for their error in religious matters all the other deviations as to divine worship which proceed from that culpable error must be imputed to them as sins that are indirectly voluntary. And sin excludes the state of grace; he who is not in the state of grace does not belong to the soul of the Church and outside the soul of the Church there is *absolutely no* salvation.

All men, unbelievers and non-Catholics as much as anyone else, are bound by God to enter the visible society or body of the Church.

No sensible man can admit … that we are free to think what we will about God and to honour Him as each man sees fit…

No sensible man can deny that God has the right and power to make Himself known to men better than He can be known by the light of reason alone and in return for these revelations to require acts of homage.

No sensible man can positively commit himself to indifference as to whether God has in fact intervened in the religious life of mankind, for such indifference would expose him to neglect of duties on which depend his honour in this world and his happiness in the world to come.

And finally no sensible man, if he has recognized as a fact the positive intervention of God in man's religious life can think we are free to take practical account of this intervention or not as we may prefer.

Against this background, let me remind you, gentlemen, that God *has* intervened, through His Son Jesus Christ He has intervened not only as Revealer but as Redeemer. He has thus acquired a twofold title to rights properly so called, correlating on our part to undeniable duties: the duty to believe the truths He has revealed and the duty to apply to ourselves the virtue of His sacrifice. *Non est in alio aliquo salus.*[734]

And the method selected by Jesus Christ to ensure the regular transmission of His truth and of the virtue of His sacrifice was to establish a society — a spiritual, religious, supernatural society…

He entrusted to His Church two forces to enlighten and purify her: the Word and the Sacraments. This is why it is in His Church that we must receive the truth to be believed and the divine power which delivers from sin. Outside the Church there is no salvation…

Salvation inside the Church and only inside the Church, such is the law. And this law was not made up by men under the influence of exaggerated rigorism; it flows from Him who had the right to dictate the conditions under which we might enjoy the benefit of the Redemption.[735]

To ensure that this obligation should be respected, God established many different means which evidently demonstrate the truth

---

[734] Cf. Acts IV, 11-12: "This is the stone which was rejected by you the builders, which is become the head of the corner. *Neither is there salvation in any other.* For there is no other name under heaven given to men, whereby we must be saved."

of the Catholic religion to those who seek it unshackled by passion or prejudice. For as the Vatican Council teaches:

> And, that we may be able to satisfy the obligation of embracing the true faith and of constantly persevering in it, God has instituted the Church through His only begotten Son, and has bestowed on her the manifest marks of that institution, so that she may be recognized by all men as the Guardian and Teacher of the revealed Word.[736]

Indeed Chapter IV of the same council's schema *De Ecclesia* declares:

> In order that the Church of Christ upon earth should be neither invisible nor hidden but placed in all openness, like to a lofty and shining city seated on a mountain, which cannot be hid, and to a candle set upon a candlestick, which, enlightened by the Sun of justice, enlightens the whole world with the light of her truth.[737]

Who then are they who have never heard of the Catholic religion? Who have never had any doubt about their own error? Who have never glimpsed a spark of the light of Catholic truth notwithstanding its evident signs of credibility? Who have never yielded in seeking the truth either to passion or to neglect? And what is to be said of those who have fallen away from Catholicism? What was the origin and cause of their heresy or apostasy?

For anyone who is guilty of grave negligence or passion in such a matter entirely forfeits the defence of good faith and becomes the cause of his own subsequent errors and liable to just punishment for them. Until such time as he shall shake off this neglect he is in the state of mortal sin and hence certainly not within the soul of the Church and quite unable to attain salvation.

---

[735] Monsabré, *Conférences de Notre Dame*, Conférence 51, *La Société des Rachetés*, 1881, pp. 117-121.

[736] Constitution, *Dei Filius*, c. III; Denzinger 1793.

[737] The demonstration of Christianity and of Catholicism from the Church's very existence and brightness, as the sun signals itself by its light, may be found abundantly set out in the writings of Cardinal Deschamps (1810-1883).

Fr. Castelein however has hit on a passage in which Saint Thomas teaches that venial sin without actual mortal sin cannot co-exist in anyone with original sin,[738] whence he concludes:

> The Angelic Doctor clearly teaches that the grace of salvation is *in fact* given to every man who does not obstruct it by a mortal sin. ... Indeed it is this broad and elevated doctrine, I would say, which has the most emboldened me to fight rigorism so energetically. (p. 207)

But in reality Saint Thomas teaches exactly the same as what I have taught under his lead, namely that anyone who is in error *through no [grave] fault of his own* and in good faith observes the prescriptions of the natural law and of his own religion, and hence is guilty of no grave actual sin, will achieve justification, not of course by his own natural powers — which is a heresy condemned by the Council of Trent[739] — but by supernatural grace communicated to him if need be by a miracle.

But no one to my knowledge has ever denied this. The real issue is not the salvation of unbaptized persons who err in good faith, adding no personal mortal sin to original sin, but whether and where any such person is to be found! This is the point I insist on and this passage from Saint Thomas does not affect it any way — hence Fr. Castelein is wretchedly mistaken in taking courage from it for his assault on those he labels "Rigorists".

Let us instead hear how this question is handled by the celebrated disciple of Saint Thomas, Fr. Monsabré, whose patronage the Progressives make bold to claim.

> This maxim — no salvation outside of the Church — condemns only those who by culpable negligence, by egregious ill will, by criminal obstinacy, will enter neither the body nor the soul of the Church.
>
> Indignation at such folk and their fate and reproaches against us on such grounds could not be more unjust or ridiculous.
>
> Have no doubt that as a rule such attitudes are adopted only by those who have practically apostatized and seek to palliate the wrongs they

---

[738] *Summa Theologiæ*, I-II, q. 89, a. 6.
[739] Session VI, *On Justification*, Canon 3.

have themselves done the Church. Our contemporary representatives of unbelief have generally no grounds whatever on which to accuse God that they did not or could not know the truth. Time deadens in their soul the recollection of the faults to which their blindness is due and they ultimately succeed in thinking themselves sincere and candid in their prejudices and hatred against the Church, which they accuse of excessive rigour. It was for them that a sceptic with no wish to condemn his own contemptible inward vacillations wrote these grave words:

> We shall one day render an account to God of all we shall have done as a result of errors wrongly taken for true dogmas, and woe, upon that dread day, to the wilfully blind, to those who were too listless and craven to examine their beliefs, to those who have welcomed errors into their mind because they harmonized with their debauched way of life.[740]

That among unbelievers there should be upright men whose morals and good faith are beyond question and who are victims of bad upbringing and corrupt surroundings, held back in error by involuntary darkness, intensely anxious to know the truth and seeking it earnestly without success, sincerely deploring the futility of their efforts and the uncertainty they live under and who continue thus right up to the gates of death but receive in their final instant of life the light they have yearned for and die converted, sanctified by grace and mysteriously adhering to the Church they seem still separated from, *is possible. I have never encountered such hidden pearls and I think them to be rare*, but grave men attest to having met some such and I respect their testimony. Yet all the same I invite those who loiter in the neighbourhood of the Church lamenting their inability to find the doors to go in by to meditate the humble avowal of a convert:

> If you wish to call God to account, he will confute you and even if you bring a thousand claims against Him, all tried in the scales of justice, not one will prove well-founded. You say you did all you could? he will show you that you did not the hundredth part of it. Did you prefer naught to the wish to please Him? Did you not display greater ardour for something other than Him and find some other business more pressing than that of knowing the truth? Did impenitence, vanity and hardness of heart never hinder the lights He

---

[740] Bayle, Pierre (1647-1706), *Œuvres*, vol. 2.

would have spread in your mind? You may say what you will, but in my own case, after receiving the grace of returning to the Church, I know that I had not done one thousandth of what I ought towards obtaining this great and infinite mercy.[741, 742]

Finally I must briefly refer to the celebrated text: *the true light that enlighteneth every man that cometh into this world,*[743] so sadly abused by Fr. Castelein and the Progressives.

It is enough to note the explanation of Liagre:

"*Enlighteneth*", i.e. **is able to enlighten**, and indeed to do so of itself alone and to this end offers itself to all in readiness. In the same way verbs in the present tense are often used to signify not a truly present effect but the natural character and power of producing the effect in question, as when we say that the sun enlightens all or that fire consumes all.[744]

10

"The early Church was not so fervent as the Church of today."

In order to promise heaven to his worldly contemporaries notwithstanding their lax faith and lukewarm charity, Fr. Castelein exalts their holiness above the holy life of the early Christians.

Let us put aside this major question of fact, viz. the comparison between the past and present states of the Church. I shall treat it later, in a work which I expect to be both very instructive and highly interesting. I shall say then what the Church was in the first centuries and why I prefer the present state of the Church to her past state. (p. 17)

The Christians to whom, or of whom, Saint Paul wrote were far from equal to the *practising Christians of our own days*. (p. 311)

And by way of evidence for this claim the learned professor adduces the Epistles to the Corinthians and two verses, taken, one from

---

[741] Paul Pellisson (1624-1693).

[742] Monsabré, Jacques-Marie-Louis, O.P., *Conférences de Notre Dame*, Conférence 51, 1881, pp. 134-136.

[743] John I, 9.

[744] Liagre, Canon Adolphe Joseph, *Commentarius in Libros Historicos Novi Testamenti*, vol. III, *In Sanctum Ioannem*, Tournai, 1883; *ad locum*.

the Epistle to the Philippians and the other from the second Epistle to Timothy. Astonishingly he seems to have overlooked the Epistle to the "senseless" Galatians![745]

Then from the texts adduced he concludes:

> What wounds are not revealed by these few words? ... Which places the state of the early Church in *its true and sad light.* ... If the clergy of Saint Paul's day were generally such, what must the ordinary faithful have been like? ... All these faithful then had fallen away... Such then were the times and the kind of Christians to whom Saint Paul addresses his exhortations so full of sweetness, consolation and hope! Undoubtedly I am entitled to invoke this great example against our rigorists, past, present and future. (p. 311 and note to p. 312)

With a sigh let us now proceed to refute these sophistries one by one:

1. According to Fr. Castelein: "It can be seen from countless passages in his epistles that the Christians to whom, or of whom, Saint Paul wrote were far from equal to the *practising Christians of our own days.*" (p. 311) And note that for Fr. Castelein "practising Christians" include — as we shall see below — even those Catholics who approach the sacraments only once a year. Now among the early faithful to whom Saint Paul wrote epistles, the Christians of Jerusalem were outstanding, for "by far the greater number of Catholic interpreters hold that the Epistle to the Hebrews was addressed to the Church of Jerusalem."[746] And in charge of this Church, as its bishop, was that most holy man Saint James the Less, an Apostle and the author of the Catholic Epistle which bears his name. It was Our Lord Himself, according to the testimony of the Fathers, who designated

---

[745] Galatians III, 1.

[746] Cf. Cornely, *Historica et critica Introductio in utriusque Testamenti libros sacros*, vol. III, p. 539 n. 178, and Beelen: "The Hebrews, or Jewish Christians, to whom this letter is addressed were converted Jews, residing in Palestine, and for the most part, in Jerusalem; so we are informed by the ancients, and their testimony is confirmed by several passages in the letter itself." (*Introduction to the Epistle to the Romans*) [This quotation from Mgr. Beelen's *Introduction* is quoted by Fr. Godts in the oroiginal Flemish. — Translator.]

him as bishop of Jerusalem and so great was the authority he commanded in the early Church that Saint Paul calls him a pillar of the Church,[747] and even among the unconverted Jews he was so greatly respected that, as the Roman Breviary says, "he alone was allowed to enter the Holy of Holies."[748] He governed the Church of Jerusalem for thirty years, raising it to such a peak of holiness that the Holy Ghost describes its Christians in the following words:

And they were persevering in the doctrine of the apostles, and in the communication of the breaking of bread [i.e. the Eucharist], and in prayers. … And all they that believed, were together, and had all things common. Their possessions and goods they sold, and divided them to all, according as every one had need. And continuing daily with one accord in the temple, and breaking bread from house to house, they took their meat with gladness and simplicity of heart; praising God, and having favour with all the people. And the Lord increased daily together such as should be saved.[749]

(…)

And the multitude of believers had but one heart and one soul: neither did any one say that aught of the things which he possessed, was his own; but all things were common unto them. And with great power did the apostles give testimony of the resurrection of Jesus Christ our Lord; and great grace was in them all. For neither was there any one needy among them. For as many as were owners of lands or houses, sold them, and brought the price of the things they sold, and laid it down before the feet of the apostles. And distribution was made to every one, according as he had need.[750]

Now since Fr. Castelein is convinced that Christians of this kidney were "far from equal to the *practising Christians of our own days*," I challenge him to point out a single diocese in the whole Church of our times in which there is such great holiness among the laity as flourished in the Church of Jerusalem at that time. And let us have no truck with the facile objection that the Epistle to the Hebrews was

---

[747] Galatians II, 9.
[748] Feast of Saint Philip and Saint James, Lesson V.
[749] Acts II, 42-47.
[750] Acts IV, 32-35.

written long after the death of Saint James, for the truth is that James was martyred in Jerusalem in the middle of the year 62 A.D.[751] while Paul wrote this epistle either in the same year or at the latest the next year: 63 A.D.[752]

With regard to the other Christians *to whom or of whom* Saint Paul wrote:

The Romans are praised for their faith which Paul says *is spoken of in the whole world*;[753] and for being *full of love, replenished with all knowledge.*[754]

To the Ephesians, whose Church Paul had himself founded but whom he had not now seen for three or four years, he writes that "...hearing of your faith that is in the Lord Jesus, and of your love towards all the saints, I cease not to give thanks for you..."[755]

The Philippians he calls: *my dearly beloved brethren, and most desired, my joy and my crown*;[756] declaring that he has them all in his heart and longs for them all most tenderly, praising them because they *not only believe in* Christ, *but also suffer for Him, having the same conflict as* Paul himself. Hence he can gratefully assure them: *I give thanks to my God in every remembrance of you, always in all my prayers making supplication for you all, with joy; For your communication in the gospel of Christ from the first day until now.*[757]

To the Colossians he writes:

> We give thanks to God ... hearing your **faith** in Christ Jesus, and the **love** which you have towards all the saints. For the **hope** that is laid up for you in heaven, which you have heard in the word of the truth of the gospel, which ... bringeth forth fruit and groweth ... in you, since the day you heard and knew the grace of God in truth, from Epaphras, our

---

[751] Cf. Cornely, *Introductio in Utriusque Testamenti Libros*, vol. III, p. 600, n. 204.

[752] Beelen, *Inleiding tot den brief aan de Rom* [i.e. Introduction to the Epistle to the Romans], *in fine*. Cornely favours late 63 or early 64 (*loc. cit.*, p. 542, n. 179). It makes little difference.

[753] Romans I, 8.

[754] *Ibid.* XV, 14.

[755] Ephesians I, 15 ; Cornely, *op. cit.*, p. 497.

[756] Philippians IV, 1.

[757] *Ibid.*, IV, and Cornely, *op. cit.*, p. 484, n. 152.

most beloved fellow servant, who is for you a faithful minister of Christ Jesus; who also hath manifested to us your love in the spirit.[758, 759]

And to *the Thessalonians* he says that he is:

... mindful of the work of your faith, and labour, and charity, and of the enduring of the hope of our Lord Jesus Christ before God and our Father, knowing, brethren beloved of God, your **election**: for our gospel hath not been unto you in word only, but in power also, and in the Holy Ghost, and in much fulness, ... And you became followers of us, and of the Lord, ... so that you were made a pattern to all that believe in Macedonia and in Achaia. ... Also in every place your faith ... towards God is gone forth, so that we need not to speak any thing.[760]

And again:

... Your **faith** groweth exceedingly, and the **charity** of every one of you towards each other, aboundeth, so that we ourselves also glory in you in the churches of God, for your **patience** and faith, and in all your persecutions and tribulations, which you endure.[761]

Surely such Christians as these, as well as Timothy, Titus, Philemon and others to whom the Apostle wrote do not fall short of the standards of those of our own day! Surely "the Christians he speaks of" — such as Phœbe, his "sister", Prisca and Aquila, his "helpers", Luke and so many others — were truly Saints?

2. But I must allow my adversary to speak for himself: "Let us collect together some *decisive* quotations whereby to paint the state of these local churches. (Note to p. 311)

A

Here is Fr. Castelein commenting on I Cor. XI 21, 22, 3 :[762]

---

[758] Colossians I, 1-8.

[759] Cornely, *op. cit.*, p. 515. n. 168.

[760] I Thessalonians I, 3-8.

[761] II Thessalonians I, 3-4.

[762] The entire passage is as follows (Translator):
When you come therefore together into one place, it is not now to eat the Lord's supper. For every one taketh before his own supper to eat. And one indeed is hungry and another is drunk. What, have you not houses to eat and to drink in? Or despise ye the church of God; and put them to shame that have not? What shall I

Notice the general terms used by Saint Paul to denounce the scandal of the meetings in which Communion was received. (*Ibid.*)

In this passage the Apostle deals with the decorum to be observed in the agape and in order to avoid either understating or overstating the gravity of the scandal he refers to let us invite that excellent exegete Fr. Cornely S.J. to explain the matter to us:

> It is easy to show that what the Corinthians were doing in these meetings had nothing to do with the Supper celebrated by Our Lord with His Disciples before His Passion: *For every one taketh before his own supper to eat.* (Verse 21) — i.e. without waiting for others to share with them. Hence it is not surprising that *one indeed is hungry and another is drunk.* From this description it is safe to conclude that the faithful brought food for the communal meal, each according to his means, to be served to all, but the rich, disregarding the poor and leaving them hungry, banqueted so richly as to transgress the limits of propriety and seem to serve rather gluttony or their belly. Estius and others agree here that the drunkenness referred to was not such as to take away the use of reason.[763]
>
> It is hard to believe that the faithful of this recently founded church which the Apostle so extols elsewhere in this same Epistle (I, 4 *et seqq.*) should so far have degenerated that already *many* of them should not hesitate to approach the Holy Eucharist in the state of mortal sin. In my opinion it is easier and more correct to accept that the way in which the Corinthians conducted their agapes before the Eucharist was such that

say to you? Do I praise you? In this I praise you not. For I have received of the Lord that which also I delivered unto you, that the Lord Jesus, the same night in which he was betrayed, took bread. And giving thanks, broke, and said: Take ye, and eat: this is my body, which shall be delivered for you: this do for the commemoration of me. In like manner also the chalice, after he had supped, saying: This chalice is the new testament in my blood: this do ye, as often as you shall drink, for the commemoration of me. For as often as you shall eat this bread, and drink the chalice, you shall shew the death of the Lord, until he come. Therefore whosoever shall eat this bread, or drink the chalice of the Lord unworthily, shall be guilty of the body and of the blood of the Lord. But let a man prove himself: and so let him eat of that bread, and drink of the chalice. For he that eateth and drinketh unworthily, eateth and drinketh judgment to himself, not discerning the body of the Lord. Therefore are there many infirm and weak among you, and many sleep.

[763] *Ad locum*, p. 333.

many of them were forgetful of due reverence when the moment came for celebration of the sacred mysteries and thus acted as unworthy heralds of the Passion of Christ Thus the account itself is better not understood of what we mean by unworthy Communion in the strict sense, neither do the penalties mentioned require such a severe interpretation as they are all temporal in nature; and although they do not absolutely exclude eternal punishment, I cannot help thinking that the Apostle would not have passed over eternal punishment if he had really thought that all these *many* souls were approaching the Table of the Lord in the state of mortal sin... In the New Testament the metaphorical use of *sleep* in the sense of death is only ever applied to those who have died in expectation of glorious resurrection and are at rest until the second coming of Christ; it can mean a premature death, certainly, but not an unhappy one.[764]

Clearly the learned, wise and reasonable interpretation of Cornely is milder than Fr. Castelein's opinion with regard to the scandals of the Corinthians.

B

But Fr. Castelein, succumbing to a sudden attack of rigorism, continues in the following terms:

Further on (XV, 12-34) he reproaches a number of them with denying the crucial dogma of the resurrection of the dead and he feels the need to offer a long demonstration of it! (Note to p. 311)

But once again we find Cornely's interpretation both milder and more tenable:

The dogma of the Resurrection, as it was of old rejected by the Sadducees, presented far greater difficulties to the pagan philosophers, who were unanimous in denying the resurrection of the body; this was why, when he proclaimed it at Athens, they derided Paul as a mere jargon-monger. Yet even among the first Christians there were some who found the resurrection of dead bodies so difficult to believe that they turned the dogma of the resurrection into an allegory, arguing that they had already risen to the new life of the spirit so that the resurrection was already past *It is not so surprising, therefore* [Pay careful attention Fr. Cas-

---

[764] *Ibid., ad locum*, pp. 350-1.

telein! — Author] that even at Corinth some *neophytes* under the influence of the teaching of the philosophers should have proclaimed that there was no resurrection of the dead to be awaited.[765]

C

In Chapter V he complains that they admit into their assemblies to communicate with him a Christian living in incest Saint Paul excommunicates this public sinner. (Note to p. 311)

In reply to which I make the following four remarks:

(i)   Among the Apostles there was a Judas and in the fervent church of Jerusalem there were Ananias and Saphira: we should never generalize from one or two examples.

(ii)   Saint Paul in fact rebukes the *elders* of the church for inadequate vigilance over the morals of their subjects.

(iii)   The woman involved seems to have been a pagan, or at least not a Christian, from the fact that the Apostle has no word of rebuke for her, which he would surely not have omitted if she too had been a believer.[766]

(iv)   The Apostle's information as to the state of the church at Corinth came only from envoys whose reports did not entirely agree.[767]

D

Further on (II Corinthians xii, 21) he expresses his opinion as to the bad state of a great many:

---

[765] *Ibid.*, p. 447.

[766] Cf. Cornely, *ad locum*, pp. 117 and 119.

[767] See Fouard, Constant, *Saint Paul and his Missions*: "Thanks to the frequency of communication between Achaia and Ephesus Paul was informed almost at once of the melancholy course events were taking over in Corinth. ... Other believers from Achaia, on their journeys to Ephesus, and especially Apollos who returned just about this time, completed the account of the divisions now so widespread... ... Only a little while after the departure of the delegates three Christians from Corinth ... arrived at Ephesus and depicted the state of their Church under less gloomy colours." (English translation by G. F. X. Griffith, Longmans, 1908, pp. 260-1)

*Lest **again**, when I come, God humble me among you : and I mourn **many** of them that sinned before, and have not done penance for the uncleanness, and fornication, and lasciviousness, that they have committed.*

On this point I wholeheartedly grant Fr. Castelein the iniquities of the Corinthian neophytes; by their prevarication they had failed to yield the fruit that Paul had expected of them, but the Apostle says that he is humiliated by God, for in this humiliation permitted by God he saw an outstanding mark of God's goodness. But it is important to stress that in that city, with its deeply-rooted cult of Aphrodite, even the Christians were inclined to lust, for many of them had indulged in that vice before being called to the faith.[768] Indeed their city was famous throughout the Empire for moral corruption, lust and luxury, so that the verb *Corinthiari* meant to lead a life of luxury and lust And on the very citadel stood a temple to Aphrodite in which *a thousand harlots* served their goddess, prostituting themselves to the lust of the people.[769] Fr. Castelein is no more entitled to use such an unpromising terrain as a standard from which to judge the other churches than we should be to judge the morals of our Catholic countryfolk from those of the seaside resorts.

E

But what places the state of the early *Church* in its true and sad light, after its initial fervour, is Saint Paul's testimony in Philippians II, 21, when praising Saint Timothy, that in general the other ministers of the Gospel seek their own interest and not those of Jesus Christ : *For all seek the things that are their own; not the things that are Jesus Christ's.* If the clergy of Saint Paul's day generally corresponded to this description, what must the ordinary faithful have been like? (Note to p. 312)

These words of Fr. Castelein are liable to give great scandal to his pious readers of both sexes.

It should be noted that :

---

[768] Cornely, *op. cit.*, p. 340.

[769] *Ibid., Prolegomenon in Epistulam I^{am} ad Corinthios*, p. 2.

(i) The claim that Saint Paul is here referring exclusively to *ministers of the Gospel* is entirely gratuitous, for, as Estius notes, *ad locum*, he is rather speaking of Christians in general or of the laity.

(ii) Secondly, it is not evident that this self-love on the part of the disciples, which incited them to *seek the things that [were] their own* was grave enough to constitute a mortal sin. Cajetan and many others rightly think that: "What the Apostle reprehends here is not mortally sinful of its nature, but rather an inclination of the imperfect, i.e. on the part of those who seek not the increase of merits in others, but are satisfied with keeping their own."

(iii)   The Apostle does not allege that *absolutely all* the laity and ministers of the Gospel of that day were such as he describes, Timothy alone excepted. Epaphroditus, who is highly praised in what follows cannot have been such; nor can those of whom he wrote in the previous chapter, verses 15 and 16: *Some ... for good will preach Christ Some out of charity, knowing that I am set for the defence of the gospel.* These at least were not of the number of those who sought *the things that were their own* rather than *the things that are Jesus Christ's.* He says *all* in the sense of *very many.* That this usage is common in the Scriptures is stated by Jerome in his Commentary on the Epistle to the Ephesians, chapter I, near the end, and by Augustine: *Liber de unitate Ecclesiæ*, cap. XII.[770] Hence it is untrue for Fr. Castelein to assert that Saint Paul is expounding the state of the Church in his day "in its true and sad light"; and it is false for him to imply ("if the clergy of Saint Paul's day generally corresponded to this description, what must the ordinary faithful have been like?") that the clergy were in general corrupt in the times of Saint Paul.

F

And the learned Professor is just as far from the mark when he asserts:

> But a still more distressing testimony is found in the Second Epistle to Timothy (I, 15) where Saint Paul declares that all the Christians of Asia

---

[770] Estius, *In Cap. II ad Philippenses*; 1679 edition, p. 645.

Minor have *cut themselves off from him*... Yes, *all* these Christians had fallen into schism! (Note to p. 312)

What Paul actually wrote, enchained at Rome, to his beloved disciple then in Asia, was: *Thou knowest this, that all they who are in Asia, are turned away from me: of whom are Phigellus and Hermogenes.* He mentions this defection of many from him in order to strengthen and comfort Timothy who might otherwise have been troubled or dejected on learning it. But it should be borne in mind that:

(i) The Apostle is speaking only of Jewish believers, not Gentile converts;

(ii) He is speaking not of the whole of Asia Minor as Fr. Castelein audaciously asserts, but of those who had begun to adhere to him when he was in Asia, but who, upon coming to Rome and finding him cast into chains and in danger, turned their backs on him as one unknown. For the Greek original which rendered *they who **are** in Asia* does not contain the word "are" at all and is often translated *they who **were** in Asia.*

(iii)   He does not say that they had cut themselves off from the faith or the Church but only from his own person. Hence Estius observes: "It is probable that he means simply that they turned away from him out of fear to be associated with a prisoner, or perhaps even blamed him for incurring such danger by his own rash fault."[771] In the same way we might say today that all nations turned away from Pius IX and Leo XIII in their captivity. There is no doubt that these Asiatics who were at Rome did wrong, but their conduct gives no credible basis for Fr. Castelein to assert that "all the Christians of Asia Minor have *cut themselves off* ... [and] fallen into schism."

G

It was therefore at such times and to such Christians that Saint Paul addresses his exhortations filled with sweetness..." But the Apostle was not always so sweet and mild. For instance, he invites the Corinthians to choose between his severity and his meekness: *What*

---

[771] *Ibid.,* ad locum, p. 809.

will you? shall I come to you with a rod; or in charity, and in the spirit of meekness?[772] And he attests that his epistles give rather an impression of severity: *But that I may not be thought as it were to terrify you by epistles, for his epistles indeed, say they, are weighty and strong...*[773] Nor is he ingratiating towards the Galatians or the Cretans: *O senseless Galatians, who hath bewitched you that you should not obey the truth?*[774] And: *The Cretans are always liars, evil beasts, slothful bellies. This testimony is true. Wherefore rebuke them sharply...*[775]

3. Fr. Castelein's final conclusion from such flimsy evidence is this:

> These quotations suffice to annihilate the panegyric of the early Church... [Note to p. 312] I prefer the present state of the Church to its past state. [p. 17]

A judgement well worth contrasting with those of weightier authorities.

His Holiness Pope Leo XIII, for instance, writes:

> And shall any one who recalls the history of the apostles, the faith of the nascent church, the trials and deaths of the martyrs and, above all, those olden times, so fruitful in saints, dare to measure our age with these, or affirm that they received less of the divine outpouring from the Spirit of Holiness?[776]

And historian Cardinal Hergenröther writes of the early Church:

> In the face of the moral corruption and the vices of its contemporaries, she maintains her holiness... She keeps her children faithful to duty by the holiness of her discipline. In this flourishing age of the first Christians, when superior gifts of grace are still so frequent, leaders seldom appear to exercise the fulness of their authority... This period of the

---

[772] I Corinthians IV, 21.

[773] II Corinthians X, 9, 10.

[774] Galatians III, 1.

[775] Titus I, 12-13.

[776] Apostolic Letter *Testem benevolentiæ* to Cardinal Gibbons, January 1899.

nascent Church, this age of martyrs, therefore presents, notwithstanding the scarcity of documents, a sublime and consoling image.[777]

Another celebrated historian of the primitive Church, Father Constant Fouard, is of the same view:

> When taking leave of his churches in Eastern lands the Apostle felt well assured that he was leaving with his converts the perfect faith in Christ, set free and unhampered by any compromise with the truth; he had furthermore the conviction that it would go on triumphant and ever fruitful in that half of the world which he had been evangelizing.[778]

4. Fr. Castelein promises us "a work which I expect to be both very instructive and highly interesting" presenting a "comparison between the past and present states of the Church" in such terms as to explain "why I prefer the present state of the Church to her past state." (p. 17)

Love of truth and of souls moves us to hope that this promise will not be kept. But if he in fact accomplishes this undertaking we shall await it unmoved, ready, as devoted children of the Apostolic Church, *to praise men of renown, and our fathers in their generation!*[779]

11
"In the early Church there was no clerical formation."

Fr. Castelein:

> At heart the Church is convinced that salvation is easy. This argument is considerably strengthened ... by consideration of the lack of regular formation for the clergy [at the time of the early Church]. (p. 278)

So egregious a calumny can be very briefly refuted.

(i)   The Apostles were formed and trained first by Christ Our Lord in person and thereafter by the Holy Ghost.

(ii)   The Apostles themselves selected for the clergy men of good reputation, full of wisdom and of the Holy Ghost.

---

[777] Hergenröther, Cardinal Joseph (1824-90), *History of the Church*, First Period, Introduction; French translation by Belet, Vol. I, pp. 137-8.

[778] *Saint Paul and his Missions*, Epilogue, p. 417.

[779] See Ecclesiasticus XLIV, 1. — Translator.

(iii)   Thereafter …

Clerics were chosen with great care. They were not to be neophytes — new to the faith — ignorant, vicious or ill-famed among the people.

The bishops then strove to raise young men for the clergy and special establishments for the purpose were set up in great cities such as Rome, Antioch, Alexandria and Cæsarea.

As great pains were taken to cultivate the spirit of chastity and of continence in them as to impart the necessary knowledge to them. It was intended above all to turn out men *able to teach*, of stainless life and accustomed to good works. Some clerics having no private means lived by the labour of their hands after the example of the Apostles.[780]

There is the simple truth. In spite of Fr. Castelein's allegations, the clergy of the first centuries emerge as educated in divine and profane learning; they led a holy life which a great number of them crowned by martyrdom.

IV

SOPHISTRIES CONCERNING ORIGINAL SIN AND ITS EFFECTS AND CONCERNING JUSTIFICATION

12

"Original sin is overcome by the grace of the Redeemer in its actual efficacy towards all."

1. The learned Professor encountered a major obstacle to his thesis in the shape of Original Sin, under which groans the *damned mass* of mankind as the Church recalls in the following words of Saint Augustine: "Evils encompassed the whole of mankind, tossing the damned mass it comprised to and fro, casting it from one ill to another…"[781]

---

[780] *Op. cit., First Century*, chapter III, n. 1.

[781] "Iacebat in malis, vel etiam volvebatur, et de malis in mala praecipitabatur totius humani generis massa damnata." Septuagesima Sunday, Lesson, IInd Nocturn, taken from the *Enchiridion* of Saint Augustine, capp. 25-27.

For it is a most certain fact that a considerable majority of mankind on earth has always been, and still is, infected with original sin, seated thus in darkness and in the shadow of death.

Now original sin, by depriving man of his supernatural gifts and wounding him in those of nature, constitutes a great impediment to salvation for the whole of mankind, which it leaves greatly debilitated. And this wound is transmitted to all men and remains present in by far the greater part of them, with all its lamentable consequences.

2. Thus for Fr. Castelein to have a solid basis in favour of the salvation of the majority who continue to live in the state of unremitted original sin, he must prove that the debilitating effects of original sin no longer exist or are in some mysterious way neutralized in the majority of unbaptized adults when they reach the use of reason, and this is indeed what he endeavours to achieve.

Let us cite in his own words this position which he himself calls "*si hardie* — so audacious". (p. 204.)

> But it may be said that original sin has made man so weak, so inclined to evil... (p. 198)

Upon which he shows that the remedy against original sin is the grace of the Redeemer, on which subject he enquires:

> Let us now enquire as to the efficacy and extension of this grace, in other words, how powerfully and how far does it act within mankind redeemed by the Blood of Jesus Christ and which the heavenly Father desires to save in its entirety?
>
> In general terms Saint Paul says, in his Epistle to the Ephesians, that the riches of this grace are "unsearchable — *investigabiles*".
>
> But it is in his Epistle to the Romans that he undertakes to reveal to us, under the vivid brightness of revelation, all its efficacy and *universality*. (p. 200)

This "universality" is of course exactly what Fr. Castelein needs, in order to be able to announce the salvation of the whole of mankind.

Now Saint Paul informs us that this grace is given us and acts within us with an efficacy and *to an extent* that are *unlimited.*

In Chapter V he compares the two Adams and attests that the new Adam has been more useful in favour of life and salvation than the old Adam was harmful in the cause of death and damnation.

This comparison, it must be noted, is applicable to the human race *in its entirety.* Mankind *as a whole* has gained more for its salvation thanks to the merits of the new Adam than it had lost through the faults of the old Adam.

The efficacy of redeeming grace for mankind is greater than the efficacy of original sin for evil — and *for the multitude.* This multitude is clearly *the same in each case* and therefore is the whole human race. (p. 202)

This means that in terms of eventual salvation, and *for the whole of mankind,* the state of original justice would have been less favourable than is the state of redemption. (p. 203)

In the first state there would have been greater succour to preserve from sin, thanks to the strength and perfection of our nature, but in the second state, thanks to the remedies of grace, there is greater *restorative succour* after sin.

In the first state there would probably have been many fewer personal faults, but these faults would have yielded their fruit of eternal death *in a greater number of men.*

Thus it is that the new Adam has been more salutary for men, *taken as a whole,* than the old Adam was baneful. (p. 204)

Thus, if I am rightly understanding Fr. Castelein, he holds that the entire human race, including pagans, Mahometans, Jews and indeed all unbelievers and misbelievers, are now in reality better placed, in a state of fallen nature, than they would have been in the state of innocence, in the sense that they now have greater help, which he calls *restorative succour.* Now this is perfectly true *in actu primo*[782] but it is certainly not true *in actu secundo,*[783] i.e. in actual fact, and herein lies

---

[782] "In first act" — i.e. as to what it is in their *power* to achieve : their potentiality. — Translator.

[783] "In second act" — i.e. as to what they in fact *have* achieved : their actuality. — Translator.

the nub of the disagreement between the learned professor and the present writer.

4. Undoubtedly in the present order of providence, i.e. following original sin, sufficient actual grace is always available to all adult sinners, no matter how obdurate and including negative infidels; but it is no less certain that not all receive the special and efficacious grace by which to reach faith and salvation.

It is in this sense that the Council of Trent says: "Not all receive the benefit of His [sc. Christ's] death,"[784] for it is quite clear from the context that the Sacred Council is referring to the benefit completed in this life by justification.

Where our Professor of Philosophy and Theology is at fault lies in his failure to distinguish God's *antecedent* will from His *consequent* will which will enable him readily to convince lay readers that all men *do* in fact receive the benefit of Christ's death just as they have received original sin from Adam, and hence that even for unbelievers salvation is an easy matter.

He admits the audacity and novelty of his doctrine, claiming to have extracted it from Chapter V of Saint Paul's Epistle to the Romans: "This doctrine, so audacious, but so consoling and so reassuring is logically drawn in its clear, formal and explicit sense, from the teaching of Saint Paul." (p. 204)

> … A doctrine affirmed by the testimony of Saint Paul in the comparison he makes between the fault of Adam and the grace of Christ, in which the latter is presented as no less extensive than the former in its application to the whole of mankind. (p. 208)

> According to Saint Paul Christ shows Himself in the fullest reality more powerful to save us than Adam was to damn us. Therefore from the viewpoint of salvation, or of the actual reign of grace which saves us (*in vita regnabunt*[785]), Christ has restored more to *the whole of* mankind than Adam had taken away. This is a demonstration which I believe to be irrefutable. (Note to p. 203)

[784] Session VI, Chapter III, *On Justification.* Denzinger 795.
[785] Romans V, 17.

5. On the subject of this demonstration Fr. Coppin has well written:

> How can it be claimed that the reference in this passage of Saint Paul is to the *number* and concerns their ultimate salvation, as this author asserts? If it were so, since Adam's fault in principle and by rights had damned *all men*, for the gift to be greater *in numerical terms* it would have to save *more than all* men — a conclusion the absurdity of which abundantly proves that Fr. Castelein's reasoning is unsound in the conclusion he reaches on the numerical aspect.[786]

6. But as usual our Professor of Theology cannot refrain from an attack on the "Rigorists" whose discomfiture he confidently anticipates:

> What avail all the lamentations of the Rigorists and the Pessimists against this robust doctrine? Nothing at all! (p. 204)
>
> (…)
>
> I trust that the Rigorists will not blame me for setting out in all its brightness this admirable doctrine which so triumphantly refutes their lamentable theories. (p. 208)

I cheerfully confess that I myself belong to the number of these "Rigorists" who fly, in matters of theology and Holy Writ, and especially in matters of predestination, original sin and the distribution of graces, from every new or audacious doctrine, no matter how admirable its adherents may boast it to be. I prefer to follow "the sounder and more approved doctrine."[787]

7. And since my antagonist appeals to Saint Paul, let us look more closely at the passage he claims for his cause, using the approved paraphrase of Mgr. Beelen:

Romans V, 15-19	Paraphrase
15. But not as the offence, so also the gift. For if by the offence of one, many died; much more the grace of	15. But the gift of divine grace which falls to men through Christ differs sharply from the injury caused to the human race by Adam. The two cases are not the same. For while, as we profess, by the fall of that one man the whole

---

[786] *Op. cit.*, p. 132.

[787] Pope Leo XIII, *Gravissime nos*, 30th Dec. 1892, citing Saint Ignatius of Loyola; *Acta*, Vatican edition, vol. XII, p. 366. See above, footnote to p. 56.

God, and the gift, by the grace of one man, Jesus Christ, hath abounded unto many.

16. And not as it was by one sin, so also is the gift. For judgment indeed was by one unto condemnation; but grace is of many offences, unto justification.

17. For if by one man's offence death reigned through one; much more they who receive abundance of grace, and of the gift, and of justice, shall reign in life through one, Jesus Christ.

18. Therefore, as by the offence of one, unto all men to condemnation; so also by the justice of one, unto all men to justification of life.
19. For as by the disobedience of one man, many were made sinners; so also by the obedience of one, many shall be made just.

multitude of men fell subject to death and his fault overflowed to the general injury, yet far more abundantly did the love of God and the gift of grace flowing from it in favour of all men pour itself out through the grace of the one man Jesus Christ.

16. And Adam did not do men harm in the same degree as Christ did them good, indeed the latter did much greater good than the former did harm, for the cause of our condemnation was the guilt of a *single* sin, but the gratuitous gift is efficacious for justification from *many* sins.

17. The gift is therefore different in character from the sin; for if, as we profess, the fall of that man established the reign of death, yet all those who with the passage of time *become partakers of the abundance of divine love and the gift of justice (righteousness) that flows from it* will much more, by the destruction of death and obtaining life, reign through the one Jesus Christ

18. And so just as the one sin yielded the condemnation of death to all men, so too did one good work yield all men justification which leads to the acquisition of eternal life.

19. For just as by the disobedience of one man, all men born of him inherited the status of sinners, so too by the obedience of one, all are made just *who by faith are born again of that One.*

8. Here now is Fr. Castelein's very different paraphrase of the same passage.

I will now quote, for the benefit of the theologians, the words from which I draw my conclusion.

v. 15. *Si enim unius delicto multi mortui sunt ... gratia unius hominis Jesu Christi in plures abundavit.*

For if by the offence of one, many [in Greek *the multitude*, i.e. the human race] died ... the grace of one man, Jesus Christ, hath abounded unto many [again in Greek *the multitude*].

> v. 19 (a) *peccatores constituti sunt* **multi** [In Greek, once more, *the*
> *multitude*, meaning mankind] : *ita et per unius obeditionem*, (b) *justi*
> *constituentur* **multi** [the human race].

So from the point of view of *salvation* or of the *effective* reign of the grace that saves us (*in vita regnabunt*) Christ has restored *more* to the whole of mankind than Adam deprived it of. This is a demonstration which I believe to be irrefutable. (Note to p. 203)

(…)

This is how the teaching of the Doctor of the Gentiles in his magnificent Epistle to the Romans *must* be understood. This is why he closes the entire dogmatic section of this Epistle by crying, at the end of Chapter XI (V. 32):

> *God has let (a)* **all** *mankind fall into the abyss of evil in order to show his mercy (b) towards* **all**.[788] (p. 206)

9. I am delighted to grant to my adversary that the sin or fault of Adam was exceeded by Christ or by His "gift", both because the gift of Christ heals us not only from one sin, contracted from Adam, but also from all those committed by our own free will, but also because through Christ we are given a new life which is more excellent than the one that the sin of Adam deprived us of.

But unfortunately this is not enough to satisfy Fr. Castelein, for the excellence of the Redemption is of no use to him in support of his erroneous thesis — he needs the *actual extension* or application of sanctifying grace to an immense multitude of unbaptized persons. This is why he insists on everywhere translating the word *multi* as referring to the whole of mankind, giving it the same extension as *plures* and equating it with *all*.

10. In which respect he is utterly wrong as I will now prove from the authority of the greatest scriptural interpreters.

Saint Augustine:

> *In* **all** *men unto justification.* Not because all men in fact come to the grace of justification but because *all who are reborn* unto justification are

---

[788] The text in fact reads : *God hath concluded all in unbelief, that he may have mercy on all.* — Translator.

necessarily reborn through Christ, just as all who are born unto condemnation are necessarily so born through Adam. …

Hence he [sc. Saint Paul] says that *grace much more abounded unto many* and **not** that *grace abounded unto many **more***.[789]

Saint Bruno:

He does not say that grace abounded unto more than did sin, but *unto many*, for not all are saved as they have not chosen to be.[790]

By the justice of Christ passing into all men *in potency*[791] [and not *in act*, although Christ paid a price sufficient for all].

Many shall be made just (verse 19); *many* because not all have willed to be justified.[792]

Thus he says: The grace of God has indeed abounded, in the following sense: just as before justification sin reigned, leading to death, so too, does grace reign, by *the acceptance and conservation* of justice [i.e. the state of grace] leading to eternal life.[793]

Saint Thomas:

It must be understood that just as all men, who are born of Adam by the flesh, incur the condemnation [of death] by his sin, so do all who are reborn spiritually of Christ obtain the justification of life. It may, however, be said that the justification of Christ brings forth the justification of all *with regard to its sufficiency*, but in terms of its *efficacy* it so acts *only* for the faithful.[794]

And more recent interpreters express the same understanding: Estius:

In verse 15 (… *grace … hath abounded **unto many***) as in the rest of this chapter the translator consistently renders the Greek πολλοὺς (*multos*, many) by the Latin *plures* (more), but no one should be surprised by this

---

[789] Letter CLVII, 13; and in the unfinished *Contra Julianum*, cited by Estius *ad locum*.

[790] *Sancti Brunonis Carthusianorum institutoris expositiones in omnes epistolas beati Pauli Apostoli, ad locum*, Montreuil, 1892, p. 30, col. 1.

[791] *Ibid.*, col. 2.

[792] *Ibid.*, p. 31, col. 1.

[793] *Ibid.*, p. 31, col. 2.

[794] *Super Epistolam Beati Pauli Apostoli ad Romanos, ad locum*; *Opera omnia*, Parma, vol. XIII, p. 56,

rendering as though more persons were saved by Christ than died in Adam given that the contrary is in fact the case.[795]

(…)

So it is clear that in this passage the Apostle's point does not concern the *number* of those made partakers of the grace of Christ, but the quantity and greatness of the benefits of Christ, as is indicated by the words *multo magis* — *much more.* So the meaning is : By the sin or transgression of one man, *many* — i.e. all his descendants — incurred death ; but by the grace of the one man Jesus Christ, i.e. on account of His merits, *much more* did God generously pour forth the gifts of His grace upon *many*, i.e. upon *all the elect*, or *all who belong to Christ.*[796]

(…)

In verse 18 (… *as by the offence of one, unto **all men** to condemnation ; so also by the justice of one, unto **all men** to justification of life*) the expression *all men* as it occurs in both clauses *could* be understood of the entire human race, but not in the same extension but differently for each subject. In the first clause the acceptation would be entirely general, because the reference is to the first parent of all men, through whom death was conveyed to all without exception. But in the second clause it would be understood in accordance with the manner of speaking, frequent in Holy Scripture, which says *all men* in order to be understood as meaning *many.*[797]

Bernardinus a Piconio :

Verse 18 : *Unto all men* — who believe in Him.[798]

Van Steenkiste :

Saint Paul's words in verse 15 do not prove that those who are saved through Christ are more numerous than those who are dragged towards hell by original sin.[799]

Omitting many others I close with Knabenbauer, whose words clearly show that Fr. Castelein errs in wanting to attribute to the

---

[795] *In Omnes Pauli Epistolas, ad locum* ; Mainz, 1858, ed. Holzammer, vol. I, p. 115, col. 2.

[796] *Ibid.*, p. 116, col. 1.

[797] *Ibid.*, p. 118, col. 2

[798] *Epistolarum Beati Pauli Apostoli Triplex Expositio, ad locum.*

[799] *Sanctum Jesu Christi Evangelium secundum Matthæum*, q. 268 ; 3rd edition, vol. 1, p. 386.

words "many" and "all" the same extension with regard to ultimate salvation as with regard to original sin, in terms not merely of intrinsic sufficiency but of actual efficacy.

> Verse 18. There is a certain difficulty here in that it is not certain whether the word *all* in each clause should be taken as having the same extension or not.
>
> There is no doubt that in the first clause the reference is to the entire human race, i.e. to each and every person descending from Adam by natural generation, and the same extension would be admissible in the second clause also if the allusion were exclusively to the *sufficiency* of the merits which Christ acquired for mankind by His obedience. For by dying on the Cross He paid a price more than sufficient for the redemption of each and every man, and did so with the set purpose of enabling each and every one of them to obtain the remission of all his sins, and true justice.
>
> But the subject here is *not* the sufficiency of the redemption but its *actual efficiency*, which extends only to the faithful, namely to those who, by using the means established by Christ, are born again of Christ, for which reason the word "all" in the second clause must be limited to them alone.[800]

Knabenbauer goes on to point out that this is the interpretation of Saint Thomas and that the Angelic Doctor, along with the Fathers of the Church and most interpreters has interpreted the passage correctly.

11. But Fr. Castelein finds in the writings of Saint Thomas and other Saints new things that no one has ever seen in them before. Everyone judges as he is inclined and, Professor of theology and philosophy as he is, he finds on every side arguments in favour of the fewness of the damned, even among infidels.

Hard on his misinterpretation of Saint Paul comes the following triumphant exclamation:

> Can there now be any grounds for surprise at Saint Thomas's broad doctrine as to the distribution of grace? This grace which sanctifies *and saves* the soul is given to every adult *without exception* in every time and

---

[800] *Op. cit.*, p. 301.

place provided only that he does not oppose to it the obstacle of a mortal sin by refusing to follow his last end as it is known to him.

This is the famous text of the *Summa*[801] in which Saint Thomas demonstrates that in a man who has reached the age of discernment needed for actual sin original sin can co-exist only with mortal sin, not with venial sin alone. Thus the Angelic Doctor clearly teaches that the grace of salvation is *in fact* given to every man who does not oppose to it the obstacle of a mortal sin. Indeed it is this broad and elevated doctrine, I would say, which has the most emboldened me to fight rigorism so energetically. (p. 207)

Earlier he had said: "I do not know why this clear and decisive text is almost never quoted." (p. 136)

12. In response to this objection I would point out that this text of Saint Thomas is extremely well known to the theologians but is far from being regarded by all of them as so "decisive" on the subject of the present controversy. The facts are:

(i) Saint Thomas states (*Summa Theologiæ*, I-II, q. 89, a. 6) that venial sin cannot exist in anyone with original sin alone, which he proves from the fact that at the first instant of the use of reason a man is bound to convert himself to God. In point of fact, very many theologians are unconvinced by this proof and reject the proposition it is alleged to demonstrate, remarking with Sylvius: "It is highly probable, and hence safe in conscience, that there is no precept to convert oneself to God as soon as a man begins to have the use of reason. In which case venial sin *can* co-exist with original sin alone, as is taught by Saint Bonaventure, Durand, Richard and no few more recent theologians." And even the Thomists teach as no more than probable this doctrine that venial sin cannot co-exist with original sin alone."[802]

(ii) But in any event it is hard to see the relevance of this passage to Fr. Castelein's thesis that the majority of men are saved. For al-

---

[801] *Summa Theologiæ*, I-II, q. 89, a. 6, and Supplement, q. 69, a. 9, reply to the 3ʳᵈ objection.

[802] See Billuart, Charles René, O.P., *Summa S. Thomæ hodiernis academiarum moribus accommodata*, Liège, 1748, vol. V, p. 433.

though he claims that "it is this ... doctrine ... which has the most emboldened me to fight rigorism so energetically," (p. 207) in reality it gives him no support at all. To infer the salvation of the majority from this passage would involve admitting a conclusion of greater extension than its premises — the same fallacy as to infer the salvation of almost all from God's infinite mercy. Moreover if this argument from Saint Thomas had any weight in favour of the salvation of the majority, it would be astonishing indeed that neither Saint Thomas himself nor any of the venerable and learned school of Thomists after him should have noticed it. Instead of which all follow their Master in saying: *Pauciores sunt qui salvantur — there are fewer who are saved.*[803]

13. Indeed the Angelic Doctor is so far from holding the doctrine which Fr. Castelein extracts from Chapter V of Saint Paul's Epistle to the Romans that he not only explains in his Commentary on the Epistles and in the *Summa*[804] the words of the Apostle as I have explained them above, but elsewhere in the *Summa*[805] he states as an objection to his own position the argument that: "... as the Apostle says[806] more was restored to man by Christ's gift, than he had lost by Adam's sin. But Adam received what enabled him to persevere; and thus man does not need grace in order to persevere." [At this point *Professor* Castelein would surely like to continue: *so the number of the elect is greater after Christ's redemption than before the fall of Adam.*[807]] But Saint Thomas replies to the objection: "As Augustine says: 'in the original state man received a gift whereby he *could* persevere, but perseverance itself was *not* given him. But now, by the grace of Christ, many receive both the gift of grace whereby they may persevere, and the further gift of actually persevering,'[808] and thus Christ's gift is greater than Adam's fault. Nevertheless it was easier for man to

---

[803] *Summa Theologiæ* I, q. 23, a. 7, reply to objection 3.

[804] *Summa Theologiæ* II-II, q. 81, a. 3, reply to objection 3.

[805] *Summa Theologiæ* I-II, q. 109, a. 10, objection 3 and reply to objection 3.

[806] Romans V, 20.

[807] Coppin, *op. cit.*, p. 134.

[808] *De Natura et Gratia*, XLIII, and cf. *De Correptione et Gratia*, XII.

persevere, with the gift of grace in the state of innocence in which the flesh was not rebellious against the spirit, than it is now. For the restoration by Christ's grace, although it is already begun in the mind, is not yet completed in the flesh, as it will be in heaven, where man will not merely be able to persevere but will be unable to sin."

It is also worth re-reading the extract from Saint Thomas cited above on p. 76 concerning the "common state of nature ... deprived of grace through the corruption of original sin" from which God has raised up "some", but "from which *very many* ... fall short [*deficiunt*]."[809]

17. It follows that Fr. Castelein's interpretation of Chapter V of the Epistle to the Romans is gravely erroneous as is his doctrine of original sin. Let him beware lest in his determination to proclaim the salvation of the greater part of mankind notwithstanding the wound inflicted by the serpent, his own doctrine may not prove to be itself a suggestion of the serpent as Recupito calls it.

Saint Augustine presents as an objection to his own position the broad doctrine of his adversaries: "Surely not, they say — when Christ comes and sees such a great multitude at His left hand He will be moved by pity and grant pardon." Which the Holy Doctor refutes as follows: "This is precisely what the serpent promised to the first man. For God had threatened him with death if he should taste the fruit, but the serpent said, 'Surely not: No, you shall not die the death,' just as if he were to say, 'You shall not be damned.' Such is the language with which the serpent deceives men.[810]

13

"Good examples do more good than bad ones do harm."

It is a problem of advanced moral philosophy to compare the good outcome of good examples with the evil outcome of bad examples.

---

[809] *Summa Theologiæ*, I, q. 23, a. 7, reply to objection 3.

[810] Recupito, Giulio Cesare, S.J., *Tractatus de numero prædestinatorum et reproborum*, cap. IV, 1681, p. 39.

Which of the two influences is the more efficacious for driving humanity back or advancing it on the road of its destinies?

The pessimists are prompt to declare that bad examples are undoubtedly more powerful, while the optimists favour the good ones.

I have not the slightest hesitation in joining the ranks of the optimists. (pp. 232-3)

Simple observation gives the lie to all this: hence the Gospel says: *Woe to the world because of scandals,*[811] and folk wisdom echoes: "One rotten apple spoils the barrel," while Tacitus declares that "corrupting and being corrupted is what the world *is*." What sane man can deny that as a rule people tend to follow bad example?

To find out *why* this should be so, we need look no further than the text which says that *the imagination and thought of man's heart are prone to evil from his youth.*[812] For this problem is theological rather than philosophical and will be ill solved indeed, or rather will forever perplex the thoughtful, if human nature is considered from the standpoint of reason alone, overlooking the crucial factor of original sin made known to us by Catholic doctrine:. "One of our commonest errors," says the great Monsabré,

> … is to imagine that our nature as actually received from our parents is *balanced* so that we can just as easily turn towards good as towards evil, by a simple act of will which we can elicit whenever we choose. We have heard tell of a thing called original sin, which is said to weaken the power of our soul's higher faculties while reinforcing our passions, but in practice we take little notice of this. But we are mistaken, gentlemen, for this first self-deception greatly broadens for us the road to perdition.
>
> Nothing is surer than the injury inflicted on our nature by the sin of our first father, the discord which has shattered the primal harmony which lay at the very heart of original justice, the tearing of the fine-woven tissue in which divine and human life were made one in a unity which depended on subordination, the deprivation of the gratuitous gifts by which the higher powers of our being held sway over the lower. Nothing is surer than the blind impetuosity with which the pas-

---

[811] Matthew XVII, 7
[812] Genesis VIII, 21.

sions, no longer chained down by reason and held in thrall to free will, now plunge headlong towards their proper objects...

The consequence of all this, gentlemen, is ... that we are powerless to observe all the commandments of God, and hence to avoid all grave sin, without the aid of grace. Hence the obligation that weighs on each of us to brook no delay in resisting our evil inclinations and in asking God for the graces we need to triumph over them.[813]

In the light of which, how can it be thought that man can resist evil when he is not only driven towards it by the inward seething of his concupiscence but also led on from without by the bad examples that surround him? Some, by ignorance rather than malice, readily deem it morally acceptable to behave as they see others do. Others gradually and imperceptibly come to attach less and less importance to the evil they see others committing. Others again, unaffected by either ignorance or passion, are led by human respect to feel ashamed of not acting as others do. Then there are those who abandon themselves totally to their concupiscences when they see that others will not disapprove of behaviour they are guilty of themselves. This is why it is so commonly recognized that men are easily led by example, the difference between good and bad being that bad example conspires with the inward inclination of fallen nature while good example pushes against the influence of human weakness and concupiscence.

It is quite true that social life is in itself the means by which men best reach not only their temporal end but also their spiritual end. But surely everyone is aware that malice and weakness all too often frustrate the good effects of society and instead work spiritual harm. The obvious reason why Holy Writ, the Fathers, the Doctors, preachers and confessors all concur in so often vehemently discouraging the faithful from bad company and dangerous occasions is that they all know from experience how vulnerable the human mind proves before the influence of evil example. *Be not seduced: Evil communications corrupt good manners.*[814] Which is why "it has always been

---

[813] *Retraite Pascale*, 1889, Instruction 2, *Le chemin de la perdition*, I.

[814] I Corinthians XV, ;33.

observed in the Church for the faithful to abstain from frequenting heretics and excommunicates."[815]

14
"Moral evil is the exception and falls below the sum total of obedience to the law."

Fr. Castelein writes:

> Moral evil is an accident and an exception. And in an order that is well known, accidents and exceptions cannot be equal in total number to conformity to the rule. (p. 235)

But this is practically identical to an objection found in Saint Thomas, viz. that "… vice is found in the greater number of men; for it is written *Broad is the way that leadeth to destruction, and many there are who go in thereat.*[816] Therefore vice is not contrary to nature." Here is the Angelic Doctor's reply:

> There is a twofold nature in man, rational nature, and the sensitive nature. And since it is through the operation of his senses that man accomplishes acts of reason, *hence there are more who follow the inclinations of the sensitive nature,* than who follow the order of reason: because more reach the beginning of a business than achieve its completion.[817]

Once again Fr. Castelein is reasoning as though original sin did not exist It is perfectly true that if the order of things had remained as originally planned and established by God, evil would be a rare occurrence. But this order has been marred by sin: reason has lost its absolute authority over the senses, which all too often now twist free will to a bad end. Hence it came about that before the Flood *the wickedness of men was great on the earth, and all the thought of their heart was bent upon evil at all times,*[818] since *all flesh had corrupted its way upon*

---

[815] Liguori, Saint Alphonsus, *De Prohibitione Librorum,* c. I, n. I.
[816] Matthew VII, 13.
[817] *Summa Theologiæ,* I-II, q. 71, a. 2, reply to the 3rd objection.
[818] Genesis VI, 5

the earth.[819] And this is due of course not to the divine order but to disorder arising from sin. And that which has once been can never be considered impossible.

15
"Excessive desire for earthly goods is not for most men an efficient cause of eternal damnation."

Fr. Castelein:

Of course *immoderate* desire for riches is not rare. Only a tiny minority of us are totally free of it. But are there many in whom this desire attains such extreme malice and monstrous gravity as to create an insurmountable barrier to salvation? (p. 257)

If only we judge the *final fate* of these sinners, prey to weakness rather than to malice, according to the merciful inspirations of the divine goodness, we shall not conclude that *too great* an attraction towards earthly goods is for the majority an efficient cause of eternal damnation. (p. 259)

Now let us listen to another voice on the same subject — this time one who is an experienced missionary and a Doctor of the Church. Saint Alphonsus writes:

The third door of Hell is theft. There are so many who go in by it because there are so many who treat money as their last end, as a god. *The idols of the gentiles are silver and gold,*[820] says Holy Scripture, and it also relays the divine judgement: *nor thieves, nor covetous … shall possess the kingdom of God.*[821] Although theft is not the greatest of the sins, it is the most dangerous: "No sin is more dangerous than theft," says Saint Antoninus. Here is the reason: to obtain the pardon of other sins, contrition is enough, but for theft contrition is not enough as restitution is also required and this is very difficult.[822]

It is an error and a great one to contend that theft, injustice and the other results of excessive attachment to earthly goods are not

---

[819] *Ibid.,* 12

[820] Psalm CXIII, 12.

[821] I Corinthians VI, 12.

[822] Liguori, Saint Alphonsus, Discourse IV, *On the Scourging.*

causes of eternal damnation for very many men. How many are they who for filthy lucre's sake forget shame, neglect the Christian upbringing of their children, injure charity and destroy the peace and concord of families. Blind indeed is anyone who denies this! And these are precisely sins that merit eternal damnation, for the daughters of avarice are betrayal, fraud, trickery, perjury, disquiet, violence and the refusal of mercy,[823] all of which most certainly obstruct eternal salvation. See above, p. 261: "A rich man shall hardly enter into the kingdom of heaven."

<h1 style="text-align:center">16</h1>

"The pride that damns is rare."

Fr. Castelein:

> What seems indisputable to me is that the vice which constitutes the greatest obstacle to salvation and most strongly alienates God's pardon is, in its extreme degree, quite rare *within the confines of the human race*. (p. 262)

It is very well known to all theologians that pride of the kind referred to as *perfect* or *consummated*, is a mortal sin *ex genere suo* — of its nature.[824]

It is found whenever anyone so far yearns for excellence as to refuse submission to God, his superiors and their laws. The reason why it is a mortal sin by nature is that it is repugnant to the love of God which is despised by pride. This is why the Apostle says of the proud and haughty: they who do such things, are worthy of death.[825]

Such is the pride that generates schisms and heresies and even now retains countless souls in schism or heresy. "The Greek schism," says Saint Alphonsus, "had its origin in the pride of an Arius, a Nestorius, a Macedonius and other similar agents of Lucifer. Again it was pride

---

[823] *Summa Theologiæ*, II-II, q. 18, a. 8.

[824] Liguori, Saint Alphonsus, *Theologia Moralis*, lib. II, n. 66; Marc, Fr. Clément C.SS.R. (1831-87), *Institutionum Moralium Alfonsianarum Epitome*, vol. I, n. 361.

[825] Romans I, 32.

that gave birth to the sects of Luther, Zwingli and Calvin."[826] "Humility is what distinguishes the Catholic from the Protestant."[827]

This is the pride that turns so many Catholics of our own times into "liberals", disciples of "Solidarism" and atheists.

This is the pride that holds thousands of Catholics back from the public worship of their religion and in particular from their Easter duties.

This is the pride that stifles sincerity in the confessional, giving rise to countless sacrileges.

This is the pride that generates *human respect*. Alas, it is far from rare in the world about us!

17

"The justification of a sinner is easy."

Fr. Castelein:

How often Scripture declares that *to be saved* it is enough to believe, enough to invoke the name of Jesus Christ with faith! (pp. 59-60)

The Rigorists have no right to appeal to the Epistle of Saint James, for there is not a word in it to suggest that *it is difficult to return to grace with God* and to be saved. *On the contrary* … the Apostle's words about the effects of Extreme Unction evince a conviction utterly opposed to that of the Rigorists. (p. 318)

1. Saint Thomas teaches:

… [t]o rise from sin is not the same as to cease the act of sin; but to rise from sin means that man has restored to him what he lost by sinning. Now man incurs a triple loss by sinning, as was clearly shown above,[828] viz. stain, corruption of natural good, and debt of punishment. He incurs a stain, inasmuch as he forfeits the lustre of grace through the deformity of sin. Natural good is corrupted, inasmuch as man's nature is disordered by man's will not being subject to God's; and this order being overthrown, the consequence is that the whole nature of sinful man re-

---

[826] *Evidence de la foi catholique*, I, cap. II. (See French translation of the Saint's *Œuvres Dogmatiques* by Fr. Jacques, vol. II, p. 411.)

[827] Tannoia, Fr. Antonio Maria C. SS.R., *Mémoires*, Paris, 1843, vol. I, p. 553.

[828] *Summa Theologiæ*, I-II, q. 85, a. 1; I-II, q. 86, a. 1; I-II, q. 87, a. 1.

mains disordered. Lastly, there is the debt of punishment, inasmuch as by sinning man deserves everlasting damnation. Now it is manifest that none of these three can be restored except by God.[829]

But for God to repair any part of that threefold loss, repentance on the part of the sinner is a prerequisite.

For this reason repentance is absolutely necessary for every man who has committed any mortal sin to recover grace and justice, by necessity both of *means* and of *precept*.

It is necessary by necessity of *means* because, as the offence of mortal sin is due to the fact that a man's will is turned away from God towards some mutable good, it is impossible for the offence to be forgiven unless the will turns back to God by a true conversion, entailing the detestation of having turned away to the mutable good and a purpose of amendment. Now is it true that these three things are so easy to accomplish, simply by invoking the most holy Name of Jesus?

And true and serious repentance is necessary by necessity of *precept*, both *natural* because everyone is bound to make satisfaction for an injury done, and *positive* as is often stated in Holy Scripture.[830] Once again, can this double precept by adequately fulfilled by invoking the divine Name?

The promise *For whosoever shall call upon the name of the Lord, shall be saved,*[831] echoes the prophecy *And it shall come to pass, that every one that shall call upon the name of the Lord shall be saved,*[832] quoted and applied by Saint Peter in his Pentecost sermon.[833] The reference is to *living* faith in Christ and its profession[834] — faith that operates by charity. And to "call upon" or "invoke" means, as Saint Thomas says, "to call to oneself by affection and devout worship," i.e. by charity.[835]

---

[829] *Summa Theologiæ*, I-II, q. 109, a. 7, body.

[830] Cf. Marc, Fr. Clément C.SS.R., *op. cit.*, vol. I, n. 1646.

[831] Romans X, 13

[832] Joel II, 32.

[833] Acts II, 17-21.

[834] Cf. Cornely, *op. cit.*, on Romans X, 13, p. 557.

[835] *Ad locum*, Lect. I, ed. Vivès, p. 528, col. 1.

Drach rightly remarks in commenting on this passage[836] that the words "to call upon the Name of the Lord" here mean to believe in Him, hope in Him and love Him, and He Himself has told us that *to love Him is to keep His commandments*.[837] As Saint Augustine says: "Love must be demonstrated by action, lest the invocation of the name prove fruitless."[838]

2. With regard to justification by Extreme Unction ("the Apostle's words about the effects of Extreme Unction evince a conviction utterly opposed to that of the Rigorists") the truth is that we "Rigorists" are united with all theologians in sharing the conviction of Saint James. Let us state what our doctrine is and invite Fr. Castelein to say exactly what part of it he finds too "rigorous".

A. Extreme Unction in itself and by its primary institution is what is termed a *sacrament of the living* — i.e. destined for subjects already in the state of grace. It therefore assumes that the dying recipient has

---

[836] Drach, Fr. Paul-Augustin (1817-95), *La Sainte Bible*, Paris, 1869.

[837] John XIV, 15-21.

[838] *On John*, tract. LXXV, n. 5 ; Drach, *op. cit.*, p. 86 ; When Fr. Castelein writes that "… to be saved it is enough to invoke the name of Jesus Christ," he resembles the preacher amusingly evoked by Fr. Emmanuel, in his article *Le Ciel au Rabais* :
"This preacher was broad-minded. Our age likes broad minds. In the past discernment, exactitude and nicety of judgement were esteemed. But such qualities are hardly fashionable today. Breadth of mind has come into its own. The broader, the better.
"The broad-mindedness of this particular preacher invariably consisted in broadening the way which Our Lord describes as narrow, by demolishing the walls which confine it on either side and which are known as the Commandments of God.
"To be saved, he maintained, it was not necessary, as the Catechisms continue as a rule to teach, to observe the Commandments of God. All that was needed was a cry of "My God!" launched heavenwards in the last instant of life and the soul would escape all the consequences of a life of wickednes and immorality.
"And such cries are uttered by almost all. Heretics, idolaters, bad Christians — all after their own fashion cry : *My God!* From whihc it follows that almost all are saved.
"This is what is commonly known as a *comforting* doctrine. *Comforting!* But is is true? For how could there be comfort in what is not true?" (*Bulletin de Notre Dame de la Sainte Esperance*, January 1893, p. 204)

already obtained the remission of his mortal sins. This is clear from the constant teaching of the Church and from the invariable custom of administering Extreme Unction *after* sacramental absolution and indeed after Holy Viaticum.

B. It is not however by mere accident but rather through a secondary purpose of its institution that this sacrament has the power of remitting even *mortal* sins if the sick person, through no fault of his own, is still in the state of sin, provided he has elicited true attrition for sins committed.

C. Extreme Unction, however, differs in this respect from the other sacraments of the living which, *by a pious conjecture*, are believed sometimes to have this effect; for it is clear enough from the text of Saint James and the teaching of the Council of Trent that the sacrament does indeed have this effect.

For this reason Extreme Unction is a far surer remedy than absolution or Viaticum for all the faithful to obtain the pardon of their sins if they are prevented by unconsciousness from manifesting to the priest directly or indirectly their desire for absolution. For provided attrition is present inwardly, Extreme Unction will justify the sick man, whereas it is at best no more than probable that absolution would do so under those conditions, as the essential condition of accusation is probably absent; neither is it more than probable that the Eucharist produces this effect.

D. It goes without saying that if the sick person is guilty of sin he ought to be reconciled with God before receiving Extreme Unction either by sacramental confession or by perfect contrition. This is implicit in the conditional words of Saint James: *If he be in sins…* And it follows from the necessity of the sacrament of Penance which has been defined to be the *necessary* means of salvation either in reality or in desire for all who have gravely sinned after baptism. If it belonged to the primary institution of Extreme Unction to remit grave sins, the Church's definition would be false.[839]

---

[839] Fr. Augustin Lehmkühl S.J. (1834-1918), *Theologia Moralis*, vol. II, n. 712 *et seqq.*

3. Another point which should not be omitted in discussing the alleged ease of justification of sinners is that most men, including most Catholics, are not merely sinners but are recidivists,[840] habitually living in the state of mortal sin. Suárez acknowledges this: "But of adults, although the *majority* of men sin very often, yet they very often rise up from it and thus pass through their lives falling and rising in alternation." (See above, p. 134.)

But when they are said to "rise", what is meant? What is the nature of their successive conversions? What sorrow, what detestation of sin committed have they — what serious, efficacious purpose of sinning no more and carefully avoiding proximate occasions?

And what ought to be said of the final spiritual resurrection which must precede death? Allow me simply to cite Bourdaloue as quoted by Monsabré:

> To claim that habits contracted during life are destroyed at the approach of death, to claim that in an instant a new spirit, a new heart, a new will are made, is the grossest of illusions... We shall die as we have lived, and the presence of death, far from weakening habits already formed, seems rather to awaken them and reinforce them.[841]

This is why so many Fathers of the Society of Jesus contradict the opinion of their confrère Fr. Suárez on this point, among them the Venerable Bellarmine, the Venerable de la Colombière, Bourdaloue, Cornelius a Lapidè, whom we have already seen, Recupito, whom I shall be quoting shortly, etc.

---

[840] Cf. Fr. Réginald Garrigou-Lagrange 1877-1964: "The recidivist is one who frequently falls into the same sin after repeated Confession, without making any effort to avoid the sin. He differs from the habitual sinner who often falls into the same sin but has not yet confessed his sinful habit. The absolution of these recidivists presents difficulties, since they cannot all be treated in the same way. There are those who repeatedly commit sins due to a malicious will [*recidivi formaliter*], and those who repeatedly commit sins due to frailty [*recidivi materialiter*]. These latter should be given advice and encouragement, and then absolved. As regards the former, Saint Alphonsus, who steers a middle course between severity and excessive leniency, states that as a general rule they are not to be absolved unless they give special signs of their sorrow." (*L'union du prêtre avec le Christ*)

[841] Monsabré, *Retraite Pascale*, 1888, *La dernière heure*, p. 199.

No one familiar with the words of Holy Scripture and of the Fathers of the Church about recidivists will find this surprising.

In Proverbs XXVI, 11 we read: *As a dog that returneth to his vomit, so is the fool that repeateth his folly*. Saint Bernard explains: "The dog that returns to his vomit becomes much more odious than before, and he who after the forgiveness of his sins falls anew into the same foulness becomes a son of hell many times over."[842] To "become a son of hell" of course can only refer to damnation.

Saint Augustine observes that "one who continues to do what he repented of and multiplies instead of diminishing his sins is not a penitent but a mocker."[843]

When Our Lord cured the infirm man at the Probatic Pool He said to him: *Behold thou art made whole: sin no more, lest some worse thing happen to thee.*[844] Once again Saint Bernard explains the passage: "There are much greater grounds for fear when a new fall follows on the grace of forgiveness: the meaning is that it is worse to go back to evil than to enter it the first time."[845]

It is for the same reason that Saint Paul writes:

> For the earth that drinketh in the rain which cometh often upon it and bringeth forth herbs meet for them by whom it is tilled, receiveth blessing from God. But that which bringeth forth thorns and briars, is reprobate, and very near unto a curse, whose end is to be burnt.[846]

But the most famous and most terrible of all these scriptural warnings is that of Ecclesiasticus:

> Be not without fear about sin forgiven, and add not sin upon sin: And say not: The mercy of the Lord is great, he will have mercy on the multitude of my sins. For mercy and wrath quickly come from him, and his wrath looketh upon sinners. Delay not to be converted to the Lord, and

---

[842] Sermon III, *On the Assumption.*

[843] Sermon I, *On Penance and Fasting.*

[844] John V, 14.

[845] Sermon 59 on the Canticle of Canticles.

[846] Hebrews VI, 7, 8.

defer it not from day to day. For his wrath shall come on a sudden, and in the time of vengeance he will destroy thee.[847]

4. I turn now to Recupito's answer to Suárez:

Whenever any adult is predestinate, everything cooperates for his good, even his sins, as is clear from Saint Augustine, who often inculcates this doctrine, saying, for instance, "I dare to say that it is beneficial for the proud to fall into some open and manifest sin, whereby they may be disgusted at themselves. It was better for Peter to be displeased with himself when he wept than to be pleased with himself when he presumed."[848]

Suárez himself gives striking support to this: "I say that the permission to fall into sin both can be and often is an effect of predestination. This view is very often followed by modern theologians in our own days and is present in Anselm and Thomas in their explanations of the words of Romans: *To them that love God, all things work together unto good,*[849] where the Interlinear Gloss adds *even sins.* This interpretation should not be haughtily rejected although it is true that Paul's *primary* intention was to speak of the tribulations and evils sent as punishments."[850] But for habitual recidivists all things do not work together unto good. Therefore, habitual recidivists are not to be numbered among the predestinate.

Proof of the minor premise: sins *work together unto good* to the precise extent that they contribute to fruitful repentance after the sin. But in habitual recidivists the sins committed do not contribute to fruitful repentance for sins, because (a) the first fruit of repentance is not to fall back, and (b) repentance is truly beneficial to the extent that it brings about not only amendment but also improvement of life, so that "the fall may be considered not only not to have produced no obstacle but even to have added to the incentives for progress"[851].

This is confirmed (i) by the fact that the frequent repetition of sin generates the habit of sinning. And this habit, in concert with the downward inclination of corrupt nature, leads almost irreparably to hell. "For upon

---

[847] Ecclesiasticus V, 5-9.

[848] *The City of God,* book XIV, cap. 13.

[849] Romans VIII, 28.

[850] *De Prædestinatione,* lib. III, cap. VIII, n. 4, ed. Vivès, vol. I, p. 475.

[851] Saint Ambrose, *De Apologia Davidis,* cap. 2.

the act follows the habit, upon the habit follows necessity, upon necessity follows despair and upon despair follows damnation."[852]

It is confirmed (ii) from what the Fathers require for repentance after sin to be a sign of predestination, namely continuous sorrow for sin, works of penance, almsgiving, flight of occasions, etc. But in recidivists for the most part these signs are wanting.

And finally it is confirmed (iii), says Recupito,[853] by the fact that if, as the gainsayers allege, "those who pass their lives falling and rising in alternation," i.e. who are habitual recidivists throughout their lives, are to be numbered among the predestinate, it would follows that this habitual recidivism is itself a mark of predestination, which is clearly absurd.

Whereas if the majority of adult believers spend their lives in alternate falls and rises, it manifestly follows that the majority of adults are of the number of the reprobate.

V

SOPHISTRIES THAT EXONERATE SINS OF LUST OF THE GUILT OF ETERNAL PUNISHMENT IF THEY ARE NOT CONTRARY TO NATURE

It is in the following terms that Fr. Castelein embarks on this subject:

> Of the three concupiscences, that of the flesh is the one in which human weakness is most revealed...
> Hence such deliverance is rare... (p. 246)
> Does it not follow from this fact alone that *the majority* of men are lost?
> *No*, I will *never* admit it.
> Why not?
> Because it would entail a complete misunderstanding of the preponderant efficacy of divine grace and mercy to save mankind.
> I will explain my view of this matter in all candour, without fearing the calumnies of the Pharisees, to whichever camp they may belong. (p. 247)

---

[852] The *Interlinear Gloss* on Job XXXI.
[853] *Loc. cit.*

Already this introduction is clean contrary to the common opinion of theologians and to the experience of pastors of souls as expressed by Saint Alphonsus:

> On account of lust the greater number of souls falls into hell; indeed I do not hesitate to assert that it is for this one sin of impurity, or at least not without it, that everyone is damned who is damned.[854]

The reason for this opinion is indicated by the Angelic Doctor: "The devil is said to take special delight in the sin of lust because it is *highly adhesive*, making it hard for a man to be delivered from it, for the delectable appetite is insatiable."[855] Elsewhere[856] Saint Thomas adds a reason quoted from Saint Isidore: "Mankind is subjected to the devil by carnal lust more than by anything else, because ... the vehemence of this passion is more difficult to overcome."[857]

Before addressing these points in detail I must quote a general remark made by the same Professor of Philosophy I have already several times quoted with heartiest approval:

> With regard to the distinction made by the Author between the two kinds of disorder (p. 248), he is guilty, among other offences, of a want of precision. He mixes up several distinctions: sins of weakness or of malice, sins of intermittence or of habit, sins according to nature or against nature, sins outside marriage or against it; periodic sinfulness or confirmation in wickedness. All these distinctions are bundled together in an overlapping hotchpotch. The importance of the subject called for sharper delineation: the author should call things by their names.

In this passage and in many others Fr. Castelein finds damnation only appropriate to sins of pure malice, of formal revolt against God and His advances, though even then in his view for most of these sins the threat is only carried out from time to time (p. 270), e.g. with Sodom and the Flood; for all less grave mortal sins, justice yields to mercy and its demands of expiation are satisfied by temporal afflictions and in Purgatory.

---

[854] *Theologia Moralis*, lib. III, n. 413.
[855] *Summa Theologiæ*, I-II, q. 73, a. 4, *ad 2ᵃᵐ*.
[856] *Summa Theologiæ*, II-II, q. 154, a. 3, *ad 1ᵃᵐ*.
[857] *De Summo Bono*, II, 39.

N.B. I have sought in vain, in these scabrous passages, the word "penance" or "mortification"; the author has seen fit to leave this absolutely essential condition of the salvation of sinners to be understood — for we cannot believe he really thinks that Purgatory takes away the guilt (Latin: *reatus culpæ*). This omission, on such a matter, is what I find the most scandalous feature of his whole book. To how much presumption will it not give rise on the part of readers? How many weak souls there are whom it will encourage to give up their last faltering efforts and restraint…

Sad, very sad indeed!

To which the present writer need only add that he knows that the following propositions of Fr. Castelein have become well-known to some of the Brussels youth who encourage one another to read them.

18

***"The sin of lust according to nature is only forbidden because otherwise
it would lead to sin against nature."***

1. Fr. Castelein writes:

The concupiscence of the flesh gives rise to two kinds of disorder. A moral disorder very frequent between puberty and marriage, in the form of weaknesses and intermittent faults, which are compatible with a state of habitual resistance and do not grossly violate the laws of nature — and a disorder that is fully willed, a disorder of every time and shape, in which the will is immersed with no effort to emerge, and worse still sheer havoc is played with these laws.

Now the first of these kinds of disorder, being due to weakness rather than malice, is incomparably less grave to mankind than the latter. *Indeed it is only forbidden absolutely because without this prohibition it would lead by instinct to the latter.*

The second kind of disorder, which comprises those grave faults which God punished by the waters of the Flood and the fire of Sodom, such as faults of vicious habit fully consented to, faults against the laws of matrimony and the natural relations between the sexes, attract for their own very specific reason the eternal chastisements of God. (p. 248)

From this it is clear that for Fr. Castelein the intrinsic reason why fornication is forbidden is only that it is inclined to lead to sin against nature: "… it is only forbidden absolutely because without this prohibition it would lead by instinct to the latter."

2. I deny outright that acts *according* to nature prepare the way and instinctively lead to acts *contrary* to nature. If this were so the act of conjugal union itself would naturally create a danger of grave sin against nature for the spouses; which is absurd for it is both injurious to Providence and contrary to experience.

> Simple fornication is *intrinsically* mortally evil; hence it is not only wrong because it is forbidden — it is forbidden because it is wrong.[858]

This is because the human sexual act [Latin: *seminatio*] is by nature ordained not only to procreation but also to feeding, raising and educating the offspring, for procreation would be in vain unless it were followed by right feeding to support the life transmitted and upbringing to enable the child to live according to reason.

This upbringing and education of their offspring requires by nature the collaboration of man and woman and hence their continued association. For it is manifest that human upbringing requires not only the care of a mother, by whom the child is fed for a time, but also, and much more, the care of a father by whom he must be instructed, defended, corrected and encouraged to good, both inward and outward: hence it is necessary that there be a natural bond linking the man to a particular woman, and this not for a short time but for a long time — their entire life, for this is what the due upbringing of the offspring of itself demands. And this association, instituted and willed by our Creator, is what we call matrimony, which is why our Creator stipulates that the human sexual act is only lawful within matrimony.

Fornication, i.e. copulation between the unmarried, of its nature excludes this association and hence of its nature implies a grave disorder, tending to be gravely harmful, not only to the child to be born of such union but also to the common good of human society, ex-

---

[858] For this and what follows cf. the *Collationes Brugenses*, vol. III, p. 431 *et seqq.* where the teaching of Saint Thomas and his commentators is very well presented by Professor Dignant following in the footsteps of Billuart.

posed to a vast number of the gravest ills if children are begotten outside marriage and badly brought up.

Therefore, fornication is a mortal sin of itself and not because it leads to unchastity against nature.

3. This is the authentic Catholic doctrine, as stated by Saint Thomas:

> In order to make this evident, we must take note that every sin committed directly against human life is a mortal sin. Now simple fornication implies an inordinateness that tends to injure the life of the offspring to be born of this union.[859]

And in his commentary on I Corinthians, *Lectio* III, he elegantly shows that Saint Paul "condemns fornication for four reasons, of which the first is based on divine ordination, the second on union with Christ, the third on pollution of the body and the fourth on the dignity of divine grace."[860]

4. Finally I ask all serious confessors: If the lustful adopt the teaching of Fr. Castelein on fornication, how can they be expected to credit the Church's condemnation of the statement that "it is only a venial sin to kiss for the carnal and sensible pleasure arising from the kiss"?[861] What will such kissing mean to them? And how then can such a doctrine increase the number of the saved?

<h1 style="text-align:center">19</h1>

"As long as concupiscence of the flesh is not carried to extremes it inclines God to immense pity towards the sinner."

Says Fr. Castelein:

> When this passion is not pressed to *extreme* disorders by deliberate and persistent malice of the will, it inclines God to an immense pity. (p. 255)

To this I reply:

---

[859] *Summa Theologiæ*, II-II, q. 154, a. 2, *in corp.* Cf. *Summa contra Gentiles*, lib. III, cap. 122; *de Malo*, q. 15, articles 1 and 2.
[860] Ed. Vivès, vol. XX, p. 653.
[861] Proposition 40 of those condemned by Pope Alexander VII; Denzinger 1140.

(i) The lustful have no right to count so presumptuously on God's mercy even if they have not sinned against nature. As a learned son of Saint Alphonsus has written:

It is certain that God abominates every mortal sin as greatly as He loves Himself, which is to say *infinitely*. But there is no kind of sin of which He manifests this hatred more strikingly than the sin of lust; he punished no other sin with punishment so horrendous, extraordinary and universal as when the Flood wiped out the entire human race because *all flesh had corrupted its way upon the earth*. This sin led God as it were to regret having created man: *It repented him that he had made man on the earth. And being touched inwardly with sorrow of heart, He said: I will destroy man, whom I have created, from the face of the earth, from man even to beasts, from the creeping thing even to the fowls of the air, for it repenteth me that I have made them.* Moreover He complained of man: *My spirit shall not remain in man for ever, because he is flesh,* when He saw that *the wickedness of men was great on the earth, and that all the thought of their heart was bent upon evil at all times.*[862]

(ii) All sinners must clearly understand that in order to forgive the sin of impurity even if not against nature God requires true and serious contrition or detestation of the sin committed together with the efficacious purpose of not sinning in the future.

But such contrition is difficult for the unhappy slave of impurity, owing to the highly adhesive quality of this sin: (a) because of the violence of the passion and the delight and the habit which very easily arises and greatly weakens the resistance of the will, and (b) because of its effects — the dreadful "daughters of lust": blindness of mind, thoughtlessness, precipitation, inconstancy, self-love, hatred of God, attachment to the present world, horror or despair of the future![863]

With regard to (a) Fr. Aertnys declares:

There is no vicious affection which binds man's will more strongly than lust, because its acts are both more frequent and more intense.

---

[862] Aertnys, Jozef C.SS.R. (1829-1915), *Theologia pastoralis*, III, cap. I, art. 4. pp. 87-88 ; biblical quotations from Genesis V.

[863] S. Thomas, *Summa Theologiæ*, q. 153. a. 5, *in corp.*

Which is why in this species of sin the bad habit is more swiftly contracted and once caught in its clutches only with great difficulty can a man extricate himself. Each day finds the mind blinder and the will weaker so that salvation is constantly becoming harder to achieve and at last it becomes apparent that this vice is indeed "a narrow well", for the easier it is to fall into it, the harder it is to get out again.[864]

And with regard to (b) the above-quoted Professor of Philosophy well writes:

Father Castelein forgets that the vice of impurity, even if accompanied by invincible ignorance, eventually submerges the soul in darkness, spreads the night of the beasts over the reason and makes natural recovery morally impossible. God is all-powerful, but without a miracle this depraved person will not turn back, and this miracle is but the exception. To one who lives piously and is attached to God it seems that perfect contrition must come quite naturally after the fault. But this is to forget that the first effect of this particular fault is to lessen our lights, our supernatural relish, our moral strength and to make more onerous this return, this repentance which seems so easy from the vantage of our present integrity.

Hence it is difficult for the lustful person to turn over a new leaf and work out his salvation with sincerity, firmness and efficacy.

20

"God can sufficiently punish such mortal sins by temporal expiation in this life or the next, without recourse to eternal punishments."

On p. 255 of his book, Fr. Castelein writes:

God can sufficiently punish such faults by temporal expiation in this life or the next, without having to have recourse to eternal punishments.

He seems to have given some thought to the phraseology of his claim for as it originally appeared in the *Revue Générale*[865] it does not contain the words "in this life or the next".

---

[864] Aertnys, *op. cit.*, 4.
[865] May 1898, p. 651.

Yet, with or without the amendment, the statement is both erroneous and scandalous.

This is because every sin of lust is of itself mortal *ex toto genere suo*[866] — a truth which sound theology does not allow us to question. But mortal sin, being a voluntary turning away from God, deserves *de condigno*[867] the eternal punishment of loss. In other words, it is a sheer outrage to Catholic theology to suggest that the guilt (*reatus culpæ*) of mortal sin can be expiated by temporal punishment whether in this life or in Purgatory.

And great is the scandal in terms of the moral dissoluteness that will surely arise if once it is thought that fornication and other sins of lust not opposed to nature lead merely to purgatory and not the everlasting fires of hell!

VI

RANDOM SOPHISTRIES HAVING NO PARTICULAR RELEVANCE

21

The promise of salvation made by saintly Founders of Orders to their religious

To prove that the number of the elect is greater, three arguments in particular are appealed to: (i) some Founders of religious orders promised salvation to their sons, (ii) Pontiffs were easily canonized in the early Church, (iii) the world may yet last a long time.

Although in reality these arguments prove nothing at all in the matter before us, here is how they are set out:

(i) A consideration of a very different kind which I like to invoke to argue that the number of the elect is greater is the privilege that certain great orders such as those of Saint Benedict and of Saint Ignatius claim to

---

[866] I.e. by its nature and without any exception for inferior degrees or lighter matter. In other words every sin of lust is of itself mortal and can only be venial for some accidental reason such as defect of consent. — Translator.

[867] I.e. in strict justice. — Translator.

have received by revelation with regard to the ultimate salvation of their members. Reliable documents affirm that it is has been revealed that all members who *de facto* have died or shall die in these two orders are of the elect. I think that this privilege extends to other religious orders too.[868]

This is quite true, and indeed our own lowly Congregation of the Most Holy Redeemer several times over received from its Founder Saint Alphonsus the explicit promise of the eternal salvation of those who die in its bosom. Nor should this promise be thought to be unusual, for it is based on a theological reason, indeed upon the promise of Christ Our Lord.

Its theological basis lies in the fact that in order to persevere in the religious life when it is properly observed, religious must observe not only the commandments of God, but also the evangelical counsels and therefore shun evil and constantly tend towards perfection.

Moreover this prediction of the Founders of Orders also finds support of the very strongest kind in the clear and explicit promise of Our Lord Jesus Christ: *And every one that hath left house, or brethren, or sisters, or father, or mother, or wife, or children, or lands for my name's sake, shall receive an hundredfold, and shall possess life everlasting.*[869] For this is what religious have in fact done, so if they persevere in the observance of their vows, God too will keep His promise and they will be saved: *He that shall persevere unto the end, he shall be saved.*[870]

As to whether the Founders' promises are valid for all who *de facto* are members of the orders, the answer is *certainly not*. The promise applies to those who are *formally* their sons, i.e. who live according to the spirit and nature of the order. It does not apply to those who belong in a purely material sense to the order's visible body — who say that they have Abraham for their father but do not the works of Abraham, being *like to whited sepulchres, which outwardly appear to men beautiful, but within are full of dead men' s bones, and of all filthiness.*[871]

For which reason the following conclusion must be rejected:

---

[868] Fr. Castelein, *op. cit.*, 2nd edition, p. 276.

[869] Matthew XIX, 29.

[870] Matthew X, 22.

[871] Matthew XXIII, 27.

Evidently among the hundreds of thousands of religious who have enjoyed this privilege, not all have been saints. Without the slightest doubt some of them were *very lukewarm*, fell into *major faults* and *were far from faithful to the grace of their vocation.* And if this is so, surely this guarantee can be invoked as a sign of *God's readiness to grant the grace of final salvation.* (p. 277)

By no means! To the religious who is such in name only [Latin: *materialiter*] applies the tremendous warning of the just Judge:

> The lord of that servant will come in the day that he hopeth not, and at the hour that he knoweth not, and shall separate him, and shall appoint him his portion with unbelievers. And that servant who knew the will of his lord, and prepared not himself, and did not according to his will, shall be beaten with many stripes. But he that knew not, and did things worthy of stripes, shall be beaten with few stripes. And unto whomsoever much is given, of him much shall be required: and to whom they have committed much, of him they will demand the more.[872]

This refutation of the opinion of Fr. Castelein is strongly confirmed by the following extract from his most learned compatriot and confrère, the Bollandist Fr. Van der Moeren S.J., who writes in the life of Saint Teresa [of Avila]:

> This is an appropriate point at which to refer to a vision recounted in the *Imago primi sæculi Societatis Jesu* (pp. 648-9) and borrowed by Fr. Lancisius in his work *De præstantia Instituti Societatis Jesu* (lib. II, cap. I) and by Cardinal Cienfuegos in his *Vita Sancti Francisci Borgiæ* (lib. V, cap. X).
>
> In this vision it is attested that it was revealed to Saint Teresa at Cordoba that the religious of the society of Jesus enjoyed the privilege that each of them, as soon as he had expired, went at once to meet Christ who received his soul. This is what these authors recount. But if I were asked what should be thought about the truth of so great and desirable a prerogative I should answer in the same terms as did Fr. Joannes Pinius[873] (vol. VIII, July, p. 852) after recounting comparable visions concerning the happy death of all who die in the Society of Jesus: "As to the truth of

---

[872] Luke XII, 46-48.
[873] Also known as Fr. Jean Pien (1678–1749). — Translator.

this prerogative, believe as much as the reasons advanced in its favour seem to you to prove. Some will undoubtedly require greater motives of credibility for something so paradoxical, *indeed I would say almost incredible*. As I have none to offer it remains for me to remain within the limits of my account, leaving each reader the fullest freedom to incline to either side. Meanwhile what is quite certain is that every member of the Society ought to strive sedulously to walk worthy of his calling,[874] sparing no effort to make certain by good works his vocation and election.[875]

Moreover there is a further reason for casting doubt on this alleged vision of Saint Teresa to the effect that Christ will receive the souls of all who die in the Society of Jesus. For in the *Chronicle* (lib. XVI, capp. XXXII, XXXIV) it is recounted at length that in the year 1594 the opinion became very current among discalced Carmelites that God had granted to Saint Teresa the prerogative that no one wearing the sacred garment of her Order should be damned. But the Saint appeared to Sister Anne of Saint Augustine and ordered her to deny this, declaring that whoever did not fulfil his duties was destined for hell, while heaven or purgatory depended on the merits of each. And when Sister Anne hesitated to make public the fact that she had been honoured by the apparition of her Mother, the Saint appeared to her a second and a third time to enjoin her to do so. At the same time she showed her the three places, one of which awaits each of us — heaven, hell and purgatory — indicating to her with a threatening glare that she would be cast into the lake if she did not do as she was told and uproot this *pernicious* confidence on the part of her religious. When Sister Anne eventually informed her confessor in full about the vision and the order she had received from her Holy Mother, he informed the superiors about the matter and they published throughout the Congregation the heaven-sent warning in order to offset the harm done and bidding all remember, as the *Chronicle* expresses it, *that salvation is not due to the habit but to good works carried out while wearing the habit.*

But I have no objection to any prophecy concerning the salvation of religious if only it is subject to some limiting condition in greater conformity with the Gospel and provided it is attested by trustworthy contemporary witnesses, just as Stilting[876] (28th August, *Life of Saint*

---

[874] Cf. Ephesians IV, 1.

[875] Cf. II Peter I, 10.

[876] Fr. Joannes Stilting (1703-1762). — Translator.

Augustine, n. 821) cheerfully admits the prophecy of Saint Norbert according to which : *My sons if your brethren fight well beneath the rule I have subscribed they will stand sure before Christ amid the terror of the Judgement.*[877]

In short, alleged promises of Paradise to every religious who dies within this or that Order are to be understood in conformity with the Gospel and thus prove nothing at all in favour of the greater number of the elect.

22

THE EASE OF CANONIZATION IN THE EARLY CHURCH

And the same applies to the following argument of Fr. Castelein :

Another consideration similar to the last may be drawn from the ease with which the Catholic Church in the first centuries allowed bishops dying within her bosom to be honoured and invoked as belonging to the elect. In Rome, the pope, and in each particular church, the bishop of the diocese, had their names inserted in the sacred diptychs except for some grave offence against their duties insufficiently retracted.

Later on, when this custom has been abolished, the Church reserved the honours of the altars for a small number of *perfect* Christians, *worthy* to be proposed to the faithful as accomplished models of all the virtues.

But the earlier practice shows that at heart the Church is persuaded that salvation is easy and above all that it requires no exceptional conditions.

This argument gains great weight for anyone who is aware of the rudimentary moral standards observed at that time and who reflects on the sometimes perfunctory and unenlightened way in which popes and bishops were chosen by the people. (pp. 277-8)

The degree of solemnity observed in electing or canonizing pontiffs is of little relevance. Or are we to think that the forty-six sovereign pontiffs whose bodies are interred in peace in the Cemetery of Callistus and "all of whom suffered the death penalty for Christ in order to become heirs in the house of the Lord"[878] are not saints after all? Or that those first Pastors of the ancient Churches canonized by

---

[877] *Acta Sanctorum*, vol. 55, pp. 491-492, nn. 1686-7.

[878] Inscription found at the entrance to this cemetery.

popular acclaim with the Church's approval are not truly in heaven? Or that they were not in fact "*perfect* Christians, *worthy* to be proposed to the faithful as accomplished models of all the virtues" quite as much as the Saints of more recent times?

Ordinary logic must dismiss the extraordinary deduction that "the earlier practice shows that at heart the Church is persuaded that salvation is easy" in favour of the only conclusion that really follows, viz. that the Church is convinced that these early Saints were just as "perfect Christians" as later ones, and just as "*worthy* to be proposed to the faithful as accomplished models of all the virtues".

And the following assertion is manifestly disrespectful towards these early Saints: "This argument gains great weight for anyone who ... reflects on ... the want of regular training for the clergy." Surely our respected adversary is not suggesting that these Saints in fact failed to match the requirements of the dignities or were but of mediocre virtue?

23

"If the number of the elect were not greater it would be desirable for baptized children not to grow up."

Says Fr. Castelein:

> If the number of those that are lost were as great as is claimed, it would be a happy inspiration for Christian parents to want their children to die before the age of reason; hence they ought to limit them to what is strictly necessary to maintain health and a life which exposes their salvation to such great perils. Yet it goes without saying that God reproves any such wish and the negligence that would flow from it. (p. 281)

This argument merits no further reply than this: Evil may be neither done nor desired in order to bring about good.

24

The increase of mankind and the continuance of the world for at least a further 20 centuries

In support of their opinion the Progressives appeal to the duration of our world, which they presume will not perish for at least another twenty centuries:

> No doubt if the world is to end tomorrow it makes sense to agree with the hypothesis of the theologians. But will it? Suppose it were to last thousands of centuries yet; suppose that all the nations of the world came successively to know Christianity, to live it, to let its influence impregnate their institutions and habits; give the United States fifteen centuries of Christianity as ardent as that of France was, give as much to China with its 377 million inhabitants and to Japan with its 250 million.
>
> Let Christianity penetrate into the Indies, the islands of Oceania and let it last there 2000 or 3000 years ... We think of our globe like those casual readers who are ready to pronounce judgement on an entire book when they have read only its preface and first two chapters. The preface to the Catholic world lasted 4000 years. Then the book began, but only two of its pages have yet been turned. Let us wait, and let us admit that we cannot say yet whether in humanity as a whole the elect will turn out to be the minority or the majority.[879]

> Suitably cultivated by scientific methods the earth could easily supply food for twelve billion inhabitants! What a grandiose prospect for the future of Christianity, which, *constantly perfecting its spirit, its doctrine, its worship ...* increasingly emerges as the power of social salvation.[880]

All that is wanting to this hypothetical argument is the proof that with the passage of time men tend to get better rather than worse, for otherwise the more time passes the less the proportion of them that are to be saved will tend to become.[881] And one thing that will certainly not encourage any such improvement is the doctrine of "heaven at a bargain price"!

[879] Bougaud, *op. cit.*, p. 366.
[880] Castelein, *op. cit.*, pp. 196-7.
[881] See Coppin, *La question de l'Évangile...*, pp. 112-3.

It is in any event unacceptable to infer the greater number of the elect as a *fact* from what is a mere *hypothesis*. And for the men of our own days whom the Progressives endeavour to reassure about their own salvation it can be of no moment even if every single person born in centuries to come were a canonizable saint: *their* salvation depends on ourselves alone — only by holiness can they be saved whereas if they continue to march in the broad way they will perish.

CONCLUSION

Such then are the arguments by which the Progressives endeavour to overturn the common teaching of the Saints on the fewness of the saved. They consider these arguments irrefutable: "Such proofs cannot be eliminated by mere denial. They stand up. *Mole sua stant!*" (p. 246)

Whether they do in fact stand the impartial Reader is in a position to judge for himself.

And after such claims — far more in need of "gossamer balances" than the common teaching of Doctors and Fathers — they throw dust in the eyes of the theologically untrained lay readers of a certain periodical by unblushingly announcing: "My solution is based on arguments of the highest order,"[882] or "I shall have no difficulty in replying to my contradictors. I only want their attack to be *learned* and *precise*."[883]

The author of the present reply is fully confident that it *is* precise and believes it also to be scientific as and where appropriate. But he is not alone in thinking that those who expect the full scholarly apparatus current in academic circles to be deployed to refute such theological bagatelles are labouring under an illusion which springs from vanity and can furnish no security.

I believe that my approach is enough to edify readers of good faith and guide them away from dangerous novelties, and if I am

---

[882] Letter from Fr. Castelein to *Le XXe Siècle*.

[883] Castelein, *op. cit.*, second edition, *Introduction*, p. XI

right I shall be more than satisfied to have achieved my intended goal.

CHAPTER EIGHT

A FEW SPECIFIC POINTS SELECTED FROM THE DOCTRINE OF FR. CASTELEIN

HAVING REFUTED these sophistries which are common to a number of the Progressives, I find that two reasons make it necessary to make a specific rebuttal to Fr. Castelein: (a) his book is both more honeyed in tone and more pernicious in effect than the other harmful books of the Progressives as will soon become all too clear, and (b) his book has been the object of a quite exceptional level of praise, recommendation and favourable publicity. As its author frankly admits: "The *Freeman Catholic* of New York has reproduced it in its entirety for its one hundred thousand readers… No doubt it answers the anxieties of a *great many* souls seeking light and undying hope." (p. VII)[884]

I have not the slightest doubt that in writing his book Fr. Castelein was guided by the very best of intentions, so it should be clearly understood that my attack is in no way against the person of this venerable and well-deserving religious but exclusively against his work, as being highly pernicious to souls.

Before addressing specific points I must cite some general remarks kindly passed on to me by my oft-quoted confrère and Professor of Philosophy concerning the title of Fr. Castelein's book:

[884] All the Catholic periodicals of Belgium reviewed Fr. Castelein's work in ecstatic terms. To give a slight idea of their panegyrics a few extracts from a single daily, *Le Patriote*, are cited in the Appendix.

1

Concerning the title and scope of the book: Rigorism, The Question of the Number of the Elect and the Doctrine of Salvation

The main title is ill chosen. *Rigorism* designates a condemned casuistic system which in our day has been entirely abandoned at least in the Catholic learned world; at most a trace of it may survive here and there in the shape of a tendency on the part of this or that director of conscience, without daring to emerge into the light.

Now the Author's attack is not directed against this heresy at all, but against the *Pessimism* which paints humanity in dark colours and exaggerates the perversity of the world in order to substantiate the fewness of the elect. No doubt the Rigorists all believed in the fewness of the saved, but it is quite possible to defend this point without being a rigorist, i.e. without burdening consciences with chimerical obligations.

The practical objective of the book is unrelated to the doctrine defended in its pages. For the Author states in his Introduction (p. VIII) that he is undertaking to reply to the doubts and anxieties of a great number of souls in quest of light and undying hope.

Who are these souls whose troubles have moved Fr. Castelein to take up his pen and who will be relieved upon learning that his opinion is in favour of a low number of the damned?

Are they the timorous and pure of conscience who are more sensitive to terrors than to the divine love? But such souls are unlikely to number among the good Father's readers, for they tend to live in the shade of the cloister whose sanctity I trust will never be breached by the entrance of the present work. Moreover their trial is too intimate, too personal in nature to evaporate upon reading a work whose tone is so worldly-wise, so quibbling, so presumptuous. The comforts needed by such troubles as these are more specific in kind and more supernatural in quality.

Where then are the victims the Author wishes to relieve? Are they our good Christians, constant in eschewing sin? Surely not, for while these souls know God's justice and fear it, they do not forget His will to save, His infinite mercies, nor the merits of Christ, the value of the Sacraments, the efficacy of prayer — *of which Fr. Castelein makes no mention.* If they read this book, then, they will learn nothing new from it on all these subjects.

Where then has the Author's intention wandered? Is he thinking of bad Christians, of the lukewarm, of lax consciences of the affectedly ignorant[885] — or is it rather of Mahometans, of Jews, of the inhabitants of Sodom and Gomorrha, of Protestants, of unbelievers, who are the infidels of our own countries?

Assuredly among this tumultuous crowd our Author will be hailed as a Liberator; the weak will find in his pages excuses for their failures, free-thinkers will be reassured in their darkness. Everyone will believe himself endowed with enough of faith and of morals to count on secret graces, on a dash of deathbed contrition and will be sure that he is not *bad enough* to be among the *élite* chosen for damnation.

This is the apostolate in reverse. Henceforth it is the doctrine of the fewness of the saved which prevents sinners from being converted. The discovery that few are damned is to bring them back in droves to the hope of eternal life. Surely the reek of Americanism is perceptible a hundred miles away! It is not in the least surprising that such a doctrine should find a hundred thousand readers in the new world.

The clearest outcome of this publication is what is fittingly known as a *succès de scandale*. The wicked will find false security in its pages while for the good will it will prove a stumbling-block. As for reviving souls cast down by "terrorism", this is a result that the Author's thesis cannot produce and to which it must remain utterly foreign. He points it out himself in Chapter VI (*Final Objection: Moral Laxism – Reply, Practical conclusion*) in which he defends himself against the accusation of Laxism. For whether the fewness of the elect or of the damned be admitted, the motives for confidence and for fear remain the same. God's infinite goodness, His promises, the merits of Jesus Christ, the inexhaustible graces, the witness of a clear conscience — all these are so many motives for trust, not only for Fr. Castelein but also for those he calls "Rigorists". But the mystery of divine justice, the inconstancy of our will, the mystery of the Redemption, the distribution of graces both of preservation and of reparation, measured and limited as it is despite the infinite power and mercy — here are so many motives to keep us in fear tempered with trust and in trust moderated by fear. Such are the sentiments by which the Holy Ghost leads real Christians.

---

[885] I.e. ignorance that is neither blameless (because involuntary) nor even due to mere negligence but is deliberately sought after and therefore actually increases culpability for the misdeeds it gives rise to.

What then is the use of this thesis of the fewness of the damned? Is it not a sheer irrelevancy? Does it make any difference to the doctrine of salvation? Has some new source of hope been discovered?

If in fact there are not many who are damned, this is reassuring as to the destiny of the bulk of mankind, but it offers no reassurance for my own case for I must still fear to be numbered among them if I should exhaust the measure of graces allotted me; any increased confidence I might derive from such a statistic, to temper my fear of divine justice, could only be false, temerarious and perilous.

And by the same token if the number of the elect is in fact small, this is distressing in terms of the whole human race, but is not particularly troubling for my own individual case as I must hope to be of their number if I am of good will and make good use of the graces I receive superabundantly; the terror this statistic would inspire in me, if it diminished my trust in God and His mercy would be vain, blameworthy and perilous.

In conclusion, by championing the fewness of the damned, Fr. Castelein cannot boast of having brought timid souls the slightest new motive of Christian confidence and supernatural hope, nor can he accuse the opposing thesis of depriving them of any such motive.

 Hence, as has already been remarked, this work bears no relation to its stated goal, in which respect it is as absurd as must be any cause that is entirely unconnected with its expected effect. It will certainly produce effects, but very different ones — effects that can only be described as deplorable.

Henceforth all the libertines of the underworld and of the *demi-monde* will have a new arm to brandish against missioners and parish priests. With greater confidence than ever they will declare: "All these threats of hell are fairytales — bugbears invented by priests; God is not so unpleasant as His ambassadors, etc."

Against this background the time has come to address the specific pernicious points referred to and to contrast them with true and salutary doctrine.

2

Fr. Castelein's grounds for claiming that he escapes the condemnation of Proposition 17 of the Syllabus are far from edifying.

Here is Fr. Castelein's case for his own defence:

The Church has condemned only *absolute* laxism and indifferentism formulated in the 17th proposition of the Syllabus in which the condemned doctrine is that "Good hope should be had of the salvation of *all* who do not live in the Catholic Church." The point condemned in this proposition is the unlimited universality of this hope. If I were to say that in bad environments one third of men are lost and in good environments one tenth, or even one hundredth as some Fathers believed of the angels, I should be safe from falling under the condemnation of this 17th proposition. (pp. 285-6)

To cite once again the Professor of Philosophy:

The author flatters himself that he would not fall under the condemnation of the 17th proposition of the Syllabus if he were to say that only one non-Catholic in a hundred is lost But this is far from evident.

The condemned proposition states that "Good hope at least should be had of the salvation of all those who are not within the Church of Christ." Which precise part of this complex proposition falls under the error?

Fr. Castelein considers that it is the unlimited universality — "of all those" — which is condemned. If the proposition were a simple one: "All non-Catholics are saved," he would undoubtedly be right, because the contradictory would be "At least one non-Catholic is not saved."

But the condemned proposition is a complex one and its error might lie in the word *saltem* meaning "at least" as implying that *hope* is a moderate term, not excluding complete assurance, in which case the truth would be: "*At the most* good hope should be had, etc."

Alternatively the error might hinge on the word *sperandum* [hope *should* be had] with its implication of duty or necessity. In this case the same sentence with "hope *may* be had" instead would be acceptable.

But enough of logical hair-splitting…

Let us accept the assumption that the error lies in the words "of all those". It remains clear that the erroneous latitudinarianism here condemned cannot be absolutely unlimited universality without any exception — Laxism has never claimed that *no* non-Catholic was *ever* damned. It is the moral universality, the generality, the idea of *the bulk* wherein lies the rub.

Thus what the Syllabus condemns is the idea that at least good hope should be had of the salvation of *the majority* of non-Catholics. But Fr. Castelein's hypothetical proposition that "only one third of mankind" and, in good milieux, "only one tenth or one hundredth are lost" would precisely imply that *the majority* (of those "who are not within the Church of Christ") *are* saved, and this *is* condemned.

So Fr. Castelein cannot press his ideas to that point without falling under the anathema.

3

Fr. Castelein's minimalism is far from edifying.

My Reverend adversary finds the disedifying modern doctrine of *minimalism in religion* quite delightful and strives in many places in his book to encourage his worldly readers to adopt it. This is already apparent from what has been said above of his sophistries relating to the necessity of revelation, the sin of lust, the salvific power of faith and the salvation of those who are religious in name only.

It is also apparent from many of his expressions, so that *minimalism* seems to be the general tendency of his doctrine, which is why it is inevitably more harmful than beneficial to souls.

1. Fr. Castelein's minimalism with regard to Holy Communion is not edifying.

We may conclude from the teaching and precept of the Church concerning the Easter Communion that *one communion per year* is necessary and as a rule *sufficient* to benefit from Christ's declaration [viz. *He that eateth my flesh, and drinketh my blood, hath everlasting life: and I will raise him up in the last day*[886]].

For if this single Communion were not a *sufficient* means of salvation for the faithful who live in the world, the Church would make her precept more demanding. (p. 330)

---

[886] John VI, 55.

The truth is that this commandment of the Church lays down that annual Communion suffices to fulfil the divine precept of Communion and hence to avoid damnation *for having failed to respect this precept.*

But as the unnamed critic I have several times quoted very well observes:

> From the fact that the Church requires Communion only once per year Fr. Castelein appears to conclude that the mind of the Church is that those who content themselves with their Easter duties are almost all saved. This logic is tenuous indeed.
>
> No doubt the Church's care for souls moves her to impose positive precepts, but her chief motive for doing so is to specify and regulate the fulfilment of certain basic duties and the exercise of certain virtues.
>
> To sanctify Sundays and to exercise the virtue of religion belong to the natural and divine law. The Church regulates them by saying: *Attend Mass at least on Sundays, such is the positive law.*
>
> Divine and natural law says in general terms: *Practise penance and temperance.* The Church positively says: *Fast and abstain at least on such and such days. Go to confession at least once a year.*
>
> In the same way Our Saviour says: *Except you eat the flesh of the Son of man, and drink his blood, you shall not have life in you,*[887] and the Church determines this, saying: *Receive Holy Communion at least at Easter.* The commandments of the Church impose the *minimum* which cannot be omitted without infraction of the divine law in these matters. The Church is thus satisfied that she has fixed the extent of the divine law so that the faithful may have peace of conscience in this respect; she claims to have done no more.

But it would be quite wrong to conclude from this that the Church defines this annual Communion as sufficient to provide the faithful with the spiritual strength they need. The Church prefers not to go further than to ensure that the divine precept is respected, both because the differences between the dispositions of individuals is too great to allow any general norm to be laid down and because the constant decline in Christian observance makes it less likely that

---

[887] John VI, 54.

greater demands would in practice be respected. Such is the sound doctrine set out in the *Catechism of the Council of Trent*:

> Lest any be kept away from Communion by the fear that the requisite preparation is too hard and laborious, the faithful are *frequently* to be reminded that they are all bound to receive the Holy Eucharist Furthermore, the Church has decreed that whoever neglects to approach Holy Communion once a year, at Easter, is liable to sentence of excommunication.
>
> *However, let not the faithful imagine that it is enough to receive the body of the Lord once a year only, in obedience to the decree of the Church.* **They should approach oftener***; but whether monthly, weekly, or daily, cannot be decided by any fixed universal rule.* Saint Augustine, however, lays down a most certain norm: *Live in such a manner as to be able to receive every day.*
>
> It will therefore be the duty of the pastor frequently to admonish the faithful that, as they deem it necessary to afford daily nutriment to the body, they should also feel solicitous to feed and nourish the soul every day with this heavenly food. It is clear that the soul stands not less in need of spiritual, than the body of corporal food. Here it will be found most useful to recall the inestimable and divine advantages which, as we have already shown, flow from sacramental Communion. It will be well also to refer to the manna, which was a figure [of this Sacrament], and which refreshed the bodily powers every day. The Fathers who earnestly recommended the frequent reception of this Sacrament may also be cited. The words of Saint Augustine, *Thou sinnest daily, receive daily*, express not his opinion only, but that of all the Fathers who have written on the subject, as anyone may easily discover who will carefully read them.
>
> That there was a time when the faithful approached Holy Communion every day we learn from the Acts of the Apostles. All who then professed the faith of Christ burned with such true and sincere charity that, devoting themselves to prayer and other works of piety, they were found prepared to communicate daily.[888]

---

[888] I draw Fr. Castelein's special attention to this passage in view of his statements (already highlighted above) such as "I prefer the present state of the Church to her past state." (p. 17) and "The Christians to whom, or of whom, Saint Paul wrote were far from equal to the *practising Christians of our own days*." (p. 311)

This devout practice, which seems to have been interrupted for a time, was again partially revived by the holy Pope and martyr Anacletus, who commanded that all the ministers who assisted at the Sacrifice of the Mass should communicate-an ordinance, as the Pontiff declares, of Apostolic institution. It was also for a long time the practice of the Church that, as soon as the Sacrifice was complete, and when the priest himself had communicated, he turned to the congregation and invited the faithful to the Holy Table in these words: Come, brethren, and receive Communion; and thereupon those who were prepared, advanced to receive the holy mysteries with the most fervent devotion.

But subsequently, when charity and devotion had grown so cold that the faithful very seldom approached Communion, it was decreed by Pope Fabian, that all should communicate thrice every year, at Christmas, at Easter and at Pentecost This decree was afterwards confirmed by many Councils, particularly by the first of Agde.

Such at length was the decay of piety that not only was this holy and salutary law unobserved, but Communion was deferred for years. The Council of Lateran, therefore, decreed that all the faithful should receive the sacred body of the Lord, at least once a year, at Easter, and that neglect of this duty should be chastised by exclusion from the society of the faithful.[889]

For further information about the spiritual need of the faithful which should be the chief norm in receiving the Holy Eucharist, let us turn to Fr. Lehmkühl:[890]

Thirdly comes the effect which according to the will of Christ makes the Holy Eucharist morally necessary for the conservation of sanctifying grace. For in the ordinary order of supernatural providence it is chiefly in the context of Holy Communion that more abundant grace is granted to help adults to overcome the dangers and temptations that threaten their salvation — without which it will be difficult or impossible to avoid every grave sin.

And not only does the Holy Eucharist obtain for those who receive it worthily when they ought this more abundant assistance of grace, but it also keeps away dangers to salvation in other ways, viz:

---

[889] Part II, chapter 4, n. 60.
[890] Fr. Augustin Lehmkühl S.J. (1834-1918).

(i) it contains and weakens man's inner concupiscence, and this is especially so of carnal concupiscence as many of the Fathers of the Church bear witness, promising the gift of continence to those who approach the sacred banquet often and with due fervour, and it is confirmed by the teaching of the theologians and the experience of confessors that frequent Communion is a very powerful and all but necessary remedy against lust;

(ii) by restraining the devil (who otherwise, with God's permission, has such great power via temptations and snares) from stirring up the temptations and dangers in which God foresees that the man would fall.

(…)

More frequent Communion is not *per se* of precept, but it can happen that it becomes morally necessary for this or that penitent — the obvious instance being a man debilitated by a habit of vice. While in theory other remedies are available to him, they are often harder to turn to put into practice, leaving no hope that so weak a soul will in fact use these more difficult means. Hence the sole recourse is to urge him emphatically to approach the Sacraments of Penance and Holy Eucharist more often in order to prove the sincerity of his present good intentions and to preserve them for longer.

Indeed those most experienced in such cases are agreed that a youth addicted to the sin of self abuse cannot hope for amendment without *frequent* reception of the sacraments; they add that weekly confession is not only not excessive for such penitents but is hardly sufficient.[891] Hence it is for the confessor to do his best to induce such penitents to frequent the sacraments.

For those who are not in such urgent need of more frequent Communion to conquer grave temptations it is still the mind of the Church to encourage frequent Communion in order to maintain and increase their Christian virtue.

This "mind of the Church" is expressed in the following terms by the Council of Trent:

And finally this holy Synod with true fatherly affection admonishes, exhorts, begs, and beseeches, through the bowels of the mercy of our God, that all and each of those who bear the Christian name would now

---

[891] Cf. Fr. Francisco de Toledo S.J. (1532-96), *Instructio Sacerdotum*, lib. 5, cap. 13, n. 11.

at length agree and be of one mind in this sign of unity, in this bond of charity, in this symbol of concord; and that mindful of the so great majesty, and the so exceeding love of our Lord Jesus Christ, who gave His own beloved soul as the price of our salvation, and gave us His own flesh to eat, they would believe and venerate these sacred mysteries of His body and blood with such constancy and firmness of faith, with such devotion of soul, with such piety and worship as to be able frequently to receive that supersubstantial bread, and that it may be to them truly the life of the soul, and the perpetual health of their mind; that being invigorated by the strength thereof, they may, after the journeying of this miserable pilgrimage, be able to arrive at their heavenly country, there to eat, without any veil, that same bread of angels which they now eat under the sacred veils.[892]

The celebrated Professor of Philosophy I have been quoting continues as follows:

> The Church's conduct in this respect does not prove that she reckons a single annual Communion generally sufficient for salvation.
>
> The truth is that Communion is the most powerful means of protecting oneself against the death of sin. In the name of Our Lord the Church has willed to bring us to the divine banquet by force — *compelle intrare*[893] — once a year, but for the rest she leaves all to the spiritual needs of the individual which alone determine the most appropriate remedies, without obliging us to Communion any more than to fasting, prayer, almsgiving or any other means of attracting the graces of God.
>
> Hence Fr. Castelein is mistaken in concluding that the Church deems Easter Communion a necessary and sufficient means for the salvation of those who do not go beyond this one practice.

The saddest feature of this affair is that Fr. Castelein seems to be supplying countless more or less lukewarm Christians with pretexts for disputing and rejecting the salutary advice of preachers and confessors.

---

[892] Session XIII, *On the Eucharist*, chap. VIII, Denzinger 882.

[893] I.e. *Compel them to come in*. Cf. Luke XIV, 23: "And the Lord said to the servant: Go out into the highways and hedges, and compel them to come in, that my house may be filled." — Translator.

2. This minimalism in matters of faith strictly so called is closely related to another minimalism: that which is determined to diminish miracles in the strict sense, punishments inflicted by God, revelations, etc.

Fr. Castelein:

> With regard to the miraculous fall of leaves from a tree during a sermon of Fr. Baldinucci[894] to symbolize the great number of the reproved, *I doubt whether this miracle was admitted in the Process of beatification of the Beatus.* (Note 1 to p. 285)

How can the author and his censors have failed to read the Bull of Beatification of their confrère in religion? It is entitled *Quod Redemptor* and dated 25th March 1893. Its stated object is "to grant the honours of the Blessed of Heaven to the Venerable Servant of God Anthony Baldinucci S.J." It states the following:

> … It is an established fact that when Anthony Baldinucci was once journeying through a fortified town near Velletri commonly known as *Guilianello* he was asked to preach to the people and readily agreed to do so. Owing to lack of space within the walls the crowd assembled in a plain and there the preacher stood beneath the dense foliage of an elm — it was in April — and inveighed against those who presumptuously rely on God's mercy to harden their hearts in their vices until at length they encounter His justice at the judgement. Suddenly inspired by the Holy Ghost he exclaimed: "How many such souls do you think there are who at this very moment are falling into hell? There are as many as the leaves that fall from this tree." Whereupon the mass of the tree's leaves fell to the ground. The portent was not wasted on these countryfolk who were profoundly moved and unable to stifle their sobs and groans until they had contritely expiated their sins.[895]

On the subject of this miracle my adversary continues:

> Its demonstrative force to settle in general terms the proportion of the reproved and the elect could be contested. So I do not rely on documents of this kind owing to the difficulty of establishing their authenticity and exact meaning. (Note 1 to p. 285)

---

[894] Blessed Anthony Baldinucci S.J. (1665-1717).

An assertion of which readers may judge for themselves.

3. Equally disedifying is that other sentimentalism which sees matter for eternal damnation only in monstrous sins.

Here is how Fr. Castelein writes of the various concupiscences:

Lust: When this passion is not pressed to *extreme* disorders by deliberate and persistent malice of the will, it inclines God to an immense pity. (p. 255)

(…)

Avarice: But are there many in whom this desire attains such extreme malice and monstrous gravity as to create an insurmountable barrier to salvation? (p. 257)

(…)

Pride: Pride that is fully developed and fixedly retained in the soul is rare. (p. 261)

(…)

Unbelief: There are few who settle irrevocably in error and evil. (p. 270)

Etc.

Is this "the doctrine of salvation" which Fr. Castelein's title invited us to expect? What is become of Our Divine Redeemer's solemn warning: "He that is faithful in that which is least, is faithful also in that which is greater: and he that is unjust in that which is little, is unjust also in that which is greater."[896]

My confrère Fr. Coppin writes pointedly:

I enquire of every attentive reader of Fr. Castelein's book and in particular of every priest who has striven in the pulpit or the confessional to lay bare the foulness of mortal sin and to inspire horror of it whether a single thought or consideration is to be found within the covers of this book liable to help to enlighten souls or to inspire hearts with this horror. I have found none.

---

[895] *Leonis XIII Acta,* Vatican edition, vol. XIII, p. 106.
[896] Luke XVI, 10.

Nor is this all: the general tone of the book and many of the expressions and ideas it contains are thoroughly in tune with the reflections uttered by sinners and cited above.

> "These are sins of weakness! Fallacy! Etc. ... The sins involved are in general but *ordinary* mortal sins... Come then, you Rigorists, how can you send people to hell for faults due to their upbringing or prejudices, etc? ... God has no interest in your gossamer balances! ... How will you convince me that God will damn a mass of these ordinary folk who have spent their whole lives in toil and labour in the sweat of their brow!! Etc."
>
> "Let us say from the start that these people are not committing mortal sins. By way of mortal sins there are only the monstrous disorders which men obstinately immerse themselves in."[897]

As the celebrated preacher Fr. Monsabré so well explains:

You imagine, for instance, that the only sins that are mortal and worthy of damnation are those monstrous ones by which a man declares himself openly an enemy of God, denies Him, cuts himself off from Him, renounces Him; or perhaps those abominable crimes that the world holds in universal reprobation; you suppose that the evil found in the vicious instincts of nature is not so great as to oblige God to use the barbarous rigours of an unhappy eternity to punish those who yield to their inclinations; you think that just keeping the faith or a certain love of uprightness is enough to protect one from the eternal punishment that the reprobate must undergo. But you are wrong, gentlemen. Sin, in theology, is the transgression of a divine law. Whether this divine law is already written in our conscience or is made known to us by the those God has sent to tell us His will makes no difference. If the transgression is grave, clearly known by the mind and fully consented to by the will, it is a mortal, and therefore damnable, sin, because whether or not we want it directly and formally, it brings about the criminal reversal of our ends which sets the creature in the place of his Creator.

This being so, count if you can the grave transgressions you have made yourselves guilty of and have not yet repaired by sincere repentance. I beg you not to let yourselves be blinded in this valuable exercise by the

---

[897] Coppin, *op. cit.*, p. 317.

gross prejudices which reduce the number of mortal sins you can commit to such crimes as are punished by human justice.

We often hear it said that such and such a man is irreproachable because his uprightness and urbanity and the correctness of his public conduct would ensure his acquittal of any criminal charge before our courts of justice. In popular language he may say: "I have never robbed or killed anyone; I am an upright man."

I will not trouble, gentlemen, to enter into the realms of moral philosophy to evaluate this cut-price uprightness. Instead I appeal to your Christian consciences before the Criminal Law of God to convince you that a man may rob and kill oftener than people think and thus, whatever the world may imagine, may fall beneath that terrible punishments that God holds in reserve to punish those that transgress His commandments.[898]

4

Thoroughly disedifying is Fr. Castelein's neglect of the method of Saint Ignatius's Spiritual Exercises and contempt for the practice of the Saints in maintaining that servile fear of God is an obstacle to charity and his use of the term "crime" to refer to sermons aimed to arouse it.

Fr. Castelein:

I also reproach Rigorism with paralysing the action of charity in souls. (p. 348)

Brethren gone astray in the false theories of Rigorism and Terrorism … when by your false theories and your pessimism you cause the fear of hell to dominate in souls … *you prevent the faithful from loving Jesus-Christ, as He wants them to love Him.* (p. 352)

You prevent the love of Jesus Christ from being a *popular* love within his Church.

Here is the *crime* that your unhappy doctrine commits despite your good intentions which I do not question.

As long as the motive of the fear of divine chastisements predominates in the soul, this soul *cannot make an act of the love* that Jesus Christ asks of us.

---

[898] Monsabré, *Retraite Pascale*, 1889, *Le chemin de la perdition*, p. 34.

Are we reduced to having to be content with a simulacrum of charity? Are we reduced to having to beg alms by threatening the faithful with the punishments of hell. (p. 353)

Much more edifying is the method followed by Saint Ignatius in his Spiritual Exercises. For therein, during the first week, corresponding to the *purgative way*, he strives to lead the soul to God's love by way of fear, i.e. by the consideration of terrifying truths.

Much more edifying is the express teaching of the Founder of the Society of Jesus. Here are the authentic words by which he recommends the fear of God as *necessary* — not only filial fear but even *servile* fear, i.e. the fear of hell. The following extract is taken from his *Rules for Thinking with the Church*.

18. Although it is very praiseworthy and useful to serve God through the motive of pure charity, yet *we must also recommend the fear of God*; and not only filial fear, which is in the highest degree pious and holy, but servile fear, which is very useful and often even *necessary* to raise man promptly from mortal sin if he should fall. Once risen from the state, and free from the affection of mortal sin, our path will be smoother towards that filial fear which is truly worthy of God and which gives and preserves the union of love.[899]

The teaching and action of Saint Ignatius is in fact common to all the holy missioners, notably Saint Leonard of Port-Maurice and Saint Alphonsus, whose aim was ever to raise souls *by fear to love*.

And this agrees with the mind of the Church as expressed in the Council of Trent:

…sinners … are usefully stirred by fear of divine justice …[900]
If anyone saith that the fear of hell whereby, by grieving for our sins, we flee unto the mercy of God, or refrain from sinning, is a sin or makes sinners worse, let him be anathema.[901]

And in the condemnation of proposition XXV of the pseudo-synod of Pistoia against which Pope Pius VI teaches that:

---

[899] *Regulæ ad sentiendum cum Ecclesia*, Antwerp, 1635, p. 142.
[900] Council of Trent, Session VI, *On Justification*, Chapter VI.
[901] *Ibid., On Justification*, Canon VIII.

It is necessary, in accordance with the usual order of preparation for justice that fear should enter first, so that charity may come through it — fear being the medicine and charity health.[902]

Much more edifying than Fr. Castelein's assertions is the clear teaching of the Angelic Doctor who poses the question: *Does servile fear remain with charity?* to which he replies affirmatively:

> Servile fear is a gift of the Holy Ghost, as stated above (Article 4). Now the gifts of the Holy Ghost are not forfeited through the advent of charity, whereby the Holy Ghost dwells in us. Therefore servile fear is not driven out when charity comes.[903]

Aquinas goes on to explain the reason for this:

Servile fear proceeds from self-love, because it is fear of punishment which is detrimental to one's own good. Hence the fear of punishment is consistent with charity, in the same way as self-love is: because it comes to the same that a man love his own good and that he fear to be deprived of it. …

… fear of punishment is, in one way, included in charity, because separation from God is a punishment, which charity shuns exceedingly; so that this belongs to chaste fear.[904]

Much more edifying are the words written by Saint Teresa, the reformer of the Order of Our Lady of Mount Carmel, and of whom the breviary tells us that: "Among the other virtues of Teresa, the most outstanding was love of God."[905]

Now among the countless extraordinary graces vouchsafed her by God she herself counted the very famous vision of hell which she often afterwards remembered with the greatest fruit. Let the Saint speak for herself:

> Some considerable time after our Lord had bestowed upon me the graces I have been describing, and others also of a higher nature, I was one day in prayer when I found myself in a moment, without knowing how, plunged apparently into hell. I understood that it was our Lord's will I should see the place which the devils kept in readiness for me, and

---

[902] *Auctorem fidei*, Denzinger 1525.

[903] *Summa Theologiæ*, II-II, q. 19, a. 6, *in corp.*

[904] *Ibid.*

[905] 27th August, Lesson IV.

which I had deserved by my sins. It was but a moment, but it seems to me impossible I should ever forget it even if I were to live many years.[906]

After describing the entrance and some of the most excruciating pains of hell, she continues:

I was so terrified by that vision — and that terror is on me even now while I am writing — that, though it took place nearly six years ago,[907] the natural warmth of my body is chilled by fear even now when I think of it. And so, amid all the pain and suffering which I may have had to bear, I remember no time in which I do not think that all we have to suffer in this world is as nothing. It seems to me that we complain without reason.

I repeat it, this vision was one of the grandest mercies of our Lord. It has been to me of the greatest service, because it has destroyed my fear of trouble and of the contradiction of the world, and because it has made me strong enough to bear up against them, and to give thanks to our Lord, who has been my Deliverer, as it now seems to me, from such fearful and everlasting pains.

Ever since that time, as I was saying, everything seems endurable in comparison with one instant of suffering such as those I had then to bear in hell. I am filled with fear when I see that, after frequently reading books which describe in some manner the pains of hell, I was not afraid of them, nor made any account of them. Where was I? How could I possibly take any pleasure in those things which led me directly to so dreadful a place? Blessed for ever be Thou, O my God![908]

---

[906] *Autobiography*, chapter XXXII.
[907] In 1558 according to De la Fuente.
[908] *Loc. cit.*

5

***It is far from edifying to compare the Catholic doctrine of hell to the
doctrine of the Mahometans and to tone down the traditional description of the pains of hell in order to avoid offending our sceptical age.***

Fr. Castelein:

We have nor right to use terrorist techniques unjustified by the Gospel
in order to produce a more vivid effect on the imagination and better
subdue the wills of our listeners...

The better to understand the Gospel on this point, ... let us first consult
the Koran. Let us see the spirit of Mahomet and the method used by the
Coran to dissuade men from sin by the penal sanction that follows it.
(pp. 303-4)

Let us avoid presenting as *real*, and especially as being of faith, descriptions of the same kind as those of the Koran. (Note to p. 208)

Jesus does not address the crowd with the threats and thunderbolts that
are typical of the procedures of Mahometan or pseudo-Christian Rigorism. (p. 309)

His yoke has nothing in common with the procedures of Mahometan
terrorism from which our Rigorists seem all too often to draw inspira-
tion.

As to the nature of the pains represented by "the fire of hell", or the
"outer darkness", let us be content to say that the main one is the pain
and remorse caused by the eternal loss of the supernatural happiness of
heaven... *In these times of critical examination and of doubt ... let us avoid presenting as real* the descriptions of the same kind as are found in the Koran.
(Note to p. 308)

1. Fr. Castelein has enterprisingly counted the verses of the Koran
and the Gospel, respectively, in which the pains of hell are mentioned.

In the first 500 verses alone of the Koran I found 55 devoted to threats
of hell.

Then with some erudition he gives all the "Surates" and the verse
numbers, concluding:

On average, discounting the historical parts, out of 100 verses of the
Koran, 15 are about hell. (p. 304)

As my friend the professor of the Faculty of Philosophy recently wrote to me:

Fr. Castelein has also put himself to the trouble of counting the passages in the New Testament in which Our Lord or the Apostles displayed "terrorism" in referring to hell. He found only eight such passages in Saint Matthew (p. 305), one in Saint Mark, four in Saint Luke and barely one half in Saint John, while in Saint Paul he has located only the merest allusions barring two texts in the Epistle to the Hebrews: "How few and far between they are!" he exclaims (p. 307).

But in point of fact he seems to have miscounted. He would appear, for instance, to have disregarded the parables which Our Lord closes by warning against damnation — such as the parables of the cockle, the talents, the minas or pounds (Luke XIX), the sterile fig tree, the net, the foolish rich man, the unjust steward and the foolish virgins, all of which are sermons on hell.

Moreover, of the passages he does include, he counts only the final verse, in which the threat of hell is expressed: "10 verses out of 28 chapters of some 40 verses each," he cries — a mere nothing! (p. 305) But in order to be fait he should count the entire context surrounding these verses. For instance the central subject of the parable of the nuptial garment is certainly hell although the allusion to the "outer darkness" is found in a single verse. Following Fr. Castelein's own arithmetic we should be entitled to allege that his own book contains only twenty pages, the rest being the merest padding.

But let us be serious: Fr. Castelein also seems to forget that not all that Our Lord said and did has been recorded — there are also the apostolic traditions. Now the early Fathers of the Church who are the echo of these traditions did not preach as Fr. Castelein recommends — they "terrorized" unrestrainedly; the fear of hell was a powerful motive among Christians during the centuries of persecution and in every age.

Moreover while the New Testament is the main basis of Catholic preaching, its use is to provide a theme to be interpreted and applied to the various situations of life. If we grant that the Holy Ghost insisted especially on the mercy and the mysteries of the divine goodness, this is no reason for us to preach less often or less emphatically on hell. If it is acceptable to wonder why it is so, it may be because the mysteries of grace and of love are more unheard-of and unbelievable for fallen man than the mysteries of eternal justice. The ancient heathens were already aware of the God of justice, but the God of goodness was all but unknown to them!

It seems to me that the main rule for fruitful preaching is to adapt both the subject and how it is handled to the audience one is addressing. Failure to do so leads to many inconveniences of which the main ones are causing trouble to souls that are too sensitive and failing to cause trouble to those that are too slack. For souls marching on the highroad to holiness, let the threat of hell be no more than the grumbling of distant thunder while heaven while heaven drops down its dewfall of peace, joy and love; for convalescent souls, recovering from recent shipwreck, let the mercy of the Lord shine down from amid the thunderclaps and storm to inspire trust and courage. But for souls frolicking on the edge of the abyss and living in proximate occasions, for sinners rotting in the tomb of their vices, let the lightning bolt rip through their darkness and let their cries of alarm rise clamorously to warn them of the danger and awake them from their fatal slumbers.

Not only is Fr. Castelein wrong to blame frequent preaching on hell, but he is also wrong to outlaw what he calls *invented terrorism*. Since hell in fact exists the sacred orator has nothing to invent — he need only offer images, comparisons, analogies. He must take care to avoid any choice of word, gesture, tone or expression that might shock his auditors by offending good taste and thereby prejudice the fruit of his sermon. But he need never fear exaggerating the horrors of eternal torment for it is quite safe to say, inverting the famous text of Saint Paul, that *eye hath not seen, nor ear heard, neither hath there entered into the heart of man,* even a distant image of the chastisements God hath prepared for those who incur His reprobation.[909] No representation could ever do justice to the appalling reality.

2. I turn now to Fr. Castelein's warning:

In these times of critical examination and of doubt ... let us avoid presenting as real the descriptions of the same kind as are found in the Koran. (Note to p. 308)

I am minded to remind the Reverend author of the fifth Exercise of the first week of the *Spiritual Exercises* of his holy Father Saint Ignatius, which comprises a *highly realistic* contemplation of hell, and

---

[909] Cf. I Corinthians II, 9.

once which would undoubtedly be of the greatest value for everyone "even" in our days.

First Prelude: This is a representation of the place. Here it will be to see in imagination the length, breadth, and depth of hell.

Second Prelude: I should ask for what I desire. Here it will be to beg for a deep sense of the pain which the lost suffer, that if because of my faults I forget the love of the eternal Lord, at least the fear of these punishments will keep me from falling into sin.

First Point: This will be to see in imagination the vast fires, and the souls enclosed, as it were, in bodies of fire.

Second Point: To hear the wailing, the howling, cries, and blasphemies against Christ our Lord and against His saints.

Third Point: With the sense of smell to perceive the smoke, the sulphur, the filth, and corruption.

Fourth Point: To taste the bitterness of tears, sadness, and remorse of conscience.

Fifth Point: With the sense of touch to feel the flames which envelop and burn the souls.

Is this exercise one of "the procedures of Mahometan or pseudo-Christian Rigorism"? (p. 309)[910]

Neither can I help wondering whether Saint Ignatius would approve of Fr. Castelein when he writes:

Once again I earnestly ask whether it is not *unworthy* of a Christian to preoccupy himself almost exclusively, in fear and trouble of soul, with the means of escaping eternal punishment? (p. 334)

For the Holy Founder and writer himself exhorts the retreatant following the exercises of the first week to make the following resolutions:

I should not think of things that give pleasure and joy, as the glory of heaven, the Resurrection, etc., for if I wish to feel pain, sorrow, and tears for my sins, every consideration promoting joy and happiness will impede it. I should rather keep in mind that I want to be sorry and feel pain. Hence it would be better to call to mind death and judgment.

---

[910] *Op. cit.*; Antwerp, 1635, p. 42. Namur, 1841, p. 62.

For the same reason I should deprive myself of all light, closing the shutters and doors when I am in my room, except when I need light to say prayers, to read, or to eat.

I should not laugh or say anything that would cause laughter.[911]

For in the science of salvation we ought ever to adhere to the teaching of the Saints as they are our masters and examples.

[911] *Loc. cit.*, First Week, Additions 6, 7 and 8.

EPILOGUE

So as it is certain, according to the common opinion of the Saints and the Theologians, that the majority of mankind are damned — a fact that the theories of the Progressives will not only never change but actually aggravate by encouraging lukewarmness — it is more edifying to admit this tremendous mystery in all humility and modify both our teaching and our behaviour in the light of it than to contest it in periodicals for the benefit of "the educated laity".

In considering the fewness of the saved *in relation to God*, let us beware of idle curiosity and of any appearance of murmuring.

Let us rather adore God's sovereign goodness, holiness and justice, saying with the Apostle:

> O the depth of the riches of the wisdom and of the knowledge of God! How incomprehensible are his judgments, and how unsearchable his ways! For who hath known the mind of the Lord? Or who hath been his counsellor?[912]

And if we chance to encounter proud objections or complaints, let us reply with the pious and learned Fr. J-B. Saint-Jure S.J.:

> If you ask me how it is possible that God, whose love for men is so great and who so much desires the salvation of all and has suffered so much for their salvation should accept to see almost all of them damned, I answer you that His love for them and His desire for their salvation are yet greater than we can imagine. *God sent not his Son into the world to judge the world*, says Our Lord to Nicodemus, *but that the world may be saved by*

---

[912] Romans XI, 33-4.

him; all the more so as no one is happy to lose what has cost him dearly and, as Solomon says, the glory of the king is in the number of his subjects.[913] Hence God desires nothing so ardently as to keep men who have cost Him so dear and to increase his court in Heaven where the elect are to honour Him throughout eternity, but it must be understood that His will to save them is conditional — He wills to save them provided they will it themselves and on their part strive for it by observing His laws. Nothing is more reasonable: (i) because they are able to do so and want for nothing necessary to be saved; (ii) because He is their God and their sovereign Lord, to whom they owe total obedience, all the more so as His laws are entirely equitable and adapted to their nature and to their reason — His laws are not as the laws of the princes of the earth, which are sanctioned but by threats and promise no rewards, for God promises endless riches, pleasure and honours to those who observe them; and (iii) because it would be derisory to expect to inherit the priceless treasures of eternal goods for no effort when even the least of the good things of the earth has some cost attached to its acquisition. It is therefore just and reasonable for men to observe God's laws. God is perfectly just in punishing them if they transgress His laws as in rewarding them if they are faithful. This is what we see in use among men in every civilized nation: men's deserts are weighed so that good deeds may be rewarded and evil ones punished.[914]

The same pious ascetical author offers the following peremptory reply to a certain well-worn objection:

> Yes, you may answer, but God who is so good ought to save us by force rather than allow us to be lost! But this cannot be. Saint Denis says: "We do not approve the unfounded claim that Providence should drag us to virtue despite ourselves, for it is not proper to Providence to destroy the nature of things, but rather to conserve it, let it act and act with it according to the strength the thing has. Hence providence allows man, whom it has created free, to use his freedom to enrol under the banners of virtue or of vice and to labour for his salvation or damnation without constraining him." "God wants to save all men," says Saint Ambrose, "but provided that they go to Him and show that they desire

---

[913] Cf. Proverbs XIV, 28: "In the multitude of people is the dignity of the king."

[914] *De la Connoissance et de l'amour du fils de Dieu Nostre Seigneur Jésus-Christ*, livre III, chap. XXIII, § 2; vol. III, p. 139 of the 1847 Lyon edition.

Him; He does not wish to save them despite themselves." After all, what man would drag his guests, bound hand and foot, to a banquet? It would be an outrage not an honour. Men are punished against their will, but not rewarded against their will. For reward there must be merit and for merit there must be intention and effort. It is perfectly true that God casts men into hell against their will, but He receives into heaven only those who have chosen it. Since the number of the reprobate is so great and that of the elect is so small, that so many are damned and so few saved, which of us ought not to fear to be included among that prodigious multitude?[915]

If we consider the fewness of the saved *in relation to ourselves* we have already been warned by the first Vicar of Christ: *Wherefore, brethren, labour the more, that by good works you may make sure your calling and election. For doing these things, you shall not sin at any time. For so an entrance shall be ministered to you abundantly into the everlasting kingdom of our Lord and Saviour Jesus Christ.*[916] "Labour the more" means work harder and harder in order to have, insofar as possible, morally certain signs of your predestination. For, as Saint Thomas notes: "Through good works the effect of predestination is most certainly fulfilled."[917]

And let us priests beware of lax doctrine and living lest having preached to others we ourselves become castaways;[918] let us both preach and practise the principles not of the Progressives but of the Saints and of the Doctors of the Church; let us not reject their holy and evangelical severity in order to please this depraved and effete world, and let us pray daily with heartfelt groans to God our Saviour:

Command that we be snatched from eternal damnation and numbered among the flock of Thy elect. To us sinners also, Thy servants, trusting in the greatness of Thy mercy, deign to grant some part and fellowship with Thy Saints. Into their company we implore Thee to admit us, not

---

[915] *Ibid.*, n. V, p. 140.
[916] II Peter I, 10-11.
[917] *Summa Theologiæ*, I, q. 23, a. 8, *in corp.*
[918] Cf. I Corinthians IX, 27.

weighing our merits, but freely granting us pardon. Through Christ our Lord and through the prayers and tears of Mary our Mediatrix. Amen.[919]

Praised be Jesus Christ and Blessed Mary ever a Virgin now and forever. Amen

---

[919] In the original Latin Fr. Godts's closing prayer reads: *"Ab æterna damnatione nos eripi, et in Electorum tuorum jubeas grege numerari! De multitudine miserationum tuarum sperantibus, partem aliquam, et societatem donare digneris, cum tuis Sanctis ... intra quorum nos consortium, non æstimator meriti sed veniæ, quæsumus, largitor admitte. Per Christum Dominum nostrum et per preces lacrymasque Mariæ Mediatricis nostræ. Amen."* This prayer is composed of two extracts from the Canon of the Mass, with a slight modification at the end. — Translator.

APPENDIX

PANEGYRICS OF
FR. CASTELEIN'S WORK
IN THE BELGIAN PRESS

ALL THE CATHOLIC PERIODICALS of Belgium reviewed Fr. Castelein's work in ecstatic terms. To give a slight idea of their panegyrics I will cite a few extracts from a single daily : *Le Patriote*.

I

A remarkable book whose erudition is full of practical teachings and which all Catholics will want to read and meditate…

It is a capital work. It straightens out a great many misunderstandings. It clears the paths. The light it sheds on life and on death is both dazzling and comforting.

Fr. Castelein is one of the finest, if not the very foremost religious writer of our days. As a philosopher, a sociologist and a theologian he is in the front rank in every field. He is not a *tinkling cymbal*, but a man of vast learning and sure doctrine, who thinks clearly and expresses his thoughts no less sharply, in a style formed by the purest sources of great French literature.

It is highly salutary for men of the competence and authority of Fr. Castelein to make their voices heard to clarify teachings all too often shrouded in obscurity. How many prejudices will fall away when Fr. Castelein's book is taken up! How many heavy hearts will be uplifted. How many will stride forth with surer steps in the right path!

Fr. Castelein's own name is a sufficient guarantee, but he has seen fit to obtain attestations of the highest order in favour of his work : learned theologians of the Company of Jesus and the Primate of Belgium have approved his work. (*Le Patriote*, 6th November 1898)

II

The *Bien Public* offered generous praise to this remarkable book, nor was the *Gazette de Liège* less enthusiastic.

The soul needs to feel that God wants to save it. Trust must reign within it, in place of this mournful despair which robs its victims of all strength to embark on the work of salvation. In a word, the soul, burdened with the awareness of its past faults must bear within itself the unconquerable knowledge of God's mercies so that, relying on the help and goodness of God, it may labour to win heaven. We often need to be reminded of these consoling thoughts and every book which places them before us deserves to find a warm welcome in Christian households.

In this respect Fr. Castelein's book cannot be too highly recommended. Upon putting it down, its reader feels strengthened, comforted and encouraged; he sees God from a vantage more comforting to the soul and, in full knowledge of His mercy and goodness, he embarks with renewed vigour on the daily struggle by which we must earn heaven. He understands, at last, that the doctrine of salvation, when once disentangled from the exaggerations and bugbears of rigorism and understood in the light of the holy traditions of Catholic theology, is a doctrine of peace, light and strength for the mind, heart and will of the believer. Many are the souls who will be indebted to Fr. Castelein for a renewal of their ardour as a result of reading these reviving pages. (*Le Patriote*, 1ˢᵗ December, 1898)

III

Fr. Castelein has the happiness, unlike Saint Francis de Sales, to find no adversaries within the Church. It is well known that when the illustrious Bishop of Geneva published his *Introduction to the Devout Life*, he was besieged with attacks of every kind. He was not an innovator but a renewer. Anathemas were hurled at him in the name of ignorance or of a misunderstood conservatism. The Saint did not reply. As a bishop he was well placed to defend his work and his intentions had he so chosen, but instead he waited for the storm to pass. And of that storm nothing at all remains in our day, while the *Introduction to the Devout Life* has joined the *Imitation* as the handbook of countless generations of chosen souls, even in Protestant lands.

In the same way Fr. Castelein draws his arguments and his teaching from the theological sources, holy writ and observation of the acts of Providence. Indeed what his book presents is not the doctrine of an outstanding man but the life-giving substantial doctrine of the Church.

This is a work which treats thoroughly the crucial question for man insofar as he is distinguished from the brute animals destined to return into nothingness. It examines from the vantage of history the role of Providence towards mankind. A mind unshackled but uninformed on such matters, having no knowledge of the solutions the Catholic Church — the greatest intellectual and moral force of all ages — gives to these problems might say: "I have no interest in this book. I pay no attention to the subject it treats. I have no wish to study it…"

But the subject of the life to come must be paramount for the thinking man. Never has it been addressed more generously or more learnedly. We have no right to err deliberately. When such a torch is placed in our hand we may not put it aside and remain in darkness. (*Le Patriote*, 9ᵗʰ December 1898)

IV

We must note the prompt success of Fr. Castelein's already celebrated little work *Rigorism, the Number of the Elect and the Doctrine of Salvation*, already at its fifth thousand, after just six months.

So uncharacteristic a success for a theological thesis will provide encouragement for religious writers to address the public at large.

No doubt the popular preoccupation with supra-terrestrial matters has played a role in this success, but it is not sufficient to explain it. There are better reasons.

We have just read the latest edition of the eminent theologian's work, attracted by the subtitle "revised and expanded". Let us say at once that it is a delight — all the more delightful as it is rare — to feel oneself led on through theological arguments by so powerful a breeze and so enticing a conviction.

These pages are full of air, of light and of heat, indeed, I stress, they transmit an apostolic flame of infectious ardour which is refreshing indeed. This is not just a theologian's book — it is an apostle's book. The author's aim is not to defend an original thesis which, as he freely admits, "is in disagreement with the opinion of some theologians and with the public spirit prevailing among certain groups of readers"; it is much higher than that for it is rather to go out to meet, amid the anguish of their doubts, souls that a legacy of antiquated Jansenism confines in torment and despair or at least exposes to the all too easy temptation of discouragement.

Fr. Castelein rightly considers that preaching terror-inspiring theories about the fewness of the saved in practice entails moral laxity and makes a mockery of our Gospel in its very heart and keystone by preventing the love of Christ from being a *popular* love.

It is well worth reading the case made for this conclusion in the new edition. In thinking as he does the author is in excellent company : Suárez, Cajetan, Saint Francis de Sales, Bergier, Lacordaire, Ravignan, Faber, Mgr. Besson, Fr. Monsabré, etc., etc.

He tells us what salvation is, its divine causes, its human obstacles, and draws a consoling conclusion of which he eloquently depicts the theoretical and practical consequences. This is the lynchpin of the work. In its pages the author evinces broad knowledge of the Scriptures and a solid exegetical erudition — advantages which entitle him to proffer interpretations that a less well-equipped mind would fight shy of but the wise boldness of which is grounded on motives that will carry conviction to the knowledgeable and unprejudiced reader.

The book's success has been too great for it to escape opposition. I have even heard it said that it would be "pulverized beneath the pile-driver of Tradition". I am familiar with the sword and the pen as weapons of combat but I had not realised that the pile-driver was one. Needless to say I wish Fr. Castelein many enthusiastic contradictions. They will get his book read — and it cannot be too much read — and will enable him all the better, as he confidently expresses it, "to shed brighter light on all his proofs and all his conclusions". (*Le Patriote*, 19th March 1899)

(Signed) "E.T., S.J."

V

Fr. Castelein's work on *Rigorism and the Doctrine of Salvation* has been approved by the diocesan authority. His Eminence the Cardinal of Mechlin has extended congratulations and thanks to the author. Archbishop Ireland, the celebrated American prelate has sent him a letter of heartfelt congratulations. Distinguished representatives of the English hierarchy have requested permission to have his work translated. (*Le Patriote*, 29th March 1899)

VI

To the Editor

Sir,

A Roulers-based publisher announces with great fanfare the appearance of a work destined to "crush beneath the pile-driver of the authority of tradition" the doctrine of my book *Rigorism, the doctrine of salvation and the number of the elect*. This doctrine is characterized as "lax and false".

I am not in the least disturbed by this rambunctious attack, which can only provide useful publicity for my book among the cultured laity and among theologians wishing to inform themselves before passing judgement.

I doubt whether the promised work contains any new objection. The quotations it will present did not prevent the two illustrious orators of Notre-Dame de Paris, Fathers Lacordaire and Monsabré, from embracing the opinion I champion, and the commentaries of a certain number of the Fathers on the text *Many are called but few are chosen* did not shackle the two most learned exegetes of the century, Mgr. Beelen of the University of Louvain and Fr. Knabenbauer S.J., for they adopted a quite different interpretation. From this angle the question is a free one. But the advertising-flyer contains three calumnies in which my thought is travestied in three inexact quotations. I will not answer them at present, though I intend to do so later.

I ask only to reassure my readers that I shall be quite able to defend my doctrines and have no fear of the famous "pile-driver" with which they are menaced.

While awaiting the book's appearance I request you to be kind enough to recommend my second edition, revised and expanded, to your numerous readership. (*Le Patriote*, March 1899)

(Signed) A. Castelein S.J.

GLOSSARY OF TERMS

Antitype: A person, thing or event foreshadowed in Holy Scripture by a *type* or symbol. Thus the Holy Eucharist is an *antitype*, of which manna was a type. See *type* below.

Benignists: The name chosen to describe themselves by the first authors to argue that most men are saved. The idea behind the word is that their position evinces benignity, or kindness.

Common: A theological opinion is said to be *common* if it is held by practically *all* approved theologians. Thus the word is almost a synonym of *universal* and stronger than the everyday sense of *frequently encountered*.

Elect: The elect are those who will ultimately be saved and spend eternity in the enjoyment of the beatific vision. The Latin word *electi* may be translated either "elect" or "chosen" as in "Many are called but few are chosen."

Exegete: A biblical interpreter.

Foreknown: Those who God foreknows from eternity will ultimately be lost by their own fault.

Gnome: Pithy statement. Rhymes with "foamy".

Hermeneutics: The science of interpretation.

More common: A theological opinion is said to be *more common* if it is held by *the majority of* approved theologians. A *common* opinion is therefore even more universally held than one which is *more common*.

More probable: A theological opinion is said to be *more probable* if the evidence (from reason or authority) in its favour is greater than that in favour of any conflicting opinion.

Pericope: A biblical excerpt comprising a single unit of thought. Rhymes with *stick-a-pea, not* with *periscope.*

Predestination: The *Catholic* doctrine of *predestination* holds that God from eternity chooses His elect in such a way as to safeguard their own free will, so that their salvation is truly the result of His choice, but also truly the result of their own merits in freely cooperating with grace.

Predestined: See *elect.*

Probable: A theological opinion is said to be *probable* if the evidence (from reason or authority) in its favour is sufficient to gain the assent of a prudent man but does not exclude some fear that the contrary may prove correct. In this technical sense it is synonymous with the everyday word *tenable* and distinct from the everyday sense of *probable.*

Progressives: This word has been chosen by the Translator as the best English equivalent of the Latin *neoterici* (devotees of something new) used by Fr. Godts to designate those who reject the traditional doctrine of the fewness of the saved in favour of the recent idea of the salvation of the greater number.

Reprobate: The reprobate are those who will ultimately be damned and spend eternity in the torments of hell.

Sentimentalists: This word has been chosen by the Translator in non-technical contexts to render the Latin coinage *benignistæ* as a label for adherents of the idea that most men are saved.

Type: An image or symbol in Holy Scripture which represents and foreshadows some future person, thing or event. Thus manna is a *type* of the Holy Eucharist. See *antitype* above.

Typical: Symbolic.

Wayfaring state: Human beings are described by theologians as being "in the wayfaring state" while alive on earth, able to sin or merit, before death and judgement.

FRANÇOIS-XAVIER GODTS C.SS.R.
1839-1928

SUFFERING marked the childhood of Frans Godts. Before he reached the age of five he had seen his father, a businessman, ruined, lost his mother to typhus, lost his elder brother, and found himself confided now to one pair of grandparents now to the other while his father sought refuge abroad from his creditors.

Young Frans's paternal grandfather, notary-royal to the Habsburgs, then sovereign over Belgium, had courageously renounced his lucrative and honourable office in 1794 when the invading forces of revolutionary France demanded he swear hatred to the monarchy. It was his paternal grandmother who entrusted an important part of her ward's education to the Jesuits in his native city at Antwerp.

School reports attest his outstanding ability and excellent conduct.

At the end of his schooling he had already decided to leave the world and enter religion — probably as a Jesuit — but a retreat with the Redemptorists changed his choice. He soon felt convinced that it was to this congregation of Saint Alphonsus, so devoted to our Blessed Lady, that God and His Mother were calling him.

He sought his father's consent to enter religion but the response was a categorical refusal and a call to London (where his father was then engaged in commerce) where his vocation was subject to what, many years later, he still referred to in his final testament as "terrible trials". His father placed him in a situation in which the attractions of the world in all its forms would do their best to draw him away from his pious ideal.

He remained sure throughout life that it was Our Lady who protected him, and after three months his father's affairs suffered a new reversal, so that he was happy to be free of the cost of keeping his son, who returned to Belgium and at once hastened to the Redemptorist convent of Antwerp. Upon arrival his entire fortune consisted of five centimes, and the following day he was admitted to the novitiate. He received the Redemptorist habit 15th October 1858 (the year of the apparitions of Lourdes) and exactly a year later made his vows, choosing to sign them in his own blood. On Saturday 15th September 1864 he was ordained priest. His younger brother Guillaume, impressed by the happiness radiating from François-Xavier's features, followed him into the Redemptorists.

The year 1865 found him already charged with teaching dogmatic theology to his younger confreres. The following year he was prefect of studies, then spiritual director, and before long he was fulfilling all of these roles simultaneously. His outstanding intelligence, ability, judgement and capacity for work were all manifesting themselves and his superiors put them to the fullest use. He worked hard at all these tasks until in 1875 he was named rector of the new foundation at Roulers.

The principal task of the Redemptorists is to preach parish missions. Fr. Godts devoted himself to it with zeal and energy, making full use also of congregations and confraternities to assist in the conversion, sanctification and perseverance of the laity notwithstanding the countless moral dangers surrounding them and particularly that of socialism which then threatened the working men. Already his influence was benefiting many thousands of souls. His name was so revered at Roulers that its population insisted on saluting him long years afterwards at the celebrations of the fiftieth jubilee of his ordination.

In 1875 alone he gave twelve missions, nine retreats, three octaves and two tridua, preaching throughout western Flanders.

He was much appreciated as a preacher and as a retreat-master and before long it became clear that he also enjoyed a special gift for the guidance of seminarians. Cardinal Dechamps summoned him again and again to the seminary of Mechlin for the benefit of the future priests studying there. Before this more learned audience he deployed the full apparatus of theological knowledge that he had accumulated over his years of study, seeming inexhaustible in his citations of Fathers, Doctors, Councils and Exegetes.

During many of these missions the confessionals were besieged from morning till night. Religious practice, where it had been reduced to a minority blossomed anew, so that Catholics failing to receive the sacraments became the exception and not the rule. In one retreat (at Tongres in 1881) five sudden deaths at the same time shook the population out of their lukewarmness and were the occasion of many conversions.

Many of the most powerful men in Church and state came to Fr. Godts for confession or counsel. When Cardinal Mercier was (prematurely) believed to be dying, he chose Fr. Godts to hear the confession by which to prepare his soul for eternity.

Godts was moved to Brussels, preaching as many as 24 retreats in a year, as well as many missions and accepting increasing numbers of calls to visit the other seminaries of Belgium.

At Morlanwez 340 out of 400 bad Catholics were converted, including an elderly Voltairean whom Fr. Godts sought out in his home. At other times Fr. Godts would unite children in fervent faithful in prayer in the church while he went alone in search of some inveterate sinner whose heart would at last be softened by the torrents of grace obtained by these prayers.

It was noted that the firmness of Fr. Godts's doctrine led to no hardness of heart. Sinners were especially attracted to him. "What Fr. Godts *says* may strike us as a little harsh," noted Fr. Dryvers,[920] "but in deeds he spares no pains to push as many souls as possible through the door of heaven notwithstanding the narrowness he has stressed."

In the 1890s, while continuing to preach retreats and missions and accomplish his other duties, he found time to embark on a new apos-

---

[920] Cf. De Meulemeester, Fr. Maurits C.SS.R., *Le Révérend Père François-Xavier Godts, Rédemptoriste*, p. 57.

tolate as a polemicist. His first work concerned the burning topic of the condition of workers. Although in Latin and addressed essentially to priests, warning them of the dangers to be avoided in addressing this issue, it ran swiftly through three printings, totalling several thousand copies. Such a success was an invitation to continue, and his next work was a series of tracts in French addressed to labourers themselves, not essentially on social issues but on religious ones. Up to a million copies of each were printed!

The year 1897 saw a new work of nearly five hundred pages, in Latin. Its thesis was the need for education to be Christianized if schools were not to be a hotbed of socialism.

And as a witness to Fr. Godts's incredible energy, his 424-page *Papa sit Rex Romæ*[921] appeared later in the same year (winning a congratulatory brief from Cardinal Rampolla) and the following year came another work on the state of education in Belgium.

While Fr. Godts was working on the last of these works the famous Jesuit Fr. Auguste Castelein (1840-1922) published the first edition of his work arguing that salvation is much easier than had been thought and the proportion of mankind who are saved much greater.

Without neglecting his other duties, Fr. Godts took up his pen to draft the refutation of this thesis which is here translated into English for the first time. For Fr. Godts two overwhelming considerations imposed on him this duty: (i) the theory that most men are saved is incompatible with the teaching of the Fathers, Doctors and Saints and indeed with the natural and traditional understanding of Holy Scripture; (ii) nothing could be more opposed to ensuring the actual salvation of souls than to reassure them that that they will very probably be saved anyway even after a life of lukewarm mediocrity or worse. The first of these arguments he knew to be true from his close familiarity with the vast literature of Catholic theology from the Fathers to his own day, and the second he knew to be true from his extensive experience as a missioner and a confessor.

---

[921] "Let the Pope by the King of Rome."

On the Fewness of the Saved[922] ran through three editions in its year of publication (1899), the last reaching 550 pages. As the twentieth century dawned all who prized fidelity to the mind of the Church as manifested by her most approved authors knew who had won the debate. Not all realised that Fr. Castelein's theology had been influenced by his growing Darwinian convictions.[923] With hindsight it is possible to see in the Castelein–Godts debate a preliminary battle, or at least skirmish, of the war between orthodoxy and Modernism. As Saint Pius X was to point out eight years later, when evolution is accepted as a universal principle, the immutable truth of Catholic dogma must lose all hold over the human mind.[924]

Fr. Castelein did not return directly to the fray and Fr. Godts was free to write on other matters. Incredibly, by 1900 he had prepared a five-volume work on education rights: *Les droits en matière d'éducation*, running to 1740 pages, followed in 1903 by a 450-page attack on Feminism. This work was brought to public attention by its powerfully worded preface:

> To Saint Alphonsus Mary Liguori, who says in his *Moral Theology* the exact opposite of what the impudent falsifiers Chiniqui, Grassmann, Wolff, Demblon etc. attribute to him ... this work is dedicated in reparation for the blasphemies vomited forth against him in November 1912 by the representatives of the socialist press.

The Belgian parliamentary left was outraged, and the odious anti-Catholic deputy Henri Crombez openly defamed Fr. Godts under cover of his parliamentary immunity, even accusing him of per-

---

[922] *De Paucitate Salvandorum* in the original Latin.

[923] Cf. Lambert, Dominique, *Revue Théologique de Louvain* (40), 2009, "Un acteur majeur de la réception du darwinisme à Louvain: Henry de Dorlodot" and *L'origine de l'homme: Le Darwinisme au point de vue de l'orthodoxie catholique*".

[924] "To finish with this whole question of faith and its shoots, it remains to be seen, Venerable Brethren, what the Modernists have to say about their development. First of all they lay down the general principle that in a living religion everything is subject to change, and must change, and in this way they pass to what may be said to be, among the chief of their doctrines, that of Evolution. To the laws of evolution everything is subject — dogma, Church, worship, the Books we revere as sacred, even faith itself, and the penalty of disobedience is death." (*Pascendi Gregis*)

sonal immorality. Crombez then committed the prudential error of repeating his calumnies in print, whereupon, for the honour of the priesthood, Fr. Godts sued for libel and Crombez was condemned to pay damages of 500 Francs to the Redemptorist and to have the judgement widely published in the press. The Socialists from then on avoided discussing Fr. Godts's works in public.

The following year appeared what was destined to be Fr. Godts's most durable contribution to theological scholarship: a 458-page study in Latin marshalling the arguments in favour of a dogmatic definition of Our Lady's title of Mediatrix of all graces: *De definibilitate Mediationis Universalis Deiparæ.*

Fr. Godts was deeply devoted to the Mother of God. The same year he wrote in French a more popular study of the initial holiness of the Immaculate Virgin, which quickly ran through three editions, helped on by a controversy with renowned theologian Fr. Lépicier. Then in 1904 came a book of prayers to Our Lady and a work on Saint Alphonsus considered as the Modern Apostle of the Blessed Sacrament. In 1905 a fall limited his mobility for the rest of his life, but he refused to submit to the constraints of his handicap. He even had himself once carried into the church to preach from the floor instead of mounting the pulpit.

At the same time Fr. Godts engaged in the burning controversies on frequent Communion. In 1907 Pope Saint Pius X was to settle the debate in terms incompatible with some of Fr. Godts's views. His submission was of course immediate, humble and unreserved.

From 1906 a period of relative literary inactivity ensues in consequence of a new project in favour of his Redemptorist brethren. Notwithstanding his father's financial catastrophes François-Xavier Godts inherited a considerable fortune from his family, including a vast farm in the village of Esschen (sometimes spelt *Essen*), a little north of Antwerp and not far from the sea, which had been acquired by his grandfather and was left by him to a daughter who died in 1903 leaving it in turn to her nephew, Fr. Godts, who donated the property to the Redemptorists to build a house of rest for fathers returning in sickness, debility, poor health or old age from the missions, especially in the Congo.

Work began in 1906 and proceeded swiftly but events moved faster yet for it was at the end of 1905 that France's Third Republic manifested its understanding of "Liberty Equality Fraternity" by its tyrannical anti-Catholic legislation, confiscating Church property and banishing the religious orders. Fr. Godts was delighted to place the buildings already completed at the disposal of the students of the Paris province of the Society of the Divine Redeemer. He oversaw the work and was able to celebrate the first Mass in a room converted into a chapel in March 1907.

Fr. Godts had planned on an immense scale and, unperturbed by the anxious enquiries of his superiors, he saw through to its conclusion the construction of a vast church dedicated to the Eucharistic Heart of Jesus with generously proportioned buildings which were ultimately to serve for the formation of future Redemptorists. His close friend Cardinal Mercier came to consecrate in person the grandiose building topped by a statue of Christ which dominates the surrounding plain and is visible from miles around.

In 1909 Fr. Godts celebrated his golden jubilee as a religious. In 1910an attack of bronchitis brought him, now over seventy, to the brink of the grave, but his strong constitution pulled him through.

Following the decree of Saint Pius X requiring the completion of studies in the humanities before admission to religious noviciates, the superiors of the Redemptorist Province of Belgium decided to erect a juvenate, for the higher schooling of future candidates for admission to the congregation. After consultation with Fr. Godts the Esschen house was selected to house it, the French exiles moved on, and Fr. Godts was appointed rector. It opened in 1911, furnishing new outlets for his zeal among these pious young men at a time when the infirmities of old age prevented him from travelling to preach missions and retreats.

There he was to spend the bulk of the remainder of his life, as a venerated father-figure exercising profound spiritual influence upon the future generations of Redemptorists who came to love him deeply. When he could do no more he continued to write, chiefly in honour of Our Lady, concerning her dignity of Coredemptrix and of Mediatrix of all graces. He also wrote on the antiquity of devotion to Saint Anne, on Saint Joseph, on Saint Dominic and the Rosary, on the Holy House of Loreto, on the definibility of the Assumption.[925]

He lived to celebrate the sixty-fifth anniversary of his profession and the sixtieth of his ordination, for which he received the congratulations of the pope.

October 1927 found him at Brussels for the last time, very weak in body at 87 years old and when he returned to Esschen he knew that he would not leave it alive. The weakness of his legs forced him to use a wheelchair to get about though he could still stand at the altar to say Mass. Then his eyesight failed and he resigned himself in November to the inability to celebrate.

The sufferings of approaching death were acute but he received them with resignation. He read and re-read the writings of his holy founder Saint Alphonsus. He was exquisitely courteous and grateful to those who waited on him in his infirmities.

His ardent soul was finally delivered from its earthly exile on Saturday 7th January 1928. May he rest in peace.

JOHN S. DALY

---

[925] In fact to be defined as a dogma of faith in 1950 by Pope Pius XII.

DETAILED TABLE OF CONTENTS

Doctors, both scholastic and expositive, very strongly supported by Holy Scripture and the Holy Fathers and by weighty arguments furnished in abundance."

41 Ven. Henri-Marie Boudon: "It is an infallible matter and of the utmost certainty that there are few who are saved."   160

42 Bourdaloue: "What is more striking in the Gospel than the small number of the elect?"   161

43 Jesuit Fathers of Würtzburg: "That the number of the elect in comparison with the reprobate will be small is quite explicitly taught by Christ and agreed by the Fathers."   161

44 Bossuet: "There are many called and few chosen. Jesus Christ has often warned us of it."   162

45 Verschuren: This author wrote an entire book to prove, against Steyaert, that even of the faithful more are damned than saved.   163

46 Dionysius Werlensis: "The commoner opinion of the Doctors is that, not only of the whole human race but even of Catholic adults alone, more are damned than are saved."   166

47 Henno: "The more common opinion and the one which better agrees with the Fathers is that more of the true faithful are damned."   167

48 Pauwels: "In the light of such clear passages from Holy Scripture it is not lawful to doubt that there are many more reprobate than elect."   167

49 Ginther: "Few are chosen, since few cooperate until the end with the grace of God."   168

50 Collet: "Is the number of the predestinate greater than the number of the reprobate? No, but rather the contrary."   169

51 Zacharie Laselve: "It is *de fide* that the number of the elect and of the saved is small as Christ said that few are chosen."   169

52 Daelman: "Many more perish than are saved, and this is why Our Saviour said that many are called, but few are chosen."   171

53 Judde: "There are few elect even in the religious life if the religious life is scarcely differentiated from the world."   171

54 Card. Gotti: "The number of the reprobate is greater."   172

55 Antonio Mayr: "It is certain that in the context of the entire human race more are destined to be reprobate than blessed. This is inferred from Christ's words."   172

56 Concina: "Holy Writ, the Holy Fathers of the Church and the more recent theologians commonly teach that the majority of adult Catholics are damned, and the minority saved."   173

57 Billuart: "Those who are saved are fewer than those who are damned."   174

58 Berti: "The number of the elect is great, but very small in comparison with the number of the damned. This is shown by Holy Scripture."   175

59 Berthier: "the number of the enemies of God surpasses almost infinitely the number of His servants."   175

60 Foggini: wrote an entire book entitled ["Assertion and demonstration of the extraordinary consensus of the Fathers of the Church as   176

to the fewness of adult faithful saved in comparison with the faithful who are reproved".

CHAPTER EIGHT   401

A FEW SPECIFIC POINTS SELECTED FROM THE
DOCTRINE OF FR. CASTELEIN

EPILOGUE   424